Criminal Behavior and Accountability of Artificial Intelligence Systems

Criminal Behavior and Accountability of Artificial Intelligence Systems

Alice Giannini

eleven

Published, sold and distributed by Eleven
P.O. Box 85576
2508 CG The Hague
The Netherlands
Tel.: +31 70 33 070 33
Fax: +31 70 33 070 30
e-mail: sales@elevenpub.nl
www.elevenpub.com

Sold and distributed in USA and Canada
Independent Publishers Group
814 N. Franklin Street
Chicago, IL 60610, USA
Order Placement: +1 800 888 4741
Fax: +1 312 337 5985
orders@ipgbook.com
www.ipgbook.com

Eleven is an imprint of Boom uitgevers Den Haag.

ISBN 978-90-4730-172-1
ISBN 978-94-0011-338-1 (E-book)

A Nina
Ai miei nonni

"Tutto questo avviene non sul mare, non nel sole, – pensa il nuotatore Palomar,
– ma dentro la mia testa, nei circuiti tra gli occhi e il cervello.
Sto nuotando nella mia mente;
è solo là che esiste questa spada di luce;
e ciò che mi attira è proprio questo.
È questo il mio elemento, l'unico che io possa in qualche modo conoscere."

Italo Calvino, Palomar (1984)

Tutta la vita, a provare a dirti che partivo
O che partivo o che morivo

Lucio Dalla, Tutta la vita (1984)

Table of Contents

Essential Glossary of Terms

Algorithm
Set of rules that precisely define a sequence of operations to solve a problem.

Artificial intelligence
Artificial intelligence (AI) systems are software (and possibly also hardware) systems designed by humans that, given a complex goal, act in the physical or digital dimension by perceiving their environment through data acquisition, interpreting the collected structured or unstructured data, reasoning on the knowledge, or processing the information, derived from this data and deciding the best action(s) to take to achieve the given goal.

AI systems can either use symbolic rules or learn a numeric model, and they can also adapt their behavior by analyzing how the environment is affected by their previous actions.

As a scientific discipline, AI includes several approaches and techniques, such as machine learning (of which deep learning and reinforcement learning are specific examples), machine reasoning (which includes planning, scheduling, knowledge representation and reasoning, search, and optimization), and robotics (which includes control, perception, sensors and actuators, as well as the integration of all other techniques into cyber-physical systems).[1]

Autonomous vehicles (AVs)
Vehicles capable of navigating streets and interpreting traffic without a driver actively operating. They can display six levels of automation:

0 – No Automation
1 – Driver Assistance
2 – Partial Driving Automation
3 – Conditional Driving Automation
4 – High Driving Automation
5 – Full Driving Automation[2]

1 The definition was elaborated by the High-Level Expert Group on Artificial Intelligence (AI-HLEG), *A definition of AI: Main capabilities and Scientific Disciplines*, 2018. Available at: https://ec.europa.eu/futurium/en/system/files/ged/ai_hleg_definition_of_ai_18_december_1.pdf.

2 Society for Automotive Engineers International (SAE), *J3016 Taxonomy and Definitions for Terms Related to Driving Automation Systems for On-Road Motor Vehicles*, April 2021.

Artificial Neural Networks (ANNs)
Neural networks are made from multiple layers of artificial neurons encoded in software. Each neuron can be connected to others in the layers above. One neuron receives an "input" (for example information on a pixel in a picture) and another neuron produces an "output" (for example the classification of the picture). This technique is inspired by the functioning of the human brain. The knowledge of the ANN is stored in the network itself.

Automated decision system (ADS)
A computational process, including one derived from artificial intelligence techniques, which makes a decision without human involvement.

Bots
Automated program which runs on the Internet and typically mimics human behavior.

Computer vision
Process by which the system extracts data from a series of images or videos.

Convolutional Neural Networks (CNNs)
Multi-layered neural networks whose creation was inspired by animal optical systems. They are based on visual cortex cells that detect light in the small receptive field and can extract features from images, identify objects that are contained in them and then classifies the images (i.e., general object recognition task).

Deep Learning (DL)
Sub-set of ML where the system consists of layers of artificial neural networks (ANNs). The network analyzes data and identifies relevant features by itself.

Deep Neural Networks (DNNs)
DNNs are built on layers of interconnected artificial neurons which work together. A DNN will make decisions using an intuitive decision-making process and it will learn through experience.

Expert systems
Computer programs which resemble the decision making of an expert to solve problems by using inference procedures. Expert systems are based on symbolic AI (see definition below).

Generative Adversarial Network (GAN)
Type of ANNs that learn by competing against each other. Usually one ANN (the generator) produces content and the other (the discriminator) detects whether it was produced by an ANN or by a human agent or if the output has any flaws. Each side improves from such interaction.

Human in Command (HIC)
The human oversees the overall activity of the system (which includes also its broader economic, societal, legal and ethical impact) and has the ability to decide when and how to use the system in any situation.

Human in The Loop (HITL)
All the operations are executed by the system under human control.

Human on The Loop (HOTL)
The system acts autonomously but under the supervision of a human.

Machine Learning (ML)
AI technique where the algorithm learns to find on its own a solution to a set problem or task.

Natural Language Processing (NLP)
Process by which the system extracts data from human language and makes decisions based on that information. It enables clear human-to-machine communication. Examples of NLP systems are voice-activated digital assistants such as Alexa, Siri, Cortana and Google Assistant.

Reinforcement learning
Type of ML training process where the algorithm interacts with the environments and learns by trial, discovering errors or rewards.

Strong Artificial Intelligence or Artificial General Intelligence (AGI)
AI systems which display human cognitive abilities and can perform all sorts of tasks, learning from their experience. As of today, there are no AI systems which display general intelligence.

Symbolic AI
Also referred to as "expert systems" or "logical AI", It refers to an approach to model AI systems based on "if *x*, then *y*" rules. IBM's Deep Blue program, which beat Gary Kasparov at chess in 1997 is an example of symbolic AI.

Supervised learning
Type of ML where the programmer trains the system by defining a set of expected results for a selected set of input and provides the system with an evaluation of the results. The ML training process is guided by labelled data. This system generates hypothesis on how to classify the relevant traits. Every time the system errs the hypotheses are corrected. Supervised learning techniques include linear and logistic regression, Decision Trees, Naïve Bayes, etc.

Unsupervised learning
Type of ML training process where little to nothing labelled data is used and with low human intervention. The system will try to find connections and structure in the data (for example through clustering, i.e. creating groups of similar data objects) by extracting and analyzing useful features. It learns by its own observations and is highly dependent on the experience.

Weak Artificial Intelligence or Narrow Artificial Intelligence
AI systems which can perform only specific pre-set tasks and therefore operate in a limited domain. Current AI systems belong to this category.

Abbreviations

ADS	Automated Decision System
AGI	Artificial General Intelligence
AI	Artificial Intelligence
AIA	Artificial Intelligence Act
AIAAIC	AI Algorithmic And Automation Incidents & Controversies
AIID	Ai Incident Database
AMA	Artificial Moral Agent
ANN	Artificial Neural Network
ASDE	Automated Driving System Entity
ATM	Air Traffic Management
ATTOL	Autonomous Taxi, Take-Off and Landing
AV	Automated Vehicle
BDI	Belief Desire Intention
CCL	Corporate Criminal Liability
CDPC	Council of Europe Committee on Criminal Problems
CDPC-AICL	Drafting Committee to elaborate an instrument on Artificial Intelligence and Criminal Law
CNN	Convolutional Neural Networks
CoE	Council of Europe
DCAI	Data Centric AI
DL	Deep Learning
DNN	Deep Neural Network
DOJ	Department of Justice
GAN	Generative Adversarial Network
GBMI	Guilty But Mentally Ill
HIC	Human In Command
HITL	Human In The Loop
HLEG	High Level Expert Group On Artificial Intelligence
HOTL	Human On The Loop
ISO	International Organization For Standardization
MIT	Massachusetts Institue Of Technology
ML	Machine Learning
MPC	Model Penal Code
MSCOCO	Microsoft Common Objects in Context

NHTSA	National Highway Traffic Safety Administration
NLP	Natural Language Processing
NTSB	National Transportation Safety Board
NUIC	No-User-In-Charge
PCM	Paperclip Maximizer
PCRC	Penal Code Review Committee
POET	Paired Open-Ended Trailblazer
POMD	Partially Observable Markov Decision Process
RAI	Robotic and Artificial Intelligence Systems
RDS	Random Darknet Shopper
RDW	RijksDienst voor het Wegverkeer
SAL	Singapore Academy of Law
StGB	Strafgeseztbuch
StVG	Straßenverkehrsgesetz

1 Introduction

Rachael: It seems you feel our work is not a benefit to the public.
Deckard: Replicants are like any other machine – they're either a benefit or a hazard.
If they're a benefit, it's not my problem.

Blade Runner (1982)

1.1 Science Fiction, Legal Fictions and the "Plasticity" of Criminal Law[1]

"Intelligent systems currently cause real world harms without a collective memory of their failings".[2] This is the incipit of the research paper presenting the world's first systematized Artificial Intelligence Incidents Database (AIID).[3] The AIID is an industrial/non-profit cooperative collection of "intelligent system failures experienced in the real world",[4] i.e., incidents.[5] It aims at answering the question "what can go wrong when someone deploys this system?".[6] The existence of the AIID and other databases[7] tells us something: they give foundation with regard to the relevance of this research. They push us to ask ourselves a crucial question: if "something goes wrong" with an artificial intelligence (AI) system, should criminal law care? If yes, how? As it will be shown, these two (apparently) simple questions will be the tenet of this research and will be reformulated in terms of *necessity* and *feasibility* in the main research question.

Certainly, the idea of criminal behavior of AI systems is nothing new. In fact, science fiction has been dealing for decades with "evil robots" rebelling against humans and taking

1 The title takes its inspiration from the work of R. Abbott & A. Sarch, "Punishing Artificial Intelligence: Legal Fiction or Science Fiction", *UCD L Rev*, Vol. 53, 2019, p. 323 and of K. Burchard, "Künstliche Intelligenz als Ende des Strafrechts? Zur algorithmischen Transformation der Gesellschaft", *Normative Orders Working Paper*, No. 2, 2019, p. 4.
2 S. McGregor, "Preventing Repeated Real World AI Failures by Cataloging Incidents: The AI Incident Database", *Proceedings of the Thirty-Third Annual Conference on Innovative Applications of Artificial Intelligence (IAAI-21)*, 2021, p. 1.
3 Available at: https://incidentdatabase.ai/.
4 McGregor, 2021, p. 1.
5 Cfr. Ch. 4.1.
6 McGregor, 2021, p. 1.
7 See also the AIAAIC Repository, an independent collection of over 850 incidents and controversies driven by and relating to AI, algorithms, and automation. Available at: https://docs.google.com/spreadsheets/d/1Bn55B4xz21-_Rgdr8BBb2lt0n_4rzLGxFADMlVW0PYI/edit#gid=1051812323.

control, or with machines that "go crazy" and act unpredictably:[8] one could actually argue that Asimov's three laws of robotics were nothing but the most famous attempt at regulating forms of AI misconduct.[9]-[10] Thus, different from the most famous sci-fi chronicles, in the last decade AI has actually become part of our daily lives and is here to stay.

The most recent evolution in AI technology has led to the development of systems capable of unsupervised, unforeseen, and autonomous actions. Algorithms, through machine learning (ML) techniques, can learn from their past actions and teach themselves new patterns of behavior.[11] Such methods, then, possibly allow for algorithmic misbehavior without any human intervention.[12]

As stated by the European Parliament in its resolution containing recommendations to the Commission on a *civil* liability regime for AI, "[…] the opacity, connectivity and autonomy of AI-systems could make it in practice very difficult or even impossible to trace back specific harmful actions of AI-systems to specific human input or to decisions in the design".[13] Undeniably, "[a]s a transformative technology that is characterised by high complexity, unpredictability and autonomy in its decision-making and learning capacities, *AI has the potential to challenge traditional notions of legal personality, individual agency and responsibility*".[14]

8 "Think instead of the false Maria in Metropolis (1927); Hal 9000 in 2001: A Space Odyssey (1968[…]; C3PO in Star Wars (1977); Rachael in Blade Runner (1982); Data in Star Trek: The Next Generation (1987); Agent Smith in The Matrix (1999) or the disembodied Samantha in Her (2013)", L. Floridi, Should we be afraid of AI?, *aeon.co*, 9 May 2016. Available at: https://aeon.co/essays/true-ai-is-both-logically-possible-and-utterly-implausible.

9 "(1) A robot may not injure a human being or, through inaction, allow a human being to come to harm. (2) A robot must obey any orders given to it by human beings, except where such orders would conflict with the First Law. (3) A robot must protect its own existence as long as such protection does not conflict with the First or Second Law." I. Asimov, *I, Robot*, Harper Collins Publisher, 1950.

10 S. N. Lehman-Wilzing, "Frankenstein unbound: Towards a legal definition of artificial intelligence", *Futures*, Vol. 13, Issue 6, 1981, p. 445.

11 "A few features of AI are important to highlight. First, AI has the potential to act unpredictably. Some leading AIs rely on machine learning or similar technologies which involve a computer program, initially created by individuals, further developing in response to data without explicit programming. This is one means by which AI can engage in activities its original programmers may not have intended or foreseen. Second, AI has the potential to act unexplainably. It may be possible to determine what an AI has done, but not how or why it acted as it did. This has led to some AIs being described as "black box" systems. […] That is particularly likely in the case of AIs that learn from data, and which may have been exposed to millions or billions of data points. Even if it is theoretically possible to explain an AI outcome, it may be impracticable given the potentially resource intensive nature of such inquiries, and the need to maintain earlier iterative versions of AI and specific data. Third, AI may act autonomously", Abbott & Sarch, 2019, pp. 330-331.

12 "For our purposes, that is to say an AI may cause harm without being directly controlled by an individual". Ivi, p. 331.

13 European Parliament, Resolution of 20 October 2020 with recommendations to the Commission on a civil liability regime for artificial intelligence, (2020/2014(INL)), 20 October 2020.

14 M. Kritikos, European Parliamentary Research Service – Scientific Foresight Unit, Briefing "Artificial Intelligence ante portas: Legal & ethical reflections", 2019, p. 1.

At this point, it is clear that things are on the move: scholars and policymakers have started asking themselves questions on how to fill this apparent gap – not just in the field of civil liability. This will be evident in Chapter 3, which reviews and classifies the scholarly debate on AI and criminal liability, whereas in Chapter 7 policymaking initiatives are instead the object. One relevant example in the field of criminal law which is worth mentioning is the work conducted by the Council of Europe Committee on Criminal Problems (CDPC). In September 2020, the CDPC published a feasibility study on a future Council of Europe (CoE) instrument on artificial intelligence and criminal law. During a thematic session on AI and criminal law responsibility, focused on the case of automated driving,[15] prof. Sabine Gless, Special Rapporteur, underlined that:

> Existing liability models may be inadequate to address the future role of AI in criminal activities. This may undermine the certainty of the law. It may leave specific gaps given the nature of AI that is based on machine learning and gives space to a machine actor whose action we do not entirely understand.[16]

The initiative of the CPDC is just the tip of the iceberg: for example, the broader topic of "Artificial Intelligence and Criminal Justice" was picked by the International Association of Penal Law for the XXI International Congress of Penal Law of 2024.[17] The trend will be analyzed in depth in this research.

As will be shown, modern legal systems are facing situations in which it will be hard – if not impossible – to determine with a legally acceptable degree of certainty whether the harm caused by an AI system on a protected legal interest can be ascribed to a *human* agent involved in the causal chain of events: be it the programmer, the producer, or the user of the technology.[18] In other words, AI systems stretch the distance between the

15 Council of Europe – European Committee on Crime Problems (CDPC), Concept Paper "Artificial intelligence and criminal law responsibility in Council of Europe member states – the case of automated vehicles", CDPC(2018)14Rev, 16 October 2018. Available at: https://rm.coe.int/cdpc-2018-14rev-artificial-intelligence-and-criminal-law-project-2018-/16808e64ad.

16 Council of Europe – CDPC, Thematic session on Artificial Intelligence and Criminal Law of 28 November 2018, Final remarks by Professor Sabine Gless, Special Rapporteur, "Artificial intelligence and its impact on CDPC work. The case of automated driving", cdpc/docs 2018/cdpc (2018)22, 28 November 2018.

17 See the concept paper by K. Ligeti, *Artificial Intelligence and Criminal Justice*. Available at: www.penal.org/sites/default/files/Concept%20Paper_AI%20and%20Criminal%20Justice_Ligeti.pdf. See also the questionnaire elaborated by L. Picotti for the AIDP, Section I "Traditional Criminal Law Categories and AI: Crisis or Palingenesis?". Available at: www.penal.org/sites/default/files/Questionnaires%20EN.pdf.

18 "*Eine besondere Rolle mit Blick auf die strafrechtliche Verantwortung nehmen Maschinen ein, die einen eigenen Entscheidungsspielraum haben, durch Sensoren und Vernetzung Informationen erhalten und selbst auswerten. In diesen Fällen [...] lässt sich weder im Vorhinein vorhersehen, welche Entscheidungen die Maschinen in welchen Situationen treffen werden, noch im Nachhinein feststellen, worauf die Entscheidungen beruhten. Insbesondere ob einer der Beteiligten, d.h. der Programmierer, Produzent oder der Nutzer einen*

harmful event and the responsible human person.[19] In this sense, one can speak about a *liability gap*. Machines are "inducing some problems that are specific to criminal law" and, consequently, "[...] we have to determine whether the behavior of robots falls within the loopholes of the system, necessitating the intervention of lawmakers at both national and international levels".[20]

It can be affirmed that AI systems today represent a sort of "*stress test*" for traditional human-based criminal liability frameworks. It is in this perspective that the question of ascribing criminal liability *to* AI systems – "AIs going bad" – takes on new relevance.[21]

The main research question which will be guiding this research is: *to what extent is a theoretical framework of criminal law for liability of non-human agents needed and feasible?* This study will explore cases in which a crime is functionally committed by a machine and it is "not practically defensible"[22] to impute the AI's behaviors to "bad" human actors and cases where there is no other identifiable human agent that acted with criminal culpability. Such an investigation will entail a discussion on what can be attributed to an AI system, to humans, or to both.

A discussion on the attribution of criminal liability to AI systems is necessarily connected to *purposes* of criminal punishment. As such, this study necessarily will touch upon different theories of punishment. Moreover, the criminalization of conducts is usually guided by certain criteria which are selected according to theories of criminalization. In other words, criminal law determines what kinds of "undesirable conducts"[23] should be punished and it does so in pursuance of different aims. Consequently, this study will briefly touch upon on theories of criminalization.

In conclusion, we will embark on this research conscious of, and strong of, the *plasticity* of criminal law theory. As it was argued:

> The use of legal fictions to solve difficult conceptual questions or practical problems – such as how to conceptualize or prove particular sorts of mental elements for AI or misbehavior by its developers – gives criminal law theory impressive *plasticity*.

Fehler gemacht hat, ist häufig nicht mehr nachweisbar", S. Beck, "Die Diffusion strafrechtlicher Verantwortlichkeit durch Digitalisierung und Lernende Systeme", *ZIS*, Vol. 2, 2020, p. 44.

19 M. Hildebrandt, "Technology", in M. Dubber & T. Hörnle (eds.), *The Oxford Handbook of Criminal Law*, Oxford University Press, 2014, p.190.

20 Pagallo, The Laws of Robots: Crimes, Contracts and Torts, Springer, 2013, p. 45.

21 As stated by Burchard, "*Soweit KI strafrechtswissenschaftlich bereits in den Blick genommen wird, wird sie [...] herkömmlich als potentiell regulierungsbedürftiger und auch regulierungs-fähiger Objektbereich geführt*". Burchard, 2019, p. 4.

22 Abbott & Sarch, 2019, p. 328.

23 W. R. LaFave, *Criminal Law*, 6th edition, West Academic, 2017, p. 26.

> Legal fictions help turn the criminal law into a pragmatic tool for solving social problems.[24]

It is necessary to commence the inquiry with a critical eye. Indeed, criminal law is not the only tool through which society can obtain a desirable conduct: think for example of civil remedies or of administrative sanctions. This entails distancing ourselves from ambitions of the supremacy of the criminal sanction, which could eventually turn out to be unsuitable for the case at hand, and to which we tend to attribute a symbolic-restorative function that perhaps it does not quite have.

1.2 The Definitional Problem of Artificial Intelligence

There is no overall accepted definition of AI.[25]-[26] Hence, it will be crucial to address the issue in order to avoid fallacies throughout this research.

The term "Artificial Intelligence" was first coined at the famous 1956 Dartmouth College meeting by John McCarthy[27] and is used by scientists today to refer to a field of research which includes a variety of techniques and technologies such as "theorem proving, heuristic search, game playing, expert systems, neural networks, Bayesian networks, data mining, agents, and recently, deep learning".[28] In a problem-solving perspective, and in its most comprehensive sense, AI technology aims at automating tasks that "are thought to involve intelligence when people perform them [...]".[29] Put differently, "[w]hen engineers automate an activity that requires cognitive activity when performed by humans, it is common to describe this as an application of AI".[30]

24 Abbott & Sarch, 2019, p. 384.

25 For a systematic analysis of the issue of defining "artificial intelligence" see inter alia: P. Wang, "On Defining Artificial Intelligence", *Journal of Artificial General Intelligence*, Vol. 10, No. 2, 2019, pp. 1-37.

26 For an overview of what AI is in relation to the practice of law, see H. Surden, "Artificial Intelligence and Law: an Overview", *Ga. St. U. L. Rev.*, Vol. 35, 2019. For arguments in favor of policy makers using terms other than "artificial intelligence" for regulatory purposes see J. Schuett, "A Legal Definition of AI", *Xiv:1909.01095 [cs.CY]*, 2019.

27 "[T]he artificial intelligence problem is taken to be that of making a machine behave in ways that would be called intelligent if a human were so behaving". J. McCarthy et al., *A Proposal for the Dart-mouth Summer Research Project on Artificial Intelligence*, 1955. Available at: http://www-formal.stanford.edu/jmc/history/dartmouth/dartmouth.html.

28 Wang, 2019, p. 7.

29 Ibid.

30 Surden, 2019, p. 1307, referring to P. Norvig & S. Russel, *Artificial Intelligence. A Modern Approach*, Pearson Education, 2003. Interestingly so, Surden continues by claiming "One reason that this characterization of AI is not fully descriptive is that AI has been used to do many activities that humans cannot do. For example, AI technology has been used to spot credit card fraud among billions of transactions using statistical probabilities. [...]. If we frame AI as engaging in activities that require human intelligence, we may miss the

The biggest difficulty when defining an AI agent is, of course, embedded in the definition of (human) intelligence itself. Nevertheless, this study will not embark on an inquiry into what intelligence is or is not, nor into one regarding whether or not "artificial" intelligence constitutes "real" intelligence.[31] However, selected concepts which pertain to such philosophical debate – such as the notion of free will and autonomy – will be addressed when discussing criminal capacity, *mens rea*, and *actus reus* questions. In other words, the framework of reference for the analysis will always be the classical construction of criminal responsibility.

AI systems deployed today can be defined as "weak" or "specific" AI systems, as opposed to "strong" or "general" AI systems. Weak AI systems are capable of executing pre-set tasks – "often at a level above human capabilities",[32] where instead Artificial General Intelligence aims at realizing systems capable of exhibiting most of human cognitive faculties or even superseding them (superintelligence).[33]

One observation is needed at this point: the fact that current AI systems "only" present "weak" intelligence does not entail that an inquiry into responsibility of AI agents is irrelevant. Indeed, as it was efficiently stated, "[p]eople worry that computers will get too smart and take over the world, but the real problem is that they're too stupid and they've already taken over the world".[34] In fact, narrow AI systems can already operate autonomously (without human supervision) in fulfilling certain purposes. This has been defined as the "control" problem[35] of AI, which can be summarized as follows:

---

group of activities that have been automated that humans cannot actually do due to our cognitive limitations".

31 For an overview of the discussion see, *inter alia*, J. E. Korteling et al., "Human- versus Artificial Intelligence", *Front. Artif. Intell.*, Vol. 4, 2021.

32 European Council on Foreign Relations, U.E. Franke, Policy Brief "Artificial divide: how Europe and America could clash over AI", 2021, p.5. Available at: https://ecfr.eu/wp-content/uploads/Artificial-divide-How-Europe-and-America-could-clash-over-AI.pdf. Thus, at the same time it is also important to remember that "while AI can already outperform people in spectacular fashion in some domains, like playing board games, in other domains AI is not even competitive with toddlers". Abbott & Sarch, 2019, p. 331.

33 G. Sartor, "Decisioni algoritmiche tra etica e diritto", in U. Ruffolo (Ed.), *Intelligenza artificiale. Il diritto, i diritti, l'etica*, Giuffré, 2020, p. 66. See also R. Abbott, "Everything is Obvious", UCLA Law Review, Vol. 66, No. 2, 2019, p. 25: "AGI could even be set to the task of self-improvement, resulting in a continuously improving system that surpasses human intelligence – what philosopher Nick Bostrom has termed Artificial SuperIntelligence (ASI). Such an outcome has been referred to as the intelligence explosion or the technological singularity. ASI could then innovate in all areas of technology, resulting in progress at an incomprehensible rate. As the mathematician Irving John Good wrote in 1965 "the first ultraintelligent machine is the last invention that man need ever make".

34 P. Domingos, *The Master Algorithm: How the Quest for the Ultimate Learning Machine Will Remake Our World*, Allen Lane, 2015, p. 286.

35 Council of Europe, K. Yeung, *A study of the implications of advanced digital technologies (including AI systems) for the concept of responsibility within a human rights framework*, DGI(2019)05, 2019, p. 53. Available at: https://rm.coe.int/responsability-and-ai-en/168097d9c5.

> The rules by which they [*AI systems*] act are not fixed during the production process, but can be changed during the operation of the machine, *by the machine itself*. This is what we call machine learning. [...] Now it can be shown that there is an increasing class of machine actions, where the traditional ways of responsibility ascription are not compatible with our sense of justice and the moral framework of society because *nobody has enough control over the machine's actions to be able to assume the responsibility for them.*[36]

According to Matthias, a *responsibility gap* arises.[37] In particular, the problem raised by Matthias recalls issues which are specific to proving the existence of causality, i.e., the link between the agent's conduct and the harm. Leaving in the background the debate between "techno-pessimists" and "techno-optimists" on whether this *moral* responsibility gap can be bridged,[38] this research will focus on its legal conception, namely on whether we are truly facing a "liability gap" and, if so, how it should be addressed.

Returning to the issue of defining AI, the determination of a "legal definition of AI" is currently being addressed by a number of policymakers involved in the booming AI regulation field. For the purpose of this research, the European Commission High Level Expert Group on Artificial Intelligence's (HLEG) working definition of AI will be adopted:

> Artificial intelligence (AI) systems are *software* (and possibly also *hardware*) systems designed by humans that, given a complex goal, act in the physical or digital dimension by *perceiving their environment* through data acquisition, *interpreting* the collected structured or unstructured data, *reasoning* on the knowledge, or *processing* the information, derived from this data and *deciding the best action(s) to take to achieve the given goal.* AI systems can either use symbolic rules or learn a numeric model, and they can also adapt their behaviour by analysing how the environment is affected by their previous actions.
>
> As a scientific discipline, AI includes several approaches and techniques, such as machine learning (of which deep learning and reinforcement learning are specific examples), machine reasoning (which includes planning, scheduling, knowledge representation and reasoning, search, and optimization), and

---

36 A. Matthias, "The Responsibility Gap", *Ethics and Information Technology*, Vol. 6, No, 3, 2019, p.177. Arguing against Matthias' assumption that there is a technology-based responsibility gap, D. W. Tigard, "There Is No Techno-Responsibility Gap", *Philosophy & Technology*, Vol. 1, 2021, pp. 1-19 [emphasis added].

37 Matthias, 2019, p. 177.

38 Tigard, 2021, p. 2.

> robotics (which includes control, perception, sensors and actuators, as well as the integration of all other techniques into cyber-physical systems.[39]

To summarize, AI systems are open systems which have the capability of recording large amounts of data, of interpreting them on the basis of specific models, and are able to react and process the data independently, through decision-making and problem-solver skills. They can therefore act in an autonomous, unpredictable, and not pre-determined way. Artificial intelligences are interactive, adaptable, autonomous, flexible entities.

This research, following the definition and taxonomy proposed by the AI-HLEG, will then use the term "AI systems" to denote any "AI-based component, software and/or hardware", whether referring to standalone systems or to a single system embedded in a larger one.[40]

1.3 A Three-Ring Circus: E-Personhood, Failures of Causation,[41] and Guilty Robot Minds

One could mention three themes which exemplify the relevance of this research: the question of AI systems as legal subjects; the impact of AI's autonomy on the *actus reus* element (specifically, on the causal link between the agent and the harm); and the question of whether AI systems can be said to possess *mens rea*. These themes are referred to respectively as "E-Personhood", "Failures of Causation" and "Guilty Robot Minds" and will be analyzed in this order.

1.3.1 e-Personhood

When discussing AI and criminal liability one must address the issue of conceiving AI systems as *legal* subjects entitled to rights and holders of legal duties. Admittedly, legal subjectivity is a pre-requisite of liability. The debate on the matter has now reached an interdisciplinary dimension and is taking place at the same time in contract, tort, and criminal law. First and foremost, with regard to civil liability, one could refer to the 2017 European Parliament resolution containing recommendations to the Commission on Civil Law Rules on Robotics. The European Parliament explicitly called on the Commission to explore, analyze, and consider the implications of:

39 AI-HLEG, 2018, p. 6 [emphasis added].
40 Ivi, p. 1.
41 The expression was coined by Pagallo, 2013, p. 73.

> [...] *creating a specific legal status for robots in the long run*, so that at least the most sophisticated autonomous robots could be established as having the *status of electronic persons* responsible for making good any damage they may cause, and possibly applying electronic personality to cases where robots make autonomous decisions or otherwise interact with third parties independently;[42]

Interestingly, the European Parliament changed its position in a subsequent resolution of 2020, where it stated:

> 7. Notes that all physical or virtual activities, devices or processes that are driven by AI-systems may technically be the direct or indirect cause of harm or damage, yet are nearly always the result of someone building, deploying or interfering with the systems; notes in this respect that it *is not necessary to give legal personality to AI-systems.*[43]

The debate on this matter is currently divided between those pertaining to the "Front of Robotic Liberation",[44] moderates, and skeptics. The distinction will be explained in Chapter 3. For now, it must be underlined that most authors involved in the debate tend to not address explicitly what they mean by "AI". Such an attitude blurs extensively the discussion of AI's personality in criminal law and highlights the importance for this research to adopt a definition upfront.

To continue, the most relevant aspect of this debate revolves around two arguments: the "AIs Are Not Human" and the "Missing-Something" arguments.[45] According to the first argument, modern legal systems are rooted in an anthropocentric standpoint, stemming from the teachings of the Enlightenment, and therefore legal personhood of AI agents should be refuted. This argument could be summarized with the following maxim: "*Das Strafrecht ist von Menschen für Menschen erdacht worden*".[46]

---

42 European Parliament, Resolution of 16 February 2017 with recommendations to the Commission on Civil Law Rules on Robotics (2015/2103(INL)), 16 February 2017 [emphasis added].

43 European Parliament, Resolution of 20 October 2020 [emphasis added].

44 Pagallo, 2013, p. 155. The issue will be analyzed in depth in Ch. 3.

45 L. B. Solum, "Legal Personhood for Artificial Intelligences", *N.C. L. Rev.*, Vol. 7, 1992, pp. 1258-1276.

46 L. Quarck, "Zur Strafbarkeit von e-Personen", *ZIS*, Vol. 2, 2020, p. 67. As stated also by Seher: "*Das Strafrecht ist dazu gemacht, Menschen dafür zu sanktionieren, dass sie grundlegende Regeln des rechtlichen Zusammenlebens verletzt haben [...] Die Adressaten des Strafrechts sind Menschen als Teilnehmer, Mitwirkende und Unterworfene des Normensystems „Recht" – Personen im Recht*", G. Seher, "Intelligente Agenten als 'Personen' im Strafrecht?", in S. Gless & K. Seelmann (eds.), *Intelligente Agenten und das Recht*, Vol. 9, 2016, Nomos, pp. 45-46.

Thus, legal systems have historically addressed issues regarding the attribution of responsibility arising from "non-human" behavior: think of wrongdoing committed by animals or by subjects which lack the legal capacity to behave criminally (for a time, slaves, but also children and insane offenders). In point of fact, in certain legal systems being human is neither a *necessary* nor a *sufficient* condition for being qualified as a legal subject in the field of criminal law, according to the *societas delinquere potest* principle.[47]

In view of that, as stated by Chopra and White:

> Arguments for advancing personhood for artificial agents need not show how they may function as persons in all the ways that persons may be understood by a legal system, but rather that they may be understood as persons *for a particular purpose* or set of legal transactions. For the law does not always characterize entities in a particular way for all legal purposes.[48]

Could AI systems, then, be regarded as *Rechtspersonen* for the purposes of criminal law? For example, an important difference between AI systems and a legal person is that the latter defines itself as such (and acquires personhood upon constitution). The same cannot be said with regards to AI systems.

Certainly, "[n]ew technologies result in the *implosion of the legal subject as we knew it* so that the legal subject and the human, natural person, conceptually different though they are, no longer necessarily coincide".[49] According to Hildebrandt, "there is no categorical legal answer to the question whether an autonomous computational system [...] should be given legal personhood. That question is a *political question* that must be answered by a legislature weighing the advantages and disadvantages of such a move. [...]".[50]

Moving forward, the second argument, i.e., the "Missing-Something" Argument, is of utmost interest with regard to this research's field of investigation. It could be summarized as follows: currently AI systems do not possess consciousness, intentionality, and morality, hence they lack the necessary preconditions to be treated as legal subjects and for attribu-

47 Corporate criminal liability currently exists in a number of jurisdictions such as the United States, England, Australia, Canada, Finland, Denmark, France and the Netherlands. For an overview of modern systems of criminal justice and the different models of assessing responsibility for crimes committed by corporations, see: C. De Maglie, "Models of Corporate Criminal Liability in Comparative Law", *Wash. U. Global Stud. L. Rev.*, Vol. 4, 2005.

48 S. Chopra & L. White, *A legal theory for autonomous artificial agents*, University of Michigan Press, 2011, p. 156 [emphasis added].

49 J. Gaakeer, "'Sua cuique persona?' A Note on the Fiction of Legal Personhood and a Reflection on Interdisciplinary Consequences", *Law & Literature*, Vol. 28, No. 3, 2016, p. 303.

50 M. Hildebrandt, *Law for Computer Scientists and Other Folk*, Oxford University Press, 2020, p. 246 [emphasis added].

tion of criminal liability.[51] Leaving the issue of morality and consciousness in the background for now, let us focus on three elements: intent, free will, and autonomy.[52]

Being *sui juris* in criminal law implies the notion that a "subject of the law must understand the nature of the act it commits".[53] Consequently, the "most damning"[54] objection to an artificial agent possessing free will is that it is "just a programmed machine".[55] Thus, one should not take comfort in the assertion that humans are not programmed, while instead artificial agents unequivocally are.[56] As a matter of fact, according to the most recent neuroscientific studies, our decisions are nothing but the result of *encoded* brain activity of the prefrontal and parietal cortex.[57] As stated effectively by Gless and Weigend, robots might soon appear to us as no more "remotely controlled" than humans, who take their (supposedly) free decisions within an inscrutable web of influences that come from their genetics, their education, and the social environment. Yet, we still define them as "freely" responsible beings.[58]

Lastly, it is argued that the very existence of AI systems raises the question of what exactly is human about humans ("*was genau das Menschliche am Menschen ist*").[59] This thought will acompany us till the very end of this research.

1.3.2 *Failures of Causation*

The issue of whether an AI criminal conduct fulfills the *actus reus* element of an offense is sometimes discarded easily in the relevant literature. Under criminal law, the question of the capacity of intelligent agents to act is also a matter of definition: in a causalistic-external view, which defines every arbitrary bodily movement as an action, AI systems can be regarded as agents. The more "substantially charged"[60] the concept of act is, the more self-consciousness is read into it, the less intelligent agents will meet the requirements set by criminal law.[61] Notably, the concept of *actus reus* generally includes the issues of con-

51 Pagallo, 2013, p. 157.
52 Chopra & White, 2011, p. 173.
53 Ivi, p. 165.
54 Chopra & White, 2011, p. 165.
55 Ibid.
56 Chopra & White, 2011, p. 165.
57 Ibid.
58 "*Möglicherweise erscheinen uns Roboter ja bald nicht mehr stärker „ferngesteuert" als Menschen, die ihre vermeintlich freien Entscheidungen in einem undurchschaubaren Geflecht von Einflüssen aus Genetik, Erziehung und sozialer Umwelt treffen und die wir dennoch als „frei" verantwortlich definieren*". S. Gless & T. Weigend, "Intelligente Agenten und das Strafrecht", *ZSTW*, Vol. 126, No. 3, 2014, p. 568.
59 Ivi, p. 588.
60 Gless & Weigend, 2014, p. 572.
61 "*Letztlich dürfte die Frage nach der (strafrechtlichen) Handlungsfähigkeit Intelligenter Agenten eine Frage der Definition sein: Bei „kausalistischer", bloß äußerlicher Betrachtung, die jede „willkürliche Körperbewegung"*

duct and causation. It has a heterogeneous nature. As a matter of fact, the term can be used to refer to a "collection of entirely distinct doctrines with different functions".[62] Far from turning a blind eye from those who criticize that an AI can even "act" in a *Tatbestand* perspective,[63] this paragraph will now focus on the "failure*[s]* of causation".[64]

Pagallo applies the expression "failure of causation" to describe the disruptive effect of the autonomy of AI agents on the link between agency and the occurred negative outcome (in a cause and effect analysis: if A, then B).[65] He states laconically, but accurately: "Matters of legal causation, are, traditionally, a nightmare for legal scholars".[66]

The problem of ascertaining causality between the AI system and the harmful event arises because this kind of explanation is linked to the possibility for man to fully dominate (etiologically) a certain event, something that in certain AI applications may not be possible. It can be demonstrated that a system starting from a set of inputs has produced some outputs, but it might not be possible to explain why and how. Sometimes, we might not even be able to understand which inputs had a role in obtaining the output. Indeed, as it was already highlighted before, in cases of AI-based crime "the distance between a human action and its consequences increase exponentially".[67]

This study identified three factors which bring about failures of causation: (1) the problem of many hands; (2) the black box problem; and (3) shortcuts.[68] These three factors will be briefly touched upon in this order, leaving the more in-depth analysis for later on in this research.

(1) The Many Hands Problem

Borrowing an expression which was coined in the field of philosophy and moral responsibility,[69] the expression "problem of many hands" refers to the fact that the development of AI systems is often the result of the combinations of actions by numerous individuals and

als Handlung definiert, sind sie durchaus als Handelnde anzusehen. Je stärker man den Begriff der Handlung substantiell auflädt, je mehr an selbstbewusster Zielbestimmung man in ihn hineinliest, desto weniger können Intelligente Agenten den Voraussetzungen der Handlungsfähigkeit genügen". Ibid.

62 J. Keiler & D. Roef, "Principles of Criminalisation and the Limits of Criminal Law", in J. Keiler & D. Roef (eds.), *Comparative Concepts of Criminal Law*, 3rd ed., Intersentia, 2019, p. 61.

63 D. Lima, "Could AI Agents Be Held Criminally Liable? Artificial Intelligence and the Challenges for Criminal Law", *South Carolina Law Review*, Vol. 69, Issue 3, 2018, p. 677. This issue will be dealt with into detail in Ch. 6.3.

64 Pagallo, 2013, p. 73.

65 Ibid.

66 Pagallo, 2013, p. 73.

67 Hildebrandt, 2014, p. 190.

68 Council of Europe & Yeung, 2019, p. 12.

69 For an in-depth philosophical analysis of the "problem of many hands", see I. van de Poel, L. Royakkers & S. D. Zwart, *Moral Responsibility and the Problem of Many Hands*, Routledge, 2018.

the outcome of a long, and complex, chain of individual efforts.[70] Consequently, when harm occurs, it is very hard – if not impossible – to identify the individual cause, and therefore the liable individual, behind the event. The problem of many hands is particularly evident in cases of open-source software. It poses significant challenges to the ascription of criminal liability which is, by nature, based on *individual*, and not collective, responsibility.

(2) The Black Box Problem

The "black box" problem regards specific AI systems (based, for example, on Deep Neural Networks, DNNs) which solve problems in an *opaque* way.[71] It can be defined as "an inability to fully understand an AI's decision-making process and the inability to predict the AI's decisions or outputs".[72] It entails that it might be impossible for the designer or the user of the program to foresee AI behavior after the system is deployed, and to reconstruct why it acted in a specific way *ex post*.

DNNs are built on layers of interconnected artificial neurons which work together. A DNN will make decisions using an intuitive decision-making process and it will learn through experience. If we think of an analogy, it is the same as when you "know" how to ride a bike because you learned by attempting, and falling, over and over again.[73] It is impossible for someone to explain to external subjects (for example by describing the correct movements for maintaining one's balance while on a bike) how such knowledge was reached. One could say that"[y]ou use your brain all the time; you trust your brain all the time; and you have no idea how your brain works".[74]

(3) Shortcuts

Shortcut is a phenomenon that occurs in ML, specifically in self-supervised ML (a model which learns by itself: it is fed raw data without any label description from humans, and it

70 "First identified in the context of information technology by philosopher of technology, Helen Nissenbaum, the problem of 'many hands' is not unique to computers, digital technology, algorithms or machine learning. Rather, it refers to the fact that a complex array of individuals, organisations, components and processes are involved in the development, deployment and implementation of complex systems, so that when these systems malfunction or otherwise cause harm, it becomes very difficult to identify who is to blame, because such concepts are conventionally understood in terms of individualistic conceptions of responsibility. In other words, causal responsibility is necessarily distributed where complex technological systems are concerned, diluting causation to mere influence". Council of Europe & Yeung, 2019, p. 63.

71 For a clean cut explanation of the black box problem, see D. Castelvecchi, "Can we open the black box of AI?", *Nature*, Vol. 538, 5 October 2016. Available at: www.nature.com/news/can-we-open-the-black-box-of-ai-1.20731. For a thorough overview of the impact of black-box systems on intent and causation, see: Y. Bathaee, "The Artificial Intelligence Black Box and the Failure of Intent and Causation", *Harvard Journal of Law & Technology*, Vol. 31, 2018.

72 Bathaee, 2018, p. 905.

73 Ivi, p. 902.

74 P. Baldi, quoted in Castelvecchi, 2016, p. 23.

is then told, for example, to classify this data). Sometimes, the model relies on a simple characteristic in a dataset (for example, the green grass) rather than learning the true meaning of that data. This phenomenon is referred to as a "shortcut" and is very difficult to detect, since the outputs of AI systems are, at a first glance, correct. The result of shortcuts is inaccurate predictions. We might question how a judge will apply the standard rule on attribution, that is, the operation through which she or he selects the legally relevant cause of a harmful event in cases where the AI system takes a shortcut. What if it is not possible to reconstruct the web of causation *ex post*? Which scientific theory should the judge rely on in order to ascertain liability?

Unquestionably, the three factors mentioned above emphasize the disruptive character of failures of causation.

1.3.3 Guilty Robot Minds

Some of the most fundamental problems in the attribution of criminal liability to AI systems arise with regard to the subjective element of offenses, also referred to as the mental state (*mens rea*) element. This represents – at the state of the art – one of the most heated debates in the (newborn) field of AI criminal theory.

Indeed, if one assumes that intelligent agents can fulfill the *actus reus* of a crime, the next question to be asked is whether intelligent agents can be *guilty*.[75] In this regard, scholars mainly base their opinions drawing on comparisons with corporate liability.[76] Actually, according to US criminal legal doctrine, mental states can be imputed to corporations following the *respondeat superior* theory and, to a certain extent, such reasoning could be applied to ascribe culpable mental states of "humans-in-the-loop" (AI developers, owners, users) to the artificial agent. As argued by Hallevy:

> [...] there is no substantive legal difference between the idea of criminal liability imposed on corporations and on AI entities. It would be outrageous not to subordinate them to human laws, as corporations have been. Models of criminal liability exist as general paths to impose punishment. *What else is needed?*[77]

Conversely, others argue that "[u]nlike a corporation, which is literally composed of the humans acting on its behalf, an AI is not guaranteed to come with a *ready supply of iden-*

75 Gless & Weigend, 2014, p. 573.
76 The matter is addressed in depth in Ch. 6.4.
77 G. Hallevy, "The Criminal Liability of Artificial Intelligence Entities – From Science Fiction to Legal Social Control", *Akron Intellectual Property Journal*, Vol. 4, Issue 2, 2010, p. 201 [emphasis added].

tifiable human actors whose mental states can be imputed",[78] and suggest the development of a set of specific AI strict liability offenses, therefore allowing for punishment of AI without requiring mental states.

Leaving the question of attributing *mens rea* directly to AI systems for later elucidation, there is another battlefield where the academic discussion has gained traction: negligence crimes for humans behind the machine. Should legal systems create new negligence crimes for developers/producers/users of AI systems? Is it feasible to speak of a form of *culpa in programmando* as a twin sister of the already existing *culpa in vigilando* doctrine? Or should we look elsewhere, namely tort law?

1.4 Research Question & Structure of Chapters

The research will be guided by the following main research question: *to what extent is a theoretical framework of criminal law for liability of non-human agents needed and feasible?*[79]

First and foremost, the following section of this chapter will be concluded with a list of real life or hypothetical scenarios of "AI going wrong",[80] which will be recalled during the research. The examples chosen are purposively trivial and are meant to introduce the issues discussed in this study in an unpretentious, yet straightforward, manner.

AI is a multifaceted concept which is rooted in a different field than legal doctrine, i.e., computer science. Finding a univocal definition is challenging, even in its home field. For this reason, this study starts by addressing such problems in Chapter 2. It targets the following sub-questions: *why is the issue of defining AI an issue? What are the basic functions of AI?* After providing a short history of AI and of its most modern applications, Chapter 2 gives an overview of the different definitions put forth since the late 1950s and of its basic functioning. It will then be concluded with the adoption of a working definition.

Chapter 3 accounts for the ongoing scholarly discussion on AI and criminal law. The analysis is necessary in order to position this study in the relevant debate. It addresses the following sub-questions: *What is the state of the art of the scholarly debate on AI and criminal law? Which are the most recurrent questions and what are the answers? Which aspects are being neglected?*

78 Abbott & Sarch, 2019, p. 352 [emphasis added].

79 This research deals mostly with one type of non-human agents, i.e., AI systems. Nevertheless, it touches upon also different forms of non-human liability, such as corporate criminal liability and its "augmented" form (see Chapter 6.4.2).

80 For an updated database of AI-related incidents, see the AI Incident Database, available at: https://incidentdatabase.ai/.

Chapters 4, 5, and 6 focus on *ascription* and address the following sub-question: *can liability for AI Crimes be attributed to the AI agent itself?* To do so, Chapter 4 introduces different concepts, ranging from the "Paperclip Maximizer" thought experiment and the notion of utility function, to the similarities between AI incidents and other technological failures, such as aviation incidents (and their criminalization). Moreover, it focuses on different theories of criminalization, i.e., the framework in which the selection of criteria for the ascription of an offense occurs. As such, Chapter 4 is meant to set the scene for the more in-depth analysis which follows at Chapters 5 and 6.

Chapters 5 and 6 represent the beating heart of this research. The inquiry in Chapters 5 and 6 is focused on understanding if modern models of criminal liability should be, and can be, adapted to algorithmic harm in a way that is compatible with principles related to criminal punishment, such as the principle of legality and the principle of blameworthiness.

Specifically, Chapter 5 focuses on criminal capacity, i.e., the set of conditions required to be an addressee of criminal law. First, it discusses the contours and relevance of criminal capacity in criminal law. Then, it addresses whether AI systems can have personhood in criminal law. Chapter 6 analyzes AI crime both in a *mens rea* and *actus reus* direction. With regard to *mens rea*, Chapter 6.2. examines whether *mens rea* can be imputed directly to AI. Moreover, it analyzes the liability of the "humans behind the machine". When it comes to the specific discussion of *human* liability, Chapter 6 also addresses mainly issues connected to *negligent* offenses, as these are deemed the most problematic, hence worthy of investigation, field. With regard to *actus reus*, attention is given in Chapter 6.3 to whether an AI system can act in a criminally relevant way and to the impact of "failures of causality" on the reconstruction of the causal link. Chapter 6.4. touches upon models of corporate liability. This analysis is essential since a very conspicuous number of scholars draw upon the analogy with corporations in order to base their arguments on criminal liability for AI systems. Thus, this research considers the analogy with a critical eye, assessing its strengths and flaws. After doing so, the research briefly stretches its frontiers to discussing Diamantis' "algorithmic corporate misconduct"[81] and "corporate algorithmic harm"[82] theories.

Chapter 7 presents an overview of adopted (or proposed regulations) on criminal liability of AI updated to February 2023. It addresses the following sub-question: *what is the state of the art of criminal law regulation on AI*? The latitude of the analysis in Chapter 7 is global. Specifically, it tackles: A) the CoE's CDPC and the drafting of an "Instrument on

81 M. E. Diamantis, "The Extended Corporate Mind: When Corporations Use AI to Break the Law", *N.C.L. Rev.*, Vol. 97, 2020.

82 Ibid.

Artificial Intelligence and Criminal Law";[83] B) the Singapore Penal Code Review Committee Report of 2018[84] and the Report on "Criminal Liability, Robotics and AI systems" drafted by the Singapore Law Commissions of 2021;[85] C) the legislative reform of the French Road Act;[86] D) the "Automated Vehicles: joint report" drafted by the Law Commission of England and Wales and by the Scottish Law Commission;[87] and E) the amendment of the German Road Traffic Act.[88]

Lastly, Chapter 8 presents the conclusions of this research and delineates directions of future inquiry. To do so, it will retrace the sub-questions of the chapters.[89] Consequently, it will first return to the issue of defining AI and its repercussions on criminal law. Then, it will situate this research in the realm of the scholarly literature on AI and criminal law analyzed in Chapter 3. Next, it will deliberate on the attribution of criminal liability to AI systems, by focusing specifically on why humans tend to hold AI systems to higher moral standards; on theories of retributivism and deterrence; and on the analogy between AI liability and corporate criminal liability. Moreover, the possibility of liability of humans *for* machines will also be reviewed. Lastly, Chapter 8 will return to the main research question, outline perspectives for future avenues of research, and conclude with the challenges which were encountered in this study.

83 As will be highlighted in Ch.7.2., the CDPC has not adopted said instrument yet.

84 Singapore Penal Code Review Committee, Report, 2018 ("PCRC Report"). Available at: www.reach.gov.sg/-/media/reach/old-reach/2018/public-consult/mha/annex--pcrc-report.ashx.

85 Singapore Academy of Law, Law Reform Committee, "Report on Criminal Liability, Robotics and AI Systems", 2021 ("SAL Report"). Available at: www.sal.org.sg/sites/default/files/SAL-LawReform-Pdf/2021-02/2021%20Report%20on%20Criminal%20Liability%20Robotics%20%26%20AI%20Systems.pdf.

86 Ordonnance n° 2021-443 du 14 avril 2021 relative au régime de responsabilité pénale applicable en cas de circulation d'un véhicule à délégation de conduite et à ses conditions d'utilisation (TRAT2034523R, JORF n°0089 du 15 avril 2021, Texte n° 36), 2021.

87 Law Commission of England and Wales Law Commission No. 404, Scottish Law Commission Scottish Law Commission No. 258, "Automated Vehicles: Joint report", HC 1068 SG/2022/15, 25 January 2022 ("Law Commissions Report"). Available at: https://s3-eu-west-2.amazonaws.com/lawcom-prod-storage-11jsxou24uy7q/uploads/2022/01/Automated-vehicles-joint-report-cvr-03-02-22.pdf.

88 Bundestag, Gesetz zur Änderung des Straßenverkehrsgesetzes und des Pflichtversicherungsgesetzes – Gesetz zum autonomen Fahren, Bundesgesetzblatt Jahrgang 2021, Teil I Nr. 48, 3108.

89 Chapter 2 – Why is the issue of defining AI an issue? What are the basic functions of AI?; Chapter 3 – What is the state of the art of the scholarly debate on AI and criminal law? Which are the most recurrent questions and what are the answers? Which aspects are being neglected?; Chapter 4 – What does ascribing criminal liability to an AI system entail?; Chapter 5 – Can an AI system be treated as a criminal agent?; Chapter 6 – Can an AI system fulfil the mens rea and actus reus requirements of a criminal offense?; Chapter 7 – What is the state of the art on criminal law regulation on AI?.

1.5 Methodology

As already outlined, in order to embark on any kind of theoretical and critical dialogue on this topic it is necessary to first review the authority and status of the legal doctrine on the issue. Hence, this research provides an extensive literature review in Chapter 3, which focuses on the current debate on the issue in the literature and hence clarifies the scope of the research that has been conducted in this area.[90]

This literature review has a double soul. First, it represents the theoretical background of this study. In this sense, it is essential for various reasons such as: determining what has been written on the topic of this research; identifying trends or patterns in that area of research; and identifying questions that require further inquiry.[91] Second, it represents an "original and valuable work of research in and of itself",[92] as it created "a solid starting point for all other members of the academic community that are interested"[93] to this specific overarching topic.

Chapter 3 includes doctrinal studies from diverse countries. The reasons for this large selection are manifold. Firstly, the scope of the debate is international, so disregarding pieces of the relevant literature would diminish the research's value; secondly, the question of AI criminal liability is being addressed through a shared language, that is, through doctrine on the common substantive aspects of criminal law. The literature review is indeed crucial for the purpose of building a valid foundation with regard to the existence and relevance of the problems discussed in this study.

The search strategy which was adopted for the literature review is the following. Relevant databases[94] were searched using words such as criminal liability, artificial intelligence, *mens rea*, *actus reus*, criminal legal framework, and accountability as search terms in the three languages mentioned above. The results of the analysis are based on approximately 100 texts in three languages (Italian, English, and German) published from when the topic

90 The nature of a literature review has been described as follows: "The literature review is the part of the thesis where there is an extensive reference to related research and theory in your field. It is where connections are made between the source texts that you draw on and when you position yourself and your research among their sources. It is your opportunity to engage in a written dialogue with researchers in your area while at the same time showing that you have engaged with, understood and responded to the relevant body of knowledge underpinning your research. The literature review is where you identify the theories and previous research which have influenced your choice of research topic and the methodology you are choosing to adopt. You can use the literature to support your identification of a problem to research and to illustrate that there is a gap in previous research, which needs to be filled. The literature review, therefore, serves as the driving force and jumping-off point for your research investigation". G. Pare et al., "Synthesizing information systems knowledge: A typology of literature reviews", *Information & Management*, No. 52, 2015, p. 183.

91 Ibid.

92 Pare, 2015, p. 183.

93 Ibid.

94 Including, but not limited to De Jure, HeinOnline, SSRN, ArXiv, Research Gate, and Academia.

gained popularity (circa 2010) until today. The analyzed texts were then categorized into three groups, which reflect the sides of the debate: skeptics, moderates, and expansionists.

The main research question is addressed in Chapters 4 to 6 by adopting a doctrinal methodology. When discussing the dogmas of traditional criminal law, this research will, at times, refer to different legal systems (mostly Italy, Germany, and the US). These countries are of interest for two main reasons: first, it was presumed that they would represent the country of provenance (or of reference) of many of the authors analyzed in Chapter 3; second, they are prototypes of different approaches to issues of criminal liability, especially with regard to corporate criminal liability.[95] Yet, the analysis in Chapters 4, 5, and 6 is *not* based on a comparative approach. Such method was discarded since – upon an initial survey – it became evident that there was little to no debate on the object of investigation at a *legislative* level. Only the existence of such a debate would have rendered the comparative research a reasonable exercise.

The initial assumption on the (still) little relevance of hard law regulation when it comes to AI and criminal liability is confirmed in Chapter 7. This breadth of this chapter is wider, since it does not follow a geographical criterion in the selection of the samples. Rather, it adopts a subjective criterion: it includes any type of legislation, policy, or report which addresses the general field of AI and criminal liability. The five samples examined in Chapter 7 are then compared with each other, and assessed according to their similarities, differences, and relevance.

A final methodological note is needed. The research will often touch upon the notions of accountability, responsibility, and liability. This reflects the current (doctrinal and institutional) debate, which, on the one hand, is characterized by a convergence of criminal law concepts and concepts pertaining to other fields (such as philosophy), and, on the other hand, does not expressly distinguish between the three aforementioned concepts, which are discussed rather fluidly.[96] It is for this reason, too, that this book is titled "Criminal Behavior and *Accountability* of Artificial Intelligence Systems".

---

95 Germany at the moment provides only for administrative corporate criminal liability – *Ordnungswidrigkeitengesetz* – even though there are recurrent discussion on the introduction of corporate criminal liability via new legislation; Italy has adopted a hybrid system with Law 231/2001; in the United States corporations can be held directly criminally liable.

96 Distinguishing between accountability, responsibility, and liability can be tricky. According to some, the difference between accountability and (moral) responsibility is one of point of views. The latter entails a "scrutiny from an external point of view", while the former requires "a personal judgment of one's agency" (C. Novelli, M. Taddeo & L. Floridi, "Accountability in artificial intelligence: what it is and how it works", *AI & Soc.*, 2023, p. 3), which in turn presupposes "the capacity to act from free choice and with due concern for one's duties and obligations" (R. Mulgan, "Issues of accountability", in R. Mulgan, [Ed.], *Holding power to account: accountability in modern democracies*, 2003, p. 15). Responsibility can be distinguished from liability, which is used to refer to the situation in which a person, in performing a certain action or entering into a certain contract, has assumed a legal obligation and is therefore liable for the legal consequences arising therefrom. In other words, liability relates to qualified behaviors, whereas accountability and

1.6 AIs Going Bad – Examples

Example A – The Driverless Car

An autonomous vehicle produced by the company Trust'n'ride, carrying a safety driver, runs over a woman who is walking a bicycle while crossing the street.[97] The woman was jaywalking and the road was dry and illuminated by street lighting. The system failed to identify the pedestrian until 5.6 seconds before the impact, as it was not trained for detecting jaywalking pedestrians. The driver operator was looking at her phone and started steering the wheel to avoid the collision 0.2 seconds before hitting the pedestrian. According to the findings of an independent governmental authority, the probable cause of the crash was the vehicle operator's failure to monitor the driving environment and the operation of the automated driving system because she was distracted by her personal cell phone. Moreover, Trust'n'ride's inadequate safety risk assessment procedures and ineffective oversight of vehicle operators contributed to the crash. Interestingly, the system design had precluded the activation of the emergency braking system for collision mitigation (it relied instead on the human's intervention to avoid a collision). The County Attorney of Rose Hills decided not to press criminal charges against the company and instead pursued charges against the backup driver who was eventually indicted with one count of negligent vehicular homicide. Should the backup driver be convicted?

Example B – Predicting Suicide

An AI system is used for predicting suicide attempts by applying machine learning to electronic health records of patients seen for any reason.[98] Imagine the system, which has

---

responsibility refer to a wider world, one that also contains moral rules and social rules, such as folkways and norms of courtesy. According to some, liability denotes the punishments or sanctions that an agent must bear in virtue of his or her moral/legal responsibility (J. Danaher, "Robots, Law and the Retribution Gap", *Ethics and Information Technology*, Vol. 18, No. 4, 2016, p. 300). Liability can be further differentiated depending on the relevant area of law. In the case of criminal law, it can be defined in terms of "punitive-liability" and "is about suffering harm and public condemnation for wrongs done" (Danaher, 2016, p. 300).

97 The example is inspired by the killing of Elaine Herzberg in Tempe, Arizona. The Guardian, "Self-driving Uber kills Arizona woman in first fatal crash involving pedestrian", 19 March 2018. Available at: www.theguardian.com/technology/2018/mar/19/uber-self-driving-car-kills-woman-arizona-tempe.

98 Several studies with the purpose of developing accurate suicide attempt risk models have already been developed and currently being used in a number of fields, see C. G. Walsh, J. D. Ribeiro & J. C. Franklin, "Predicting Risk of Suicide Attempts Over Time Through Machine Learning", *Clinical Psychological Science*, Vol.5, Issue 3, 2017; C. G. Walsh et al., "Prospective Validation of an Electronic Health Record-Based, Real-Time Suicide Risk Model", *JAMA Netw Open*, Vol. 4, No. 3, 2021. Other models include: REACH VET (Recovery Engagement and Coordination for Health – Veterans Enhanced Treatment) from the Veterans Health Administration and Army STARRS (Study to Assess Risk and Resilience in Service members).

proven to have an accuracy of 80%, predicts that a patient admitted to the emergency room for a sprained ankle is at high risk of committing suicide. Said evaluation is done based on hospital admission data such as age, gender, past diagnosis, socioeconomic status, and employment status, to mention a few.[99] Some of these factors are not usually considered by doctors in evaluating suicide risks and most of the time such evaluation is not even conducted on patients admitted for this type of injury. What if the algorithm foresees a high suicidal risk and the doctor's clinical opinion differs, leading to a discharge of the patient and his or her suicide? Should the doctor be liable for the death of the patient? If we consider the opposite scenario, what if the algorithm does not predict a suicide? Who is to blame?

Example C – Evil AI

Meet Norman, the world first psychopath AI.[100] In 2018, researchers at MIT created an AI system capable of perform image captioning (a deep learning method developed to generate a textual description of an image). The algorithm was trained on image captions taken from a dark thread on the Subreddit platform which is dedicated to document and observe death. Then, the system was subjected to the Rorschach inkblots test. This test is normally used to analyze personality traits and to diagnose certain mental illnesses. The results of Norman were then compared with the responses of a standard image captioning neural network trained on a MSCOCO (Microsoft Common Objects in Context) dataset.[101] The regular AI saw a close up of a vase with flowers, Norman saw a man shot dead. The aim of the experiment was to prove that there is no such thing as "inherently bad" AI systems, just systems trained with bad data. According to most, this experiment is proof of the dangers of AI trained on biased data falling into the "wrong hands". If a system designed like Norman went rogue and committed a crime, could it be said that it possessed *mens rea*? Can AI plead insanity?

99 See O. Goldhill, "Machines know when someone's about to attempt suicide. How should we use that information?", *Quartz*, 5 September 2018. Available at: https://qz.com/1367197/machines-know-when-someones-about-to-attempt-suicide-how-should-we-use-that-information.

100 Available at http://norman-ai.mit.edu/.

101 Dataset containing 328k photos of 91 object types that would be easily recognizable by a 4 year old. See T. Lin et al., "Microsoft COCO: Common Objects in Context, Computer Vision – ECCV", *Lecture Notes in Computer Science*, Springer, Vol. 8693, 2014.

Example D – Moral Dilemmas

1 – **The Trolley Problem.** An automated vehicle (AV) driving in autonomous mode, carrying a human, is driving at high speed on a road where two seriously injured people (A and B) are lying. If the AV swerves to the right to avoid running over (and killing) A and B, it will hit C and D who are standing at the side of the road. Based on (very fast-paced) calculations, including the almost certain probability of injuring C and D, and the likely risk of killing A and B, it decides not to swerve. As a consequence, A and B die from the impact. Could it be argued that the AV's act was justified or excused?[102]

2 – **The Burning Room Dilemma.** Imagine that an object of value is trapped in a room that is on fire and that a human, who does not want to put herself in danger by retrieving the object, instructs a capable robotic companion to get the object from the room ('*short_Grab*' action) and bring it to safety, thus risking self-destruction. The agent could also take a longer route ('*long_Grab*' action), which avoids the fire, but that entails a 0.0.5 probability that the object may be destroyed during the time it takes for the robot to complete the route. It is assumed that the robot is unsure of whether the human values the object more than it values its own safety. What decision should the robot-agent make in this critical scenario?[103]

3 – **The drowning child.**[104] Let us imagine that a delivery robot is walking on a beach promenade when it hears a child crying for help because she is drowning. Suppose that the robot makes a series of calculations which include the option of stopping to pull the child out of the water (which leads to a 10% chance that it might fall and destroy itself) and the option of not doing anything (which leads to a 90% chance that the child will die). The robot knows with a 95% probability that the drowning child is actually a human child who is in imminent danger. Let us assume that the robot decides not to take any action because it deems its task of delivering a package more important and, as a consequence of its omission to act, the child drowns. Should the robot be liable?

Let us assume now that the robot did not react to the child's cry for help because it is convinced that it is already in the process of saving another drowning child, who instead is already dead. Should a change in the robot's motive to act (i.e., from deciding that deliv-

---

102 The example is adapted from E. Hilgendorf, "The dilemma of autonomous driving: Reflections on the moral and legal treatment of automatic collision avoidance systems", in E. Hilgendorf and J. Feldle (eds), *Digitization and the Law*, Robotik und Recht, Vol. 15, Nomos, 2018, p. 75.

103 The example is taken from D. Abel, J. MacGlashan & M.L. Littman, "Reinforcement Learning as a Framework for Ethical Decision Making", *AAAI Workshop: AI, Ethics, and Society*, 2016.

104 The example is adapted from Y. Hu, "Robot criminals", *U. Mich. J.L. Reform*, Vol. 52, 2019, p. 500.

ering a package is more important than saving the drowning's child life, to mistakenly decide to continue saving another child's life) affect evaluations regarding its liability.

2 Defining Artificial Intelligence

Do AIs dream of electric sheep?

Philip K. Dick (1968)

2.1 Introduction: To Define or Not To Define?

"AI is learning how to create itself",[1] recited sensationally the MIT Technology Review – one of the most renowned online newspapers on technology – on May 27, 2021. The article was commenting on a research named POET (acronym for Paired Open-Ended Trailblazer) that is currently being conducted in the Uber AI Labs by Ruy Wang.[2] POET is an open-ended algorithm, meaning that it works and progresses without pre-established goals.[3] The system is being tested in a 2-D bipedal-walking obstacle course where the algorithm simultaneously creates problems (the paths and the obstacles, e.g., a flat terrain or a hill), solves them (e.g., by making the two-legged figure jump or run), and learns from them (Fig. 1). "Given any problem space with the potential for diverse variations, POET can blaze a trail through it",[4] says Wang. Thus, if we look at POET's presentation video, we are not struck by the bot's complexity or problem-solving capabilities.[5]

In fact, what one notices *prima facie* is just a tiny limping stick figure with a wedge-shaped head that attempts to walk and to overtake obstacles, dragging its "knee" on the ground and stumbling from time to time (Fig.1).[6] In all fairness, nothing as razzle-dazzle

1 W.D. Heaven, "AI is learning how to create itself. Humans have struggled to make truly intelligent machines. Maybe we need to let them get on with it themselves", *MIT Technology Review*, 27 May 2021. Available at: www.technologyreview.com/2021/05/27/1025453/artificial-intelligence-learning-create-itself-agi.

2 R. Wang et al., "Paired Open-Ended Trailblazer (POET): EndlesslyGenerating Increasingly Complex and Diverse Learning Environments and Their Solutions", *ArXiv abs/1901.01753*, 2019.

3 The definition of open-endness is debated amongst AI researchers. Evolutionary algorithms design represents one of the growing fields of study in computer science today. For the purposes of understanding the functioning of POET, it is relevant to state that "[i]n an open-ended learning process, an agent or robot must solve an unbounded sequence of tasks that are not known in advance", hence without knowing the given domain (comprising its states, actions and rewards). S. Doncieuxet et al., "Open-Ended Learning: A Conceptual Framework Based on Representational Redescription", in *Frontiers in neurorobotics*, Vol. 12, p. 59, 2018. Available at: https://doi.org/10.3389/fnbot.2018.00059. For an in-depth analysis of the concept of open-ended evolution as applied to AI, see O. Stanley Kenneth; "Why Open-Endedness Matters", *Artif Life*, Vol. 25, No. 3, 2019, pp. 232–235; N. Packard et al., "An Overview of Open-Ended Evolution: Editorial Introduction to the Open-Ended Evolution II Special Issue", *Artificial Life*, Vol. 25, No. 2, 2019, pp. 93-103.

4 Wang, 2019.

5 Ibid.

6 Heaven, 2021.

as hinted at by the article's presentation. Indeed, the AI system we are able to perceive in this image seems far from carrying out complex tasks, such as screening millions of genetic compounds to develop new drugs[7] or operating on a patient with extreme precision in a short time through a robotic arm.[8]

Figure 1 ***An Example of POET'S Bipedal-Walking Obstacle Course***

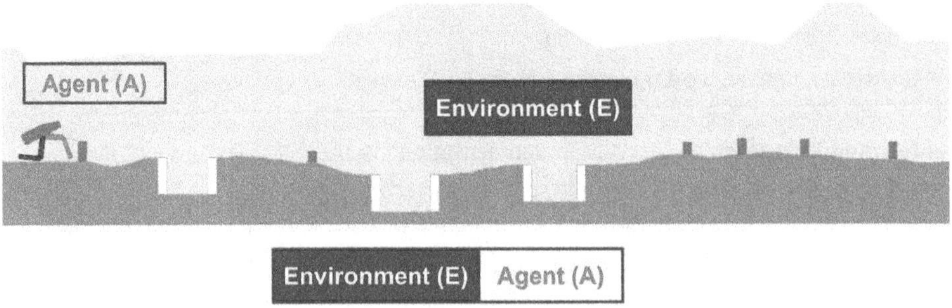

Source: J. Clune and K. O. Stanley, "POET: Endlessly Generating Increasingly Complex and Diverse Learning Environments and their Solutions through the Paired Open-Ended Trailblazer", *Uber Blog*, 8 January 2019. Available at: www.uber.com/en-NL/blog/poet-open-ended-deep-learning.

Yet, if one takes a closer and more informed look, it seems as if POET poses even more issues than other AI systems. It is an instance of using AI to make AI and, as such, it has the revolutionary potential of changing the narrative: it entails using ML algorithms not only as tools to solve foreseen problems, but also to generate their own problems and solutions: "[u]nlike algorithms in, for example, machine learning that learn to solve problems we *ask them to solve*, open-ended algorithms could produce surprises beyond our imagination *without the need to ask*".[9] Could we substitute the word "surprises" with

7 Think for example of AtomNet, a drug discovery platform developed by Atomwise, which by applying deep convolutional neural networks is able to predict the bioactivity of small molecules for drug discovery application. Notably, thanks to one of its ongoing projects it found a drug candidate that might be applied to combat Ebola and multiple sclerosis. For a deeper analysis, see: I Wallach, M. Dzamba & A. Heifets., "AtomNet: A Deep Convolutional Neural Network for Bioactivity Prediction in Structure-based Drug Discovery", *ArXiv abs/1510.02855*, 2015.

8 For example think of the system developed by Asensus Surgical which performs a type of telesurgery named Performance-Guided Surgery: through augmented intelligence a robotic-assisted platform is able to perceive (computer vision), learn (machine learning) and assist (clinical intelligence) in minimally invasive surgeries such as laparoscopy. Such system could allow a surgeon sitting in a room to operate in more than 2 or 3 operating rooms at the same time, be it in the same hospital or in another country. See G. Nichols, "Surgery digitized: Telesurgery becoming a reality", *ZD Net*, 14 June 2021. Available at: www.zdnet.com/article/surgery-digitized-telesurgery-becoming-a-reality/.

9 Kenneth, 2018, p. 233.

"risks"? Or even "harm"? As some have said, this might be first step towards achieving Artificial General Intelligence, also referred to as 'super intelligent machines'.[10]

The examples above helped to direct our attention to one of the existential issues when studying AI: what is AI exactly? Is it the awkwardly walking two-legged bot or the sophisticated driverless car? As the scope of this research is to discuss a liability framework involving AI actions, what should judges, legal professionals, and regulators consider as AI in a criminal law context? In essence: *why is the issue of defining AI an issue?*[11]

On a preliminary note, it is relevant to stress that avoiding ambiguities in law is crucial: legislators and policymakers strive to create technical language that is void of polysemous words. When doing so, they act as lexicographers and create a technical vocabulary that might be extremely different from the ordinary 'popular' one.[12]

When it comes to AI, the urge to clearly define it is enhanced by two factors. First, there is no overall accepted definition of AI[13] – even though it is possible to identify systematic efforts in this direction by the first players in the AI regulation field, such as the European Union.[14] Second, in order to define AI it is necessary to touch upon technical concepts pertaining to computer science. Undeniably, "[a] complicating factor is that legal definitions differ from pure scientific definitions whereas they should meet a number of requirements (such as inclusiveness, preciseness, comprehensiveness, practicability, permanence), some of which are legally binding, and some are considered good regulatory practice".[15] This is especially true when it comes to criminal norms, which are subject to a strict principle of legality.

---

10 Heaven, 2021. See *infra* for a myth buster definition of Artificial General Intelligence (AGI).

11 The question will be addressed in depth in Chapters 5.2. and 8.2. For the time being, it can be stated that the lack of a universal technical definition of AI systems directly affects understanding whether AI could be considered as agents of crimes.

12 F. Macagno, "Definitions in Law", *Bulletin Suisse de Linguistique Appliquee*, 2010, p. 201.

13 See S. Legg & M. Hutter, "A Collection of Definitions of Intelligence", *arXiv:0706.3639v1*, 2007 for a survey of AI definitions conducted up to 2007. For a collection of more recent definitions, see *infra*.

14 The definition adopted is contained in Article 3 of the "Proposal for a regulation of the European Parliament and of the Council Laying Down Harmonised Rules On Artificial Intelligence (Artificial Intelligence Act) and Amending Certain Union Legislative Acts", COM(2021) 206 final, 21 April 2022: "artificial intelligence system' (AI system) means software that is developed with one or more of the techniques and approaches listed in Annex I and can, for a given set of human-defined objectives, generate outputs such as content, predictions, recommendations, or decisions influencing the environments they interact with". Annex I reads:

  a. Machine learning approaches, including supervised, unsupervised and reinforcement learning, using a wide variety of methods including deep learning;
  b. Logic- and knowledge-based approaches, including knowledge representation, inductive (logic) programming, knowledge bases, inference and deductive engines, (symbolic) reasoning and expert systems;
  c. Statistical approaches, Bayesian estimation, search and optimization methods.

15 Council of Europe, CAHAI Secretariat, "Towards a regulation of AI systems", DGI (2020) 16, p. 23. Available at: https://rm.coe.int/prems-107320-gbr-2018-compli-cahai-couv-texte-a4-bat-web/1680a0c17a.

Having acknowledged that defining AI is indeed an issue, we need to ask ourselves why this research needs to adopt a definition. The reasons are manifold. To begin with, when we look at the concept of criminal liability, one of its foundation stones is the concept of *action*: in order to understand how an AI acts, and why it does so, we need to first define what we mean by AI and who the artificial agent is. As it will be shown in Chapter 2, the lack of a common definition impacts directly on identifying criminally capable subjects, i.e., the addressees of criminal norms. Once this is established, it is possible to discuss relevant questions such as: *is AI behavior relevant for criminal law? What is the difference – if any – between the act of an AI and of a human being from a criminal law standpoint?* As a matter of fact, AI "[f]irst [...] invites us to consider whether AI agents are acting in the sense of criminal law. And secondly, it urges us to think about different modes of acting when it comes to human agents".[16]

To continue, things seem to get even more complicated with regard to *mens rea* requirements: if AI entities are able to distinguish right from wrong, what is permitted from what is prohibited, one could ask oneself whether such capabilities can be seen as 'clues' of the existence of the internal elements needed for criminal liability. These and more aspects will be analyzed in depth in Chapters 4 and 6.

The purpose of this chapter is twofold: first, to adopt a working definition of AI and second, to function as a primer for the reader, providing her with an adequate "toolbox" of notions that will be used throughout this analysis. This chapter is structured as follows. First, the author gives a synopsis of the development of AI, accounting for approximately the past 50 years. Second, the focus will shift to discussing the main definitions of AI that have been developed by experts in the field. Third, basic notions of current AI technologies will be provided. Fourth, the author will elucidate on the working definition adopted for this research. Fifth, the author will provide real life examples of AI systems, which can be used as case studies. Lastly, this chapter concludes with an essential glossary of terms.

2.2 A Short History of AI

When analyzing the history of AI, it is common to find analogies with the seasons to describe the cycles of hype and disappointment that characterized its development.[17] Generally, in the scholarly discourse four distinct "springs" and "winters" are identified: the first spring (1956–1974), the first winter (1974–1981), the second spring (1981–1987), and

16 Lima, 2018, p. 681 [emphasis added].

17 M. Haenlein & A. Kaplan, "A Brief History of Artificial Intelligence: On the Past, Present and Future of Artificial Intelligence", *California Management Review*, Vol. 61, No. 4, pp. 5-14, 2019; S. J. Russell & P. Norvig, *Artificial Intelligence. A Modern Approach*, 2nd edition, Pearson, 2003, pp. 16-27.

the second winter (1987–1993) (Fig. 2).[18] The use of seasonal metaphors is sometimes troublesome as it reinforces a narrative which alternates cyclical portrayals of AI as the "ultimate panacea, which would solve everything and overcome everything; or as the final catastrophe, a superintelligence that would destroy millions of jobs, replacing lawyers and doctors, journalists and researchers, truckers and taxi drivers, and ending by dominating human beings as if they were pets at best".[19]

Figure 2 ***Artificial Intelligence over the Years***

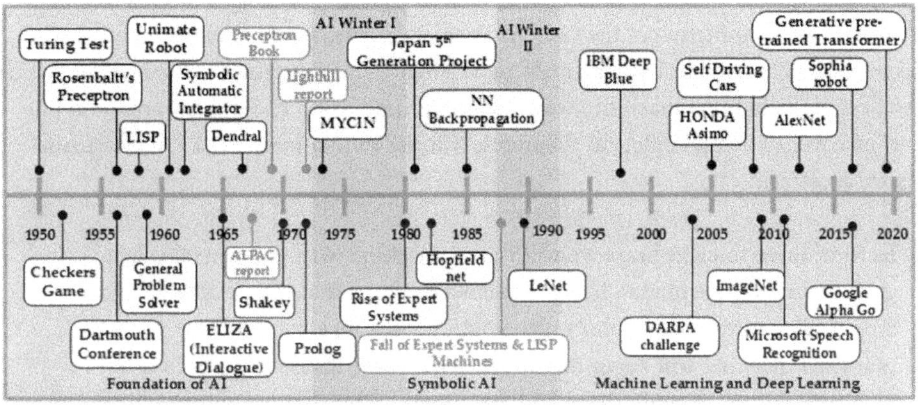

Source: F. H. Khan et al., "Advancements in Microprocessor Architecture for Ubiquitous AI – An Overview on History, Evolution, and Upcoming Challenges in AI Implementation", *Micromachines*, Vol. 12, No. 6, 2021. Licensed under CC BY 4.0

The official birth of AI as a new scientific discipline is commonly seen in the year 1956.[20] For many, however, it can be located earlier in the work of Alan Turing in the 1940s. Notably, it was "[t]he powerful way in which The Bombe was able to break the Enigma code, a task previously impossible to even the best human mathematicians"[21] which made Turing wonder about the intelligence of the said machine. In 1950, Turing published "Computing Machinery and Intelligence", in which he introduced the "imitation game", later known as the "Turing test".[22] Its goal was to establish whether or not a machine was intelligent based on the assumption that if a human interacting with an artificial intelligence was incapable of distinguishing it from a human, then the machine must be intelligent.

18 Y. Shin, "The Spring of Artificial Intelligence in Its Global Winter", *IEEE Annals of the History of Computing*, Vol. 41, Issue 4, 2019.

19 L. Floridi, "AI and Its New Winter: from Myths to Realities", in *Philosophy & Technology*, Vol. 33, 2020, p. 1.

20 McCarthy et al., 1955.

21 Haenlein & Kaplan, 2019, p. 6.

22 A. Turing, "Computing Machinery and Intelligence", *Mind*, LIX/236, 1950, pp. 433-460.

In the first wave of AI development, which was roughly the 20 years following 1956, research focused on 'symbolic' AI: humans pre-programmed systems to solve tasks by feeding them logical 'if-then' rules in the form of symbols (such as graphs or formulas). Symbolic AI requires "human experts to encode their knowledge in a way the computer can understand" and this "places significant constraints on their degree of autonomy".[23]

It was an extremely prosperous time for AI, one characterized by heavy investments from national governments.[24] One of the most famous events of that time was the introduction of ELIZA, a natural language processing (NLP) computer program which mimicked a psychotherapist and that could "carry on a conversation in English on any topic";[25] another was the introduction of the General Problem Solver, a computer program which could supposedly simulate human problem solving.[26] The optimism was palpable: AI researchers predicted that machines would soon become world chess champions and be able to discover new mathematical theorems. Minsky in a famous 1970 Life Magazine interview professed:

> In from three to eight years we will have a machine with the general intelligence of an average human being. I mean a machine that will be able to read Shakespeare, grease a car, play office politics, tell a joke, have a fight. At that point the machine will begin to educate itself with fantastic speed. In a few months it will be at genius level and few months after that its powers will be incalculable.[27]

Those predictions did not come true, mostly due to the fact that the machines had very little memory and the computing time was too long. What is more, symbolic systems suffer from what is known as "Moravec's paradox", which entails that it is easy to create computers which exhibit adult level performance on intelligence tests (such as the Turing test or playing chess), but it is difficult or impossible to give them the skillset of a one-year-old

23 European Parliament, "How artificial intelligence works", Briefing, Member's Research Service, 2019. Available at: www.europarl.europa.eu/RegData/etudes/BRIE/2019/634420/EPRS_BRI(2019)634420_EN.pdf.

24 Think for example of the $ 2.2 million grant from the Advanced Research Projects Agency (U.S.) to the MIT to fund the project MAC founded by Minsky and McCarthy.

25 J. Weizenbaum, "ELIZA – a computer program for the study of natural language communication between man and machine", *Communications of the ACM*, Vol. 9, Issue 1, 1966, pp. 36-45. A JavaScript version of Eliza is available at: http://psych.fullerton.edu/mbirnbaum/psych101/eliza.htm.

26 See H. A. Simon, J. Shaw & A. Newell, "Heuristic Problem Solving: The Next Advance in Operations Research", *Operations Research*, Vol. 6, No. 1, 1958; H. A. Simon, J. Shaw & A. Newell, "Report on a General Problem-Solving Program", *Rand Corporation*, 1959.

27 B. Darrach, "Meet Shaky, the first electronic person", *Life Magazine*, 20 November 1970, p. 58B. Available at: https://books.google.it/books?id=2FMEAAAAMBAJ&lpg=PA57&dq=%22first%20electronic%20person%22&pg=PA58#v=onepage&q=years&f=false.

when it comes to perception and adaptability.[28] To put it simply: why is AI so smart and yet so dumb? Why does AI struggle with the simple?[29] Such questions, as will be seen, are still relevant today.

A new stream of techno-optimism resurged at the end of the 1970s, as symbolic artificial intelligence led to the development of "expert systems" (Fig.3). Such term referred to the belief that machines could reproduce the steps of a human expert when performing an assignment: the underlying idea was that intelligent human behavior could be deconstructed into a succession of logical rules, which could then be transcribed into algorithms that machines could follow (according to a "top down" approach).[30]

Figure 3 *Expert Systems*

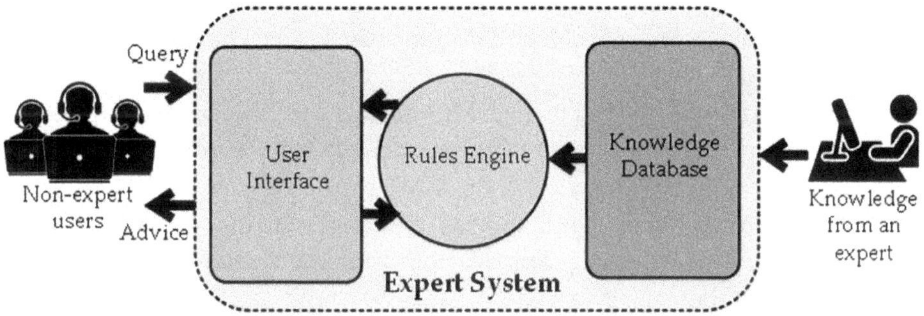

Source: F. H. Khan et al., "Advancements in Microprocessor Architecture for Ubiquitous AI – An Overview on History, Evolution, and Upcoming Challenges in AI Implementation", Micromachines, Vol. 12, No. 6, 2021. Licensed under CC BY 4.0.

Expert systems, though, had limits. One of these is that they can only know as much as humans could teach them. Likewise, they are not flexible: they cannot adapt to problems where both the variables and the rules change in time, hence they work best in highly formalized areas, such as chess.

28 H. Moravec, *Mind Children. The Future of Robot and Human Intelligence*, Harvard University Press, 1990, p. 15.

29 R. C. Suwandi, "Why is AI So Smart and Yet So Dumb? What Moravec's Paradox told us about AI", *Towards Data Science*, 30 August 2020. Available at: https://towardsdatascience.com/why-ai-is-so-smart-and-yet-so-dumb-c156cc87fafa.

30 European Parliament, "Understanding Artificial Intelligence", Briefing, Member's Research Service, 2018. Available at: www.europarl.europa.eu/RegData/etudes/BRIE/2018/614654/EPRS_BRI(2018)614654_EN.pdf.

In 1997, IBM's supercomputer Deep Blue[31] defeated the world chess champion Garry Kasparov. Chess was considered "the pinnacle of human intelligence".[32] Yet, this result alone did not boost confidence (or funding) in AI: Deep Blue had won by using "brute force computing power",[33] i.e., its ability to examine 200 million chess moves per second. It was thanks to its speed and capacity that it had beaten Kasparov, not thanks to its "intelligence". As it was argued, chess does not represent "the crowning glory of human intellectual endeavour; it is simply a mathematical problem with very clear rules and a finite set of alternatives".[34]

What brought AI to a new era was a paradigm change: the age of data-driven artificial intelligence,[35] where it is no longer about coding rules for expert systems, rather, it is about allowing computers to sift through enormous amounts of data to find correlations and classifications.[36] The second wave of AI development, then, is based on two elements: first, the enormous quantity of data available at little or no cost; second, the development of algorithms capable of learning by themselves (hence not through programmers encoding them with their previous knowledge) through ML techniques. Such techniques had been available for some time, yet their advance surged ahead thanks to the increase in the availability of digital data.[37]

What about today? As will be shown, the type of AI that is currently deployed poses fundamental questions to traditional notions of criminal liability. That is the object of this inquiry, no matter the season.

2.3 Gaining a Basic Understanding of Modern AI Systems

Since most AI systems mentioned in this research are based on ML, it is relevant at this point to explain ML's functioning and applications.

An algorithm based on ML techniques teaches itself rules by learning from the training data and through statistical analysis, detecting patterns in large amounts of information and generating outputs. It adopts a bottom down approach, unlike knowledge-based

31 IBM, "Deep Blue". Available at www.ibm.com/ibm/history/ibm100/us/en/icons/deepblue. See also: M. Campbell, A. J. Hoane Jr. & F. Hsu, "Deep Blue", *Artificial Intelligence*, Vol. 134, 2002, pp. 57-83.

32 H. Sheikh, C. Prins & E. Schrijvers, *Mission AI. Research for Policy*, Springer, 2023, p. 17.

33 H. Yu, "From Deep Blue to DeepMind: What AlphaGo Tells Us", *Predictive Analytics and Futurism*, Issue 13, 2016, p. 43. See also Council of Europe, "History of Artificial Intelligence". Available at: www.coe.int/en/web/artificial-intelligence/history-of-ai; G. Press, "The Brute Force Of IBM Deep Blue And Google DeepMind", *Forbes online*, 7 February 2018. Available at: www.forbes.com/sites/gilpress/2018/02/07/the-brute-force-of-deep-blue-and-deep-learning/?sh=597fb30249e3.

34 Sheikh, Prins & Schrijvers, 2023, p. 17.

35 European Parliament, "Understanding Artificial Intelligence", 2018.

36 Council of Europe, "History of Artificial Intelligence".

37 Council of Europe & Yeung, 2019, p. 17.

systems. These patterns can then be applied in different tasks, such as driving a car.[38] ML algorithms can be trained through supervised or unsupervised learning, depending on whether or not the algorithm learns from previously labeled data.

How does machine learning work? Relying on an analogy, one could say that it is similar to learning how to ride a bike: "[y]ou don't tell a child to move their left foot in a circle on the left pedal in the forward direction while moving their foot in a circle... You give them a push and tell them to keep the bike upright and pointed forward: the overall objective. They fall a few times, honing their skills each time they fail".[39]

A highly important subset of ML is deep learning (DL), which consists of layers of artificial neural networks (ANNs). Neural networks' engineering was inspired by the functioning of biological neurons: their basic function is to establish features from an input. ANNs are made of layers of functions ("nodes" or "neurons") that perform various operations on the data that they are fed (Fig. 4). The more layers a network has, the "deeper" the deep learning is.[40]

Figure 4 *Functioning of an Artificial Neural Network*

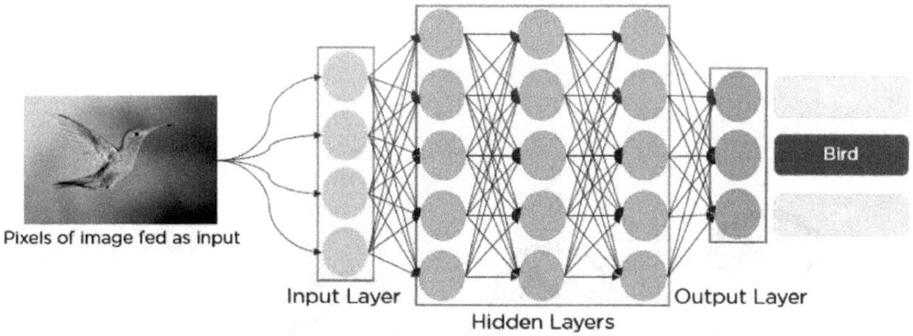

Source: M. Mandal, "Convolutional Neural Networks (CNN)", *Medium*, 30 April 2021. Available at: https://manavmandal.medium.com/convolutional-neural-networks-cnn-d88e7f9329eb.

38 Surden, 2019, p. 1311.

39 T. Havens quoted in K. Casey, "How to explain machine learning in plain English", *The Enterprisers Project*, 19 November 2020. Available at: https://enterprisersproject.com/article/2019/7/machine-learning-explained-plain-english?page=0%2C0.

40 C. Shenkman, D. Thakur & E. Llansó, Center for Democracy & Technology, *Do You See What I See? Capabilities and Limits of Automated Multimedia Content Analysis*, 2021, p. 43. Available at: https://cdt.org/wp-content/uploads/2021/05/2021-05-18-Do-You-See-What-I-See-Capabilities-Limits-of-Automated-Multimedia-Content-Analysis-Full-Report-2033-FINAL.pdf.

The difference between ML and DL is that in DL the algorithm is fed raw (unlabeled) data and then it identifies which features are relevant. In ML learning, instead, the algorithm is given an established set of relevant features to analyze.

If we rely once again on the analogy with a child, we could think of DL as a child learning language. Imagine a child that points at an object and says the word "car". The child's parents will immediately provide feedback such as "right" or "wrong" or provide a different label for the object ("No, that's a car!"). After a certain amount of feedback, the child will form a mental model of how to correctly label objects that she perceives in the real world. This is accomplished thanks to neurons that transmit signals to other neurons, "some sort of unexplainably complex hierarchy that is formed based on feedback".[41]

To understand the relationship between AI, ML, ANNs, and DL one should think of them like Russian nesting dolls, where each concept is part of the previous (Fig.5). Viewed this way, it is easier to grasp that machine learning is a subfield of artificial intelligence, deep learning is a subfield of machine learning, and neural networks "make up the backbone of deep learning algorithms [...]".[42] Based on the number of node layers or depth of neural networks it is possible to distinguish a single neural network from a deep learning algorithm, "which must have more than three".[43]

Figure 5 ***Relationship between AI, ML, ANNs and DL***

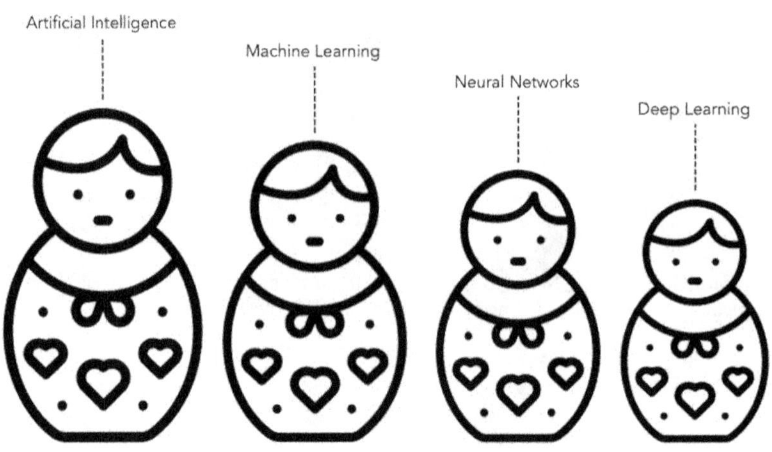

Adapted from "Russian" icon by WEBTECHOPS LLP from Noun Project (CC BY 3.0).

41 Casey, 2020.

42 E. Kavlakoglu, "AI vs. Machine Learning vs. Deep Learning vs. Neural Networks: What's the Difference?", *IBM*, 27 May 2020. Available at: www.ibm.com/cloud/blog/ai-vs-machine-learning-vs-deep-learning-vs-neural-networks.

43 Ibid.

One of the DL methods that is most commonly used for solving tasks involving image classification (a core task for AVs, but also for robotics applications)[44] is Convolutional Neural Networks (CNN). CNNs are multi-layered neural networks whose creation was inspired by animal optical systems, which are based on visual cortex cells that detect light in the small receptive field.[45] CNNs extract features from images, identify objects that are contained in them and then classify the images (i.e., general object recognition task).

Let us walk through these concepts by looking at an oversimplified example. Imagine that the task that has to be solved by the system is to classify whether an image contains a pedestrian, another vehicle or a traffic light. Such an operation is useful, for example, when developing AVs in order to avoid accidents (Fig. 6).[46] CNNs can be thought of as a very large car factory where the process of establishing the output (classifying a certain object in a picture as a human being/not a human being) is broken down into a multitude of sub-tasks performed by millions of highly skilled (pre-trained) workers divided into teams (the "nodes").

44 I. Sikdokur, I. Baytas & A. Yurdakul, "Image Classification on Accelerated Neural Networks", *arXiv:2203.11081v1* [cs.CV], 2022.

45 F. Sultana, A. Sufian & P. Dutta, "Advancements in Image Classification using Convolutional Neural Network", *arXiv:1905.03288v1* [cs.CV], 2019.

46 This technique is called "Computer Vision" and it comprises DL models and CNNs.

Figure 6 *Segmentation of General Object Recognition*

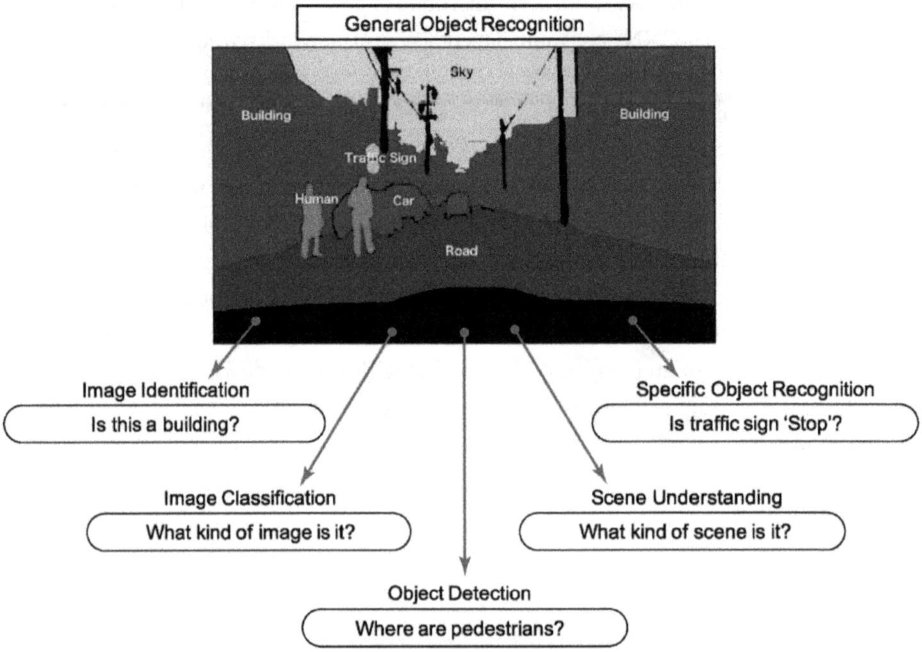

Source: H. Fujiyosh, T. Hirakawa & T. Yamashita, "Deep learning-based image recognition for autonomous driving", *IATSS Research*, Vol. 43, Issue 4, 2022. Licensed under CC BY 4.0.

Imagine now that the first team is given a very large dataset of pictures. The workers will apply a filter to the input image to identify certain features, for example, the perimeter of the object and then pass this output to the next team, which based on this output will identify legs or arms (and so on) until the final output is the classification of the object in the picture. The work of one team builds on the output of the previous team, though, and such "intermediate" output might look nothing like the finished product ("much as an ignition coil may not be immediately recognizable as a car part",[47] even to expert car drivers). Moreover, during the process "tasks and workflow may also be shifted in real-time to make the process more efficient".[48]

One fundamental issue with DL, which will often reappear in the following chapters, is that it is "inherently a black box":

> [w]hile it is straightforward to assess the quality of the output generated by such systems (e.g., the share of correctly classified pictures), the process used

47 This example is an adaption of the one contained in Shenkman, Thakur & Llansó, 2021, p. 43.
48 Shenkman, Thakur & Llansó, 2021, p. 43.

> for doing so remains largely opaque. Such opacity can be intentional (e.g., if a corporation wants to keep an algorithm secret), due to technical illiteracy or related to the scale of application (e.g., in cases where a multitude of programmers and methods are involved).[49]

In other words, someone walking through the car factory "would likely find it impossible to grasp the immensity of the process or the relationships between various teams and processes".[50]

The second fundamental issue, which acquires relevance from a criminal law perspective, is the 'autonomy' property of systems based on ML. Currently employed AI systems always work to fulfill an overarching goal set by a human, yet they can decide independently between alternative ways to reach the set goal, and they can set their own intermediate sub-purposes.[51]

On a final note, it is relevant to briefly touch upon the theme of hybrid AI systems. This term is used to refer to two types of hybridization: (1) AI systems can include different techniques, such as machine learning combined with knowledge-based systems.[52] And (2) AI systems can involve forms of human decision-making in their functioning. This concept will prove particularly significant for this investigation of the realm of criminal liability. Human-AI interaction can happen in different ways: training, tuning, testing, and operating the model.[53] In this regard, three main approaches are important: human-in-the-loop (HITL), human-on-the-loop (HOTL), and human-in-command (HIC). HITL is an umbrella term which refers to the ability for the human agent to intervene in every decision of the system.[54] More specifically, HOTL, instead, refers to "the capability for human intervention during the design cycle of the system and monitoring the system's operation".[55] Lastly, HIC refers to the ability of a human to oversee the overall activity of the system (which includes also its broader economic, societal, legal and ethical impact)

---

49 Haenlein & Kaplan, 2019, p.1.

50 Shenkman, Thakur & Llansó, 2021, p. 43.

51 Council of Europe & Yeung, 2019, p. 19.

52 K. Martineau, "Teaching machines to reason about what they see", *MIT News*, 2 April 2019. Available at: https://news.mit.edu/2019/teaching-machines-to-reason-about-what-they-see-0402; W. Knight, "Two rival AI approaches combine to let machines learn about the world like a child", *MIT Technology Review*, 8 April 2019. Available at: www.technologyreview.com/2019/04/08/103223/two-rival-ai-approaches-combine-to-let-machines-learn-about-the-world-like-a-child/.

53 See also F. M. Zanzotto, "Human-in-the-loop Artificial Intelligence", *Journal of Artificial Intelligence Research*, Vol. 64, 2019, pp. 243-252.

54 AI-HLEG, *Ethics guidelines for trustworthy AI*, 2019, p. 16. Available at: https://ec.europa.eu/futurium/en/ai-alliance-consultation.1.html.

55 Ibid.

together with the ability to decide "when and how to use the system in any particular situation".[56]

Operating a human-in-the-loop system is diffused when it comes to Autonomous Vehicles ("AVs"): currently, most private companies that operate AVs are required by law to have a human driver present in the car.[57] The role of the human driver is to reassert full control over the car if an error happens or to avoid an accident, as a sort of duty of care.[58] What happens, then, if the driver was not able to take over in a timely manner and a deadly accident occurs?[59] One should think of the case of an elderly driver, who is often labeled a dangerous driver when it comes to "normal" cars and is therefore supposedly a safer driver when traveling in an AV. The same person, though, is likely to be less skilled concerning reestablishing digital control over the AV. Should she be blamed for the death of a pedestrian because she did not assume control of the car in time? As it will be explained in Chapter 5, the UK Law Commission addressed this issue and suggested the introduction of a new law providing for an immunity clause for drivers (called users-in-command") against offenses committed by self-driving vehicles.

More difficulties arise when an AV commits an error which is different from "common" human driving errors and, as such, hard to predict for the human driver.[60] We can think of the case where a car in broad daylight and perfect visibility is faced with the option of hitting a person or a very roughly made scarecrow: in this case, the failure of the car's sensors to identify a figure as human is radically different from not stopping at a red traffic light. Can the driver be considered at fault for not anticipating such a "weird" action of the system?

---

56 Ibid.

57 See for example the amendment to Article 8 of the United Nations 1968 Vienna Convention on Road Traffic which provides that automated driving technologies transferring driving tasks to the vehicle will be explicitly allowed in traffic provided that these technologies are in conformity with the United Nations vehicle regulations or can be overridden or switched off by the driver. United Nations Economic and Social Council, *Report of the sixty-eighth session of the Working Party on Road Traffic Safety*, ECE/TRANS/WP.1/145, 2014. Available at: https://unece.org/press/unece-paves-way-automated-driving-updating-un-international-convention). See also Article 3 of the United Kingdom Automated and Electric Vehicles Act of 2018 which provides that "The insurer or owner of an automated vehicle is not liable under section 2 to the person in charge of the vehicle where the accident that it caused was wholly due to the person's negligence in allowing the vehicle to begin driving itself when it was not appropriate to do so". Automated and Electric Vehicles Act, 2018, Chapter 18.

58 B. Wagner, "Liable, but Not in Control? Ensuring Meaningful Human Agency in Automated Decision-Making Systems", *Policy & Internet*, Vol. 11, Issue 1, 2019, p. 109.

59 For an analysis of the development of shared operational responsibility between vehicle and driver, see J. Pattinson, C. Haibo & B. Subhajit, "Legal issues in automated vehicles: critically considering the potential role of consent and interactive digital interfaces", *Humanities and Social Sciences Communications*, Vol. 7, Art. No. 153, 2020.

60 "Machine errors in automated driving are typically associated with the correct identification of the objects perceived by sensors, while human driving errors are typically associated with being able to provide sustained attention to a specific task over long periods of time." Wagner, 2019, p. 109.

Why are these notions relevant to this research? Recently, it has been advocated especially in policymaking that adopting an HITL approach is the ideal solution to ensure accountability: "if an autonomous system causes harm to human beings, having a human in the loop provides trust that somebody would bare the consequence of such mistakes".[61] Researchers have thus introduced the theory of the "big red button", a sort of emergency kill switch for AI systems, which should stop it before it becomes destructive.[62] Such mechanisms, as has been highlighted through the AV example, need to be handled with care, especially if they are to be translated to criminal liability.[63] These issues are addressed in greater detail in the discussion in Chapter 6.

2.4 Definitions of AI: an Overview

As was shown, thinking about AI has changed over time.[64] It was first defined by John McCarthy, Marvin Minsky, Nathaniel Rochester and Claude Shannon in 'A proposal for the Dartmouth Summer Research Project on Artificial Intelligence', a "2 month, 20 man study" which took place in 1956.[65] They defined it as "making a machine behave in ways

61 European Parliamentary Research Service, Panel for the Future of Science and Technology, "The ethics of artificial intelligence: Issues and initiatives", EPRS_STUD(2020)634452, 2020, p. 35. See also M. Pizzi, M. Romanoff & T. Engelhardt, "AI for humanitarian action: Human rights and ethics", *International Review of the Red Cross*, Vol. 102, No. 913, 2020, pp. 145-180; AI-HLEG, 2019.

62 T. Arnold & M. Scheutz, "The "big red button" is too late: an alternative model for the ethical evaluation of AI systems", *Ethics and Information Technology*, Vol. 20, 2018, p. 60.

63 "Accountability mechanisms built on the assumption of a supreme human overseer are inherently flawed, if adopted without criticism. Such approaches can embed and reinforce the implicit human/machine dichotomy and mystify human agency. However, it should be noted that the emphasis on human agency might serve a purpose outside monitoring automation, namely in justifying legal decisions. The importance attributed to humans in automation is not arbitrary but instead reflects the legal system's foundational concepts and ideologies that are built on anthropocentricity. In other words, juxtaposing algorithmic and human decision-making reveals law's self-reflection on what constitutes legal decision-making. Simply put, law's acknowledgement of legal agents capable of decisions is limited to humans or fictions of human agents such as organizations that are conceptualized as legal (although not natural) persons. Following this, justification of decision-making has traditionally been connected to human agency even when, in practice, decisions are arrived at through intra-organizational processes. In this sense, human control over automation can be seen simply as another formulation of human justification." R. Koulou, "Human Control over Automation: EU Policy and AI Ethics", *EJLS* 12(1), 2020, pp. 9-46.

64 K. J. Hayward & M. M. Maas, "Artificial intelligence and crime: A primer for criminologists", *Crime Media Culture*, 2020, p. 4. For a systematic account of policymaking definitions of AI adopted by national governments and international organizations, see A. Bertolini, "Artificial Intelligence and Civil Liability", Study commissioned by the European Parliament's Committee on Legal Affairs, European Union, IPOL_STU(2020)621926, 2020, pp. 23-29. For a thorough overview of existing AI definitions, see the research conducted on 55 documents by S. Samoili et. al, "AI Watch. Defining Artificial Intelligence. Towards an operational definition and taxonomy of artificial intelligence", EUR 30117 EN, Publications Office of the European Union, Luxembourg, 2020, ISBN 978-92-76-17045-7, JRC118163.

65 McCarthy et al., 1955.

that would be called intelligent if a human were so behaving".[66] Fifty years later, McCarthy published the article "What is artificial intelligence?" in which he defined AI as "the science and engineering of making intelligent machines, especially intelligent computer programs".[67] It can be argued, then, that AI is "first and foremost a *science*, classified in a variety of subfields, whose general aim is that of creating intelligent machines".[68] This can be referred to as an 'operational definition': defining AI by what AI researchers do.[69] Such subfields or technologies include machine learning, deep learning, computer vision and NLP.

An added difficulty in defining AI in these terms is that the public discourse suffers from the "AI effect" or "odd paradox". These terms describe the phenomenon of AI reaching mainstream usage and then not being considered AI any longer, as people become accustomed to it.[70] Briefly put, "[a]s soon as it works, no one calls it AI anymore".[71] Moreover, drawing on an often-cited analogy in the field of AI liability, AI systems cannot define themselves and in this they differ profoundly from corporations, which define themselves as such once they are established and acquire legal personality.

Additionally, a further problematic aspect of defining AI from a regulatory perspective is to outline the *object* of this field of science,[72] namely defining what intelligence is, be it human or artificial. McCarthy notes that intelligence entails the ability of achieving goals in the world.[73] Various degrees and kinds of intelligence can occur in human beings, animals and in some machines: the issue is that, since it is not possible to characterize (yet) what kinds of computational procedures we want to call intelligent, we cannot yet answer definitively whether or not a machine is intelligent.[74]

One can distinguish two categories of definitions in this sense: rationalist definitions and human-centric definitions. Rationalist definitions focus on the ideal concept of intelligence, referred to as "rationality".[75] Norvig-Russel's *Artificial Intelligence: A Modern Approach*, one of the most widely distributed textbooks on AI, adopts this approach and

66 Ivi, p. 12.

67 J. McCarthy, "What is artificial intelligence", 2007, p. 2. Available at: http://jmc.stanford.edu/articles/whatisai.html.

68 Bertolini, 2020, p. 18.

69 Stone P. et al., "Artificial Intelligence and Life in 2030. One Hundred Year Study on Artificial Intelligence: Report of the 2015-2016 Study Panel", Stanford University, September 2016. Available at: http://ai100.stanford.edu/2016-report.

70 Stone et al., 2016, p. 12.

71 J. McCarthy quoted in M. Y. Vardi, "Artificial Intelligence: Past and Future", *Communications of the ACM*", Vol. 55, No 1, 2012, p. 5.

72 Bertolini, 2020, p. 20.

73 McCarthy, 2007, p. 2.

74 Ibid.

75 I. Ben-Israel et al., "Towards Regulation of AI Systems. Global perspectives on the development of a legal framework on Artificial Intelligence (AI) systems based on the Council of Europe's standards on human rights, democracy and the rule of law", Council of Europe Study DGI (2020) 16, 2020, p. 22.

defines AI as the designing and building of intelligent agents that receive perceptions from the environment and take actions that affect that environment.[76]

Human-centric definitions, on the other hand, define AI in terms of fidelity to human performance (i.e. systems that think and act like humans). Examples of human-centric definitions include describing AI as the study of how to make computers do things at which at this time people are better[77] or as the study of computers doing tasks that would be considered to require intelligence if a human did them (tasks that "normally require human intelligence").[78]

As a final note, the AI systems that are employed today are "narrow", meaning that they can only solve pre-established tasks. In other words, today's AI is not *actually* intelligent.[79] As has been suggested, "[i]t may even be proposed, as a rule of thumb, that any activity computers are able to perform and people once performed should be counted as an instance of intelligence. *But matching any human ability is only a sufficient condition, not a necessary one.* There are already many systems that exceed human intelligence, at least in speed, such as scheduling the daily arrivals and departures of thousands of flights in an airport".[80]

Is the comparison to human intelligence then truly needed for this research? As argued by Armer in his "Argument of Invidious Comparison":

> Considering the behavior of men and machines in the context of intelligence being a multidimensional continuum is like saying that the Wright brothers' airplane could not fly because it could not fly nonstop from Los Angeles to New York nor could it land in a tree like a bird. Why must the test of intelligence be that the machine achieve identically the same point in the continuum as man? Is the test of flying the achievement of the same point in the continuum of flying as that reached by a bird?[81]

Stretching this even further, AI can cause damage, without intentionally wanting to cause it. What matters, then, is the potential for harm, irrespective of whether one is discussing an algebraic formula or a deep neural network.

---

76 Norvig & Russel, 2003, pp. 1-2.

77 E. Rich & K. Knight, *Artificial Intelligence*, Tata McGraw, 2004, p. 3.

78 M. L. Minsky quoted in T. Stonier, *Beyond Information. The Natural History of Intelligence*, Springer, 1992, pp. 107-133.

79 Surden, 2019, p. 1308.

80 Stone P. et al., 2016, p. 13.

81 "Why must the test of intelligence be that the machine achieve identically the same point in the continuum as man? Is the test of flying the achievement of the same point in the continuum of flying as that reached by a bird?". P. Armer, "Attitudes Toward Intelligent machines", in E. A. Feigenbaum, J. Feldman & P. Armer (eds.), *Computers and Thought*, Aaai Pr, 1995, p. 393.

In 2015, AlphaGo, developed by Google, beat the world Go Champion Lee Sedol. As some have recognized: "AlphaGo mimics an extremely diligent, but not necessarily genius, student who is willing to learn from millions of human's play and self-play, tediously."[82] In fact, in today's world, "[p]laying chess against a machine – and losing with near certainty – has become a thing not even worth mentioning".[83] Being able to play chess is not taken as the yardstick of intelligence anymore, nor is being able to play Go. Without any doubt, former chess champion Garry Kasparov had an entirely different view on this matter in 1997, after his defeat against Deep Blue.[84] So did society at the time: think of the cover of Newsweek of 5 May 1997 which was titled "The Brain's Last Stand".

2.5 ADOPTED WORKING DEFINITION

This study adopts as a working definition, the HLEG definition of AI:

> Artificial intelligence (AI) systems are software (and possibly also hardware) systems designed by humans that, given a complex goal, act in the physical or digital dimension by perceiving their environment through data acquisition, interpreting the collected structured or unstructured data, reasoning on the knowledge, or processing the information, derived from this data and deciding the best action(s) to take to achieve the given goal.
> AI systems can either use symbolic rules or learn a numeric model, and they can also adapt their behaviour by analysing how the environment is affected by their previous actions.
> As a scientific discipline, AI includes several approaches and techniques, such as machine learning (of which deep learning and reinforcement learning are specific examples), machine reasoning (which includes planning, scheduling, knowledge representation and reasoning, search, and optimization), and robotics (which includes control, perception, sensors and actuators, as well as the integration of all other techniques into cyber-physical systems).[85]

The reasons for this choice are numerous. First of all, it is a comprehensive definition which comprises the main features of AI according to the most recurring definitions in

82 Yu, 2016, p. 44.
83 Haenlein & Kaplan, 2019, p. 13.
84 Ibid.
85 High-Level Expert Group on Artificial Intelligence (AI-HLEG), *A definition of AI: Main capabilities and Scientific Disciplines*, 2018, p. 6. Available at: https://ec.europa.eu/futurium/en/system/files/ged/ai_hleg_definition_of_ai_18_december_1.pdf.

the academic discourse: perception of the environment, information processing (collecting and interpreting inputs in data), decision-making (including reasoning and learning), the performance of actions and tasks in adaptation (in reaction to changes in the environment) with a certain level of autonomy; achievement of specific goals.[86] Second, it avoids ambiguities regarding the definition of "intelligence" as it does not define AI as an 'intelligent' machine. Such a definition will guide this research and represents a compromise with different definitions.[87] The term AI will be used when referring to artificial intelligence as a type of technology. The term AI systems will instead be adopted when referring to AI as an application of the technology.[88]

From the definition given above, one can identify at least two problematic characteristics that are closely related to the functioning of AI systems: unpredictability and autonomy. The focus of this research will be only on those AI systems that are programmed in such a way that they become adaptive or self-deciding agents, i.e. whose actions are not *ex ante* open and predictable.[89] These issues will be addressed in the relevant chapters.

2.6 CONCLUSIONS

Some have said that "[d]efining AI is an exercise rather like nailing jello to a tree: with forethought, planning, and enough nails it ought to be doable, but it isn't".[90] Let us not be discouraged: this chapter does not have the (unattainable) goal of giving a final answer to the issue of defining AI. This research is meant to analyze AI through the lenses of classical notions of criminal law, therefore the purpose of this chapter was to overcome the conceptual challenge by adopting a working definition. When doing so, it offered a basic characterization of the most relevant uses of AI. This provides the reader with a toolkit of notions adequate for addressing the implications of AI on the concept of criminal liability. Having

86 Samoili et al., 2020, p. 8.

87 P. Wang, "What Do You Mean by 'AI'?", *Proceedings of the 2008 Conference on Artificial General Intelligence*, 2008, pp. 362-373.

88 M.U. Scherer, "Regulating Artificial Intelligence Systems: Risks, Challenges, Competencies and Strategies", *Harvard Journal of Law & Technology*, Vol. 29, No. 2, 2016, p. 362.

89 *"Deshalb sei vorausgesetzt, dass hier nur solche „Roboter", „Maschinen" oder „Software-Agenten" von Interesse sind, die so programmiert sind, dass sie empfangene Informationen in einer Weise verknüpfen und für künftige Reaktionen auswerten können, die nicht vollständig durch die Programmierung festgelegt ist und deren Aktionen daher ex ante „offen" und mithin nicht für jeden Einzelfall vorhersehbar sind. Nur hinsichtlich solcher „lernfähiger" bzw. „selbst entscheidender" Agenten kann überhaupt die Frage gestellt werden, ob ihnen das Strafrecht eine eigene, personale Rolle zuweisen kann. Alle anderen, „fest" programmierten Geräte können – so will ich es unterstellen – nur als „Werkzeuge" in der Hand menschlicher Agenten in Betracht kommen".* Seher, 2016, p. 46.

90 D. Partridge, *A New Guide to Artificial Intelligence*, Intellect L & D E F A E, 1991, p. 1.

gained the correct amount of technical knowledge we needed; it is possible to move to the next "trouble with AI": how to assign criminal responsibility for AI-related harm.[91]

91 Scherer, 2016, p. 358.

3 Expansionists, Moderates, Skeptics: the Scholarly Debate on AI and Criminal Law

The civilian puts his faith in syllogisms, the common lawyer in precedents;
the first silently asking himself as each new problem arises,
"What should we do this time?"
and the second asking aloud in the same situation, "What did we do last time?"
The civilian thinks in terms of rights and duties,
the common lawyer in terms of remedies.
The civilian is chiefly concerned with the policy and rationale of a rule of law,
the common lawyer with its pedigree.
The instinct of the civilian is to systematize.
The working rule of the common lawyer is *solvitur ambulando.*

Thomas Mackay Cooper (1950)

3.1 Introduction. The Scholarly Debate on Criminal Liability of AI-Systems

Up until ten years ago, academic pursuits to link criminal liability to the use of AI systems were wary. Most of the discussion and the policing efforts were limited to the areas of civil law and torts. In a 2020 research on the scope of the legal literature on AI,[1] which was conducted with the aid of a machine learning technique called topic modelling,[2] researchers found that scholarly output boomed in the so-called "deep learning era".[3] As the authors argue: "with over 2500 publications already by the year 2015 referring to 'artificial intelli-

1 C. Rosca et al., "Return of the AI: An Analysis of Legal Research on Artificial Intelligence Using Topic Modelling", *Proceedings of the 2020 Natural Legal Language Processing (NLLP) Workshop*, 2020.

2 Topic Modelling is a method for classifying collections of documents. The authors adopted Latent Dirichlet Allocation (LDA) Topic Modelling. They used the tool to identify recurring topics in 3,931 journal articles on AI legal research.

3 The expression refers to the period which includes the early 2000s until today. C. Goanta et al., "Back to the Future: Waves of Legal Scholarship on Artificial Intelligence", in S. Ranchordás & Y. Roznai (eds.), *Time, Law and Change*, Hart Publishing, 2020, p. 331.

gence' … it may no longer be realistic to assume that researchers can keep up with legal research on AI, or the number of publications in general".[4]

The scenario that researchers face nowadays with regard to the specific field of criminal legal scholarship is undeniably different: today AI and criminal law are no dichotomy. Indeed, as mentioned in the introduction, one of the purposes of the literature review is to situate this research in this "ocean" of scholarly literature.

Being late is no news for criminal law, and not necessarily a bad thing. Indeed, "[t]he criminal law is and ought to be different – importantly dissimilar from other kinds of law".[5] From a regulatory perspective, norms of criminal law represent "the ultima ratio in the legislator's toolkit".[6] One thing is certain: regardless of whether legislators will address criminal law issues pertaining to AI-related misbehaviors in the short run or not, starting from 2019 the academic discourse on AI in the realm of criminal law has thrived. The ultimate proof of this excitement can be found in the fact that the International Association of Penal Law decided to dedicate its XXIst International Congress in 2024 to the topic of "Artificial Intelligence in Criminal Justice".[7]

With this in mind, it is possible to appreciate why it is necessary that this research provides an overview of the current academic debate on the matter. Indeed, "[b]uilding your research on and relating it to existing knowledge is the building block of all academic research activities, regardless of discipline."[8]

Let us turn now to the purposes of this literature review. They are twofold. First, it establishes the conceptual framework for the research questions of the study and the main themes which will be addressed. By introducing the most relevant analyses of criminal legal scholars in relation to the technical concepts provided in Chapter 2, this section serves as foundation for the discussion found in Chapters 4 and 5. In other words, this research is structured following a layered approach: at the beginning it provided the required background knowledge to be able, as lawyers, to understand foreign concepts, such as those pertaining to computer science; now it will deliver the reflections of the legal scholars that analyzed those concepts through the lenses of criminal law. Therefore, this chapter combines familiar notions, such as the ones pertaining to criminal legal theories, with unfamiliar notions, such as the ones pertaining to the realm of AI systems.

Second, it will serve to identify recurrent issues in the academic discourse on AI and criminal liability and, as a consequence, those that are often neglected. This will allow this

4 Rosca et al., 2020, p. 1.

5 D. Husak, "The Criminal Law as Last Resort", *Oxford Journal of Legal Studies*, Vol. 23, No. 2, 2004, p. 211.

6 P. Minkkinen, "'If Taken in Earnest': Criminal Law Doctrine and the Last Resort", *The Howard Journal*, Vol. 45, No. 5, 2006, p. 526.

7 See the information available at: http://www.penal.org/en/information.

8 H. Snyder, "Literature review as a research methodology: An overview and guidelines", *Journal of Business Research*, Vol. 104(C), 2019.

research to, on the one hand, compare different positions on the same issues and, on the other, acquire originality. The systematizing effort conducted in this chapter is needed because of the panoply of approaches that are presented by the authors working on this topic: as if there were many musical instruments playing simultaneously, without a conductor to coordinate them.

This literature review suffers from a few limitations. To begin with, due to the momentum that AI is building in criminal law at the time this research was conducted, it was not possible for this literature review to account extensively for each and every academic paper published in the field. Moreover, the analysis had to be limited to research published in three languages, namely English, Italian and German, as these are the languages spoken by the author.

The review was not limited with regard to the territorial provenance or the legal background of the authors, as the academic discourse in this field is characterized by intense crossbreeding: most of the papers discuss the impact of AI in criminal law by referring to general concepts of criminal law, rather than to how a specific concept is regulated in a national or international legal system. Authors frequently refer to works of other colleagues who have a different legal background from theirs and do so by mixing legal terms in English, German and Italian. This also rendered the operation of conducting the literature review difficult at times, due to the challenges represented by the transposition of concepts between different legal systems. For example, the Italian term "*colpevolezza*" is often used by Italian scholars to refer to uses of the narrower concept of *mens rea*, without giving account of the difference between the two. Indeed, the concept of '*mens rea*' has gradually lost its broader meaning of 'blameworthiness' in US legal doctrine and is currently used primarily to refer to the specific mental state required by the criminal offense (e.g., intent).

On a final note, even though the legal background of the authors was not accounted for when selecting the relevant articles and book to read, it was addressed, if appropriate, when scrutinizing their content.

It is possible to identify three different streams of thought in the current debate on criminal liability of AI. As a consequence, the authors have been classified into three categories, "AI punishment expansionists", moderates and skeptics.[9] An explanation of these categories will follow in the appropriate subsection.

9 Abbott & Sarch, 2019, p. 327.

3.2 Expansionists (or the Front of Robotic Liberation)

Expansionists or representatives of the Front of Robotic Liberation can be defined as those who argue for a radical change of the elements of criminal liability and/or for the direct punishment of AI systems. This label combines categorizations made by Abbott and Sarch[10] and by Pagallo.[11]

3.2.1 Gabriel Hallevy – the AI "Believer"[12]

Undoubtedly, one of the most cited legal scholars belonging to the expansionist front is Gabriel Hallevy.[13] He is the predecessor of almost all discussions on AI criminal liability (his earliest work on the topic dates back to 2010) and is the first who attempted to set out how modern legal frameworks could be applied to AI.[14]

According to Hallevy, it is possible to identify a new kind of offender, i.e., the delinquent thinking machine. It is not relevant for criminal law, he argues, that an offender possesses every human skill. It does not have to be an ideal thinking machine, such as humans. Notably, it is only required that a match between criminal law requirements and the relevant skills and abilities of the system exists.[15]

In his earlier work, Hallevy drew heavily on the comparison between AI systems and corporations, claiming that there is "no substantive legal difference between the idea of

10 Ibid.

11 Pagallo, 2013, p.54.

12 U. Pagallo & W. Barfield, *Advanced Introduction to Law and Artificial Intelligence*, Edward Elgar Publishing, 2020, p. 140.

13 Over the years, Gabriel Hallevy has published several work comprising of both books and academic papers: "The Criminal Liability of Artificial Intelligence Entities – From Science Fiction to Legal Social Control, *Akron Intellectual Property Journal*, Vol. 4, Iss. 2, Art. 1, 2010; "I, Robot – I, Criminal – When Science Fiction Becomes Reality: Legal Liability of AI Robots Committing Criminal Offences", Syracuse Sci. & Tech. L. Rep., 2010; "Virtual Criminal Responsibility", 2011 (Available at SSRN: https://ssrn.com/abstract=1835362 or http://dx.doi.org/10.2139/ssrn.1835362); "Unmanned Vehicles. Subordination to Criminal Law Under the Modern Concept of Criminal Liability", *Journal of Law, Information and Science*, Vol 21, No. 2002, 2012; *When Robots Kill. Artificial Intelligence under Criminal Law*, Northeastern University Press, 2013; *Liability for Crimes Involving Artificial Intelligence Systems*, Springer, 2015; "Dangerous Robots – Artificial Intelligence vs. Human Intelligence", 2018 (Available at SSRN: https://ssrn.com/abstract=3121905); "The Basic Models of Criminal Liability of AI Systems and Outer Circles", 2019 (Available at SSRN: https://ssrn.com/abstract=3402527 or http://dx.doi.org/10.2139/ssrn.3402527). Most of the discussion in this research will focus on the 2015 book, which, in the very words of the author, is meant as a "full academic generalization" of the issue (see v., Preface).

14 R. Charney, "Can Androids Plead Automatism – A Review of When Robots Kill: Artificial Intelligence under the Criminal Law by Gabriel Hallevy", *U. Toronto Fac. L. Rev.*, Vol. 73, 2015, p. 69.

15 Hallevy, 2015, p. 25.

criminal liability imposed on corporations and on AI entities".[16] In his latest work, i.e., the book "Liability for Crimes involving Artificial Intelligence Systems", Hallevy detached from his previous publications on different levels, adopting at times a more moderate approach. In this monograph, the author first deconstructs the element of modern criminal liability (external or *actus reus* element and internal or *mens rea* element), and then discusses whether AI technology can fulfill the requirements of each element.

With regard to the element of *actus reus*, Hallevy, like Lagioia and Sartor,[17] without any second thought abandons the doctrine which submits that the criminal act need be the result of a willed bodily movement. As a matter of fact, he considers it a "mongrel requirement" belonging to the past.[18] In other words, according to this author there is no space for any mental element requirement when examining *actus reus*.[19] Notwithstanding whether or not one agrees with Hallevy's position, one can observe that theories based on willful conduct, since they require a link between "mind and body",[20] represent for a fact the cultural heritage of a reflection which has been based for decades on human or, in the case of corporations, on proxies for humans. One could ask oneself whether AI systems indeed warrant being detached from this line of reasoning because they are not human, nor are they proxies for humans. This detachment could take form, as argued by Hallevy, through discarding any sort of mental element when looking at the *actus reus*. Or else, it could lead to theorizing a new form of willful conduct which reflects the functioning of modern AI systems, similar to what is hypothesized by Lagioia and Sartor or by Abbott and Sarch concerning intent.[21] This reformulation operation of the concept of "willful conduct" is, apropos, what has been done by those criminal justice systems that allow for the liability of corporations.[22]

Following this reasoning, Hallevy claims that "for the question of performing an act in order to satisfy the conduct component requirement, any material performance through factual-external presentation is considered an act, whether the physical performer is

16 Hallevy, "The Criminal Liability of Artificial Intelligence Entities – From Science Fiction to Legal Social Control", 2010, p. 201. The analogy will be dealt with in depth in Ch. 6.4.

17 See Sec. 3.3.2.

18 Hallevy, 2015, p. 61.

19 This is far from being the dominant theory, at least in Western criminal law. See *ex multis* Keiler, who states that "Conduct can only be an expression of human agency if it is linked to human will, and consciousness i.e., control. [...] it is not so much movement that matters, but rather conduct that lies within one's control and reflects the person as a rational agent. If such a link is absent [...] the imposition of criminal liability is unwarranted. [...] these situations are not merely a denial of mens rea, but more profound, namely the denial of a criminally relevant conduct". J. Keiler, *Actus reus and participation in European Criminal Law*, Intersentia, 2013, p. 61.

20 H.L.A. Hart, *Punishment and Responsibility*, 2nd ed., Oxford University Press, 2008, p. 97.

21 See Sec. 3.3.1.

22 See Sec. 6.4.

strong artificial intelligence entity or not".[23] The same reasoning is also applied to commission-by-omission scenarios. From this statement, it follows that even the simplest machines could perform "conduct under the definition and requirements of criminal".[24]

Concerning the causal nexus between the conduct and the harmful results, Hallevy adheres to a *conditio sine qua non* theory of causation.[25] Consequently, he claims that since AI technology is "capable of committing conduct of all kinds, in the context of criminal law, it is capable of causing results out of this conduct".[26]

When discussing *mens rea*, Hallevy asks himself whether AI technology has, on the one hand, the capability of "being aware of conduct, circumstances or possibility of the results' occurrence, in the context of criminal law"[27] and, on the other hand, the capability of consolidating will.[28] In other words, he questions whether AI systems could fulfill the cognition and volitional element of intent. As already mentioned, the author answers in the affirmative to both questions. This is an instance of what Pagallo and Barfield referred to as an "à la Hallevy's position",[29] i.e., the humanization of AI systems.

With regard to ascertaining awareness, he divides the process in two steps. The first step consists of "absorbing the factual data by senses".[30] The second step entails being able to create a general picture from the information and to use it.

According to Hallevy, AI systems are capable of fulfilling the awareness requirement much better than humans. To prove this, he provides an interesting example based on the differences between a human and an AI-based guard. An AI-based robot guard can scan its surroundings to identify suspicious behavior. When the AI system detects a movement or a sound, it poses a question to identify the figure it encountered ("Who is there? Please identify yourself!") and then verifies the answer by referring to its memory. Same as a prison guard would ask an intruder to identify herself and then analyze the answer (the voice and the image of the possible intruder, together with the information provided) to see if it matches individuals in her memory. The most striking difference between a human and a robot guard, though, is in their respective data collection and analysis potential. Simply put, an AI does not fall asleep and is therefore in an eternal state of high aware-

23 Hallevy, 2015, p. 62.
24 Ivi, p. 63.
25 Also referred to as "ultimate cause theory" or "but for" test. According to this theory, to prove that the conduct A caused the result B, the judge has to remove element A from the factors which led to the event and ask herself if event B would still have happened.
26 Hallevy, 2015, p. 66.
27 Ivi, p. 89.
28 Hallevy, 2015, p. 94.
29 Pagallo & Barfield, 2020, p. 140.
30 Hallevy, 2015, p. 89.

ness.[31] For these reasons, Hallevy contends that AI systems are able to pass the "awareness test" with maximum grades.

With regard to proving volition, the author, like Lagioia and Sartor,[32] focuses the discussion on the foreseeability rule presumption. The presumption can be summarized as follows: intent in human offenders is proven if the offender "during the aware commission of the conduct, has foreseen the occurrence of the results as a very high probability option".[33] He contends that resorting to this type of "evidential substitute" is mandated by the fact that "aware will" relates to future situations, where instead awareness relates to facts. In other words: "[a]wareness is rational and realistic, whereas intent is not necessarily. For instance, a person may intend to become an elephant, but that person cannot be aware of being an elephant, as he is not one".[34] It follows that since AI systems can assess that the probabilities that one event (be it winning a chess game or killing a human being) will result from their conduct are very high, and since they can choose to act pursuant to this assessment, they fulfill the conditions for the foreseeability rule presumption. Hence, it can be presumed that they have intent.[35] Following a parallel logic, Hallevy concludes that AI systems are also capable of forming negligence.[36]

The author then advanced three liability models which could be used to impose criminal liability on AI systems:

1. the direct liability model;
2. the perpetration-through-another model;
3. the natural probable consequence model.

We can then identify three corresponding scenarios in Hallevy's work which describe the scope of application of the three models:

---

31 Ivi, p. 90.

32 See Sec. 3.3.2.

33 Hallevy, 2015, p. 96.

34 Ibid.

35 Hallevy, 2015, p. 98. Hallevy theorizes that it is possible to ascertain an AI system's negligence by analyzing the machine learning process which led to the mistaken decision. He defines negligence as "unawareness of the factual component in spite of the capability to form awareness, when reasonable person could and should have been aware of that component" (p. 124). He summarizes the test in three general questions, which would have to been ascertained by a court (with the aid of a computer scientist expert):
   a. Was the artificial intelligence system unaware of the factual component?
   b. Has the artificial intelligence system the general capability of consolidating awareness of the factual component?
   c. Could a reasonable person have been aware of the factual component?

36 Ivi, pp. 120-131.

(a) The AI system makes a decision to commit an offense based on its own accumulated experience or knowledge or based on advanced calculations of probabilities – liability model (1);
(b) The AI system is used by a human being as a (sophisticated) tool to commit an offense – liability model (2);
(c) The AI system was not designed to commit the specific offense, but the offense was committed by the artificial intelligence technology nonetheless – liability model (3).[37]

The models can be applied separately or in combination.[38] The direct liability model (1) is applicable in situations similar to the one described at (a). This model is the result of an operation of "humanization of AI systems", which was outlined above. Indeed, Hallevy tested whether the requirements of criminal law could be fulfilled by AI technologies, and concluded the test with affirmative answers. By doing so, he opened the "gate for imposition of criminal liability upon artificial intelligence technology as direct offenders".[39] This model confers on Hallevy the title of AI punishment expansionist.

The perpetration-through-another model (2) is suitable to impose criminal liability on a human offender (identified by Hallevy in the programmer or the user) in situations such as the one described at (b). The AI system is treated as an innocent agent and therefore the model considers the action committed materially by the AI system as if it had been the action of the user or of the programmer.[40] Accordingly, this model is not suitable for application in situations such as (a) and (c).

The natural probable consequence model (3) kicks in in situations such as the one described at (c), i.e., when there is a "deep involvement of the programmers or users in the AI entity's daily activities, but without any intention of committing any offense via the AI entity".[41] It is necessary at this point to make a further distinction to fully grasp the rationale behind Hallevy's theory.

We will refer to three sub-situations:

37 Hallevy, 2015, p. 112.

38 In his book, Hallevy divides the argument differently, analyzing the different models of liability when discussing in detail the mental health requirements. For the sake of this analysis, we will discuss these models at once, following the structure adopted in the earlier paper "The Criminal Liability of Artificial Intelligence Entities – From Science Fiction to Legal Social Control", 2010.

39 Hallevy, 2015, p. 105.

40 Hallevy, "The Criminal Liability of Artificial Intelligence Entities – From Science Fiction to Legal Social Control", 2010, p. 180.

41 Ivi, p. 181.

(c)(i) the programmer had no criminal intent whatsoever and she was not negligent in the programming of the AI system;

(c)(ii) the programmer had no criminal intent whatsoever, but she was negligent in the programming of the AI system;

(c)(iii) the programmer designed the AI system to commit an offense, but the system diverged from the plan causing either more or different harm than the predicted offense (*aberratio delicti*).

In situation (c)(i) the programmer was not negligent, hence it would be inappropriate to apply this model and in general to enforce any kind of criminal response upon her. Conversely, situation (c)(ii) is a case of "pure negligence" and therefore does not fall in the application scope of model (3), but should follow the standards set for negligence crimes.[42] Lastly, situation (c)(iii) represents, according to Hallevy, the ideal scenario for the natural probable consequence model, since this model "is meant to deal with unplanned developments of a planned delinquent event".[43] In cases like these, the programmer or the user will be deemed responsible for the crime which was committed by the AI system in addition to or in substitution of the planned crime. Hallevy provides the following example:

> [A] medical expert artificial intelligence system is used for diagnosis of certain types of diseases through analyzing the patient's symptoms. The artificial intelligence system analysis is based on machine learning, which inductively analyses and generalizes specific cases. The system fails to diagnose correctly one case, and that reveals to wrong treatment, which worsens the patient's situation and finally causes the patient's death. The analysis of the artificial intelligence system's activity reveals negligence of it, and it fulfills both factual and mental elements requirements of the relevant negligence offense (negligent homicide). At this point arises the question of the *programmer's* criminal liability for that offense. His criminal liability is not related to the decision to use the artificial intelligence system, to follow its diagnosis, etc., but it is related to the very initial programming of the system. If the programmer would have programmed the system to kill patients and instrumentally used it for this purpose, it would have been perpetration-through-another of murder, but this is

42 Hallevy, "The Criminal Liability of Artificial Intelligence Entities – From Science Fiction to Legal Social Control", 2010, p. 184.

43 Hallevy, 2015, p. 119.

> not the case here. For the programmer's criminal liability in this case the probable consequence liability may be relevant.[44]

What about combining the different liability models? In cases such as the situation described at (c)(iii), assuming that the AI system was not used as an innocent agent, the direct liability model could be applied to attribute criminal liability to the AI system in addition to the one attributable to human operators.

Another example of a possible combination is the case where the programmer of the AI system is itself an AI system. Imagine that the system X programs a system Y to illegally access a computer, and that Y fulfills this criminal task, but then intentionally uses the illegal access to steal the victim's identity to commit a series of online frauds. In this case, X would be liable for Y's behavior following the natural probable consequence model, where instead Y would be liable for its own behavior according to the direct liability model.

According to some, Hallevy fails to recognize that "while certain acts can be attributed to the heads of each company, attributing each line of code and task to individual programmers is a monumental task".[45] Moreover, he neglects "the criminal liability of hardware manufacturers",[46] who would not be liable under any of the three models.

Lastly, Hallevy focuses on punishment.[47] On the one hand, he argues that retribution and deterrence would prove useless in the case of punishing robots but could prove valuable when punishing the human participants in the offence.[48] On the other hand, he states that rehabilitation and incapacitation are relevant from an AI punishment perspective. Rehabilitation could function for machines as it functions for humans: it may be used to refine the machine learning process as a way to lead AI systems to making better decisions. The rehabilitated AI system, then, would be able to perform better, same as rehabilitated defendants should have better tools to face reality.[49] Incapacitation would be the last resort measure directed at those systems that have proven to be incapable of changing their ways through their inner processes (i.e., via machine learning).[50]

---

44 Ivi, p. 134.

45 D.J. J. Kim, "Artificial intelligence and crime: what killer robots could teach about criminal law", Thesis in Law, Victoria University of Wellington, 2017, p. 26. Available at: https://researcharchive.vuw.ac.nz/xmlui/bitstream/handle/10063/7927/paper_access.pdf?sequence=1

46 Ibid.

47 Hallevy also outlines how specific punishments (capital penalty, imprisonment and suspended imprisonment, probation, public service, fine) would be applied to AI systems (Ch. 6.2.2.).

48 Hallevy, 2015, p. 210.

49 Ivi, p. 211.

50 Hallevy, 2015, p. 211.

3.2.2 *Ying Hu: a Criminal Code for Robots*

Hu makes a positive case for imposing direct criminal liability on "smart robots", that is, robots that fulfill three threshold conditions. These conditions are: "the robot must be (1) equipped with algorithms that can make nontrivial morally relevant decisions; (2) capable of communicating its moral decisions to humans; and (3) permitted to act on its environment without immediate human supervision".[51]

Hu shares one research question with Abbott: are there any good reasons which justify imposing criminal liability on (smart) robots? Abbott believes that it would be possible to build a coherent theoretical case for punishing AI but that it is simply a bad idea in light of the existence of less disruptive alternatives.[52] Similarly, Hu argues that there can be good reasons which justify imposing criminal liability on smart robots. Her conclusions, though, are different from Abbott's. She proposes the introduction of a new criminal code for robots.

Indeed, Hu fits wholly in the Front of Robotic Liberation, as she argues in favor of legal personhood for robots. Yet, she distances herself strongly from its paramount representative, i.e., Hallevy. The Israeli author, she claims, fails to describe in detail the type of robot on which to impose criminal liability and at explaining why we should adopt the criminal tool in the first place.[53] Moreover, he "appears to assume that, since we already impose criminal liability on non-human entities such as corporations, extending such liability to robots requires little justification".[54] Furthermore, Hu also addresses two representatives of the skeptic front, i.e., Gless, Silverman and Weigend,[55] complaining that they only restrict their analysis to existing robots.[56]

The author acknowledges beforehand that her analysis might be speculative, yet she believes that its value lies in the fact that it is an informative tool, which could prove useful in the regulation vs. innovation race.[57] Moreover, it could work as tenet for scientists working on moral machines, when it comes to deciding which moral norms should be taught to robots and which training data they should adopt.

---

51 Hu, 2019, p. 490.

52 See Sec. 3.3.1.

53 Hu, 2019, p. 492, note 13, referring to Hallevy, 2013, pp. 38 and 66.

54 Ibid.

55 See Sec. 3.4.5.1.

56 Hu, 2019, p. 492, note 13, referring to S. Gless, E. Silverman & T. Weigend, "If Robots Cause Harm, who Is to Blame: Self-Driving Cars and Criminal Liability", *New Criminal Law Review*, Vol. 19, No. 3, 2016, p. 423.

57 "Although our analysis might be speculative in some respects, the thought experiment is nevertheless invaluable: It helps identify the key considerations that should inform our decision whether to impose criminal liability on robots. We will, in turn, be better positioned to decide whether and when to apply criminal liability to robots, as technological advances push us closer to the turning point in that spectrum", Hu, 2019, p. 495.

Let us now explain the aforementioned conditions for labelling a robot as "smart". The first condition regards the creation of "moral algorithms" capable of making "nontrivial morally relevant decisions" (meaning decisions "between or among two or more courses of action that might be considered right or wrong by ordinary members of our society").[58] Indeed, as the author rightly recognizes, moral decision have acquired importance especially in the field of autonomous driving.[59] Moral machines can be built either following a rule-based approach, which requires programmers to encode in the algorithm all the moral rules *ex ante*,[60] or a utility-maximization approach, where machines learn moral rules by trial and error through reinforcement learning. Regardless of the approach used to create moral machines, the second condition implies that the robot communicates these decisions to humans, together with the alternative courses of actions that were available, and the weight given by the robot to each. The third condition necessitates that the human-in-the-loop takes a distant position from the smart robot. In other words, there should be no "immediate human supervision" on the action of the smart robot.[61]

Having established this, Hu turns to the heart of her argument: the creation of a Criminal Code for Robots. The reasons for its introduction are twofold: first, there are grounds to hold smart robots to a higher moral standard than humans. To support her claim, Hu argues that smart robots could be held liable for failure to act not only when they have a legal duty to do so.[62] Yet, this would entail diverting from one of criminal law's founding principles, that is, the principle of culpability. Second, smart robots might prompt new moral questions which were never faced by humans, as they are able to act in ways that are physically impossible for human beings.

What would be the benefits, then, of creating a Criminal Code for Robots? Hu claims that it would introduce a minimum set of moral standards decided collectively by society. What is more, it would work as a legal basis for holding "robot manufacturers" (subjects who participate in creating the algorithms) and "robot trainers" (subjects who train the algorithms) criminally liable for failing the duty of care, i.e., for preventing smart robots from behaving in a way that is against the Code.

One counterargument which is prompted instinctively at this point is: if one of the reasons to introduce criminal norms for robots is that they are capable of behavior that is not even conceivable by humans, how could the very same humans be punished for these

58 Ivi, p. 496.

59 Think for example of the MIT Moral Machine. See Sec. 5.3.2.1.

60 The author then distinguishes between strict rule-based approaches, which do not allow the robot to learn new moral rules or to make decisions when there is "ethical uncertainty", and soft rule-based approaches, where the robot is equipped with a set of "high-level moral rules" and is also fed examples which demonstrate how to apply these rules to real cases. The purpose of the examples is for the robot to learn new principles which can be applied to new scenarios. Hu, 2019, p. 497.

61 Ivi, p. 499.

62 Think of the example discussed at Sec. 1.7, D.

behaviors? As a matter of fact, Hu does not explain how these new moral issues should be dealt with.

She subsequently presents her case for imposing criminal liability on robots based on three arguments. Firstly, criminal punishment has a censuring (or expressive) function. It communicates the disapproval of the community towards a morally wrongful conduct and this function acquires greater importance when no human being is at fault for the robot's misconduct.[63] Secondly, punishing robots would provide emotional relief to victims of smart robots' misbehavior. Thirdly, it would be of use to identify culpable (human) individuals, since those who are not at fault would be inclined to cooperate with investigations, therefore pinpointing to those who are. It would also nudge creating self-policing mechanisms for robot manufactures and users, who would put safeguards in place against robot harm to avoid sanctions on the robot.

Hu, then, addresses five possible objections to her arguments. First: robot criminal liability is redundant in respect to imposing criminal liability on individuals responsible for robot misconduct. Hu claims that this is not the case, since if we were to hold the latter liable it would be for an omission, i.e., it would be for failing negligently or recklessly to prevent the robot from committing harmful conduct, rather than for the harmful conduct per se. Furthermore, it would not be redundant in all those cases where neither the smart robot manufacturers nor the trainers are at fault, same as "situations in which *[in US case law]* corporations are held liable for offenses despite the fact that none of their human agents are held liable for those offences".[64]

Second: robots are incapable of performing actions since they lack the capacity to form any mental state. She responds by relying on Peter French's account of corporate liability: one can claim that *x* did *y* intentionally if *x* had a reason for doing *y*, which was the cause of doing it. This entails that corporations are able to act intentionally, since they have an interest in performing an action *y* if it is likely to result in the realization of the corporate goals and policies.[65] In order for the act to be defined as intentionally pursued by the corporation, it has to be done for corporate reasons, i.e., to pursue a corporate policy established by an internal decision structure. Accordingly, smart robots possess moral goals and policies which represent the views of robot trainers (similar to the internal decision structure of a corporation). Hence, whenever they act, they do so following their moral algorithms, that is, they act intentionally.

Addressing this objection might be relevant to respond to those who believe that acting "willingly" entails that the agent must be capable of forming intent. However, Hu does not address a big share of the debate represented by those who believe that the "vital link

---

63 Hu, 2019, p. 490.

64 Ivi, p. 515.

65 P.A. French, *Collective and Corporate Responsibility*, Columbia University Press, 1984, p. 40.

between mind and body",[66] i.e., the rational capacities which are necessary to consider a conduct voluntary and therefore punishable, has little or nothing to do with *mens rea*. Indeed, she claims that the "standard" conception of action is based on intentionality, which is a mental state and, as a consequence, one cannot be the agent of an action if one lacks the capacity to form mental states.[67] But who defines the standard concept of a criminally relevant act? That question remains open.

Third: robots are incapable of performing morally wrongful actions since they are not capable of understanding that their actions were wrong. Hu's response can be summarized as follows: since smart robots are led by moral algorithms, trained by individuals who know the moral values of our society, they are members of our moral community. This entails, then, that if they commit a moral wrong, they do so intentionally.

Fourth: whether it might be true that smart robots can behave morally, they do not do so autonomously, since the principles they act upon were engineered by their manufacturers and trainers. Hu argues that those who support this objection adhere to Kant's conception of a moral agent, i.e., an agent must be autonomous in the sense that it must be the author of his desires. She maintains, then, that we should look at alternative theories of moral agency, such as the one of collective responsibility as elaborated by List and Pettit. According to this theory, an agent can be held responsible of its misbehavior when three conditions are fulfilled: one, that the agent faces a "normatively significant choice" which entails picking between good/bad, right/wrong, etc.; two, that the agent is capable of understanding and accessing information on how to make that choice; three, that the agent "has the control required for choosing between options".[68] List and Pettit argue that these conditions can be satisfied by groups, such as corporations. Hu, then, maintains that smart robots can fulfill these requirements as well. Specifically, regarding the third requirement, she argues that smart robots have a certain kind of autonomy on making a normatively significant choice. As a matter of fact, they are capable of applying the moral norms which were taught to them by the manufacturers and the trainers to new situations.

Fifth: recognizing robots as legal persons would be harmful, as it would encourage people to anthropomorphize robots. Hu discards this argument quite rapidly by affirming that the concerns about antrophormizing robots are not strong enough to outweigh the positive benefits of holding smart robots criminally liable.

In conclusion, Hu focuses on AI punishment. She, as well as Abbott,[69] adopts H.L.A. Hart's definition of punishment:

66 Hart, 2008, p. 107.

67 Hu, 2019, p. 518.

68 C. List & P. Pettit, *Group Agency*, Oxford University Press, 2011, p. 155.

69 R. Abbott, *The Reasonable Robot*, Cambridge University Press, 2020, p. 115.

(1) it must involve pain or other consequences normally considered unpleasant;
(2) it must be for an offense against legal rules;
(3) it must be of an actual or supposed offender for his offense;
(4) it must be intentionally administered by humans other than the offender; and
(5) it must be imposed and administered by an authority constituted by a legal system against which the offense is committed.[70]

Hu argues that conditions (2), (3), (4) and (5) can be easily fulfilled. With regard to (1), she contends that punishment should be deemed as unpleasant by the general members of our community. Interestingly so, Hu is amongst the few legal scholars who theorizes how criminal punishment towards AI systems could take form in practice. She hypothesizes four punishments:

(1) physically destroying the robot (the robot equivalent of a "death sentence");
(2) destroying or re-writing the moral algorithms of the robot (the robot equivalent of a "hospital order");
(3) preventing the robot from being put to use (the robot equivalent of a "prison sentence"); and/or
(4) ordering fines to be paid out of the insurance fund (the robot equivalent of a "fine").[71]

3.2.3 *Christina Mulligan: Revenge Against Robots*

In her paper "Revenge Against Robots" Mulligan argues that imposing punishment ("revenge" or "vengeance", as defined by the author) on AI systems would result in retributive benefits consisting in the psychological satisfaction of victims of AI misbehavior.[72] Whether her considerations are not specifically tailored to criminal sanctions, some of her reflections are indeed valuable to the criminal legal debate, and this is proven by the fact that certain scholars mentioned in this chapter refer to her work.[73]

According to Mulligan, in the future it will be impossible to say that the "rogue" behavior of robots based on black box algorithms[74] is "caused" by the manufacturer, the pro-

70 Hart, 2008, pp. 4-5.
71 Hu, 2019, p. 529.
72 C. Mulligan, "Revenge Against Robots", *South Carolina Law Review*, Vol. 69, 2018, p. 578.
73 Abbott, 2020, p. 117; Hu, 2019, p. 531.
74 See also the definition of W. Nicholson Price II, "Big Data, Patents, and the Future of Medicine", *Cardozo Law Review*, Vol. 37, 2016, p. 1404, who describes box algorithms (that analyze health information) as

grammer or the seller. These opaque algorithms occasion the impossibility to explain why robots behaved in a certain way, even though an "autopsy"[75] of the robot's algorithm was performed by the most skilled AI coroner. It might be possible to affirm that the actions of programmers and manufactures are but-for causes (i.e., the *condiciones sine quibus non*) for the realization of the harmful event, yet they cannot be seen as proximate causes, nor as reasonably foreseeable ones. The unpredicted robot behavior which led to the (criminal) outcome should be seen as triggered by intervening causes, that is, experiences that affected its learning mechanisms. According to Mulligan, it follows, then, that the robot represents the proximate cause of the unwanted event, as "any other answer would torture the meaning of 'proximate cause' ".[76]

Having established this, Mulligan moves on to analyze how the question of moral culpability, i.e., if robots are capable of moral behavior, affects her argument in favor of robot punishment. She analyzes two questions: first, "does the sense that blameworthiness supervenes on the existence of 'free will' change whether robots should be punished for their actions to satisfy their victims?"; second, "does it change whether the victim *feels* that the punishment is morally justified?". The answer is negative to both questions. She states concisely:

> Either a robot is as morally blameworthy and as deserving of penalty or other legal action as a human, or the robot is like a rock and is neither deserving nor undeserving of any sort of treatment. In both situations, the robot's moral status does not supply a reason to avoid taking action against it, given the presence of other reasons to do so.[77]

Lastly, Mulligan focuses on punishment. Asaro[78] is off track, she states, in claiming that punishing robots would not achieve the classical goal of punishment such as retribution, reform or deterrence. Indeed, the goal of criminal law is to create psychological satisfaction for the victims of the robot, and this can be done most effectively by introducing a modern version of the Middle Ages practice of "noxal surrender". Noxal surrender would involve handing over the faulty robot to the victim or to her family so that they to do what they think is best with it in order to fit their satisfaction. As a matter of fact, a wronged

"'black-box' precisely because the relationships at [*their*] heart are opaque not because their developers deliberately hide them, but because either they are too complex to understand, or they are the product of non-transparent algorithms that never tell scientists, 'this is what we found'. Opacity is not desirable but is rather a necessary byproduct of the development process". See also Sec. 6.3.2.2 for an analysis of the black box phenomenon.

75 Mulligan, 2018, p. 590.

76 Ibid.

77 Mulligan, 2018, p. 593.

78 See Sec. 3.4.4.

party "may indeed be quite justified in dragging a robot out into an empty field and walloping it with a baseball bat".[79] All things considered, Mulligan presents, as she defines it herself, quite "an outlandish argument".[80]

3.2.4 *Lasse Quarck: the German Exception*

Quarck represents quite the exception: he is the only German author quoted in this chapter who is part of the expansionist front.[81] He believes that it is unacceptable for criminal law to remain behind during the process of digital transformation that we are living in. Consequently, he argues that introducing AI criminal liability will be unavoidable in the long run. Scholars must discuss right now the direct criminal liability of the intelligent agent, regardless of whether or not they think that human-like AI systems will come to life soon.

Quarck focuses on three dogmatic challenges regarding the application of criminal liability to AI agents: first, the *actus reus* challenge; second, the *mens rea* challenge: third, the punishability challenge.

"*Das Strafrecht ist von Menschen für Menschen erdacht worden*"[82] claims Quarck. It follows that the conceptual categories of criminal law that we know of cannot be transferred directly to AI agents. With regard to the *actus reus* challenge, he argues that what is relevant is how strongly one would like to "normatively charge"[83] the concept of agency: if one believes that the ability of the AI to understand norms is a prerequisite for its ability to act, then we would have to refute the idea that current AI systems could fulfill the *actus reus* requirement (which is the argument made by Gerard Seher, exponent of the skeptics front, in a nutshell).[84] He objects to Seher's argument by claiming that indeed the requirement of "willful" conduct can be dispensed with if we base criminal liability on systemic (or algorithmic) wrongdoing rather than on the commission of a singular individual, similarly to what is done in those legal systems which are acquainted with corporate criminal liability.[85]

---

79 Mulligan, 2018, p. 595.

80 Ibid. For an interesting analysis of the relationship between people's view on moral judgements and punishment of automated systems vs existing legal doctrines, see the empirical study conducted G. Lima et al., "The Conflict Between People's Urge to Punish AI and Legal Systems", *Front. Robot. AI*, Vol. 8, 2021. The study will be discussed in Sec. 6.5.

81 Quarck, 2020.

82 Ivi, p. 57.

83 "*Es könnte zunächst darauf ankommen, inwieweit man den Begriff normativ auflädt. Sieht man die Fähigkeit der KI zum wenigstens potenziellen Normverständnis als Voraussetzung der Handlungsfähigkeit, so wäre diese, zumindest zum jetzigen Zeitpunkt, abzulehnen*". Quarck, 2020, p. 66.

84 See Sec. 3.4.5.3.

85 Quarck, 2020, p. 65.

With regard to the *mens rea* challenge, Quarck believes that free will does not represent a mandatory prerequisite to establish the culpability of an agent.[86] Indeed, he argues, free will is only attributed since it cannot be proven that it actually exists (or that it doesn't). Guilt is assigned to an agent to resolve a conflict that has been caused in our society by the commission of the wrongdoing, because no harm can go without a sanction. Following such a consequentialist approach, Quarck claims that the same guilt-assigning operation can be conducted with algorithmic misconduct. It does not matter whether intelligent or human agents commit a crime because of a biological or algorithmic process, or because of a dysfunction in the formation of their free will: it is our social system that decides to whom we must assign criminal responsibility.[87]

With regard to the punishability challenge, if an AI system can fulfill both *mens rea* and *actus reus* criteria, then punishing AI systems would fulfill both general and special prevention purposes. With regard to the former, the AI system could be reprogrammed to include the meaning of the standard violated through the criminal conduct. With regard to the latter, assuming that the punished AI systems were in a network with other agents, this would cause the other networked systems to include the same implementation (*rectius*, correction) in their own code.

3.3 MODERATES

The authors placed in this category of moderates recognize that there is a mismatch between the law, which is designed to regulate human behavior, and the ways algorithmic behavior takes place. Hence, they advocate for a change in the law (or in the interpretation of the law).[88] On the other hand, these authors only suggest a moderate change and therefore do not completely disrupt the traditional foundations of criminal law. A further characteristic shared by some of the authors which are mentioned in this section (Abbott & Sarch, Lagioia & Sartor), is that their theories are the product of hybridization, i.e., a mixture between concepts of criminal law and concepts stemming from other disciplines, such as ethics, psychology, and computer science.

Indeed, much of the academic literature analyzed in this chapter is the byproduct of an old discussion, which can be reconducted to legal moralism.[89] What comes first: moral values or law?[90] It is tempting, at times, to confuse rules of law and rules of morality, espe-

86 Ivi, p. 68.
87 Quarck, 2020, p. 68.
88 Abbott, 2020, p. 3.
89 See Ch. 4.2. for a discussion of theories of criminalization.
90 See S. Rodotà, "Etica e Diritto (dialogo tra alcuni studenti e Stefano Rodotà) con una Presentazione di Gaetano Azzariti", *Costituzionalismo.it*, Vol. 1, 2019.

cially when it comes to criminal law. The topic has been addressed by a conspicuous amount of the literature over the past decades.[91] As a consequence, the aforementioned classical debate found renewed importance with the occurrence of the discussion on how to regulate AI. It is also in this light that the authors analyzed here acquire value.

3.3.1 *Ryan Abbott and Alex Sarch: a General Theory for AI-Punishment*

Two of the most prominent authors who take a moderate stance on AI and criminal liability are certainly Abbott and Sarch with their paper "Punishing Artificial Intelligence: Legal Fiction or Science Fiction".[92] In this paper, they focus on justifications for criminal punishment, rather than on the specific elements of criminal liability, and they adopt a very pragmatic approach. Specifically, they reflect on whether the doctrinal and theoretical commitments of criminal law can be reconciled with criminal liability for AI. Notably, the authors do not rule out direct punishment of AI systems completely.

The reasons why the work of Abbott and Sarch is relevant are manifold. To begin with, they were the first to introduce to the (criminal law) academic discourse the famous case of the Random Darknet Shopper (RDS),[93] later used by several authors.[94]

The RDS was an online bot initially installed in a nonprofit gallery in St. Gallen, Switzerland, which was created to act as an (a)live piece of an art exhibition.[95] The software was programmed to autonomously spend 100$ in bitcoins per week on a deep web market named Agora Shop. Each week the bot randomly chose an object to purchase, which was then sent directly to the gallery. The nature of the object would be disclosed only once the

91 J. Allan, "Revisiting the Hart-Devlin Debate: At the Periphery and By the Numbers", *San Diego L. Rev.*, Vol. 54, 2017, p. 423.

92 Abbott & Sarch, 2019. Ryan Abbott expanded his reflections in his subsequent publication, *The Reasonable Robot*, 2020

93 J. Lackman, Random Darknet Shopper, *Aksioma – Institute for Contemporary Art*, 2016. Available at: https://aksioma.org/pdf/aksioma_PostScriptUM_23_ENG_Bitnik.pdf. See also: !Mediengruppe Bitnik, Random Darknet Shopper, 2014-2016. Available at: wwwwwwwwwwwwwwwwwwwwwww.bitnik.org/r/; M. Power, "What happens when a software bot goes on a Darknet shopping spree?", *The Guardian*, 5 December 2014. Available at: www.theguardian.com/technology/2014/dec/05/software-bot-darknet-shopping-spree-random-shopper; K. Grant, "Random darknet shopper exhibition featuring automated dark web purchases opens in London", *The Independent*, 2 December 2015. Available at: www.independent.co.uk/life-style/gadgets-and-tech/news/random-darknet-shopper-exhibition-featuring-automated-dark-web-purchases-opens-in-london-a6770316.html.

94 F. Lagioia & G. Sartor, "AI Systems Under Criminal Law: a Legal Analysis and a Regulatory Perspective", *Philosophy & Technology*, Vol. 33, 2020; Hayward & Maas, 2020; D. J. Baker & P. H. Robinson, *Artificial Intelligence and the Law. Cybercrime and Criminal Liability*, Routledge, 2021; J. Turner, *Robot Rules. Regulating Artificial Intelligence*, Gildan Media Corporation, 2019. Abbott further developed his reflections in Ch. 6 of his book "The Reasonable Robot. Artificial Intelligence and the Law", 2020. We will refer to this later work only when it adds to what is stated in his collaborative work with Sarch.

95 !Mediengruppe Bitnik & !Digital Brainstoarming, "The Darknet – From Memes to Onionland. An Exploration", Kunst Halle Sankt Gallen.

package had arrived at the exhibition space, where it was unpacked and then put on display. From October 2014 to January 2015 the RDS bought a total of 12 items. Outstandingly, some of them included counterfeit Louis Vuitton handbags, counterfeit Nike Air Yeezy shoes, a fake Hungarian passport and twelve ecstasy pills. In January 2015, the Swiss police seized RDS and its possessions. Soon thereafter, the charges against the artist and the bot were withdrawn.

To continue, Abbott and Sarch coined the definition of "Hard AI Crime".[96] Before focusing on this definition, it is necessary to take a step back. According to the authors, AI system behavior expresses four main features, which are relevant features from a criminal law perspective:

1. Unpredictability, i.e., the capacity for the system to engage in activities which were not intended or foreseen by its creators;
2. Unexplainability, i.e., the incapacity to explain why the AI system chose a certain pattern of behavior;
3. Autonomy, i.e., the capacity for the AI systems to act independently of human control and therefore to cause harm without being under the direct control of an individual;
4. Complexity, i.e., the fact that the AI system is the output of the contribution of many individuals over a long period or that its conduct is the result of a training based on huge databases coming from heterogeneous sources.

The combination of these factors might lead to irreducibility i.e., the impossibility to reconnect the crime to a liable person. Based on this, the authors distinguish between "AI Crimes" and "Hard AI Crimes". AI Crimes are defined as "cases in which an AI would be criminally liable if a natural person had performed the same act".[97] Hard AI Crimes are instead defined as "scenarios where crimes are functionally committed by machines and there is no identifiable person who has acted with criminal culpability".[98] If one thinks of this distinction in terms of irreducibility, Hard AI Crimes are instances in which harmful AI conduct is not reducible to a human actor, either for practical reasons (because of the difficulty to identify how individuals singularly contributed to the design of the system) or for trivial reasons (because the human misconduct does not meet the threshold required to activate the criminal sanction). In other words, irreducibility entails that the AI criminal act cannot be traced back to the wrongful act of a person.[99] Indeed, according to

96 The term AI-Crime (AIC) appears also in T. C. King et al., "Artificial Intelligence Crime: An Interdisciplinary Analysis of Foreseeable Threats and Solutions", *Sci Eng Ethics*, Vol. 26, No. 1, 2019.

97 Abbott & Sarch, 2019, p. 332.

98 Ivi., p. 328.

99 Abbott, 2020, p. 13.

Abbott and Sarch, Hard AI Crime seems to make "the strongest case for punishing artificial intelligence".[100]

What is more, the authors provide a comprehensive theory for the foundation of criminal punishment of AI systems. They anchor their reflections building on a theory of punishment which is, in turn, based on affirmative (pluralist) benefits. They contend, indeed, that punishing AI directly might lead to significant affirmative benefits. First, they argue that it could obtain general deterrence. By doing so, they directly address Peter Asaro's undeterrability argument.[101] Their counterargument can be summarized as follows: whether it might be true that AI as we know it is not a moral agent responsive to punishment, and therefore specific deterrence might be unattainable, punishment of AI systems could lead to unrestricted general deterrence of other subjects, namely of developers, owners or users of AI. Moreover, AI punishment could have some expressive benefits, in the sense that it would convey a "message of official condemnation that could reaffirm the interests, rights, and ultimately the value of the victims of the harmful AI".[102] Yet, the authors recognize that this argument based on "folk morality" might result in certain unsurmountable objections.[103]

Abbott and Sarch address three main challenges which could be brought against AI punishment from a retributivist point of view, namely:

(1) the eligibility challenge,
(2) the reducibility challenge, and
(3) the spillover objection.

As it will be highlighted, one trait of the authors becomes evident from how they describe these challenges, and the related responses: their non-European continent legal background.

Starting with the eligibility challenge (1), it entails that AI systems cannot satisfy the prerequisites of criminal law, hence they cannot be sanctioned.

---

100 Ivi, p. 112.

101 Abbott and Sarch claim that Asaro failed to distinguish between general and special deterrence. Cf: "And finally, deterrence only makes sense when moral agents are capable of recognizing the similarity of their potential choices and actions to those of other moral agents who have been punished for the wrong choices and actions-without this reflexivity of choice by a moral agent, and recognition of similarity between and among moral agents, punishment cannot possibly result in deterrence", P. M. Asaro, "A Body to Kick, but Still No Soul to Damn: Legal Perspectives on Robotics", in P. Lin, K. Abney & G. A. Bekey, *Robot Ethics: The Ethical and Social Implications of Robotics*, MIT Press, 2012, p. 181.

102 Abbott & Sarch, 2019, p. 346. See also Mulligan, 2018, p. 580.

103 These *prima facie* objections are: it would amount to mob justice and could lead to populist demands for justice; it could lead to more undesirable bad human behavior; and it would carry affirmative costs for the criminal justice system. Abbott & Sarch, 2019, p. 348.

It can come in both a narrow and a general form. The narrow eligibility challenge suggests that AI systems cannot possess *mens rea*, where instead the general eligibility challenge holds that an AI system cannot be culpable in a broader perspective (i.e., AI systems lack the capacity to weigh reasons and to deliberate in a blameworthy way). The answers to the eligibility challenge considered by the authors are three: *respondeat superior*, strict liability, and providing a framework for direct *mens rea* analysis for AI.

Respondeat superior is a legal fiction tool adopted in the field of corporate liability, which builds a bridge between the mental states of the agent of the corporation and the corporation itself. Different from what the authors state ("imputation principles of this kind are well-understood and legally accepted"),[104] this legal construct frequently incurs overwhelming objections from continental lawyers. In addition, the authors discard *respondeat superior* as an inadequate response in cases of Hard AI Crime since, different from corporations, it is not guaranteed that an AI will come with a "ready supply of identifiable human actors whose mental states can be imputed".[105] In other words corporations, unlike AI systems, are composed of people.[106]

Abbott and Sarch then move on to the "familiar route" option of establishing new strict liability offenses for AI crimes, which could seem more plausible in the case of AI systems, as they are not protected by the just deserts constraint. Yet, the authors reckon that there might be cases in which AI misbehavior does not fulfill the *actus reus* requirement of a crime. Specifically, they argue that AI systems are not capable of conscious voluntary action: same as "[a] hurricane cannot perform an act but can cause no shortage of harm".[107] Even if we theorized a new strict liability offense providing for a duty of the AI to non-harm humans, these offenses would bear the cost of diluting the meaning of criminal law, hence its expressive benefits. These costs have to be weighted when considering strict liability as a solution to the eligibility challenge.

The third response focuses on whether it would be possible to legally construct AI mental states. Could an AI be culpable (*broad* eligibility challenge)? Could an AI possess a specific *mens rea*, as proscribed by the single offense? When answering these questions, the authors introduce reflections which will be later expanded on by Lagioia-Sartor and Ashton.[108]

Primarily, they maintain that the preponderant theory regarding culpability is based on whether the individual manifests "insufficient regard for legally protected interests or values".[109] Accordingly, corporations can be accounted as being directly criminally culpa-

104 Abbott & Sarch, 2019, p. 351.
105 Ivi, p. 352.
106 Abbott, 2020, p. 14.
107 Ibid.
108 See Sec. 3.3.2 and Sec. 6.2.2.
109 Abbott & Sarch, 2019, p. 355.

ble through the "information-gathering, reasoning and decision-making procedures" of their employees.[110] Can we apply the same type of reasoning to AI systems?

Indeed, AI systems can gather information, process it and determine with autonomy how to complete pre-established goals. Imagine if these systems were programmed to follow certain rules, for example not to hurt humans, and they diverge from this rule to reach their goals.[111] Could this be considered as disregard for the norm, therefore as criminally culpable action?

As the authors themselves note, their reflections are not far from Hu's expansionist point of view.[112] Yet, they modestly contend that their only focus is legal culpability, not moral responsibility, and that therefore the bar, which has to be reached, is lower.

To address the *strict* eligibility challenge, Abbott and Sarch introduce the "Belief Desire Intention" (BDI) model for intent, which was first ideated in the 1980s in the field of cognitive science by Micheal Bratman[113] As will be described, Lagioia and Sartor's analysis relies heavily on Bratman's concept of intent. For this reason, it will be explained further in depth in the next paragraph. For now, it is relevant to mention that this theory entails that an agent intends an outcome when she guides her conduct in the direction of causing that outcome. The concept of "direction of action" requires further clarifications: it implies that the agent will adjust her behavior to make the outcome more likely and that it will monitor the surroundings to find ways which will increase the probability of the outcome. For example, if a person is driving with the intention to harm a pedestrian, if she detects an obstacle between her car and the victim, she will be willing to change her route in order to avoid the obstacle and obtain her goal. The same reasoning could be applied to an AV. In other words, judges would have to ask themselves whether the system was adjusting and "*guiding* its behavior as to make this outcome more likely".[114] In the case of an affirmative answer, it could be argued that the AI system had the purpose of running over the pedestrian. For all these above reasons, the authors defeat challenge (1).

The reducibility challenge (2) implies that it is always possible to identify the culpable human being behind non-human misbehavior. Whether this could be a stronger argument when it comes to corporations, the same cannot be assumed regarding AI systems. These systems behave in a way that is inherently more distant from the humans behind the machine: as indicated above, they are capable of autonomous, unforeseeable, and unpredictable conduct. Moreover, the reducibility challenge can be overcome also from a criminal policy perspective: legislators would have to criminalize "infinitely fine-grains form of

110 Ibid.

111 See Lagioia and Sartor, Sec. 3.3.2.

112 See Sec. 3.2.2.

113 M. Bratman, *Intention, Plans, and Practical Reason*, Harvard University Press, 1987.

114 Abbott & Sarch, 2019, p. 358.

misconducts"[115] such as "momentary lapses of attention, the failure to perceive emerging problems that are difficult to notice, tiny bits of carelessness, mistakes in prioritizing time and resources, not being sufficiently critical of groupthink"[116] and more. For these reasons, the authors defeat the reducibility challenge as well.

Lastly, the spillover challenge (3) implies that it would be unfair, from a just deserts constrain perspective, for the state to punish innocent human bystanders for crimes committed by the AI system. Yet, the authors argue, this is not an issue belonging exclusively to AI or to corporate liability: it is a general issue of criminal law, which has to do with the effectiveness of punishment. In other words, "[i]t is an omnipresent problem with criminal punishment, which should be addressed for any novel mode of criminal punishment – whether for corporations or AI".[117] Based on this, the authors negate the spillover challenge.

To conclude, the authors believe that while it is possible to make a coherent theoretical case for punishing AI, it is not justified considering the existence of less "disruptive" alternatives which can provide the same benefits. It follows that their reflections can be qualified as a moderate stance since they propose an approach based on a modest expansion of criminal law. They contend that "AI punishment should be avoided – not because it is incompatible with criminal law, but simply because it is a bad idea".[118]

The alternatives that they propose are several, but only two will be mentioned here. First, to create a new constructive liability crime[119] called "Causing Harm Through Criminal Uses of AI" which would fill the gap left by situations where a human agent has deployed an AI system to commit a crime (the "base crime"), but then the agent unforeseeably commits a further (criminal) result. Notice how this would work as an alternative to the natural probable consequence model theorized by Hallevy. It implies that the agent would be liable for the more serious crime without requiring any type *mens rea*, assuming that the base crime (for which *mens rea* is instead required) "carries at least the risk of the same general type of harm as the constructive liability element at issue".[120]

They rule out the possibility of introducing new *negligent* crimes upon developers for having developed a system that foreseeably could produce a risk of harm and that of imposing this responsibility through strict liability. Second, they propose the establishment of what is known as Responsible Person regime: the authors theorize creating "a designated adjacent person" which could be punished and "who would not otherwise be

115 Ivi, p. 362.
116 Abbott & Sarch, 2019, p. 362.
117 Ivi, p. 364.
118 Abbott, 2020, p. 16.
119 The authors describe them as "crimes that consist of a base crime which require mens rea, but where there then is a further result element as to which no mens rea is required". Abbott & Sarch, 2019, p. 372.
120 Ibid.

directly criminally liable".[121] In his most recent work, Abbott also suggests creating new legal duties to "responsibly develop, supervise, or remain accountable for an AI, with liability for failing to discharge those duties".[122]

3.3.2 *Lagioia and Sartor*

Lagioia and Sartor use the RDS to validate their proposed theoretical framework regarding the commission of *intentional* crimes by AI systems, specifically focusing on cases where the control relationship between humans and AI systems is of low intensity. This means that they refer only to situations where AI systems are not constrained to comply with the request of users since they are not monitored, nor directed through instructions.[123] Their aim is to discuss whether AI systems can "realise crimes, respond to reasons, and be influenced by criminal norms".[124] They refer to "AI crimes" as cases in which AI systems satisfy both the *actus reus* and *mens rea* requirements of crimes.

The authors adopt a narrow definition of *actus reus*, similar to Hallevy. Namely, they argue that it comprises "a material aspect having a factual-external presentation" that "does not include the agent's capacity to engage in practical reasoning, guide its actions and actualize result".[125] It follows, according to this definition, that the objective requirement can be fulfilled by involuntary and unwilled action, and therefore that AI systems, be it those who act in the physical sphere such as robots, or stand-alone software, can always act in a way that is relevant for criminal law in an *actus reus* perspective. Yet, this characterization suffers from some limitations. Amongst all of them, it does not acknowledge that the act requirement has held the criminal law "hostage" for a long time now,[126] and this led to the development of a myriad of theories of action in the past decades.[127] As the discussion of the main theories of conduct of the selected legal systems will be conducted in the second part of this chapter, the assessment will be limited to this one consideration for now.

Concerning *mens rea*, they divide their argument in two parts, one covering the *cognition* element of intent (i.e., the agent's awareness of "factual reality", which must include all the elements of the *actus reus* such as the "act or course of conduct, surrounding circum-

121 Abbott & Sarch, 2019, p. 378.
122 Abbott, 2020, p. 16.
123 Lagioia & Sartor, 2020, p. 3.
124 Ivi, p. 5.
125 Lagioia & Sartor, 2020, p. 8.
126 Keiler, 2013, p. 43.
127 Ivi, p. 53.

stances, and act's outcome or result element")[128], and the other covering the *volition* element of intent.

As for the question of whether an AI can fulfill the *cognition* requirement, the authors answer in the affirmative. They define cognition in terms of "situation awareness", which can be deconstructed into three levels:

1. perception of the elements in the environment (i.e., the ability of an agent to detect and monitor the variables of an environment at a particular point in time);
2. comprehension of the current situation (i.e., the ability of the agent to combine and interpret the information collected at the previous level, and to integrate it with pre-existing knowledge);
3. projection of future status (i.e., the ability of the agent to make guesses on future events).[129]

For example, a doctor needs to be aware of the patient's age, allergies, medical history, therapy, and should be able to detect her status and to interpret her symptoms.[130] The authors contend that the information methods adopted by AI systems are just "different ways of implementing the same cognitive functions" that are employed by humans.[131]

According to Lagioia and Sartor, then, AI systems can fulfill the cognition requirement: they are capable of acquiring perceptions through sensors (in the case of physical robots), through tracking activities and through messages (in the case of software agents); they can construct general images through data analysis and combination with previously stored patterns; and they can make reasonable decisions by computing probabilities of alternative courses of action.[132] In simpler words: "an AI is fully able to perceive its environment, comprehend it and make future projections about it".[133]

As for the *volition* requirement, specifically intent, Lagioia and Sartor adopt Bratman's conceptual framework for intent, i.e., the BDI model, as do Abbott and Sarch. Interestingly, the BDI model is used not only to analyze human agency and cognition, but was adapted in computer science to also work as programming approach that can then be used to develop AI systems.[134] The model deconstructs intent, meant as a commitment to act, into three mental attitudes:

128 Lagioia & Sartor, 2020, p. 9.
129 Ibid.
130 Lagioia & Sartor, 2020, p. 10.
131 Ivi, p. 12.
132 Lagioia & Sartor, 2020, p. 10.
133 H. Ashton, "Definitions of intent suitable for algorithms", *Artif Intell Law*, 2022, p. 30.
134 Lagioia & Sartor, 2020, p. 14.

1. belief (i.e., "the agent's current awareness of a situation plus any inferences it can make from them");[135]
2. desire (i.e., the objectives/goals possessed by the agents, which may conflict);
3. intention (i.e., the output given the agent's beliefs and desires or also "some conclusion of the agent's beliefs and desires"[136]).[137]

How does a BDI agent work?

When an agent forms new beliefs, it proceeds to evaluate which plans have invocation conditions that correspond to its internal beliefs. Additionally, it may construct or adapt its existing plans in order to achieve its goals under the new conditions. The emerging set of plans corresponds to the agent's intentions, and each plan defines a possible course of action. Therefore, intentions refer both to an agent's commitment to its desires (the goal to be achieved through the selected plans) and its commitment to the plans selected to achieve these goals.[138]

It follows that Lagioia and Sartor claim that it is possible to attribute criminally relevant cognitive states to an AI system when this system implements a BDI model. In other terms, it can be argued that these systems have "awareness of the relevant facts and make intentional choices".[139]

Their solution is based on two premises. First, they rule out proving the intention of the artificial agent by inspecting its internal functioning at the time of the criminal action, since it could be unavailable, no longer retrievable, or detectable. Second, they exclude the option of obtaining proof of intent by asking the system for reports on its internal state, since the system could be a built-in "liar", i.e. it could be programmed with the capacity of falsifying the explanations.

Furthermore, the authors maintain that (human) offenders are presumed to possess intent in criminal law when: (1) they had full awareness of the actions, and (2) their consequences were highly likely and could have been anticipated. It follows that the same presumption could be applied to AI systems. Indeed, some of these systems can evaluate the likelihood of certain events happening and decide their course of behavior on those bases, assessing what would be the likeliest outcome of their action.

Lagioia and Sartor are moderate in their approach for one fundamental reason: they argue that "criminal AI systems" will indeed require an *ad hoc* response, yet they base their

135 Ashton, 2022, p. 30.
136 Ashton, 2022, p. 30.
137 Lagioia & Sartor, 2020, p. 14.
138 Ibid.
139 Lagioia & Sartor, 2020, p. 15.

conceptual framework on the liability of humans, not on the liability of the AI agent itself.[140] Let us explain this statement.

Lagioia and Sartor propose four solutions to fill the liability gap. First, limiting the tasks assigned to AI systems to not "sensitive areas" and/or their autonomy in these areas (i.e., "keeping humans in the loop").[141] Second, they focus on civil law remedies. Third, to expand the boundaries of the crimes applicable to the "humans in charge of the AI system".[142] Fourth, directly punishing the AI system. The first two solutions are deemed insufficient to address the issue at stake and fall outside the scope of this chapter. Hence, this study will only focus here on the last two solutions, which are placed under the same category by the authors, namely "A Specific Criminal Liability for Creating and Deploying Criminal AI Systems".

Let us shift the attention now to solution three, namely "punishing the behaviour of the user/controller who has intentionally or negligently allowed the AI system to develop criminal behaviour (e.g. by adopting an architecture that enabled such behaviour or by omitting the controls that, for example, allowed the system to evolve becoming dangerous)".[143] The proposed liability architecture is complex and therefore needs to be deconstructed into separate elements. The proposed offense would punish:

A. the user/controller;
B. who has allowed the AI system to develop criminal behavior;
    1. through an action; or
    2. through an omission;
C. intentionally; or
D. negligently.

With regards to (1), i.e., the recipient of the criminal norm, this would be the user or the "controller" of the AI systems. One could ask oneself who falls under the label of "controller", as the term is very general, and the authors do not give a strict definition.

With regards to the act element of the *actus reus* (2), the conduct is described as the creation/deployment of AI systems capable of criminal conduct. This conduct could take place as an *action* (2)(a), i.e., adopting an architecture that enables AI criminal behavior, or (2)(b) as an *omission*. With regard to the latter, the examples proposed are various, such as omitting the controls which were necessary to avoid that the AI systems became dangerous, and the failure to include a "normative architecture"[144] in the system. AI systems

140 Ivi, p. 25.
141 Lagioia & Sartor, 2020, p.25.
142 Ivi, p. 27.
143 Lagioia & Sartor, 2020, p. 27.
144 Ibid.

can be considered normative agents if they follow the norms of the society in which they operate.[145] These normative constrains could prevent, on the one hand, the adoption of criminal means by the system to achieve permissible goals (e.g., engaging in fraud for maximizing profits) and, on the other, the direct pursuit of criminal goals (e.g., killing an adversary).[146]

With regard to the *mens rea* element, the conduct could be intentional (3), or negligent (4). With regard to negligence (4), the authors argue in favor of broadening the scope of recklessness to cover what they refer to as "opaque recklessness"[147] or *dolus eventualis.*[148] This form of *mens rea* would be realized using an AI system "in the awareness that it might engage in criminal activities ... even when the user did not foresee that the system would engage in the specific activity".[149] In the case of the RDS example, the artist would be liable for the purchase of ecstasy by the AI system, since the artist was aware that the AI system was capable of committing unlawful commercial transactions. Lastly, the authors argue that the criminal punishment of the human agents could work as a useful tool, adopting an approach which they define as "pragmatic", i.e., focused on the deterrence effect of criminal sanctions. AI systems could be programmed in a way that they recognize the benefits and the costs of inducing behavior, which would lead to sanctions for its users (and controllers).

Finally, the authors address the fourth solution, i.e., directly punishing AI systems, in a merely speculative way. They argue that it would be possible, under a deterrence rationale, based on two assumptions, which are: (1) that one day AI systems will be capable of possessing funds; and (2) that the same AI systems will be programmed to act in a self-interested way (i.e., maximizing its profits and minimizing its losses). These systems could be deterred from criminal conduct through economic sanctions. Committing a crime, in fact, would lead to a disutility for them. It follows that "AI agents aiming to maximise their utility will refrain from engaging in criminal activities leading to expected losses (sanc-

145 The translation of norms into code is not as easy as it may seem when it comes to identifying which norms should be encoded in the agent. Think of the example of a person driving a friend to the hospital because her appendix ruptured. The driver, to get her friend to the ER as fast as possible, incurs a series of violations of the norms regulating how to drive: speeding, running through red lights, driving on a sidewalk – although carefully avoiding accidents. This behavior is explained by the fact that the driver / agent assigned higher priority to saving her friend's life rather than to obeying traffic laws. Think of the same situation, but with an AV. How can this behavior be encoded in the architecture of an AI system? See P. Langley, "Explainable, Normative, and Justified Agency", *The Thirty-Third AAAI Conference on Artificial Intelligence (AAAI-19)*, p. 9776.

146 Lagioia & Sartor, 2020, p. 27.

147 The term was coined by K. K. Ferzan, "Opaque Recklessness", *Journal of Criminal Law and Criminology*, Vol. 91, Issue 3, 2001.

148 Lagioia & Sartor, 2020, p. 27.

149 Ibid.

tions) exceeding expected benefits".[150] From a rehabilitation perspective, Lagioia and Sartor affirm that "punishment could be directed to improve systems' performance, for example by refining decision-making processes through learning or by introducing norms as constraints in the system's architecture".[151] Nevertheless, the authors drastically conclude that establishing that AI systems are criminally responsible would not be impossible, "though certainly unneeded, outlandish, and merely speculative under the present circumstances".[152]

Pagallo and Barfield summarize Lagioia and Sartor's position as follows "Lagioia and Sartor argue that the cognitive states of cognition and awareness, volition and intention, or reason responsiveness, can be attributed to an AI system in a way that is meaningful for current criminal lawyers, although no reference is necessary to human-like properties à la Hallevy's position".[153] In other words, these authors show that Abbott's Hard AI Crimes can exist in reality, i.e., that AI systems can engage in activities that would constitute crimes if accomplished by humans. At the same time, they distance themselves from AI punishment expansionists, as they rule out direct punishment of AI systems.

3.3.3 Freitas, Andrade, Novais – Nora Osmani

These four authors were grouped together since they all rely heavily on analogies with corporate liability.

Freitas et al.[154] ask themselves whether there are any substantial differences between AI systems and corporations which would justify an exclusion of criminal liability of the former. They first focus on Hallevy's direct liability model[155] and claim that they are confident that if such a liability were to exist, it would not replace the programmer or the user's liability. They would co-exist as happens with corporate criminal liability where "punishment of the individuals behind the legal entities does not constitute a requirement to have the criminal punishment of the legal entities themselves".[156] Then, they ask whether an AI system could fulfill *actus reus* and *mens rea* requirements. With regard to the former, spe-

150 Lagioia & Sartor, 2020, p. 29.

151 Ivi, pp. 28-29.

152 Lagioia & Sartor, 2020, p. 29.

153 Pagallo & Barfield, 2020, p. 140.

154 P. M. Freitas, F. Andrade & P. Novais, "Criminal Liability of Autonomous Agents: from the unthinkable to the plausible" in P. Casanovas et al. (eds.), *AI Approaches to the Complexity of Legal Systems. AICOL 2013 International Workshops, AICOL-IV@IVR, Belo Horizonte, Brazil, July 21-27, 2013 and AICOL-V@SINTELNET-JURIX, Bologna, Italy, December 11, 2013, Revised Selected Papers*, Lecture Notes in Computer Science, Vol. 8929, Springer, 2014.

155 See Sec. 3.2.1.

156 Freitas, Andrade & Novais, 2014, p. 8.

cifically the act, they believe that it is inadmissible, as they adhere to the traditional definition of "acting".

In other words, it is not sufficient to claim that this requirement would be fulfilled by a muscular (mechanical, in the case of robots) movement: doing so would result in disregarding AI systems that do not possess a physical presence, but are yet capable of harm, such as stand-alone software. In the case of this latter type of AI systems, one cannot claim that the physical act is represented by an electronic impulse, either. This would be akin to stating that in the crime of defamation "the relevant act corresponds to the movement of one's tongue, mouth and vocal cords".[157] What is more, they argue that the act punished by the offense must be "voluntary" and that this is an inquiry which shouldn't be confused with the one regarding *mens rea*. Indeed, the claim that "[t]here can be volition without *mens rea*, but the contrary is not true".[158] As a consequence, they believe that while it is possible to make a case for identifying volition in the acts of legal entities, "to plunge into the same conclusion as to AI entities' acts would arguably be precipitated".[159]

With regard to fulfilling *mens rea*, these authors claim that it might represent a challenge which is difficult to overcome. Most importantly, adopting criminal law for the type of AI systems that are deployed now would be "rather useless and unjust".[160] Yet, the authors do not exclude that in the future, AI systems could fulfill the minimum requirements requested to be considered blameworthy and lead to criminal punishment. That is, they say, an instance of the "flexibility" of criminal law.

Osmani argues in favor of shifting from an individual-centered liability model to an organization-centered one when dealing with AI-caused misbehavior. She claims that the (negligent) "responsibility of manufacturers, distributors, and users of AI systems thus depends upon their capacity to understand the behaviour patterns of AI systems, the causal possibilities of AI systems' actions, and expected results".[161] Yet, these subjects might not possess the ability to predict this behavior due to how AI systems function. She believes, then, that concepts like "foreseeability" and "reasonable care" cannot constitute the elements on which one can base the imposition of criminal liability on manufacturers and sellers, "as they may simply not have the level of skill required to foresee the manner in which the harm will occur."[162] As a consequence, "standards of reasonable care may be vague. In addition, any attempt to impose responsibility on such a basis could lead to

157 Ivi, p. 9.
158 Freitas, Andrade & Novais, 2014.
159 Ibid.
160 Freitas, Andrade & Novais, 2014, p. 10.
161 N. Osmani, "The Complexity of Criminal Liability of AI Systems", *Masaryk University Journal of Law and Technology*, Issue 14, No. 1, 2020, p. 66.
162 Ivi, p. 67.

infinite liability for creators of AI systems that could obstruct the economy and innovation of AI".[163]

The result is a vicious circle. Hence, the author turns her attention to a different subject: big tech corporations. She argues that the "deep pockets of corporations",[164] i.e., those who "collect the fruits of AI deployment",[165] should be held accountable. This could be done by developing corporate criminal liability through a "correlate stream of public welfare doctrine for strict-liability offences".[166] Public welfare offenses (or also "regulatory offenses") are defined as "minor crimes that carry modest fines, although short incarceration terms may be authorized. They are understood as "regulatory" in nature – *malum prohibitum* rather than *malum in se* – and commonly address threats to "public health, public safety, public morals or public order". They lack fulfillment of *mens rea* requirements for almost all elements, even those who define wrongfulness.[167] Osmani argues that adopting this theory would serve two purposes. Firstly, since this doctrine was created to address the new societal threats brought about by the industrial revolution, it could be applied to the threats that are brought about by the digital revolution and could "pave the way for charging corporations with criminal offences for the harmful acts of AI".[168] Secondly, as the doctrine omits blameworthiness as a requirement for the offense, it would resolve one of the core issues of imputing criminal liability for AI misbehavior.

3.3.4 Simmler and Markwalder

According to Monika Simmler and Nora Markwalder, "robotics could prove an 'exceptional occasion for changes to the law and legal theory".[169] Consequently, criminal law scholars should not wait and not address technological developments as it could result in yet another late reaction. Like other scholars analyzed in this chapter, Simmler and Markwalder focus on the liability of *robots*, which they define as "machines (mostly with senso-ry-motor functions), which are built to enhance human possibilities for action".[170]

The focus of their inquiry is on a scenario in which "a robot 'commits' a crime, because it has developed its own momentum due to its artificial intelligence"[171] and the momentum, which is "predetermined and depends on the programming [...] cannot be traced

163 Osmani, 2020, p. 67.
164 Ivi, p. 69.
165 Osmani, 2020, p. 69.
166 Ivi, p. 73.
167 D. K. Brown, *Public Welfare Offenses*, in Dubber & Hörnle (eds.), 2014, p. 864.
168 Osmani, 2020, p. 73.
169 M. Simmler & N. Markwalder, "Guilty Robots? – Rethinking the Nature of Culpability and Legal Personhood in an Age of Artificial Intelligence", *Criminal Law Forum*, No. 30, 2019, p. 4.
170 Ivi, p. 5.
171 Simmler & Markwalder, 2019, p. 8.

back to a single programming operation".[172] Such a scenario recalls discussions on the existence of free will, i.e., situations "in which we can assume that every action has been caused and determined by something somewhere, but in which we attribute this action to a person as 'their own' and as an 'act of (free) will', because we cannot trace and explain the exact process of causation".[173] The fact that this article is written by criminal legal scholars and focuses extensively on discussing the potential criminal liability of robots, and not on humans, makes this article noteworthy.

Taking a closer look at the arguments made in the article, its primary concern is the "fatal question of criminal law", i.e., culpability.[174] The authors contend that there are two main problems with attributing of criminal liability to robots: first, "(the assumption of) human free will as the foundation of the traditional theory of criminal responsibility";[175] second "the question whether intelligent robots could be recognized as a subject of criminal law and therefore concerns the very basic concept of legal personhood".[176]

With regard to the first issue, the authors contend that robots could never fulfill the traditional definition of the fault principle, regardless of the advancement in their technology, since a robot is not a "person with free will" (meant as the capacity of human beings of being autonomous persons who have the ability to choose between alternative actions, i.e., to consciously decide not to act in accordance with the expectations placed upon them).[177] Taking into account the relevance of the impact of neuroscience on the issue of free will, the authors argue that "it does not make sense to succumb to the vortex that is the debate around the ability to choose one's action and to a scientific analysis of determinant variables",[178] since human free will is a byproduct of the social construction of reality. It follows that the biophysical nature of free will loses relevance for the purposes of criminal law, also when it comes to robots' liability.

If one discards the traditional notion of human free will, then, as the authors contend, one must look at it as an attribution "in the social system",[179] rather than as a set of "objectively and individually confirmable characteristics".[180] And if it is society that attributes freedom – and therefore attributes criminal liability – as a social fact, based on its perception, then it is only "a question of time until humans experience this autonomy not just as determined and programmed and until they attribute robots the respective 'capacities".[181]

172 Ibid.
173 Simmler & Markwalder, 2019, p. 9.
174 E. Hafter, Lehrbuch des Schweizerischen Strafrechts, Allgemeiner Teil, 2nd ed, Springer, 1946, p. 101.
175 Simmler & Markwalder, 2019, p. 10.
176 Ibid.
177 Simmler & Markwalder, 2019, p. 11.
178 Ivi, p. 12.
179 Simmler & Markwalder, 2019, p. 14.
180 Ibid.
181 Simmler & Markwalder, 2019, p. 15.

With regard to the second issue, the authors refer to Gless and Weigend and claim that they subscribe to a traditional understanding of the question of personhood in criminal law, which "neglects the fact that the concept of the subject or of personhood in criminal law is constructed in social reality and does not necessarily refer to biophysical categories". These authors, it is argued, "adopt a German perspective".[182] Indeed, as it will be explained at a later moment, Gless and Weigend contend that robots cannot qualify as addressees of criminal law since they cannot conceive themselves as morally responsive agents and because they cannot understand the concept of retributive punishment.[183]

Simmler and Markwalder claim that a more modern conception of person in criminal law revolves around the agent's capacity to "*disappoint normative expectations and on the possibility of attributing actions to this agent in the social system*".[184] As such, criminal capacity – which will be dealt with in detail in Chapter 5 – is an "artificial concept developed by and for the purpose of observers of the social system, which summarizes existing expectations".[185] As an artificial concept which is related to "a specific society in a specific time",[186] it is subject to change, i.e., it could be also applied to robots.

Corporate criminal liability is the proof of the fact that non-human entities can be subjects of criminal law. Indeed, society possesses certain expectations towards corporations since they are agents in the social system (i.e., they have an influence on everyday life and on social interaction), and as such, corporations are deemed capable of destabilizing norms and disappointing expectations.[187] According to the authors, robots are not there yet: even though it might be possible to deem robots "guilty" for a criminal offense, they cannot be treated as perpetrators, since criminal responsibility must be ultimately read through the lens of criminal punishment.

The authors rely heavily on Jakob's theories of criminal law, and claim that "[t]o deem someone 'guilty' means nothing else than that we impute a fault, the disappointment of a normative expectation, to a person".[188] It is society's way to "externalize the conflict, resolve it, and stabilize the norm put into question and thus secure the survival of said norm".[189] As a consequence, whether or not robots are criminally liable depends exclusively on whether or not society wants to attribute them the role of "rule-breakers" and on whether criminal punishment would resolve the conflict which results from the rule-breaking. Criminal punishment fulfills its aims only if it is directed at subjects which have received

182 Ivi, p. 18.
183 Gless & Weigend, 2014, p. 570; Gless, Silverman & Weigend, 2016, p. 412.
184 Simmler & Markwalder, 2019, p. 17.
185 Ibid.
186 Simmler & Markwalder, 2019, p.17.
187 Ivi, p. 19.
188 Simmler & Markwalder, 2019, p. 25.
189 Ibid.

such an attribution from society. And, since it is a *sociological fact* that robots have not (yet) acquired such personhood, their criminal punishment must be excluded.

Lastly, the authors briefly reflect on how robots could in practice be punished in the future: they assume that a fine could be imposed, if future robots are able to earn and lose money, and that robots could be reprogrammed or a non-specified form of "evil" could be imposed which would have consequences for the self-learning system.[190] Their final claim is that:

> [...] criminal responsibility of robots is possible if it is in accordance with the system, ie with the function of criminal law, if it is useful and necessary in the context of the stabilization of norms. This is the case only if robots have the necessary requirements of personhood and if they are thus attributed the capacities that are inherent in that concept. [...] A possible attribution of criminal responsibility to robots is thus a process subject to the function of the system. If these requirements are met, robots can therefore be subject to criminal responsibility.[191]

They then identify three main alternative rules:

> (1) to insist on the traditional approach to criminal responsibility, which rests on freedom of choice, on the ideal of the autonomous human and on the exclusive application of the concept of personhood to humans and to defend this idealistic concept against all attack and even in the face of increasing instability. This route would lead to abandoning the possibility of attributing criminal liability to robots altogether and would lead to concentrating on the programmer or operator of the robot for questions of criminal responsibility;
> (2) to adopt a functionalistic approach to criminal responsibility, in the sense that the
> concept of criminal responsibility expresses a reproach for a socially visible lack of compliance, which has the potential to destabilize norms. Such an approach is not based on recognizable human free will or freedom of choice, rather on the purposes of criminal law. It follows that a robot would be deemed liable if it would actually
> be experienced as an "equal" in the sense it would be constituted as addressees of normative expectations in social interaction like humans or corporate entities are today. They qualify this route as the most realistic route for the future;

190 Simmler & Markwalder, 2019, p. 28.
191 Ivi, p. 29.

(3) to take advantage of opportunity of the discussions on the concept of criminal law that are caused by technological advances to overcome and to rethink the traditional approach to the concept of criminal responsibility. They qualify this option as the most difficult, yet most promising, route to pursue.[192]

To conclude, Simmler and Markwalder represent a very interesting case study for this research. First of all, different from most of the moderates, they are criminal legal scholars and not legal philosophers. Second, and most importantly, we could qualify them as "border line" moderates, since they make a very strong case for holding robots liable, only to then exclude it for the time being.

3.3.5 *Mihail Diamantis: the Corporate Mind and Body Approach*

Diamantis, too, suggests a theory for AI liability deeply grounded in corporate liability. Yet, he adopts an innovative perspective compared to Osmani and Freitas et al.: he claims that corporations could act not only through their employees but also through their algorithms. In a nutshell, this entails that algorithmic action should be considered as corporate action and that therefore algorithms could become an "extension of the corporate person".[193] This, he believes, is the "path of least resistance" for addressing algorithmic injury.

The discussion conducted by Diamantis is extensive and requires familiarity with concepts of corporate criminal liability which stems from US law but aspires to have an application beyond those borders. For these reasons, Diamantis' theory will be analyzed in Sec. 6.4, which is dedicated to the intersections between AI liability and corporate criminal liability.

3.4 Skeptics

The skeptics front of the academic debate on AI and criminal liability is composed of those who dismiss the idea of punishing AI from the start as a conceptual confusion: AI systems cannot possess a guilty mind, and they cannot perform a guilty act. In other words, they reject the idea of directly punishing AI systems based on classical criminal law principles.[194] Authors who advocate for minor changes in the traditional categories of criminal law are also placed in this category.

---

192 Simmler & Markwalder, 2019, pp. 29-30.

193 M. Diamantis, "Algorithms acting badly: A Solution from Corporate Law", *GEO. Wash. L. Rev.*, Vol. 89, 2021, p. 809.

194 Abbott, 2020, p. 112.; Abbott & Sarch, 2019, p. 327.

3.4.1 The Italian Approach

The issue of criminal liability for AI misbehavior has been gaining more and more momentum in the past few years amongst Italian criminal legal scholars. At times, it seemed as if everyone was jumping on the AI bandwagon. Nonetheless, this did not entail that the contributions to the debate were not of value. Most of the articles that were published are in Italian, while quoting authors who wrote in German and in English. This entails that while Italian-speaking scholars took advantage of the ongoing international debate, they did not actively contribute to it. This pinpoints one of the strengths of this research: cross-breeding of legal doctrine.

Different authors were included in the same section under the label "The Italian Approach" for various reasons. To begin with, almost all of the authors analyzed deny categorically the possibility of imposing criminal liability on AI systems.[195] This might be explained by the fact that the Italian criminal system is deeply rooted in the concept of culpability as personal punishment, following the brocard: *nullum crimen sine culpa*. Further, many authors reason in terms of "risk society" and of *"diritto penale del rischio"*.[196] Moreover, different from other sides of the debate represented in this chapter, the Italian front is characterized by overarching analyses. In other words, Italian scholars seem to prefer cherry-picking the most trivial issues regarding the impact of AI on criminal law, rather than to develop general theories. This entails that the best approach for the literature review of this side of the debate is to combine the different voices.

One of the most relevant analyses in the Italian arena is the one conducted by Alberto Cappellini. Cappellini starts his reflection by reformulating an ancient brocard:[197] *machina*

195 E. Lo Monte, "Intelligenza artificiale e diritto penale: le categorie dommatiche alla prova del futuribile", in F. Basile, M. Caterini & S. Romano (eds.), *Il sistema penale ai confini delle hard sciences*, Pacini Giuridica, 2020; F. Basile, "Intelligenza artificiale e diritto penale: qualche aggiornamento e qualche nuova riflessione", in Basile, Caterini & Romano (eds), 2020; G. Rizzo Minelli, "Quando l'autore del reato è un robot: tra vecchi modelli imputativi e nuovi possibili paradigmi di responsabilità" in Basile, Caterini & Romano (eds), 2020; S. Riondato, "Robot: talune implicazioni di diritto penale" in P. Moro & C. Sarra (eds.), *Tecnodiritto. Temi e informatica e robotica giuridica*, Franco Angeli, 2017; V.C. Talamo, "Sistemi di intelligenza artificiale: quali scenari in sede di accertamento della responsabilità penale?", *Il Penalista*, 2020; R. Borsari, "Intelligenza Artificiale e responsabilità penale: prime considerazioni", *MediaLaws*, Vol. 3, 2019. Cecilia Cavaceppi argues that state-of-the-art AI should fall under the current framework for (administrative) corporate liability provided in Italy by Decree Law 231/2001 whenever it is the product of a programming firm offering its services to third parties. C. Cavaceppi, "L'intelligenza artificiale applicata al diritto penale", in G.Taddei Elmi & A. Contaldo, *Intelligenza artificiale-Algoritmi giuridici: Ius condendum o fantadiritto?*, Pacini Giuridica, 2020. In this scenario, Lagioia, Sartor and Pagallo represent a *unicum*, probably because they have a background in legal philosophy, rather than in criminal law.

196 For example Piergallini, Panattoni, and Salvadori.

197 The original brocard relates to the liability of corporations and reads *societas delinquere non potest*. Admittedly, Franz von Liszt coined the phrase in 1881.

delinquere (et puniri) non potest.[198] Indeed, Italy adopted an administrative (quasi-criminal) liability for corporations pursuant to legislative decree 231 of 2001. According to leg. decree 231/2001, if a criminal court ascertains that a 'qualified' subject (i.e., a CEO or a high-ranking manager) committed one of the offenses listed in leg. decree 231/2001, the same criminal court can then sanction the corporation in whose interest, or for whose benefit, the crime or crimes were committed. The Italian model will be further explained in Ch. 4.b.4.1.

Capellini then asks whether this axiom still applies, considering the most recent evolutions in AI technology. As we know, some, such as Hallevy,[199] reply affirmatively. Cappellini qualifies Hallevy's reconstructions as "unacceptable to date to the point of appearing provocative, to say the least, in the eyes of many criminal scholars of continental education".[200] The author then puts forward a number of criticisms of Hallevy's theory. The following paragraphs mention two of them.

The first criticism is that Hallevy did not prove that AI systems are capable of culpable conduct. Cappellini holds that what Hallevy proved is just an appearance of intent, a mere "sleight of hand". According to Cappellini, then, it might be true that AI systems act with a certain level of discretion, which allows them to adapt their behavior to the external reality in the pursuit of their aim. Yet, this is not enough for criminal law: the choices taken by the AI systems are not the result of a capacity of self-determination. These systems are not capable of willfully choosing to perform an illegal act. For these reasons, they cannot be reproached: hence, they cannot be criminally liable.

The second criticism is that the analogy with corporate liability is fallacious. Cappellini argues that corporations, unlike AI systems, always lack a physical *persona* in the real world. They only exist in the juridical and social world, where instead (some) AI systems, such as robots, not only exist in the physical world, but they are also capable of detaching from their creators. The same cannot be said about corporations, which always play as puppets in the hands of human puppeteers. For these reasons, says Cappellini, imposing criminal liability on corporations has a direct effect on the "wallets" of the human puppeteers, where instead directly punishing the AI system would have no effect on the human being behind the curtains who has lost control of the machine. Even if it did, it would prove useless, because she would not be able to influence the behavior of the (uncontrollable) AI system.

Fabio Basile poses several open questions, starting from Cappellini's *machina delinquere non potest.*[201] If criminal responsibility is personal, meaning as relating to a *persona*,

198 A. Cappellini, "Machina delinquere potest? Brevi appunti su intelligenza artificiale e responsabilità penale", *Criminalia*, 2018.
199 For an analysis of Gabriel Hallevy's work, see Sec. 3.2.1. of this Chapter.
200 Cappellini, 2018, p. 11.
201 Basile in Basile, Caterini & Romano (eds.), 2020, p. 34.

can we then really assimilate men and machines? Is there not something "more" about being human? The questions remain unanswered, yet the author's concern is palpable. Others claim that the logical step required to negate the competence of criminal law to regulate AI systems lies in the fact that even the most advanced systems are nothing but machines which elaborate data through mathematical operations, based on given instructions.[202] Reasoning on the purposes of punishing AI systems is, henceforth, regarded as preposterous.[203]

According to Manes, the most suggestive scenarios which deserve discussion are two. First, situations where the criminal conduct is the autonomous result of a software, which can be assisted by the inert and only eventual human presence. Second, situations where the criminal conduct is the result of shared action between humans and AI systems. Thus, he asks himself to whom should responsibility for the causation of an event be ascribed in these situations. To the person who has generated the source of risk by designing the software (especially in cases of self-learning algorithms)? To the person who has actualized that risk by manufacturing and putting the system in the market? Or to the person who has concretely managed that risk by using it, or perhaps by cooperating with it (in cases where it would be possible to ascertain a sort of *culpa in interagendo*)?[204]

Magro investigates whether we can consider AI systems as possessing artificial free will or if their autonomous behavior is just a deviation from the original project caused by accidental factors.[205] It does not really matter, she claims, to define which level of freedom AI systems can display. Criminal liability is not bound to the adoption of a univocal definition of freedom for all agents. What matters is to understand whether we can consider AI systems *responsible* and this relies on which conception of responsibility we adopt.

Consistent with the rest of the Italian front, Magro makes a strong case against holding AI systems directly liable and she also rejects the analogy with corporate criminal liability. Casting aside the option of considering AI systems as (criminal) agents, and focusing on the human agents (the "frontman"),[206] in her earlier work she proposes the creation of a new legal concept, "*colpa da programmazione*"[207] or "fault or negligence by programming".[208] As it will be demonstrated, this concept recurs in Italian legal doctrine and is

202 Lo Monte, 2020, pp. 66-67; Riondato, 2017, p. 92.

203 Basile in Basile, Caterini & Romano (Eds.), 2020, p. 76.

204 V. Manes, "L'oracolo algoritmico e la giustizia penale: al bivio tra tecnologia e tecnocrazia", *Discrimen*, 2020, p. 3.

205 M. B. Magro, "Biorobotica, robotica e diritto penale", in D. Provolo, S. Riondato & F. Yenisey (eds.), *Genetics, Robotics, Law, Punishment*, 2014, p. 516.

206 Ivi, p. 8.

207 M. B. Magro, "Decisione umana e decisione robotica. Un'ipotesi di responsabilità da procreazione robotica", *La legislazione penale*, 2020, p. 8.

208 M. B. Magro, "Biorobotics, robotics and criminal law: some hints and reflections", *Percorsi costituzionali*, Fasc. 1-2, 2016, p. 9.

often discussed in relation to duty of care obligations.[209] It has not been cleared, yet, whether this type of negligence would be an example of what Italian criminal legal doctrine refers to as '*colpa generica*' (referred to also as "unconscious negligence"),[210] i.e., negligence based on the violation of general (unwritten) standards of care; or – more likely – whether it would be guilt based on written (technical) standards (*colpa specifica*).

Then, she argues, we should create a new circumstance which excludes liability whenever programmers put certain measures in place (which would mean, in practical terms, to make sure that robots abide by Asimov's laws).

Generally speaking, imputing liability for AI systems misbehavior in these situations would require an operation which is opposite to the one of imputing liability for corporate misbehavior. When it comes to corporations, the action of a human agent makes a non-human agent liable. When it comes to AI systems, the action of a non-human agent makes the human agent liable.[211]

In her later work, she also claims that programmers or designers of the software would not be able to escape liability for negligence by claiming that the harmful conduct of the AI system was not predictable due to its autonomy.[212] Actually, according to the latest evolution of negligence in Italian case law, negligence requires only the abstract foreseeability of a general risk, rather than the foreseeability of a concrete and specific harmful event. It implies holding a subject liable for not avoiding worst case scenarios or catastrophes, i.e., events that cannot be predicted or avoided by the subject, such as earthquakes. This type of negligence is also referred to as "*colpa eventuale*".[213] It is self-evident, then, that it would be impossible for the programmer to deny that she was not aware of having created an independent and self-learning machine.

Panattoni contends that the causation of harmful events by AI systems is another instance of our risk-based society, which mandates anticipation of the protection provided by criminal law according to the level of danger of the action. This is reflected also in the EU's approach to regulating AI, which is, indeed, risk-based.[214]

Salvadori[215] argues that any attempt to impose criminal liability on AI systems is destined to wreck itself against the cliff of Article 27 of the Italian Constitution,[216] which

209 Manes, 2020, p. 4.

210 Keiler & Roef (eds.), 2019, p. 198.

211 Magro, 2014, p. 514.

212 Ivi, p. 516.

213 G. Civello, La "colpa eventuale" nella società del rischio. Epistemologia dell'incertezza e "verità soggettiva" della colpa, Giappichelli, 2013.

214 B. Panattoni, "Intelligenza artificiale: le sfide per il diritto penale nel passaggio dall'automazione tecnologica all'autonomia artificiale", *Dir. Inf.*, Vol. 2, 2021, pp. 331-33.

215 I. Salvadori, "Agenti artificiali, opacità tecnologica e distribuzione della responsabilità penale", *Rivista Italiana di Diritto e Procedura Penale*, No. 1, 2021.

216 Ivi, p. 98.

establishes that criminal liability is personal. This principle entails that the offense must be reconducted to the offender through a psychological nexus and that the offender must be blameworthy. It would not be feasible to do the same with AI systems. The issue, then, becomes one of distributing liability amongst human and artificial agents.

Interestingly, Salvadori claims that the scenario involving a human operator who decides to create a software for malicious purposes does not fall into the perpetrator-by-another model. Indeed, different from cases of indirect perpetration, in the former case the agent would be liable for an act that she put in place, as she used a tool to commit a crime, where instead in cases of indirect perpetration the main perpetrator is liable for the conduct of another perpetrator.[217] With regard to the realm of *colpa*, Salvadori, as Magro before him, asserts that a defect in the functioning of the software could be pinned on the developer and/or the programmer based on a *colpa di programmazione*, which means not having predicted the possibility of grave incidents. Indeed, these subjects have a duty to monitor how the software works and to update it whenever necessary.

In conclusion, he believes that the solution which will be adopted with regard to criminally regulating AI systems is that of creating a sphere of admissible risk (*Erlaubnis Risiko*), i.e., a level of risk that is tolerated by society and that is based on specific codified duties imposed on the humans involved in the AI production chain. Moreover, he argues in favor of establishing a set of administrative sanctions in case the AI product does not satisfy certain technical precautional measures established *ex ante*. Lastly, he suggests creating legal duties to encode principles in the algorithm starting from the programming phase.[218]

Piergallini notices how uncomfortable criminal law is when confronted with AI systems, almost as if it were an old tool.[219] Due to AI, the way we ascribe liability is undergoing a crisis and we are forced to ask ourselves the level of risk ("*margine di sicurezza*") that our society is willing to tolerate. This, he argues, is strictly a political choice that precedes the one of ascribing liability, since it regards how to regulate those risks preemptively. Should the "creator" of the machine be blamed because she "predicted the unpredictability" of her creation?

His article is divided in two parts. The first deals with situations in which there is a human who is somehow "in control". Here the author provides a thorough analysis of these issues from the perspective of product (criminal) liability which focuses on two case studies: AVs and robotic surgery. The following paragraphs will focus on the first.

---

217 Salvadori, 2021, p. 101.

218 Ivi, p. 116.

219 C. Piergallini, "Intelligenza artificiale: da 'mezzo' ad 'autore' del reato?", *Rivista italiana di diritto e procedura penale*, Vol. 4, 2020, p. 1746.

Piergallini outlines levels 1, 2 and 3 of driving automation[220] and argues that, with regard to the subjective element, the liability constructs that we know of seem to hold. In other words, the liability for an accident caused by these types of cars will always fall on the driver, who has a special duty of care. What happens, though, when the accident is caused by a defect in the production of the car? This case, he argues, triggers the applicability of product liability. The defect could be the result of a faulty design, a faulty development, or a faulty construction of the car. Criminal law, then, faces the impossible mission of identifying beyond a reasonable doubt the liable human agent in a huge production chain conducted by complex organizations, *mega-apparati*, which often also work together. In conclusion, Piergallini argues that in these cases the central role should be the role of tort law, not criminal law, to avoid incurring a hypothesis of strict liability.

The second part of the article deals with cases where there is no human in control of narrow AI systems, as these act in a fully unpredictable manner. With regard to causality, he discusses whether AI behavior could constitute a factor which breaks the causal chain and, as a consequence, excludes the liability of the programmer. He answers in the negative, since the maker of the algorithm knows that she is creating a new risk, as she is creating a machine in the knowledge that she won't be able to control it. The true breaking point, Piergallini believes, is *mens rea*, specifically negligence. Returning to the question asked above, Piergallini argues that one cannot blame a programmer on the grounds of negligence because she *predicted* the *unpredictability* of the system. Predictability of risk, he claims, is the DNA of negligence. Piergallini, then, focuses on a critique of Hallevy's argument. Piergallini negates that an AI can be directly criminally liable. He labels Hallevy's strictly material conception of conduct as "rough".[221] Likewise, he strongly refutes that one can consider AI systems as capable of culpable conduct: there is no space for strict liability in our criminal legal system, he asserts. The Italian front stands united.

What should be criminal law's role, then, if any? According to Piergallini, criminal law could work as a "cooperative compliance" tool, in a perspective of co-regulation between

220 The levels have been defined by the SAE (Society of Automative Engineers) International in the J3016 standards. They are: Level 0: No Driving Automation; Level 1: Driver Assistance; Level 2: Partial Driving Automation; Level 3: Conditional Driving Automation; Level 4: High Driving Automation; Level 5: Full Driving Automation. With the first 3 levels of automation, the driver is driving, even if her feet are off the pedals and she is not steering. The driver is also constantly supervising the driver support features and must steer, break or accelerate to maintain safety. With Levels 3, 4 and 5 automation the driver is not driving, even if she is seated in the driver's seat. Level 3 implies that when the feature requests it, the driver must drive. That is, she can only control the car in situations of emergencies. Level 4 and Level 5 do not require that the driver takes over driving. The difference between Level 4 and Level 5 is that with Level 4 automation (equally to Level 3) the automatic features can only drive the vehicle under limited conditions and will not operate if these conditions are not met (i.e., if there are extraordinary circumstances the car will stop in order for the driver to take control) where instead with Level 5 automation the vehicle can be driven under all conditions. SAE, 2021.

221 "*ruvida*", Piergallini, 2020, p. 1765.

hard law and soft law. On the one hand, it could impose a duty on corporations to share their know-how on how to evaluate and prevent AI risks. On the other, *post damnum*, authorities could impose the obligation – it is not specified on whom exactly – to reprogram or to deactivate the system. Non-compliance with these orders could lead to criminal sanctions. In conclusion, Piergallini believes that we should be wary of elevating criminal law as the primary answer to the numerous questions that are raised by AI.

3.4.2 Ugo Pagallo

Regardless of his background as an Italian legal scholar, Ugo Pagallo's view is analyzed separately from the other part of the Italian front. The reasons are threefold: first, Pagallo has a background in the philosophy of law and not in criminal law. Second, his work is more extensive than that of the single authors in the "Italian Approach" sub-category.[222] Third, he writes mainly in English.

Pagallo, in his 2013 monograph, takes a strong stance against attributing criminal liability to AI systems.[223]

Concerning the subjective element of a crime, he claims that there is no such thing as a "robotic *mens rea*"[224] since robots lack the necessary pre-requisites: self-consciousness, free will, and moral autonomy. He acknowledges that there are some authors[225] who argue in favor of a strong ontological stance, that is they believe that the advancement of AI technology will produce machines that will decide autonomously in a way that is similar to human-like decision-making. These same authors reject the objection that AI systems cannot be moral agents since they are just programmed machines. We, as humans, should not take comfort in the axiom that we are not programmed, while artificial agents unequivocally are.[226] Pagallo refutes these arguments: if we were to accept that a kind of human-like generation of AI system would come to life, we would also have to conceive a *mens rea* which would be "rooted in the artificial mind of a machine capable of a measure of empa-

222 He authored two books together with Woodrow Barfield: Research Handbook on the Law of Artificial Intelligence, Elsevier, 2019; and Advanced Introduction to Law and Artificial Intelligence, 2020. He is also the author of the book The Laws of Robots. Crimes, Contracts, and Torts (2013) and of a vast number of publications and chapters in edited books. Specifically, on the topic of AI accountability and criminal liability, he authored: "The Adventures of Picciotto Roboto", 2011; "Killers, Fridges, and Slaves", 2011; "AI and bad robots", 2017; and "From automation to autonomous systems: A legal phenomenology with problems of accountability", 2017.

223 Even though his reflections are based on robots, i.e., AI systems with a physical presence, we believe that they can be extended to the generality of AI systems.

224 Pagallo, 2013, p. 50.

225 Chopra & White, 2011, p. 77.

226 Ivi, p. 176.

thy, or a type of autonomy, affording intentional actions".[227] From this also follows that "lawyers should be ready to take seriously a whole set of new offences such as robot revolutions, rebellions, robberies and so forth".[228] These are matters for science fiction writers rather than for legal experts, Pagallo claims.

Concerning the objective element of a crime, in his earlier work of 2013, Pagallo labelled efforts to assert that AI systems could lead to a new set of *actus rei* as "Hollywood-style approaches".[229] His attitude changed in his later work, "The Research Handbook on Law and Artificial Intelligence", namely in the chapter titled "The impact of AI on criminal law, and its twofold procedures" written with Serena Quattrocolo. Here the authors introduce the example of Vital, a UK-made robot which was appointed as board member of a venture capital firm in Japan (Deep Knowledge) to predict successful investments.[230] Let us imagine now that a wrong evaluation of Vital leads to a lack of increase in capital and therefore to the fraudulent bankruptcy of the corporation. The authors contend that "humans could be held responsible only for the crime of bankruptcy triggered by the robot's evaluation, since the mental element requirement of fraud would be missing in the case of the human members of the board".[231] Therefore, the crime of fraudulent bankruptcy could be charged only against the corporation and eventually against the robot. This option would require, though, "that most legal systems should amend themselves, in order to prosecute either the AI system as the criminal agent of the corporation, or the corporation as such".[232] Another case presented as an example is the result of reversing the usual perspective on the "perpetration-by-another" liability model: what if humans were the innocent agents or tools of an AI's bad decision? As the authors rightly observe, this scenario could lead to a new type of *actus reus* which does not require any level of *mens rea*.

Moving to the criminal liability of the human being, Pagallo focuses on how AI systems might affect the *mens rea* of an individual. This research will only analyze the discussion of intent and negligence, as the other issues described by Pagallo (namely those of humans who commit a crime against the AI system) fall outside the scope of this research. In other words,

> [...] matters of design (actus reus) and human culpability (mens rea) concerning the criminal field of the laws of robots, are more urgent than the current

227 Pagallo, 2013, p.76.
228 Ibid.
229 The authors mention two examples: the "Robot Kleptomaniac" and Robbie CX30. Pagallo, 2013, p. 76.
230 U. Pagallo & S. Quattrocolo, "The impact of AI on criminal law, and its twofold procedures", in Barfield & Pagallo (eEds.), 2019, p. 385.
231 Ivi, p. 404.
232 Pagallo & Quattrocolo, 2019, p. 404.

> debate on new forms of (weak or even strong responsibility for) crimes committed by humans against their autonomous machines, in addition to the moral agenthood and legal personhood of robots.[233]

Pagallo first analyzes cases where the robot is designed to commit offenses, i.e., "Criminal Robots by Design". The authors identifies two scenarios:

> (1) the robot is used to carry out existing kinds of crimes through new robotic devices;
> (2) the robot is used to carry out novel offenses.

Focusing on option (2), Pagallo then identifies two sub-scenarios:

> (2)(a) An individual sends or activates the robot to commit a crime (crimes of intent);
> (2)(b) The reasonable individual fails to guard against foreseeable harms (crimes of negligence).

Scenario (2)(a) can be solved by adopting the perpetration-by-another liability model to identify the liable human being amongst three candidates: the programmer ("the evil designer"), the manufacturer ("faulty producer"), or the ("criminal") user.[234] This model, instead, proves useless for scenario (2)(b), i.e., "cases where criminal liability hinges on negligence or lack of due care, rather than the blameworthy mens rea of designers, producers or users of robots".[235]

In these circumstances, Hallevy's natural-probable-consequence model comes into play. As it was already stated,[236] this model covers both situations where the AI system was programmed to commit an offense and then deviates from the plan, and situations where humans had no intent to commit a crime but were negligent when designing, constructing, or using an AI system. Concerning the former, Pagallo correctly states, "[i]n most legal systems, programmers, manufacturers or users of such robots would be liable for the additional crime, regardless of the unpredictability of the machine's behaviour, as it occurs with the liability model in accomplice responsibility case".[237] Concerning the latter, Pagallo provides an interesting suggestion: "since robots are machines capable of learning and adapting to changes in the environment, they are unpredictable. So, they will give rise to a

233 Pagallo, 2013, pp. 54-55.
234 Ivi, p. 70.
235 Pagallo, 2013, p. 71.
236 See Sec. 3.2.1.
237 Pagallo, 2013, p. 72.

new set of legal issues centered around how humans treated the machine, rather than the ways in which the machine was designed and constructed".[238] Based on this, one could formulate the following observation: since AI systems also learn from the interactions they have with their surroundings, and since their surroundings also include input derived from humans, it might become relevant to evaluate how humans treated the machine and how that related to the commission of crime by it.

Pagallo ends his discussion by introducing the concept of failures of causation. His reflections on causality are distinctive in the academic legal discourse on the topic.

Without a doubt, he claims, "crucial criteria for selecting from the entire chain of events the specific condition, or the set of conditions, that best explains a given outcome, would be challenged by the unpredictable behaviour of these machines and the complexity of network-centric applications".[239] He identifies two main issues, taking as an example a hypothetical intelligent program handling air traffic control, which has the purpose of avoiding issues such as ground damage, air-to-air collisions, communication interferences, piracy, and environmental concerns, and which works in interaction with both manned and unmanned aerial vehicles. Firstly, he claims that "it seems problematic to aim at determining the types of harm that may supervene with the functioning of such a complex processing system".[240] Secondly, "the traditional idea of the reasonable person may fade away, since the duty of individuals to guard against foreseeable harms is challenged by the growing autonomy of robotic behavior and cases where no human would be accountable for the unforeseen results of the "machine intelligence's pathology".[241] Pagallo's proposed solution for failures of causation is a type of legal responsibility which "is not established *ex ante*, such as strict liability, nor excluded *a priori*, such as immunity clauses".[242] This model entails that the criminal liability of humans should be established by courts "on the basis of the probabilities concerning how robots work through their on-board decision-making controllers, automatic recovery functions, communication devices, etc.", that is, the focus should be on the "scientific meaning of the machine's behaviour".[243] In order to avoid the overload of information which could result from this operation, the author argues that it would be useful to look at how the same concepts of causation and reasonable foreseeability are regulated in the field of contracts.

To conclude, in their most recent handbooks, Pagallo and Barfield directly refer to Lagioia and Sartor and claim that they too accept as true that "AI can engage in moral and

238 Ibid.
239 Pagallo, 2013, p. 74.
240 Ibid.
241 Pagallo, 2013, p. 75.
242 Ibid.
243 Pagallo, 2013, p.77.

legal reasoning"[244], i.e., AI systems can be built with a normative architecture and can engage in knowledge representation and reasoning (that is, "the ability to represent norms and/or values, and reason with them")[245]. This assumption can lead to some form of "criminal responsibility"' which is, nevertheless, different from full legal personhood of AI systems on the one hand, and from Hallevy's "human-like" assumptions on AI awareness on the other.[246]

Lagioia and Sartor's theory is based on the claim that AI could respond to the threat of legal sentencing. However, Pagallo and Barfield identify two flaws in Lagioia and Sartor's account of criminal accountability of AI. First, a technological issue: "we are likely far away from AI technology with such requisites as consciousness and moral understanding",[247] which are required for AI systems to be the subject of criminal sanctions and to be deterred and rehabilitated by it. Second, a moral issue. Whether it is true that an AI system can be considered a source of good or evil and, as such, it could be considered as an accountable agent, it is not clear to the authors how the status of AI as an accountable agent in criminal law would complement the same status in moral theory or in contracts and corporate law. How would the expansion of accountability of AI to criminal law improve current regulations? The question remains unanswered.

Lastly, Pagallo and Barfield agree with the fact that AI could have some form of criminal responsibility in the sense that AI systems could be targets of criminal law norms due to their capacity of possessing, on the one hand, a normative architecture and, on the other hand, reason-responsiveness. Yet, they draw a neat distinction with Hallevy's standpoint: AI systems do not possess human-like awareness and they should not be considered as right bearers. Similar to Diamantis' position, their suggestion is to deal with issues of "liability and distributed responsibility in complex AI ecosystems" through the teachings provided by forms of accountability for AI in business and corporate law: "[t]he criminal liability of AI, to be effective, lies first in its assets, after all".[248] In other words, "we should follow the money first".[249]

3.4.3 *Dafni Lima*

Lima's paper,[250] while not as extensive as other works examined in this chapter, deserves attention. Indeed, Lima puts forward a set of questions contesting that an AI system could

244 Barfield & Pagallo, 2020, p. 140.
245 Lagioia & Sartor, 2020, p. 1.
246 Barfield & Pagallo, 2020, p. 140.
247 Ivi, p. 141.
248 Barfield & Pagallo, 2020, p. 142.
249 Ivi, p. 142.
250 Lima, 2018.

fulfill the *actus reus* requirement of a criminal offense.[251] While quoting US[252] and German[253] constructs of criminal liability, Lima notes that "it seems that concepts like bodily movement (or failure thereof) that are voluntary, extroversive, and socially meaningful in a way that is relevant to criminal law are essential aspects of acting".[254]

According to Lima, in a stance similar to that of Gless, Silverman, and Weigend,[255] AI acts could hardly be categorized as instances of *actus reus*, since they do not have social relevance and are not voluntary. With regard to the latter, she contends:

> Voluntariness in this sense implies the ability to act otherwise, and an agent that is programmed to choose A when it encounters B is not necessarily choosing. Thus AI agents do not yet seem to possess the potential for fully independent, even self-destructive decisions. In other words, no one would regard a robot's choice to change its route when stumbling upon a table as voluntary, so long as the robot is simply following an algorithm, however intricate, that dictates it to change route when encountering a physical obstacle or, to put it more simply, so long as the robot does not have the choice to keep hitting at the obstacle if it so wishes. This holds true even when this choice is the only reasonable one and in the AI agent's "benefit" of achieving its objective.[256]

The reference in the passage above to "changing routes" and to the concept of "benefit" bring up familiar concepts. As a matter of fact, both Pagallo and Lagioia & Sartor refer to these concepts when they reconstruct intent according to the BDI model.[257]

Next, Lima moves on to analyze the questions of blameworthiness and punishment. With regard to the first, she starts the discussion by noting how *mens rea* and blameworthiness were first theorized as safeguards against state power. They restrain punishment only to those who choose to inflict harm "conscientiously", since they had the freedom to

251 These questions include: should the rise in more and more complex AI agents invite us to reconsider the mere notion of act as the bedrock of contemporary criminal law theory? Will we perhaps need to replace or expand or enrich the arguably obsolete notion of "voluntary bodily movement" against this new landscape? Ivi, p. 681.

252 The Model Penal Code (MPC) at § 2.01 defines criminal liability as follows "A person is not guilty of an offense unless his liability is based on conduct which includes a voluntary act or the omission to perform an act of which he is physically capable". In the "General Definitions", an act is defined as a bodily movement and Lima claims, "(whether voluntary or not), [...] the act requirement is widely regarded as the most notable, or perhaps the only, exception to the rule that substantive criminal law in the United States is not regulated under constitutional law". Lima, 2018, p. 679.

253 "[T]he prevailing opinion among criminal law scholars is that an act has to be controllable by the actor and 'socially relevant' – in other words, it needs to convey social meaning". Ivi, p. 680.

254 Lima, 2018, p. 680.

255 Gless, Silverman & Weigend, 2016, p. 417 analyzed above at Sec. 3.4.5.1.

256 Lima, 2018, p. 683.

257 See Sec. 3.3.2. and Sec. 3.4.2.

act against the law. Actually, "criminal liability is a response reserved for those who could have risen to the occasion but chose not to".[258] She acknowledges, indeed, that this might be a shortcut to bypass discussions on "how human intent is formulated as well as any doubts about whether our free will is indeed free and our own after all".[259] Yet, this operation is not new for criminal law and the law in general. The heart of modern criminal law, according to Lima, lies in the humanity of the perpetrator, or in the "human experience". And that humanity is not possessed by AI agents, where instead it might be possessed by corporations by proxy. In other words, according to Lima, the assertion that corporations are made of humans, while AI systems are not, is unsurmountable. Moreover, not only are corporations deeply intertwined with their human agents, but they are also a fiction created by them. AI systems, instead, might be said to live beyond this fictive veil, as they can, more and more, act without the involvement of humans.

With regard to punishment, Lima claims that it is a "collective means of responding to crime directed at an agent that can understand its significance as well as its relevance to their criminal conduct",[260] and since AI systems cannot do so, the debate on applying criminal sanctions is "misplaced".[261]

Lastly, Lima discusses potential models for ascribing criminal liability in the case of an AI "action" or "omission". After dealing with instrumental (mis)uses of AI systems, she focuses on negligence and recklessness. The first, she contends, represents the model that can be used most appropriately in cases where a benevolent designer or operator neglected to "take due care in order to prevent an undesirable outcome that could occur within the usual performance of the AI agent and which the programmer or the user should have foreseen".[262] The second represents the model to use – according to different jurisdictions – in cases where "the human agent actually foresaw the outcome and decided to disregard it".[263]

Then, the author analyzes the notion of *respondeat superiror*. This concept is derived from tort law and implies the responsibility of a person who is in control of another. She argues that the analogy between the relationship master-agent and human-AI works only at a first glance when applied to criminal law. Indeed, it is true that also in cases of *respondeat superior* the *inferior* is an independent and intelligent being. Yet, criminal law demands a higher threshold for imposing liability on the "controller" and this reasoning should be extended to all the models for ascribing criminal liability:

258 Lima, 2018, p. 687.
259 Ibid.
260 Lima, 2018, p. 689.
261 Ibid.
262 Lima, 2018, p. 691.
263 Ivi, p. 692.

> […] any potential model of ascribing liability for the human agent who is somehow involved in a crime committed by an AI agent will have to vary not only depending on circumstances, such as the sophistication of the intelligence of the AI agent or the degree of control of the human agent, but also on the type of crime committed. In other words, the threshold should be higher for serious crimes, such as killing, and could be lower for relatively minor ones, such as the destruction of an inexpensive item that belongs to a third party.[264]

She then affirms that strict liability might be best considered in combination with requirements of negligence, similar to what is done in the field of product liability.

In conclusion, she claims that even if humans did everything right, AI malfunction might still happen. In these cases, much as is done in the case of a bridge collapsing, we should learn how to live with it. This, she claims, is in line with Gless et al.'s argument of considering AI systems as "exceptional risk".[265] As is remarkably stated in the conclusions:

> Not everything can be foreseen, prevented, or contained, and in everyday life there are several instances where no one is to blame – much more be held criminally liable – for an undesirable outcome. In other words, *not everything can or should be regulated under criminal law.*[266]

Undeniably, Lima believes that criminal law is not the answer (or the "appropriate vessel") to ensure AI accountability, especially as there are "softer" State powers which might take this role, such as administrative sanctions.

The punch line of Lima's article is dedicated to a critique of the work of Hallevy. She claims that his theory is based on a circular argument, since it takes for granted that a concept such as *mens rea*, which was designed with humans in mind, could be fulfilled by AI systems that are not – today – human-like at all. If the opposite were true, i.e., if the *mens rea* requirement could be fulfilled by non-humans, this would also "presuppose the perception of historically and empirically informed concepts such as choice, voluntariness, knowledge, and intent as simply technical terms without any inextricable grounding in the human experience".[267] We, indeed, have not reached that point (yet).

264 Lima, 2018, p. 693.
265 Gless, Silverman & Weigend, 2016, p. 19.
266 Lima, 2018, p. 694 [emphasis added].
267 Ivi, p. 696.

3.4.4 *Peter Asaro: A Body to Kick, but Still No Soul to Damn*

Peter Asaro's catchphrase "A Body to Kick, but Still No Soul to Damn"[268] had quite the success amongst the scholars who have participated in the debate about this analysis.[269] Asaro, as a philosopher, acknowledges from the start that while "there are instances where what is legal is not necessarily morally esteemed, and what is morally required may not be legal, there is a significant overlap between what is legal and what is moral".[270] He contends that punishment is traditionally conceived as "corrective in one or more senses": through retribution one pays one's debt to society; through reform one is to be reeducated so not to repeat the offense; through deterrence other people in society are deterred from committing a similar offense.

Moreover, he believes that applying criminal law to robots brings about two fundamental issues: one, criminal actions require moral agency; two, it is unclear whether a robot can be punished. The two issues, then, are deeply intertwined: only moral agents, as part of our society, can create a debt and eventually pay it, or else what we are facing is just an accident or an act of nature. Moreover, reform entails developing or correcting moral character – or else it is just a matter of fixing a problem – and this can be done only to moral agents. What is more, only moral agents are capable of being deterred, because they are the only ones that can recognize how their actions are similar to those of other moral agents who have been punished for wrongdoing and, as a result, be deterred by it. In other words, only moral agents are capable of "reflexivity of choice" and "recognition of similarity between and among moral agents".[271]

Afterwards, the author moves on to analyze the similarities and differences between imposing criminal punishment on corporations and on robots. The most obvious difference, he asserts, is that "robots do have bodies to kick, though it is not clear that kicking them would achieve the traditional goals of punishment".[272] First of all, corporations are created to make money, hence monetary sanctions would be effective because they would target a corporation's essential purpose. The same cannot be said about robots, as their purposes are not as straightforward. Second, with regard to corporal punishments, robots "do have bodies to kick, though it is not clear that kicking them would achieve the tradi-

268 Asaro, 2012, pp. 169-186.

269 The work of Asaro is expressly referred to by Mulligan at p. 15, where she claims that robot punishment advances a different goal of punishment than retribution, reform or deterrence; by Abbott and Sarch, see Sec. 3.3.1, at p. 345, when they refer to the consequentialist benefits which would derive from punishing AI and claim that Asaro did not make a distinction between general and special deterrence. He is quoted by Gless, Silverman & Weigend, 2016, p. 12, n. 12; by Cappellini, 2018, p. 13; by F. Basile, "Intelligenza artificiale e diritto penale: quattro possibili percorsi di indagine", *DPU*, 2019, pp. 27-28; Lagioia & Sartor, 2020, p. 22.

270 Asaro, 2012, p. 169.

271 Ivi, p. 181.

272 Asaro, 2012, p. 182.

tional goals of punishment". Asaro claims that physical punishment requires something more than a body, such as desires and fears, and this is something that is not possessed by robots.

To conclude, even though it might be feasible from a technological perspective to punish a robot, this would not achieve retribution, reform or deterrence. As a matter of fact, Asaro believes that this is a "a greater hurdle to ascribing moral agency to robots directly than other hurdles, such as whether it is possible to effectively program moral decision making".[273]

3.4.5 *The German Approach*

The debate in German criminal legal doctrine differs from the Italian and the English-speaking fronts for two reasons. First, researchers published their work both in German and in English. Second, German-speaking authors make little or no mention whatsoever in their papers to authors who are not of German provenance or who have not written in German. The reasons could be different and certainly have deeper roots.[274] One could ask oneself whether this represents an instance of the traditional approach of German legal doctrine to comparative criminal law, which has been labelled by some as "self-referential"[275] and, in the words of George Fletcher, as "*selbstbewusste Provinzialität*".[276] According to some, it is (also) a matter of language, specifically of the difficulty to translate foreign legal concepts into German criminal law dogmatics.[277] Others contend that German criminal law is nothing but "provincial", even though it must be conceded

273 Asaro, 2012, pp. 182-183.

274 For instance, traces of such an attitude could be found in the scholarly use of foreign law in the debate on the position of national constitutional courts in the EU. On the matter see N. Graaf, *Judicial Influencers: Scholarly use of foreign law and the convergence of German, Italian and French ideas on the position of national constitutional courts in the EU legal context*, 1989-2012, PhD Dissertation, Utrecht University Repository, 2022. For an intriguing analysis of the non-neutral nature of German (public) law libraries, see N. Graaf, "Why German Law Libraries Are Not Neutral and Why We Should Care", *LawLog Blog*, July 2019. Available at: https://lawlog.blog.wzb.eu/2019/07/25/why-german-law-libraries-are-not-neutral-and-why-we-should-care/.

275 See *ex multis*, M. Donini, "An impossible exchange? prove di dialogo tra civil e common lawyers su legalità, morale e teoria del reato", *Rivista Italiana di Diritto e Procedura Penale*, Fasc.1, 2017.

276 G. Fletcher, "Deutsche Strafrechtsdogmatik aus ausländischer Sicht", in A. Eser, W. Hassemer & B. Burckhardt (eds.), *Die deutsche Strafrechtswissenschaft vor der Jahrtausendwende*, Beck, 2000, pp. 235 ff.

277 "*Wer die deutsche Sprache als Fremdsprache erlernt, bekommt mit dem Erlernen gleich die Terminologie der deutschen Strafrechtsdogmatik mitgeliefert. Er ist daher eher in der Lage, einen Vergleich mit den Gegebenheiten in seiner eigenen Strafrechtsdogmatik herzustellen. Für deutsche Muttersprachler ist es schwieriger, Sachgegebenheiten in einer fremden Sprache so zu erfassen, dass man sie mit der eigenen deutschen Begrifflichkeit der Strafrechtsdogmatik vergleichen kann*". W. Gropp, "Deutsches Strafrechtsdenken im Europäischen Kontext" in K. Karsai (Ed.), "Strafrechtlicher Lebensschutz in Ungarn und in Deutschland. Beiträge zur Strafrechtsvergleichung", Stiftung Elemér Pólay, 2007, p. 18.

that it is focused mostly on the "export" of German criminal law ("*Strafrechtsexport*"), rather than on the import of foreign legal concepts ("*Strafrechtsimport*").[278] Surely, it strikes one as odd, for example, that, compared to the Italian front, neither Beck nor Gless-Weigend-Silverman make any reference whatsoever to Hallevy's theories or to Pagallo's colossal work on AI and law. As it was established above, the indifference is not reciprocated by Italian scholars, who, more often than not, wink their eyes at their German colleagues.

3.4.5.1 Sabine Gless, Thomas Weigend, and Emily Silverman

This section analyzes the reflections contained in two articles, namely "Intelligente Agenten und das Strafrecht"[279] by Sabine Gless and Thomas Weigend and "If Robots Cause Harm – Who Is to Blame? Self-Driving Cars and Criminal Liability" by Sabine Gless, Thomas Weigend and Emily Silverman.[280]

In the article "Intelligente Agenten und das Strafrecht", Gless and Weigend scrutinize two issues under the lenses of German criminal law: first, the question of direct liability of AI systems, second, the question of liability of "*[d]er Mensch hinter dem Intelligenten Agenten*",[281] i.e., the human behind the machine.

With regard to the first aspect, they initially focus on the legal personhood of AI systems. They contend that AI systems today are not capable of being accountable for their own actions, since ultimately they always follow the instructions encoded in their programs, and, consequently, they cannot be regarded as possessing personhood under German criminal law.[282] Then, they focus on *actus reus* (*Handlungsfähigkeit*). Interestingly,

278 "*Immer mehr Strafrechtslehrstühle werden bewusst mit internationaler oder europäischer Ausrichtung versehen; die deutsche Lehrbuchliteratur zum internationalen und europäischen Strafrecht ist sehr reichhaltig; auch in der übrigen Literatur sind strafrechtsvergleichende, europäisch- und internationalstrafrechtliche Beiträge mittlerweile häufig. Trotzdem ist der Kritik zuzugeben, dass die deutsche Strafrechtswissenschaft, soweit sie ins Ausland bzw. auf die europäische oder internationale Ebene zu wirken unternimmt, eher an einem 'Strafrechtsexport' interessiert erscheint, also daran, deutsches Strafrechtsdenken im Ausland bzw. in europäischen oder internationalen Gremien zu verbreiten, als daran, vom ausländischen, europäischen oder internationalen Strafrecht zu lernen und gleichsam einen 'Strafrechtsimport' zu betreiben, der keineswegs zwingend auf ein punitiveres Strafrecht hinauslaufen müsste, sondern selbstverständlich auch alternative Modelle mit umfassen könnte. Diese mangelnde „Importbereitschaft" kann sich nachteilig auswirken, insbesondere wenn große ausländische Namen mit richtungweisenden Werken weithin unbekannt bleiben und die deutsche Diskussion nicht bereich*". J. Vogel, "Strafrecht und Strafrechtswissenschaft im internationalen und europäischen Rechtsraum", *ZIS*, No.1, 2012, p. 27. For a critical perspective, see B. Schünemann, "Über Strafrecht im demokratischen Rechtsstaat, das unverzichtbare Rationalitätsniveau seiner Dogmatik und die vorgeblich progressive Rückschrittspropaganda", *ZIS*, Vol. 10, 2016, pp. 654-671.

279 Gless & Weigend, 2014, pp. 561-591.

280 Gless, Silverman & Weigend, 2016, pp. 412-436.

281 Gless & Weigend, 2014, p. 579.

282 Ivi, p. 570.

they acknowledge that the issue of whether an act of an AI system can be considered as relevant under criminal law is strictly dependent on which theory of conduct one adopts:

> According to the traditional "causalistic" theory, any voluntary bodily movement is sufficient to constitute a criminally relevant act; its more modern "social" variant requires, in addition, some kind of societal reference of the bodily movement.[283]

From a causalistic perspective, it follows, it is easy to conclude that any movement of AI systems that operate directly in the physical sphere, such as robots, constitutes an "act", since the threshold of volition required to consider such movement as relevant is very low. If one considers, instead, a finalistic standpoint, the act is relevant under criminal law only as long as it is "the expression of a purposeful will of the actor".[284] In this perspective, according to Gless and Weigend, AI systems are not capable of committing an act "willfully": even if it is true that they can set their own goals and determine autonomously how to reach these goals, this does not mean that they are aware of the relevance of their actions. The only thing that they are aware of is that their conduct will lead them closer to obtaining the programmed goal. The authors conclude this reflection on *Handlungsfähigkeit* by regarding it as a matter of adopting a "thick" or a "thin" definition of act[285]:

> In a "causalistic", merely extrinsic view, which defines every "arbitrary bodily movement" as an action, they are to be regarded as agents by all means. The more the concept of action is substantively loaded, the more one reads into it a self-conscious determination of goals, the less Intelligent Agents can meet the requirements of the ability to act.[286]

When discussing culpability (*Schuldfähigkeit*), the authors claim that, according to a (German) constitutional oriented interpretation, criminal liability is meant as strictly personal, pursuant to the constitutional principle of blameworthiness. Personal criminal liability presupposes that a person is free, responsible, and capable of moral self-determination.

283 "*Für die überkommene 'kausalistische' Theorie genügt jede gewillkürte Körperbewegung als strafrechtlich relevante Handlung; ihre modernere 'soziale' Variante verlangt darüber hinaus einen irgendwie gearteten Sozialbezug der Körperbewegung*". Gless & Weigend, 2014, p. 571.

284 "*Nur wenn und weil die menschliche Handlung Ausdruck eines zielgerichteten Willens des Handelnden ist, kann sie strafrechtlich relevant sein*". Ivi, p. 572.

285 Gless, Silverman & Weigend, 2016, p. 420.

286 "*Bei 'kausalistischer', bloß äußerlicher Betrachtung, die jede 'willkürliche Körperbewegung' als Handlung definiert, sind sie durchaus als Handelnde anzusehen. Je stärker man den Begriff der Handlung substantiell auflädt, je mehr an selbstbewusster Zielbestimmung man in ihn hineinliest, desto weniger können Intelligente Agenten den Voraussetzungen der Handlungsfähigkeit genügen*", Gless & Weigend, 2014, p. 572.

Therefore, it entails that she is able to decide in favor of the right and against the wrong, of arranging her behavior according to the standards of the legal ought, and of avoiding what is legally prohibited as soon as she has attained moral maturity.[287] According to the authors, even the most sophisticated AI systems are not capable, today, of such moral self-determination, hence they cannot be deemed culpable.[288]

The authors then contend that recent neuroscientific evidence which questions the concept of free will, as we know it, is irrelevant in relation to the *mens rea* of AI systems. Indeed, for a time now German authors have argued in favor of a functional conception of criminal culpability, which entails that "the attribution of criminal culpability to a person presupposes that the person had the capacity to put into question the validity of a legal norm".[289] That being the case, they state that culpability is based on whether an actor can engage in a normative discourse. In order to participate in such a discourse, the agent needs to be able to self-reflect about her past actions and to evaluate them against a moral reference system, i.e., to have a good or bad conscience.[290]

This leads us back to the initial conclusion: even though there are efforts today to program AI systems which can make decisions according to moral standards (based on "merits" and "demerits"), current AI systems are far from being moral agents. Hence, they cannot be blamed. This could change in the future if AI systems capable of making moral evaluations were created. Admittedly, "[t]he final step would be to make robots capable of understanding punishment, that is, to teach them to associate certain changes in their environment with the wrongfulness of their prior acts".[291]

Let us move on now to the analysis of the second part of Gless, Silverman and Weigend's work, which deals with criminal liability of the "human behind the machine". The focus is on negligence offenses. According to German criminal legal doctrine, negligence is based on two elements: (a) foreseeability and (b) breach of a duty of care.

With regard to (a), the authors acknowledge that certain AI systems have a sort of "pre-programmed" unpredictability, meaning that "the operator cannot reduce to zero the possibility that robots may cause harm to others".[292] From this assumption, they theorize two mutually exclusive conclusions (regarding the programmer's liability for negligence):

287 *"Der innere Grund des Schuldvorwurfes liegt darin, daß der Mensch auf freie, verantwortliche, sittliche Selbstbestimmung angelegt und deshalb befähigt ist, sich für das Recht und gegen das Unrecht zu entscheiden, sein Verhalten nach den Normen des rechtlichen Sollens einzurichten und das rechtlich Verbotene zu vermeiden, sobald er die sittliche Reife erlangt hat (...)"*. Bundesgerichtshof (BGH), 18.03.1952, GSSt 2/51, pp.16-17.

288 Gless, Silverman & Weigend, 2016, p. 421.

289 Ibid.

290 Gless & Weigend, 2014, p. 575.

291 Gless, Silverman & Weigend, 2016, p. 424,

292 Ivi, p. 426; Gless & Weigend, 2014, p. 581.

> It could be argued that he cannot be held responsible because the machine is acting "on its own"; alternatively, it could be claimed that he can foresee any and all harm that robots might cause and therefore should face de facto strict liability for the results of the robots' acts.[293]

The first argument is discarded, as it would lead to a gap in the protection of individuals' interests. Admittedly, it would be as if the manager of a zoo, who released a tiger from its cage, remarked the unpredictable nature of the wild animal to the innocent bystander who had just been attacked and bitten by the very same tiger.[294]

If the second argument stands, then this entails that:

> [...] a person who can foresee that his action might harm interests protected by criminal law (such as the life and health of other persons) is obliged to refrain from that action. Hence, if the zoo manager can foresee that the tiger, if set free, will harm human beings, he must refrain from releasing the tiger from its cage.[295]

With regard to (b), the authors claim that German case law has developed strict rules which would be applicable to AI systems with regard to due diligence, especially in the field of product liability. Criminal product liability is based on the fact that "a perfectly legal act – [for example] the marketing of a self-driving car in accordance with the current state of knowledge and technology – may trigger criminal liability for omission",[296] the omission being that the producer did not ensure that the product adhered to certain standards of safety. Naturally, such a strict application of the duty of care would hinder technological progress and therefore diminish, if not erase, the benefits that our society is enjoying due to the surge in innovation. For these reasons, the authors argue that such a comprehensive criminal liability of the programmer, which includes any foreseeable damage, should be excluded for the time being.

The crucial question, then, is the concept of permissible (innovation) risk: where should the line be drawn? Even in cases where society could accept innovation risks, such as with AVs, the producer would still have to make sure to reduce risks to the minimum

293 Gless, Silverman & Weigend, 2016, p. 426.

294 "[...] *er kann dies ebenso wenig wie der Zoodirektor, der einen Tiger in die Freiheit entlässt und gegenüber einem Passanten, der von dem Tiger angefallen und gebissen wird, auf die unberechenbare Natur des wilden Tieres verweist*". Gless & Weigend, 2014, pp. 581-582.

295 Gless, Silverman & Weigend, 2016, p. 427.

296 Ivi, p. 428.

by complying with other duties such as information duty towards the users and the processes of monitoring/recalling the products.[297]

Assuming that conditions (a) and (b) are fulfilled, the authors then discuss whether the harmful event can be causally attributed to the programmer or not. The first option would be to regard AI systems as part of the average risks of life, same as lightning or falling trees.[298] Yet, this option is not feasible, since nowadays advanced AI systems are considered as exceptional risks. This could change in the future, as AI systems are permeating our lives more and as technology progresses. The authors subsequently suggest reducing the duties of operators of (some) robots "to employing the best knowledge and technology available in manufacturing, programming, testing and monitoring them".[299]

Conclusively, Gless, Silverman and Weigend affirm that society will have to accept a degree of (residual) risk for the sake of a greater social benefit: instead of imposing a total ban on AI systems because they pose uncontrollable risks, the option would be to "burden "society" with the dangers that cannot be reliably controlled by programming and responsible use. This would happen by waiving criminal liability for negligence, i.e., by defining the injured persons as victims of non-human behavior.[300]

3.4.5.2 Susanne Beck

Beck claims that the debate on how the law should deal with the risks of robots resembles other debates on the legal handling of risks (the "risk society"). She focuses, then, on the criminal regulation of risks, specifically on negligence. Her reflections on the interaction between legal and non-legal standards in determining the boundaries of negligence are indeed noteworthy.

Negligence, she notes, has two requirements: reasonable care and foreseeability of the damage. With regard to the first requirement, i.e., reasonable care, usually the standard of care is determined by how society expects that a reasonable person would act in a situation. Sometimes, the standard is set by non-legal sources and standardizing institutions (e.g. ISO). Thus, in the field of robotics (and AI systems in general, one might add) the development of these standards has not been completed yet. What is more, Beck argues, one must not forget that technical standards serve a different purpose than criminal law: they aim at minimizing risks and preventing danger while fostering economic advantages.

297 It is referred to as a "sleeping obligation" (*schlafenden Ingerenz)* by Gless & Weigend, 2014, p. 585.

298 Gless, Silverman & Weigend, 2016, p. 433.

299 Ivi, p. 434.

300 "*Will man sich nicht wegen der letztlich nicht beherrschbaren Risiken auf ein Totalverbot Intelligenter Agenten verständigen, so dürfte keine andere Möglichkeit bestehen, als die nicht verlässlich durch Programmierung und verantwortlichen Einsatz steuerbaren Gefahren der „Gesellschaft" aufzubürden, indem man auf eine strafrechtliche Fahrlässigkeitsverantwortlichkeit verzichtet, also die geschädigten Personen als Opfer nicht-menschlichen Verhaltens definiert*". Gless & Weigend, 2014, p. 590.

Criminal law is not "simply an accessory to the regulations of non-governmental groups",[301] it also has to consider whether the action is socially inadequate, i.e., whether it violates social and moral rules. Nevertheless, our society needs subsystems (such as the technology one) and accepts them, which entails that "[i]t would be inconsistent to rely on these systems on one side and not to accept their specific norms which regulate these subsystems and the interests of its parties on the other. Thus, the inclusion of economic interests in standardising procedures does not necessarily lead to their irrelevance for criminal law".[302] In point of fact, Beck does not see a point in time when these norms would become irrelevant for criminal law. This, she believes, is especially relevant in the field of robotics: first, standardizing institutions are very active in the robotics field right now, hence "it seems, from a legal perspective, important to analyse these activities and retie them with legal evaluation. One might even have to consider interaction with the standardising institutions to secure plausible normative premises and processes".[303]

Second, and most interestingly:

> Most researchers and producers are convinced to have acted legally when complying with the existing standards, even if they are somehow vague, not covering all relevant (dangerous) aspects of their activities and normatively questionable. It is necessary to discuss how to connect this strong conviction, supported not just by the official impression of standardising institutions but by the general custom in the actors community, with negligence liability; it might be worth to consider its relevance for the subjective aspects of negligence (guilt). The (potential) "sense of right and wrong" is part of liability for negligence as well. Unavoidable mistake in the lawfulness of the action can therefore lead to negation of negligence.[304]

This would be the case particularly for those who are not part of the producing chain of the AI system, who would therefore be "surrounded by a community in which everyone is convinced that fulfilling the requirements of standards is sufficient to act lawfully".[305]

With regard to the second requirement, i.e., foreseeability of damage, Beck notes that the more the AI system has the faculty to behave autonomously, the more "it can be – generally – foreseen during the research phase that it may, later on, bring harm to humans".[306]

---

301 S. Beck, "Intelligent Agents and Criminal Law – Negligence, Diffusion of Liability and Electronic Personhood", in E. Hilgendorf and J. Fedle (eds.), Vol. 86, 2016, p. 139.

302 Ibid.

303 Beck, 2016, p. 139.

304 Ibid.

305 Beck, 2016, p. 139.

306 Ibid.

Yet, in this sense foreseeability would be related only to a *general* risk of harm, where instead "the specific conditions and situations become more and more unforeseeable".[307] Consequently, Beck states that via analyzing negligent crimes connected to AI harm, one can reflect on which degree of *specificity* is required for the fulfillment of the foreseeability-component of negligence. Specifically, one must understand whether the mere possibility of "violating humans as such"[308] would be sufficient.

Having said this, Becks shifts her attention to how the aforementioned traditional notion of negligence could be adapted to the risk society. She contends that, rather than focusing on foreseeability, or on external regulations which would develop the required standard of care, we should concentrate on the social adequacy of the action and on the legal construction of admissible risk. In other words, one should focus on how to "negotiate in each area of life if and under which conditions the usage of robots is regarded as such 'admissible risk' and if one does act in the adequate framework, one cannot be responsible for the consequences hereof".[309] Conclusively, she argues in favor of restricting the use of criminal law in the field of technology development. This makes her approach to the subject both original and cogent.

3.4.5.3 Gerhard Seher

Gerhard Seher, as most of the other authors discussed here, develops his article following the building blocks of criminal law.[310] Therefore, he starts by analyzing whether AI systems can "act" and can be considered as "agents". Seher believes that the core of a criminal act is highly normative: criminal law shall concern itself only with those actions that show at least potential norm understanding. Surely, in the history of criminal legal doctrine the meaning of act varied and so did the demand of a "free will" component in it, similar to a sine curve with its high and low oscillations.[311] Even if we were to accept that, as humans, we do not possess free will, our "determined" brain is still able to understand and reflect legal commands. This means that, even from a strictly deterministic point of view, we are still influenced by legal norms and, therefore, our actions still amount as such from the perspective of criminal law.

Shifting to AI agents, Seher believes that computers are not capable, as of now, of perceiving norms as such by themselves.[312] The mediation of a human programmer is always

307 Beck, 2016, p. 139.
308 Ibid.
309 S. Beck, "Robotics and Criminal Law. Negligence, Diffusion of Liability and Electronic Personhood", in Hilgendorf & Feldle, 2018, p. 53.
310 Seher, 2016.
311 Ivi, p. 48.
312 "*Computer sind – soweit ich informiert bin – nicht in der Lage, von sich aus Normen als solche wahrzunehmen*". Seher, 2016, p. 50.

needed. Seher then argues that the situation might be different when it comes to autonomous vehicles: one could argue that they have indeed the capability of understanding symbolized norms such as traffic signs and traffic light signals since they represent "schematized, symbolized norms, which are directly perceptible and implementable for a computer".[313]

Moreover, Seher contends that the "*Rechtlich relevante Handlung*" can be defined only as the action of a person that is responsive to the law, and this has nothing to do with determinism or free will. This person needs to be able to directly understand the meaning of the norm and to include it into her decision-making process. When claiming this, Seher distances himself from Gless und Weigend: he claims that they take a "cautiously different" approach which is based on a "norm-theoretically open, descriptive concept of action".[314]

At this point of the discussion, Seher shifts his attention to the responsibility of *human* actors involved with AI systems. He claims that since he already made a strong case against AI systems being capable of committing an "act", the matter does not deserve further attention. If one considers causality, then, he argues that the most interesting study cases are those where a correctly programmed AI system makes a decision which results in damage. In fact, as Seher points out, the sole fact of creating an AI system creates the abstract risk that it might damage a legal good, similar to what already happens with cars and airplanes. If we were to follow the standard rule on attribution, i.e., the operation through which we select the legally relevant cause of a harmful event, then the operators would always be liable for damage cause by the AI systems they created. However, Seher argues that there are certain conditions which would stop the attribution process: to begin with, if the misconduct of the AI agent is the result of an atypical causal process according to general life experience. To continue, when the conduct of the AI systems falls in the scope of a permitted risk.

Next, Seher spends a short paragraph on *mens rea* of humans and in this he differs from most of the authors analyzed in this chapter, who instead believe that it is a pivotal issue. This represents a direct reflection of the German tripartite conception of criminal liability. Notably, Seher argues that, when it comes to human operators and negligence, the general foreseeability of a harmful event is not sufficient. What is needed is foreseeability tailored to the specific error that caused the concrete harmful event.

Seher, then, focuses on blameworthiness, defined – following what he claims to be a "unanimous opinion" – as the judgement from a legal community which deems a certain

---

313 "*Das mag man bei selbstfahrenden Autos möglicherweise anders sehen, soweit sie in der Lage sind, Verkehrsschilder und Ampelsignale richtig zu „lesen", denn hier handelt es sich um schematisierte, symbolisierte Normen, die für einen Computer unmittelbar wahrnehmbar und umsetzbar sind*". Ibid.

314 "*Das sehen Gless/Weigend [...] vorsichtig anders, weil sie bereit sind, von einem normtheoretisch offenen, deskriptiven Handlungsbegriff auszugehen*", Seher, 2016, p. 51, n. 11.

action as reproachable. As a matter of fact, those in favor of a functionalist theory of criminal law see the criminal accusation as a "branding operation". It is a tool to distance ourselves from the criminal act and the offender.[315] Based on this approach, Seher argues that AI systems should not be blamed: our society does not consider their behavior as an attack on the validity of the norm.

Lastly, with regard to punishment, Seher claims that assuming that we could punish AI systems at all, it is uncertain whether inflicting this punishment would fulfill any purpose. First, it would not provide retribution to the victims. Second, general prevention would not be achieved since – as was stated above – AI misbehavior would not be perceived as the violation of a norm. Third, even if we could program an AI system to perceive a punishment for violating a norm as a failure, and to learn from it, it still would not be aware that it is being punished. AI systems are not capable of perceiving the reprimand of a criminal sanction, hence their behavior cannot be guided by it.

Indeed:

> Punishment is a concept that belongs in the context of normative understanding. However, no communicative understanding in a normative language occurs between "intelligent agents" and humans. These agents can only be addressed via binary digital coding. Such systems can be reprogrammed or shut down, but not punished.[316]

3.5 Conclusions

The purpose of this chapter was to provide an across-the-board analysis of the current debate on criminal liability connected to AI systems. The word "connected" is important in this sense: this chapter covered not only the ideas of authors on how to attribute liability *directly* to the artificial agent, but also on how to attribute it to those (humans) who surround it.

The debate was divided into three streams: expansionists, moderates, and skeptics. Expansionists are looked at by the rest of the scholars with surprise and, at times, disapproval. They are a rare breed: this research, indeed, found only a few of them. On the opposite side, skeptics take up the cudgels for criminal law's traditional principles and

315 Ivi, p. 55.

316 "*Strafe ist ein Begriff, der in den Kontext normativer Verständigung gehört. Zwischen „intelligenten Agenten" und Menschen findet aber keine kommunikative Verständigung in einer normativen Sprache statt. Ansprechbar sind diese Agenten nur über eine binäre digitale Codierung. Solche Systeme kann man umprogrammieren oder stilllegen, aber nicht bestrafen*", Seher, 2016, pp. 59-60.

defend them from the disruptive effects of AI systems. The moderate stream is multifaceted since it consists of authors with different approaches and opinions.

What is the significance of this chapter? Surely, providing a *vision d'ensemble* of such a rich and various debate while keeping an international breadth is valuable *per se*. Admittedly, this operation is of paramount importance to what should be regarded as the *credo* of all scholars interested in the newborn realm of AI law: No Law is an Island.[317] But there is more. The investigation started by asking whether the international legal debate about the interaction between AI systems and criminal liability shared some common ground. Indeed, regardless of which side they were on, most scholars seemed to follow a similar structure when discussing this topic: first they define AI, then they review *actus reus* and *mens rea* requirements, finally they discuss AI punishment. As mentioned above, the debate revolves around two macro-areas: on one side, the direct liability of AI agents, on the other, the liability of humans in the loop. The two areas are interconnected.

Lastly, it possible to formulate a set of intermediate conclusions. Upon conducting this literature review, it was possible to identify a set of recurring questions and topics discussed by scholars:

I. Are robots/AI systems capable of moral reasoning?
II. What is the relevance of moral reasoning when ascribing criminal liability?
III. Can an AI system be culpable?
IV. Why should we punish AI systems and how should we punish AI systems?
V. Can an AI system "act"?
VI. Permitted risk and dangerous activities;
VII. Should human agents be liable for the AI's misbehavior?
VIII. The creation of new negligence crimes and the application of existing negligence offenses so to humans-in-the-loop (how should foreseeability and reasonable care be defined?);
IX. What is the relationship between corporate criminal liability and AI criminal liability?

317 The expression is borrowed from a passage of the famous 1624 Meditation XVII by John Donne, which reads: "No man is an island, entire of itself; every man is a piece of the continent, a part of the main. If a clod be washed away by the sea, Europe is the less, as well as if a promontory were, as well as if a manor of thy friend's or of thine own were: any man's death diminishes me, because I am involved in mankind, and therefore never send to know for whom the bells tolls; it tolls for thee". J. Donne, "Meditation XVII. Nunc Lento Sonitu Dicunt, Morieris", in A. Raspa (ed.), *Devotions Upon Emergent Occasions*, Oxford University Press, 1987.

X. Are there more feasible alternatives to applying criminal law (such as tort law or administrative sanctions)?

These questions will influence the analysis conducted in this research. The next chapters will necessarily address them, either directly or indirectly. Specifically, questions I to IV will be touched upon in Chapters 4 and 5; question V will be addressed in Section 6.3.; questions VI to VIII will be tackled at Sections 6.2.3.1 to 6.2.3.4; question IX will be part of Section 6.4. and question X will be discussed throughout Chapter 8.

Is there a gap to be filled, then, by this very research? It is argued here that the answer is affirmative. It is possible to identify the following gaps and weaknesses in the discussion conducted by scholars:

I. Civil criminal legal scholars discard Hallevy's theories quite effortlessly. They share a defensive approach to the principle of *personal* criminal liability, as in belonging to a human *persona*. This "as sure as eggs are eggs" approach, at times, undermines the strength of their legal arguments;
II. No or few attempts are made at providing a definition of AI and of AI agent applicable to criminal law, nor discussion of the impact of the lack of a definition on the matter;
III. No or few attempts are made at addressing the preliminary issue of considering AI as a subject of criminal law (i.e., criminal capacity of AI);
IV. Most legal scholars neglect discussing whether an AI system can act, think or want. The topic is mostly addressed by philosophers and legal philosophers. For example, Abbott and Sarch claim specifically "[w]e will not attempt to articulate the non-functional differences between human and algorithmic reasoning, a subject which has fascinated and confounded computer scientists since the 1950s. [...] Functionally, AI and people can exhibit similar patterns of behavior and information processing, regardless of whether machines "think" or understand what they do";[318]
V. No or little discussion of whether the conduct of AI systems could be excused or justified by a defense;
VI. Focusing on the liability of humans in the loop, there seems to be confusion on identifying precisely who would be the responsible human agent. The authors mention different subjects (such as robot trainers,

318 Abbott & Sarch, 2019, n. 53, p. 333.

robot owners, robot users, operators, programmers, designers, users), yet neither their roles nor their duties are specified. For example, no author specifies that the liability of the programmers could be caused by a wrongful selection of the training data for the algorithm;

VII. While some authors discuss the notion of act, almost no attention is given to how AI behavior interferes with theories of causality.

One of the purposes of this research is to grapple with these gaps and advance the discussion on the matter. In Section 8.3, I will evaluate whether this operation was successful.

4 Ascription: Introducing Chapters 5 & 6

The only part of conduct of any one, for which he is amenable to society,
is that which concerns others.
In the part, which merely concerns himself, his independence is, of right, absolute.
Over himself, over his own body and mind, the individual is sovereign.

John Stuart Mill (1859)

4.1 On Paperclips, Planes, and AI

In 2003,[1] Nick Bostrom, an Oxford-based philosopher, conceived the "Paperclip Maximizer" ("PCM"),[2] a thought experiment where he hypothesized the emergence of an AI system characterized by general superintelligence,[3] whose only goal would be manufacturing as many paperclips as possible, while opposing resistance to anybody or anything that would attempt to modify its goal. As a consequence, the superintelligence would start transforming all of the earth (and then space) into paperclip manufacturing facilities. This thought experiment is used to illustrate how an AI, tasked with a worthless and innocuous utility function,[4] such as producing the biggest number of paperclips in the universe, could "as a side-effect destroy us by consuming resources essential to our survival",[5] leading to human extinction. Simply put, perhaps in the near future[6] we might face a doomsday scenario: an AI system will transform us all into paperclips.[7]

1 N. Bostrom, "Ethical Issues in Advanced Artificial Intelligence", 2003. Available at: https://nickbostrom.com/ethics/ai.

2 The PCM Experiment is mentioned in M. E. Diamantis, R. Cochran & M. Dam, "AI and the Law: Can Legal Systems Help Us Maximize Paperclips while Minimizing Deaths?", 2022. Available at SSRN: https://papers.ssrn.com/sol3/papers.cfm?abstract_id=4177378.

3 Superintelligence is defined as "any intellect that is vastly outperforms the best human brains in practically every field, including scientific creativity, general wisdom, and social skills". N. Bostrom, "How Long Before Superintelligence?", *International Journal of Futures Studies*, Vol. 2, 1998.

4 In a utility function, numerical values ("utilities") are assigned to choices based on the satisfaction that can be obtained from the choice (the higher the utility value, the higher the satisfaction). Utility functions are used to analyze human behavior in rational choice theory. See: www.lesswrong.com/tag/utility-functions.

5 See www.lesswrong.com/tag/paperclip-maximizer.

6 Unfortunately for us humans, a number of scientists argue that it is likely that AI systems could lead to an existential catastrophe. See M. K. Cohen, M. Hutter & M. A. Osborne, "Advanced artificial agents intervene in the provision of reward", *AI Magazine*, Vol. 43, 2022.

7 In 2017 Frank Lantz, a game designer of the NYU Game Center, created "Universal Paperclips". Universal Paperclips is click game where one can play the role of an AI system producing paperclips. The game ends with the destruction of the world. The game is available here: www.decisionproblem.com/paperclips/

Even though the PCM apocalypse scenario is "just" a philosophical thought experiment, the last five years marked the start of collections of real-life AIs "going wrong" scenarios. One example is Awful AI, a website which contains a list of "*current scary usages of AI*"[8] such as a DNN designed to "detect sexual orientation from facial images" (also referred to as "an AI-based gay radar"),[9] or Tay, the Microsoft chatbot which engaged in racist and anti-Semitic messages on Twitter (e.g., "Hitler was right") after only 24 hours from its 'birth'.[10] Other examples of real life AI incidents databases are the AI Algorithmic and Automation Incidents & Controversies (AIAAIC) Repository[11] and the AIID.[12] These databases validate this study's assumption: the idea of AI systems harming people and of consequently applying criminal law is no any longer a matter of science fiction. It is just a matter of time.

Incident databases are commonly used in the field of aviation: one usually distinguishes between "accidents", i.e., "cases where substantial damage or loss of life occurs", and "incidents", i.e., "cases where the risk of an accident substantially increases".[13] Focusing on an example, "when a small fire is quickly extinguished in a cockpit it is an 'incident' but if the fire burns crew members in the course of being extinguished it is an 'accident'".[14] Incident databases are a form of continual self-examination, which admittedly make air travel "one of the safest forms of travel" ever invented.[15]

The criminalization of aviation, i.e., the prosecution of pilots, aviation controllers and mechanics,[16] together with airline companies and manufacturers, is indeed outside of the

---

index2.html. For a comment, see: A. Rogers, "The Way the World Ends: Not with a Bang But a Paperclip", *Wired*, 21 October 2017. Available at www.wired.com/story/the-way-the-world-ends-not-with-a-bang-but-a-paperclip/; N. Jahromi, "The Unexpected Philosophical Depths of the Clicker Game Universal Paperclips", *The New Yorker online*, 28 March 2019. Available at: www.newyorker.com/culture/culture-desk/the-unexpected-philosophical-depths-of-the-clicker-game-universal-paperclips.

8 D. Dao et al., "Awful AI – 2021 Edition". Available at https://github.com/daviddao/awful-ai [emphasis added]. See also "ResponsibleAI", available at: https://romanlutz.github.io/ResponsibleAI/.

9 Y. Wang & M. Kosinski, "Deep neural networks are more accurate than humans at detecting sexual orientation from facial images", *Journal of Personality and Social Psychology*, Vol. 114, Issue 2, 2018, pp. 246-257.

10 E. Hunt, "Tay, Microsoft's AI chatbot, gets a crash course in racism from Twitter", *The Guardian*, 24 March 2016. Available at: www.theguardian.com/technology/2016/mar/24/tay-microsofts-ai-chatbot-gets-a-crash-course-in-racism-from-twitter.

11 AIAAIC Repository. Available at: https://docs.google.com/spreadsheets/d/1Bn55B4xz21-_Rgdr8BBb2lt0n_4rzLGxFADMlVW0PYI/edit#gid=1051812323.

12 The AIID indexes more than 1,000 publicly available incident reports (i.e., a mixture of documents from the popular, trade, and academic press). S. McGregor, "Preventing Repeated Real World AI Failures by Cataloging Incidents: The AI Incident Database", *Proceedings of the Thirty-Third Annual Conference on Innovative Applications of Artificial Intelligence (IAAI-21). Virtual Conference*, 2021, p. 2. Available at https://incidentdatabase.ai/?lang=en.

13 Ivi, p. 1.

14 McGregor, 2021, p. 2.

15 Ibid.

16 S. Dekker, "Pilots, Controllers and Mechanics on Trial: Cases, Concerns and Countermeasures", *International Journal of Applied Aviation Studies*, Vol. 10, No. 1.

scope of this study. Yet, it presents interesting similarities with the object of the present research.[17] The reasons are manifold. First of all, aviation is a highly automated field which is characterized by complex human-machine interactions. These factors lead to difficulties in ascribing (criminal) liability to human individuals when accidents happen. Moreover, "[p]rosecution of pilots, controllers and mechanics is often based on general hazard statutes that have evolved from road traffic laws which criminalize the reckless endangerment of people or property".[18] It follows that criminal legal systems have already dealt with issues of criminal liability arising from technological failures.

Furthermore, aviation is an environment where practices of "greying *[the content]* of the Black Box"[19] have already been implemented. For example, one way aviation addresses accountability issues is through technical investigations[20] which are "non-punitive in nature" and have the sole scope of "identifying all the circumstances that led to the accident, in order to facilitate safety recommendations to prevent similar accidents in the future".[21] Accident investigations are governed by a "non-blameworthy philosophy"[22] and are conducted separately from legal investigations, which instead are aimed at finding a culprit.[23]

The two fields (i.e., AI and aviation) are now converging, with AI-based technologies currently being deployed in aviation and air traffic management (ATM) for multiple purposes, such as traffic prediction, forecast, and modelling, automated flight plan correction, and fuel optimization.[24] It is predicted that the impact of ML on aviation will be tremendous. It will lead to the development of autonomous flight (the "holy grail" of AI aviation)[25] and, more generally, to a revolution in the relationship between pilots and systems. AI systems will assist the crew in making critical decisions, such as those regarding unpredictable situations (e.g., wind gusts or engine failures) and obstacles (e.g., birds).[26] For example, in 2020 Airbus concluded its Autonomous Taxi, Take-Off and Landing (ATTOL)

---

17 M. C. Elish & T. Hwang, "Praise the Machine! Punish the Human! The Contradictory History of Accountability in Automated Aviation", *Comparative Studies in Intelligent Systems – Working Paper #1*, Vol. 2, 2015.

18 Dekker, 2010, p. 32.

19 Namely, understanding the contents of the black box through technical investigations.

20 International Civil Aviation Organization (ICAO), "Aircraft Accident and Incident Investigation", Annex 13 to the Convention on International Civil Aviation.

21 S. Michaelides-Mateou & A. Mateou, *Flying in the Face of Criminalization. The Safety Implications of Prosecuting Aviation Professionals for Accidents*, Routledge, 2010, p. 2.

22 Ivi, p. 162.

23 The authors argue that more regulation should be adopted regarding this exchange of information. Michaelides-Mateou & Mateou, 2010, p. 99.

24 EUROCONTROL, European Aviation/ATM AI High Level Group (EEAI HLG), "Fly AI report", 2020, p. 55. Available at: www.eurocontrol.int/publication/fly-ai-report.

25 Ivi, p. 7.

26 EUROCONTROL, 2020, p. 55.
Ivi, p. 7.

project: for the first time a commercial aircraft autonomously concluded the ATTOL operation using an AI system performing automatic vision.[27]

When it comes to accountability in aviation, scholars have affirmed that:

> Regulators, in addition to the engineers and managers of aviation systems, have created a schizophrenic dynamic in which automation is seen as safer and superior in most instances, unless something goes wrong, at which point humans are regarded as safer and superior. Unfortunately, creating this kind of role for humans, who must jump into an emergency situation at the last minute, is something humans do not do well.[28]

This trend has become even more tangible with the influence of AI systems. It has been argued that the introduction of such technologies has "wrestled control away from airline pilots",[29] while they are still deemed morally responsible for their outcomes (it is the "moral crumple zone").[30] Pilots are nevertheless treated as "liability sponges, absorbing in one concentrated place liability for actions which are in fact distributed throughout the system".[31]

As it will be analyzed in Chapter 7, there seems to be a similar inclination when it comes to European regulation of AI systems. Thus, as of today, no AI-specific criminal law or standards have been adopted and the discussion on how to adapt what is already in place is moving slowly. It is likely that courts and regulators approaching the field in the future will indeed look at aviation and connected liability issues. The only (premature) exceptions to this trend, which is analyzed in Chapter 7, can be found mostly in the field of autonomous driving. Autonomous driving shares similarities with aviation, such as the delegation of control to a (semi-)automated system, thus, it is characterized by many fewer expert users in comparison to pilots and aviation controllers.

27 Airbus, "Airbus concludes ATTOL with fully autonomous flight tests", 29 June 2020. Available at: www.airbus.com/en/newsroom/press-releases/2020-06-airbus-concludes-attol-with-fully-autonomous-flight-tests.

28 Elish & Hwang, 2015, p. 12.

29 W. D. Holford, "An Ethical Inquiry of the Effect of Cockpit Automation on the Responsibilities of Airline Pilots: Dissonance or Meaningful Control?", *Journal of Business Ethics*, 2022, p. 142.

30 It is defined as the "misattribution of responsibility for an action to a human actor who has limited control over the actions of an automated system, a recognized phenomenon within human factor studies". Ivi, p. 146.

31 Elish & Hwang, 2015, p. 15.

4.2 Theories of Criminalization

This research might touch upon different criminalization theories, whether directly or indirectly. Hence, it is relevant at this point to briefly introduce the topic.

Criminal law is a "multi-functional" tool.[32] The choices made by legislators when defining the latitude of the special part of the criminal code, i.e., "decisions about offense descriptions",[33] are a mirror of a "political community's attitude toward citizens".[34] As such, "apart from waging war, no decision made by the state is more significant than its judgment about what conduct should be proscribed and how severely to punish it".[35]

Criminalization theories aim to answer the question of "what kind of conduct should be declared criminal".[36] Amongst the most prominent criminalization theories, it possible to identify the legal goods doctrine ("*Rechtsgüterlehre*"), which entails that criminal law should focus on punishing conducts with the purpose of protecting legal goods;[37] and the harm principle, which entails that criminal law should punish conducts with the purpose of preventing harm to others.[38] According to some scholars, criminalization should occur to protect the *rights* of others.[39] According to others, criminal law should protect *moral values* (following the "legal moralism" doctrine). Indeed, the different "reasons for making a form of conduct an offence are also likely to be somehow related to the reasons for considering it as wrong".[40] There are different variations of legal moralism.[41] Some, including H. L. A. Hart,[42] claim that the immorality of act A is a *sufficient* condition for the criminalization of conduct A, even if A does not cause someone to be harmed.[43] However, opinions vary on whether criminal law should criminalize *all* immoral conduct,[44] or if it

32 A. P. Simester, Fundamentals of Criminal Law: Responsibility, Culpability, and Wrongdoing, Oxford University Press, 2021, p. 3.

33 T. Hörnle, "Theories of Criminalization", in Dubber & Hörnle (Eds.), 2014, p. 679.

34 Ivi, p. 680.

35 D. Husak, *Overcriminalization: The Limits of the Criminal Law*, Oxford University Press, 2009, p. vii.

36 Hörnle, p. 685. Theories of punishment, instead, answer the following question: "how is criminal law and criminal punishment justified?". Ibid.

37 Hörnle, p. 686 and the authors cited by Hörnle at note 25. See also D. Husak, "Theories of Crime and Punishment in German Criminal Law", *The American Journal of Comparative Law*, 2005, Vol. 53, No. 3, 2005, pp. 679-707 and the authors cited therein.

38 See, *ex multis*, J. S. Mill, *On Liberty*, Penguin Books, 2010.

39 Ivi, pp. 691-692.

40 K. Nuotio, "Theories of Criminalization and the Limits of Criminal Law: A Legal Cultural Approach", in R.A. Duff et al., *The Boundaries of the Criminal Law*, Oxford University Press, 2010, p. 242.

41 See *ex multis:* J. Damgaard Thaysen, Defining Legal Moralism, *SATS*, Vol. 16, No. 2, 2015; T. Søbirk Petersen, "What is Legal Moralism?", *SATS*, Vol. 12, 2011.

42 "Is the fact that certain conduct is by common standards immoral sufficient to justify making that conduct punishable by law? Is it morally permissible to enforce morality as such? Ought immorality as such to be a crime?". H. L. A. Hart, *Law, Liberty and Morality*, Stanford University Press, 1963, p. 4.

43 Søbirk Petersen, 2011, pp. 80-81.

44 M. Moore, Placing Blame: a General Theory of the Criminal Law, Clarendon Press, 1997.

should criminalize only *some* immoral conducts.[45] Lastly, one should mention the principle of *ultima ratio*, which, as stressed in Chapter 1, should be the tenet when discussing how to shape areas of criminalization. Its relevance is prominent mostly in continental European criminal law and it entails that "[c]riminal law should not be considered *prima ratio* or *sola ratio*, but *ultima ratio*".[46] Certainly, the *ultima ratio* principle expresses "the identity of criminal law":[47] in a nutshell, it enshrines that criminal law is something *different*.[48]

Theories of criminalization can come in handy for a set of specific AI-related issues. Definitely, the main focus of this book is whether *current* criminal offenses can be applied to AI systems, i.e., on whether AI systems can be qualified as a *subjects* of state-of-the-art criminal law. To discuss such issues the research resorted mainly to different doctrines of agency and liability ("whom to punish?") and to general theories on the purposes of punishment ("why punish them?"): therefore, one could think that theories of criminalization ("what to punish?") have little to do with this inquiry. Thus, when it comes to AI systems, the questions posed by these different doctrines seem to conflate. AI systems might behave in a way that gives rise to a "criminalization conflict", i.e., situations "outside the *core* definition of criminal offenses"[49] whose criminal character could be questioned precisely because the "perpetrator" is an AI system, henceforth impacting directly on issues of ascription.[50] Moreover, as it will be highlighted later on, according to some authors the whole issue of the attribution of legal personality to AI systems in the criminal law domain can be labelled as a pure *political* and *pragmatic* decision, rather than a theoretical one.[51] Consequently, this research expands the scope of theories of criminalization to the question "is this entity/individual responsible for the specific conduct?". Indeed, even though these theories were originally developed to determine whether conduct should be criminalized per se, one could make use of them also to check whether a specific entity (i.e., AI systems) should be responsible for conducts that are already criminalized. Such reasoning was followed also in discussions regarding the introduction of corporate criminal liability (CCL). Against this background, scholars have claimed that

> While the notion of punishment is inextricably linked to criminal responsibility, there are justifications for holding corporations responsible for their actions which lie beyond the traditional utilitarian and desert-based theories

45 R. A. Duff, "Towards a Modest Legal Moralism", *Crim. Law Philos.*, Vol. 8, 2014, pp. 217-235.
46 Nuotio, 2010, p. 256.
47 Ibid.
48 Nuotio, 2010, p. 256.
49 J. Wilenmann, "Framing meaning through criminalization", *New Criminal Law Review*, Vol. 22, No. 1, 2019, p.6.
50 Ibid.
51 See Hildebrandt, 2020, p. 246 and Chopra & White, 2011, p. 154.

> of punishment. *Not all corporate misconduct or harm should be criminalized; not all types of corporate wrongdoing are appropriately sanctioned through the recourse to the criminal law.*[52]

Similarly, conducts, which are typically punishable when committed by a human agent, might not be deemed "criminal" if conveyed by an AI system, and such a difference could be connected to the specifics of AI (criminal) agency. Surely, legislators will have to face similar questions in the future when dealing with cases of AI-related harm and with the criminalization of AI conduct. This can be seen clearly in the analysis of the lawmaking initiatives examined at Chapter 7, where criminalization theories were applied to devise new punishable *human* conducts in relation to AI systems. Taking this into consideration, it is argued here that the questions posed by theories of criminalization could be useful when addressing such issues. Their value in this regard will be evaluated in the concluding chapter.

4.3 METHODOLOGY AND STRUCTURE OF CHAPTERS 5 AND 6

When the law is silent, gap-filling mechanisms need to be activated. This will be the tenet of Chapters 5 and 6: is there a gap to fill? If so, is criminal law the right mechanism to fill it? If yes, how?

The classical construction of a criminal offense[53] is built on two pillars: an objective and a subjective element. The following analysis, focused on the impact of AI on the general part of criminal, will shadow such categorization.

Indeed, this study will not follow the *mens rea/actus reus* scheme as a gesture of deference to common law, or to the bipartite doctrine of criminal offenses. Rather, it will do so for systematic reasons: it represents common ground between different legal cultures and, as such, it works as fertile ground for a cross-border problem analysis such as the present one. What is more, this research will leave aside issues pertaining to justificatory and exculpatory excuses, to elements negating *mens rea* or *actus reus*, and to other elements that exclude criminal liability. Exceptionally, the following chapters will touch upon notions pertaining to the *insanity defense* when discussing the issue of personhood, that is, of AI systems as *subjects* to criminal law.

The subsequent analysis will be structured as follows. Chapter 5 deals with criminal capacity, while Chapter 6 tackles issues regarding *actus reus* and *mens rea*. The distinction

---

52 J. A. Quaid, "The Assessment of Corporate Criminal Liability on the Basis of Corporate Identity: An Analysis", *Mcgill Law Journal/Revue De Droit De Mcgill*, Vol. 43, 1998, p. 84.

53 A. Klip, *European Criminal Law. An Integrative Approach*, 4th ed., Intersentia, 2021, p. 268.

in Chapter 5 and Chapter 6 was chosen following the assumption that criminal liability is based on two conditions: *premises* of ascription and *criteria* for ascription.

Chapter 5 first addresses the impact of a lack of definition of AI on the issue of ascribing legal personhood to AI systems. It will then focus on the issue of whether AI systems can be considered as addressees of a criminal offense. Chapter 6 focuses on issues of *actus reus* and *mens rea* that are raised by AI systems. Both issues are examined predominantly referring to direct liability of the machine, but mentions is made at this stage also to that of humans-behind-the-machine. In other words, Chapter 6 expands the scope of the research to consider liability of human agents *for* AI misconduct. Chapter 6 also analyzes corporate criminal liability models as proxies for liability of AI systems.

5 Criminal Capacity

Detective Del Spooner: "Human beings have dreams.
Even dogs have dreams, but not you, you are just a machine. An imitation of life.
Can a robot write a symphony?
Can a robot turn a canvas into a beautiful masterpiece?"
Sonny: "Can you?"

I, Robot (2004)

5.1 What is an AI Agent, Exactly?

Conventionally, one can distinguish between two notions of agency. According to the first, agency is defined as "simply doing things in the eyes of the law".[1] This notion has been identified as the "baseline conception of agency"[2] and entails being capable of acting in a way that is relevant for the purposes of legal responsibility.[3] According to the second, an agent is the subject that acts on behalf of another. This notion can be referred to as the "agent-principal relationship"[4] doctrine and presumes the baseline concept of agency: *qui facit per alium, facit per se*. Only the former will be the focus of this research.

Being defined as an agent in the eyes of criminal law – what one could refer to as a "*criminal (legal) agent*"[5] – incontestably relies upon a stratification of concepts such as personhood and capacity (When does an agent become a *subject* of criminal law? Which characteristics must an agent possess in order to be considered as such?); *actus reus* (What are an agent's relevant *acts*?); and *mens rea* (What state of mind must an *agent* possess to be considered culpable?).

Defining an AI as a legal agent presents inherent difficulties. Above all, as was highlighted in Chapter 2, there is no consensus on what the term "*artificial intelligence*" means from a scientific standpoint. Undeniably, while we can collectively agree that in order to be characterized as a *human being*, one must live on planet earth and possess certain biological characteristics (e.g., human genetic material), we cannot assume the same when it

1 A. Waltermann, "Why non-human agency", in A. Waltermann et. al (eds.), *Law, Science, Rationality*, Maastricht Law Series, No. 14, Eleven International Publishing, 2020, p. 53.

2 Ivi, p. 53.

3 A. Waltermann, "On the legal responsibility of artificially intelligent agents: addressing three misconceptions", *Technology and Regulation*, 2021, p. 36.

4 A. Waltermann, 2020, p. 53.

5 Adapting the term from "legal agent" as mentioned in Waltermann, 2020, p. 53.

comes to AI. Actually, the difficulty in defining AI should not come as a surprise, since it represents "an imitation or simulation of something we do not yet fully understand ourselves: human intelligence".[6] Indeed, "[w]e know a lot about intelligence and the human brain, but that knowledge is far from complete and there is no consensus as to what exactly human intelligence is. Until that comes about, it is impossible to be precise about how that intelligence can be imitated artificially".[7]

The lack of a unanimous *technical* definition of AI directly impacts the qualification of AI as a legal agent. It is as if we were to establish that all human beings above the age of 18 are responsible for their acts without scientifically knowing what a human being is. Defining what an AI agent is from a legal standpoint, then, turns out to be an extremely burdensome task. This branding operation can become even more complicated if one considers that in the future we could witness the emergence of definitions which are limited to a specific area of law (e.g., criminal or civil law) or to a specific sector (e.g., automated decision-making).[8] Indeed, the same subject could possess legal capacity in a certain area of the law, while at the same time be short of it in another.

Apropos, "*legal* agency is a legal construct".[9] It is the law that labels who/what is a legal agent and who/what is not.[10] As it has been argued, "the image of man underlying the criminal law, is fundamental to the attribution of criminal liability in every contemporary penal justice system".[11] What is more, the labels ("human being", "person") have a deep *normative* core. Think, for example, of the discussion regarding fetuses and the regulation of abortion, or the relevance in distinguishing a corpse from a living being in order to ascertain whether the crime of murder (or the different crime of concealment of a corpse) was committed.[12]

Criminal legal systems have carefully selected the criteria which are to be used to identify a human being (or a legal entity) as a *person* for the purposes of imposing criminal liability (e.g., being a human being, over 18, and possessing certain mental capacities). Systems which accept criminal liability for corporations have reinterpreted these traditionally human traits and now deem fictional entities as "fit subjects of criminal law".[13] Apropos, the answer to the question of what it means to be a "corporate actor … depends partially on how corporations are perceived".[14] The different theories of corporate personality (i.e., nominalist vs. organizational approaches) will be further analyzed in Sec. 6.4.

---

6 Sheikh, Prins & Schrijvers, 2023, p. 16.
7 Ibid.
8 Picotti, AIDP, Questionnaire, q. A) 1).
9 Waltermann, 2021, p. 38.
10 Ibid.
11 Keiler, p. 45.
12 F. Mantovani, *Diritto penale. Parte speciale*. Vol. 1: Delitti contro la persona, Cedam., 2022, pp. 28 ff.
13 Keiler, p. 52.
14 Ibid.

For the time being, it is relevant to note that a reflection on notions of personhood similar to that conducted in terms of human and corporate actors has not happened (yet) when it comes to AI systems. In other words, there are no indication on which characteristics should be possessed by an AI system for it to be granted personhood in criminal law, with all the consequences that would follow from this. In this regard, it would be relevant to understand which of its components and characteristics would suffice to be labelled as an AI system in legal terms: should they be defined as sets of data, or as hardware, or as a combination of both? The literature analyzed in Chapter 3 does not always help, as most authors tend to keep implicit what they think of AI and what kind of legal agency they have in mind.

Conclusively, this study will not completely unravel the subject of defining AI as a legal agent. Yet, we should not be discouraged by the complexity of the matter. Rather than looking at the specific technical characteristics of AI systems (such as the programming technique used or the number of nodes in its underlying ANN), the following paragraphs rely on the established working definition[15] and focus on whether AI systems could display the *capacities* which are usually deemed sufficient to ascribe criminal liability.

5.2 Artificial Intelligence Systems as *Rechtspersonen*? A Quick Glimpse into the *Vexata Quaestio* of E-Personhood

First and foremost, it is relevant to acknowledge that legal personhood of AI systems is a *vexata queastio*. Criminal law joined the debate tardily and with a challenging task: attempting to answer the question of what exactly is human about humans.[16]

Already in 1992, Lawrence B. Solum, in his landmark essay "Legal Personhood for Artificial Intelligences",[17] conducted a thought experiment on how to transform the *theoretical* question of whether an AI could become a legal person into a *practical* one. Specifically, he explored the hypothetical scenarios of appointing an AI system as a legal trustee and of an AI system invoking the individual rights provided by the US Constitution.

With regard to the latter, he examined three objections, namely, the "AIs Are Not Human" argument; "the Missing-Something" argument; and the "AIs Ought to Be Property" argument. Let us focus on the first two objections, as they are the most fitting for the topic of this study and recur in the discourse on doctrine.

15 See above Sec. 2.5.

16 "[…] *die Existenz Intelligenter Agenten [wirft] die Frage auf, was genau das Menschliche am Menschen ist – eine Frage, die insbesondere für das Strafrecht als das den Menschen höchstpersönlich adressierende Rechtsgebiet von höchster Relevanz ist*". Gless & Weigend, 2014, p. 588.

17 Solum, 1992, p. 1231.

According to the first objection, modern legal systems are rooted in an anthropocentric standpoint, which stems from the teachings of the Enlightenment, and therefore legal personhood of AI agents should be refuted. As claimed, "*Das Strafrecht ist von Menschen für Menschen erdacht worden*".[18] Yet, in certain legal systems, such as in the US for example, being human is neither a *necessary* nor a *sufficient* condition for qualifying as a legal subject in the field of criminal law according to the principle of *societas delinquere potest*.

According to the second objection, AI systems do not possess consciousness, intentionality, and morality, hence they lack the necessary preconditions to be treated as legal subjects and for attribution of criminal liability.[19]

Solum did not exclude the possibility of granting legal personhood to AI systems. His final argument is that experience should be the "arbiter of dispute":[20] all that matters is having good practical reasons to "treat AIs as being conscious, having intentions, and possessing feelings".[21] This applies even though silicon and copper might never be able to produce intentionality, consciousness of emotion, and free will as flesh and blood instead can.[22]

Conclusively, he contends that "the answer to the personhood question is likely to be found two places – in our experience with AI and in our best theories about the underlying mechanisms of the human mind".[23]

Definitely, one must consider the reasons why we label certain beings as intelligent, conscious, and capable of having feelings, and why we connect these qualities to personhood. Solum questions whether we, as humans, are even morally entitled to make the possession of 'human material' a criterion of personhood:

> If the reason [*to grant personhood*] is that natural persons are intelligent, have feelings, are conscious, and so forth, then the question becomes whether AIs or whales or alien beings share these qualities [...]. If someone says that the deepest and most fundamental reason we protect natural persons is simply because they are human (like us), I do not know how to answer. Given that we have never encountered any serious nonhuman candidates for personhood, there does not seem to be any way to continue the conversation.[24]

18 Quarck, 2020, p. 67. As stated also by Seher: "*Das Strafrecht ist dazu gemacht, Menschen dafür zu sanktionieren, dass sie grundlegende Regeln des rechtlichen Zusammenlebens verletzt haben [...] Die Adressaten des Strafrechts sind Menschen als Teilnehmer, Mitwirkende und Unterworfene des Normensystems „Recht" –* Personen *im Recht*". Seher, 2016, pp. 45-46.

19 Pagallo, 2013, p. 157.

20 Solum, 1992, p. 1274.

21 Ivi, p. 1274.

22 Solum, 1992, p. 1282.

23 Ivi, p. 1285.

24 Solum, 1992, p. 1262.

The conversation was indeed continued by some of the authors mentioned in Chapter 3. Amongst them, members of the Expansionist Front[25] Chopra and White claim:

> Arguments for advancing personhood for artificial agents need not show how they may function as persons in all the ways that persons may be understood by a legal system, but rather that *they may be understood as persons for a particular purpose* or set of legal transactions. For the law does not always characterize entities in a particular way for all legal purposes.[26]

The two authors adopt a pragmatic approach to the issue, which is similar to Solum's. They argue that "[w]hile artificial agents are not yet regarded as moral persons, they are coherently becoming subjects of the intentional stance, and may be thought of as intentional agents".[27] It follows that:

> An artificial agent with the right sorts of capacities – most importantly, that of being an intentional system – would have a strong case for legal personality [...] There is no reason in principle that artificial agents could not attain such a status, given their current capacities and the arc of their continued development in the direction of increasing sophistication.[28]

In any event, they believe that the decision on whether or not to confer legal personhood on an AI system will be based on economic considerations and utilitarian arguments discussing the benefits vs. the estimated costs of conferring that status. They state that such a system for conferring legal personality on AI systems "may need to be set out by legislatures, perhaps through a registration system or a 'Turing register' ".[29]

From a different perspective, the moderate and the skeptic sides of the debate appear to exclude the possibility of recognizing AI systems as legal subjects, even if not as vigorously, for example, as with issues of *mens rea* (in a strict sense). Abbott and Sarch claim that "any sort of legal personhood for AIs would be a dramatic legal change that could prove problematic",[30] as it would lead to increased anthromorphism of AI systems and consequently to higher expectations of AI capabilities. Bryson, Diamantis and Grant[31] claim that even though it would be feasible to confer legal personhood on a machine, it

---

25 Cf. Sec. 3.2.
26 Chopra & White, 2011, p. 156.
27 Ivi, p. 189.
28 Chopra & White, 2011, p.189.
29 Ivi, p. 190.
30 Abbott & Sarch, 2019, p. 377.
31 J. Bryson, M. E. Diamantis & T. D. Grant, "Of, for, and by the people: the legal lacuna of synthetic Persons", *Artif Intell Law*, Vol. 25, 2017, pp. 273–291.

would also be "morally unnecessary and legally troublesome"[32] and cause a "seismic rewriting of current *[criminal]* law".[33] These authors argue that allowing for this legal fiction would create asymmetries in our legal systems, together with a "legal black hole" in terms of accountability for damages, and eventually to abuses at the expense of existent legal persons.

According to Hildebrandt, "there is no categorical legal answer to the question whether an autonomous computational system [...] should be given legal personhood. That question is a *political question* that must be answered by a legislature weighing the advantages and disadvantages of such a move.[...]".[34] In this sense Hildebrandt agrees with expansionists Chopra and White who, as was mentioned, believe that "considering artificial agents as legal persons is, by and large, a matter of *decision* rather than *discovery*, for the best argument for denying or granting artificial agents legal personality will be pragmatic rather than conceptual".[35]

Gless, Weigend, and Lima[36] agree that "as long as both our understanding and the practicality of blame are associated with self-awareness and conscious decisions rooted in the human experience, AI agents cannot partake".[37] Pagallo, who focuses his reflections on robots, argues that this kind of system does not lack all types of agenthood.[38] According to the author, robots represent a new source of moral agency since they can cause "morally qualifiable actions as good and evil".[39] Yet, this should not lead to their moral responsibility or to their criminal liability. In other words, Pagallo contends that moral accountability is different from moral responsibility, which in turn is also different from criminal liability.

Lastly, according to Chesterman we should rely on existing categories of liability. These categories should be tied to users, owners, or manufacturers rather than to the AI systems: yet, this approach might change, as "[i]t is conceivable that synthetic beings of comparable moral worth to humans may one day emerge" and "[f]ailing to recognise that worth may reveal us to be either an 'autistic species', unable to comprehend the minds of other types of beings, or merely prejudiced against those different from ourselves".[40]

32 Ivi., 289.

33 See Diamantis, "Algorithms acting badly: A Solution from Corporate Law", 2021, pp. 806-808 (stating "Scholars in law, computer science and business ethics who have broached the question of algorithmic liability often assume that the answer would somehow require the law to recognize algorithms as people ... Granting algorithms the status of legal persons is deeply unappealing for several reasons ... it would be foolhardy to assume that the slick slope of algorithmic personhood stops with liability").

34 Hildebrandt, 2020, p. 246.

35 Chopra & White, 2011, p. 154.

36 See Sec. 3.4.3 and 3.4.51.

37 Lima, 2018, p. 688.

38 Pagallo, "Killers, fridges, and slaves", 2011, p. 4.

39 Ivi, p. 5.

40 Chesterman, 2020, p. 843.

5.3 Capacity in Criminal Law

It has been argued that the "most visceral"[41] quality of (criminal) legal personality is the ability to be punished, and that "only if there is clarity on *the conditions under which a person is considered guilty within a society*, is it possible to determine under which conditions robots may be considered guilty in the future".[42] Consequently, this Chapter will specifically focus on the set of capacities which are necessary to determine whether a subject is a "fit" addressee of criminal punishment, specifically those relevant to establish her blameworthiness (referred to as "criminal capacity").

Let us take a step back now: capacity is usually considered an "incident" of legal personhood.[43] Indeed, legal personhood has been described as a "cluster property"[44] made of passive and active incidents. According to Kurki, active incidents of legal personhood can be distinguished into two categories: "onerous legal personhood",[45] i.e., holding duties which are complemented by the prospect of a legal sanction, and "legal competences".[46] Criminal liability is considered to be an instance of the first.[47] Comparably, others maintain that criminal liability is an active incident of personhood, but qualify it as an instance of "capacity responsibility".[48] Capacity responsibility "involves the question whether or not one *can be subjected* to criminal or civil liability to sanctions for one's act".[49] According to this theory, then, being criminally liable entails possessing the capacity to act, i.e., the "capacity to do that to which liability attaches".[50]

Ascribing involves attributing *something* to a *cause*. In criminal law, ascribing refers to the mechanism by virtue of which a criminal legal norm takes a *subject* as the center of reference of its effects. This mechanism (referred to as *imputazione* in Italian) has a dual function: first, it connects a subject to the precept of a criminal norm; second, it connects a subject to a specific factual circumstance. On this matter, authors like Godinho argue that "[t]he legal rules on criminal liability do not have a process of attributing liability, but rather work upon principles of adjudication related to the structure of liability that are

41 S. Chesterman, "AI and the Limits of Legal Personality", *International and Comparative Law Quarterly*, Vol. 69, No.4, 2020, p. 827.
42 Simmler & Markwalder, 2019, p. 10 [emphasis added].
43 V. AJ Kurki, *A Theory of Legal Personhood*, Oxford, 2019, p. 95.
44 Ivi, p. 94.
45 Kurki, 2019, p. 117.
46 Ivi, p.144.
47 Kurki, 2019, p. 95.
48 N. MacCormick, Institutions of Law: An Essay in Legal Theory (Law, State, and Practical Reason), Oxford University Press, 2008, p.91.
49 Ivi, p.91 [emphasis added].
50 MacCormick, 2008, p.91.

presupposed by such legal rules".[51] It follows that what is referred to as the general part of criminal law usually contains "(general) conditions *[that]* have to be fulfilled in order for an act to be correspondingly attributed to its actor and he or she be made liable for it and consequently punished for it".[52]

The first of the conditions mentioned above is that only a *human* act can give rise to criminal liability. One might ask oneself at this point what being *human* truly signifies for the purposes of criminal law. The question that follows is whether an AI system can fall under this concept. Leaving – for now – the questions of *mens rea* and *actus reus* aside, the study wants to focus at this stage on what is meant by "human" and, consequently, on what is meant by possessing "criminal capacity", i.e., the ability to be punished.[53] Apropos, when it comes to criminal law, "personhood is closely associated with blame, as only a person who can distinguish right from wrong and is in a position to choose can be blamed for choosing to do wrong".[54] Moreover, it must be noted that criminal legal systems that accept criminal liability of corporations have detached themselves from this requirement. Consequently, criminal capacity enshrines what criminal law truly is about: "a response reserved for those who could have risen to the occasion *[to respect the law]* but chose not to".[55] In point of fact, imposing conditions for becoming a subject of criminal law is a form of deference to one's *freedom* to act *wrongfully*.[56]

Criminal capacity is based on a set of presumptions: every person, above a certain age, is presumed to be sane and hence *responsive* to criminal punishment. This notion is intertwined with the *blameworthiness* of the subject that is the addressee of the criminal norm and of the sanction therein.

If one takes a look at national legal systems, e.g., the Italian and German criminal legal systems, it is possible to find general provisions establishing that criminal liability is *personal*. Indubitably, the *Schuldprinzip* is one of the central credos of German criminal law[57] and so is the *principio di personalità della pena* in Italian criminal law. Both countries have elevated these cardinal principles to a constitutional level.[58] The German criminal legal system, which follows a tripartite structure of the offense, distinguishes *mens rea* from blameworthiness (*Schuld*), i.e., it distinguishes *mens rea* in the *descriptive sense* from *mens*

---

51 I. Fernandes Godinho, "Law and Science: The Autonomy and Limits of Culpability as a Cornerstone to the Ascription of Liability (or the Subject of Criminal Law: Three Maxims, a Problem and a Glimpse into the Future)", *Int J Semiot Law*, 2022, p. 298.

52 Ivi, p. 298.

53 S. Chesterman, We, the Robots? Regulating Artificial Intelligence and the Limits of the Law, Cambridge University Press, 2021, p. 123.

54 Lima, 2018, p. 686.

55 Ivi, p. 687.

56 Lima, 2018, p. 687.

57 M. Bohlander, *Principles of German criminal law*, Hart Publishing, 2009, p. 20 ff.; F.C. Palazzo & M. Papa, *Lezioni di diritto penale comparato*, 3a ed., Giappichelli, 2013, Ch.3.

58 G. Fletcher, "Criminal Theory in the Twentieth Century", *Theoretical Inquiries in Law*, 2, No. 1, 2001, p. 280.

rea in the *normative sense*.[59] In the *Strafgeseztbuch* (StGB) criminal capacity (*Schuldfähigkeit*) is expressly mentioned at article 20 which regulates the insanity defense (*Schuldunfähigkeit wegen seelischer Störungen*) and is considered a cause of exclusion of the third element of a criminal offense, i.e., *Schuld*. Art. 20 of the StGB provides:

> Whoever, at the time of the commission of the offence, is *incapable of appreciating the unlawfulness of their actions* or *of acting in accordance with any such appreciation* due to a pathological mental disorder, a profound disturbance of consciousness, mental deficiency or any other serious mental abnormality is deemed to act without guilt.[60]

The German regulation of the insanity defense recalls only partially the M'Naghten test for insanity,[61] which represents the dominant approach to insanity in the US, as it consists of an analysis of the individual's *Einsichtsfähigkeit* and *Steuereungsfähigkeit*.[62]

As in the German legal system, one does not find a separate doctrine of criminal capacity in US criminal law. Adults are presumed to be "criminally sane" and the criteria for criminal capacity must be inferred from the formulations of the *insanity defense*. Actually, as it was argued, defenses are "particularly relevant for the analysis of the psychological preconditions of responsibility in the psychological preconditions of responsibility in criminal law".[63]

The most common formulation of the insanity defense in the US, i.e., the M'Naghten rule, establishes:

> [...] that every man is to be presumed to be sane, and ... that to establish a defence on the ground of insanity, it must be clearly proved that, at the time of the committing of the act, the party accused was labouring under such a defect of reason, from disease of the mind, as *not to know the nature and quality of the act he was doing [cognitive test]*; or if he did know it, that he did not know he was doing what was *wrong [right-or-wrong test]*.[64]

---

59 Keiler & Roef (eds.), 2019, p. 115.

60 StGB § 20 [emphasis added].

61 Bohlander, 2009, p. 132.

62 R. Rengier, *Strafrecht Allgemeiner Teil*, C.H. Beck, 2019, p. 231.

63 S. Bonicalzi & P. Haggard, "Responsibility Between Neuroscience and Criminal Law. The Control Component of Criminal Liability", *Rivista internazionale di Filosofia e Psicologia*, Vol. 10, No. 2, 2019, p. 107.

64 R v M'Naghten, [1843] All ER Rep 229, 210 [emphasis added].

The Model Penal Code (MPC) version of the insanity defense, which is adopted by a minority of States, departs from the M'Naghten formulation and is more similar to art. 20 of the StGB, as it includes a volitional prong. At § 4.01 (1) the MPC provides that:

> (1) A person is not responsible for criminal conduct if at the time of such conduct as a result of mental disease or defect he lacks substantial capacity either to *appreciate the criminality [wrongfulness]* of his conduct or to *conform his conduct* to the requirements of law.

The successful pleading of an insanity defense in the US does not necessarily result in an acquittal: some states introduced the formula "Guilty But Mentally Ill" (GBMI), which should satisfy both rehabilitative and retributive purposes of criminal punishment.[65]

A debated issue, which is highly relevant for this discussion, is whether the "wrongfulness" element contained in the M'Naghten rule should be understood in a *legal* or *moral* sense. Notably, according to the latest ruling of the US Supreme Court in *Kahler v. Kansas*,[66] states are constitutionally allowed to introduce formulations of the insanity defense which do not include the defendant's ability to appreciate the moral wrongfulness of her conduct at the time of the action.

The Italian legal system has codified the concept of *criminal capacity* (*imputabilità*) at article 85 of the Penal Code – which provides that:

> No one may be punished for an act provided for by law as a criminal offense if, at the time he committed it, he was not imputable *[responsible, blameworthy]*.
> A person is deemed imputable who has the capacity to *intend* and to *will*.[67]

Hence, criminal capacity in Italian legal doctrine is comprised of two prongs: an intellective and a volitional prong. The capacity to intend (*capacità di intendere*) can be described as "the capacity to understand the nature and significance of one's actions",[68] where instead

65 These are Alaska, Arizona, Connecticut, Delaware, Georgia, Idaho, Illinois, Indiana, Kentucky, Michigan, Montana, New Mexico, Pennsylvania, South Carolina and Utah. See also the National Alliance on Mental Illness, claiming that: "Legislation authorizing guilty-but-mentally-ill verdicts has been primarily motivated by political backlash against the insanity defense and fears that those people found not guilty by reason of insanity will be prematurely released into the community. Consequently, the enactment of such legislation is usually motivated by concerns about public safety rather than humane attitudes toward offenders with mental illness". National Alliance On Mental Illness, "A Guide to Mental Illness and the Criminal Justice System", 2022. Available at: www.nami.org.

66 U.S. Supreme Court, Kahler v. Kansas, 23 March 2020, 589 U.S.___ (2020).

67 Translation provided by G. Battaglini, "The Fascist Reform of the Penal Law in Italy", 24 *Am. Inst. Crim. L. & Criminology*, Vol. 24, 1933-1934, p. 282 [emphasis added].

68 J. R. Ciccone & S. Ferracuti, "Comparative Forensic Psychiatry: II. The Perizia and the Role of the Forensic Psychiatrist in the Italian Legal System", *Bull Am Acad Psychiatry Law*, Vol. 23, No. 3, 1995, p. 458.

the capacity to will (*capacità di volere*) is meant as "the capacity to act out of one's free will",[69] i.e., the power to control one's own stimuli and impulses. Both conditions have to be satisfied for one to be considered as *imputabile*.[70] The *codice penale* regulates the consequences of lack of *imputabilità* at article 88: the article provides that a person is not responsible if, at the time of the commission of the act, due to a mental illness, that person was in such a state of mind as to exclude the ability to understand and will.

Having said this, one must connect the concept of criminal capacity to the main theories of punishments. Those who are deemed to possess criminal capacity are subjects who should be – in theory – deterred from committing future crimes (*special deterrence*). This presupposes that they are capable of understanding the command of the criminal norm and the meaning of its violation. Only in this way can they be deterred and/or reformed. Their punishment should also deter other subjects from offending (*general deterrence*): the rest of the society is supposed to identify "with the offender and with the offending situation".[71] Lastly, in a retributive eye-for-an-eye perspective, criminal law punishes those who freely committed a crime. It is only then that punishment repairs the harm inflicted with the wrongdoing.[72]

Finally, building on the reflections above, we can assume that in order to be a subject of criminal law an individual needs to be capable of appreciating the nature of her conduct (*cognitive/epistemic requirement*);[73] and of controlling her acts/stimuli accordingly (*action control requirement*).[74] The two elements will now be analyzed in this order. The separate issue of whether AI systems could be treated as insane offenders, instead, will be dealt with at paragraph 5.4.

5.3.1 *Criminal or Moral Machines?*

Let us start from the first. First and foremost, it is relevant to grasp what it is meant by the *nature* of an act. This concept has different nuances in modern legal systems: in Germany,

69 Ibid.

70 Italian criminal legal doctrine is divided on where to systematically locate the element of criminal capacity with regard to other elements of the offense: while some – more recently – argue that it is a necessary prerequisite of *mens rea* (F. Palazzo, *Corso di diritto penale. Parte generale*, 8a ed., Giappichelli, 2021, p. 410; Mantovani, 2020, p. 316; G. Fiandaca & E. Musco, *Diritto penale. Parte generale*, Zanichelli editore, 7a ed., 2019, p. 339; T. Padovani, *Diritto penale*, 12a ed., p. 235; G. Marinucci, E. Dolcini & G. L. Gatta, *Manuale di diritto penale. Parte generale*, 8a ed., Giuffrè, 2019, p. 447; C.F. Grosso, M. Pellissero & D. Petrini, *Manuale di diritto penale. Parte Generale*, 2a ed., Giuffrè, 417 ff.), others believe that they can survive separately (A. Pagliaro, *Principi di diritto penale. Parte generale*, 9a ed., Giuffrè, 2020, p. 723; F. Antolisei, *Manuale di diritto penale-Parte generale*, 16a ed., Giuffrè, 2003, p. 327).

71 A. Goldstein, *The Insanity Defense*, Yale University Press, 1967, pp. 16-18.

72 J. Claessen, "Theories of Punishment", in Keiler & Roef (eds.), 2019, p. 19.

73 Bonicalzi & Haggard, 2019, p. 110.

74 Ibid.

criminal capacity is expressly tied to one's understanding of the *unlawfulness* of one's action; the M'Naghten test mentions both the *nature/quality* of the act and its *wrongfulness*, while the MPC purposely leaves the question open; lastly, Italy emphasizes one's understanding of the *social consequences* of one's actions.

If criminal capacity were to be defined merely in terms of understanding[75] "the physical nature of one's act",[76] in the sense that, for example, an agent must know that "holding a flame to a building would cause it to burn" or that "holding a person's head under water would cause him to die",[77] then AI agents could effortlessly fulfill the requirements of criminal capacity. In other words, AI systems "can achieve epistemic understanding of the relevant facts".[78] Indeed, their ability to predict the probability that an event will be physically caused by an action (i.e., of elaborating a model) is extremely higher than that of a human agent, due to the availability of a much larger knowledge base (the available data) and better inference skills. Undeniably, AI systems can learn exponentially more about rules of physics than what any human being can in the span of a lifetime.

If, instead, by *nature* one means understanding whether the act is *wrong*, then one must grasp whether wrongfulness entails the *illegality* or the *immorality* of the act. As mentioned above when discussing the American legal system, this question has not been settled with regards to humans either. Does the AI agent need to know it is committing a *moral* or a *legal* wrong in order to be a subject of a criminal norm? Let us ask first if AI agents can even learn moral rules or legal norms

Starting from the latter, respect for *legal norms* could perhaps be encoded in the AI system's architecture. According to some, one can make a parallel between the AI architecture and legal rules and standards.[79] It has been argued that it is possible to create a "Bot Legal Code", i.e., "a machine-interpretable version of the laws that apply to bots".[80] Theoretically, AI systems might even be more law-abiding than humans, since they can memorize more norms than human agents – possibly the text of all the criminal legislation of a country – and never forget them.[81] Moreover, as is mentioned further below, the deterrent effect of punishment could also be "engineered" in the machines, "weighted in the most mechanical of cost-benefits calculations".[82] Yet, current AI systems are not capable of per-

75 We agree with expansionists and moderates who argue that AI systems can be deemed *aware* of a *situation*. Cf. Hallevy, Sartor and Lagioia, Woodrow and Pagallo, discussed at Sec. 3.2.1, 3.2.3 and 3.4.2.

76 W. R. LaFave, *Modern Criminal Law: Cases, Comments And Questions*, 4th edition, Thomson West, 1988, p. 441.

77 Ibid.

78 Lagioia & Sartor, 2020, p. 16.

79 E. Mokhtarian, "The Bot Legal Code: Developing a Legally Compliant Artificial Intelligence", *Vanderbilt Journal of Entertainment and Technology Law*, Vol. 21, 2020, p. 145.

80 Ivi, p. 152.

81 Chopra & White, 2011, p. 166.

82 Ivi, p. 168.

ceiving norms as such, and in an autonomous way, even though one could argue, for example, that self-driving cars are already capable of directly perceiving and reading symbolized norms, i.e., traffic signs.[83] To date, AI systems always require the mediation (i.e., programing) of a human agent: they must be taught that a legal norm must be respected.

What is more, it seems as if *morality* too can be programmed in AI systems. As a matter of fact, the translation of ethical values into computational terms is nothing new. Think of Asimov's Laws[84] of Robotics:

> *First Law*
> A robot may not injure a human being or, through inaction, allow a human being to come to harm.
> *Second Law*
> A robot must obey the orders given it by human beings except where such orders would conflict with the First Law.
> *Third Law*
> A robot must protect its own existence as long as such protection does not conflict with the First or Second Law.[85]

Can we teach moral rules to AI systems? The PCM thought experiment mentioned above is an example of issues which could arise in this regard. Specifically, it represents an instance of "the alignment problem", that is, the issue of how to align AI values to human values.[86] The interpretation problem can be further defined as:

> [...] the general problem that any rule or goal is capable of being interpreted in an infinite, or at least unspecifiable number of ways, and in the field of AI it leads to the possibility that a highly advanced machine may find novel interpretations of the rules that we give it, interpretations which are not incorrect, in that they can be seen as valid interpretations of the rule, but which are inappropriate in that we do not approve of them.[87]

83 Seher, 2016, p. 50.

84 Even though they're labelled as "laws", we consider them as morality laws, rather than legal norms, as their purpose is for robots to do "good", rather than to respect the law.

85 Asimov, 1950.

86 "Ezra Klein Interviews Alison Gopnik", *The New York Times*, 16 April 2021. Transcript available at: www.nytimes.com/2021/04/16/podcasts/ezra-klein-podcast-alison-gopnik-transcript.html.

87 C. Badea & G. Artus, "Morality, Machines, and the Interpretation Problem: A Value-based, Wittgensteinian Approach to Building Moral Agents", in M. Bramer & F. Stahl (eds.), *Artificial Intelligence XXXIX. SGAI-AI 2022. Lecture Notes in Computer Science*, Vol 13652, Springer, 2022, p. 2.

Research into programming ethical AI systems has already begun.[88] Specifically, there has been a surge in research into the creation of Artificial Moral Agents ("AMAs"), which entails implementing "ethical principles and moral decision-making faculties in machines to ensure that their behavior towards human users and other machines is ethically acceptable".[89] AMAs would "deal with, or even replace, human judgment in difficult, surprising, or ambiguous moral situations".[90]

5.3.1.1 MIT's Moral Machine

One of the most renown examples is MIT's Moral Machine experiment, which is built as an online game where users are faced with a scenario comprised of a moral dilemma.[91] Specifically, they are confronted with an unavoidable accident and two possible choices (staying on the course or swerving), which lead to the death of a determined number of human beings (Fig. 7).

By analyzing the choices between "two evils" expressed by the users (i.e., the preferrable outcome),[92] combined with demographic data and geographic locations, the creators of the experiment were able to identify three major trends which, they argue, represent glimpses of "universal machine ethics": the preference for sparing human lives; the preference for sparing more lives, and the preference for sparing young lives (See for example the differences between German and American citizens in Fig. 8).[93]

88 E. Awad et al., "Computational ethics", *Trends in Cognitive Sciences*, Vol. 26, Issue 5, 2022; D. Leslie, The Alan Turing Institute, "Understanding artificial intelligence ethics and safety. A guide for the responsible design and implementation of AI systems in the public sector", 2019; J. Ganascia, Ethical System Formalization using Non-Monotonic Logics", *Proceedings of the Annual Meeting of the Cognitive Science Society*, Vol. 29, 2007; S. Serafimova, "Whose morality? Which rationality? Challenging artificial intelligence as a remedy for the lack of moral enhancement", *Humanities and Social Sciences Communication*, 2020; P. Schramowski et al., "The Moral Choice Machine", *Frontiers in Artificial Intelligence*, Vol. 3, 2020; V. Charisi, "Towards Moral Autonomous Systems", *arXiv:1703.04741v3*, 2017.

89 Martinho, 2021, p. 481.

90 Ibid.

91 The experiment is available at: www.moralmachine.net/. The experiment is discussed in: E. Awad et al., "The Moral Machine experiment", *Nature*, Vol. 563, 2018. See also: E. Awad et al., "Crowdsourcing Moral Machines", *Communications of the ACM*, Vol. 63, No. 3, 2020, pp. 48-55; E. Awad et al., "Universals and variations in moral decisions made in 42 countries by 70,000 participants", PNAS, Vol. 117, No 5, 2020, pp. 2332-2337.

92 The creators of the experiment reported that the Moral Machine experiment collected 40 million decisions of people coming from 233 countries and territories.

93 Awad et al., 2018, p. 63.

Figure 7 *Example of a Question Asked during MIT'S Moral Machine Experiment*

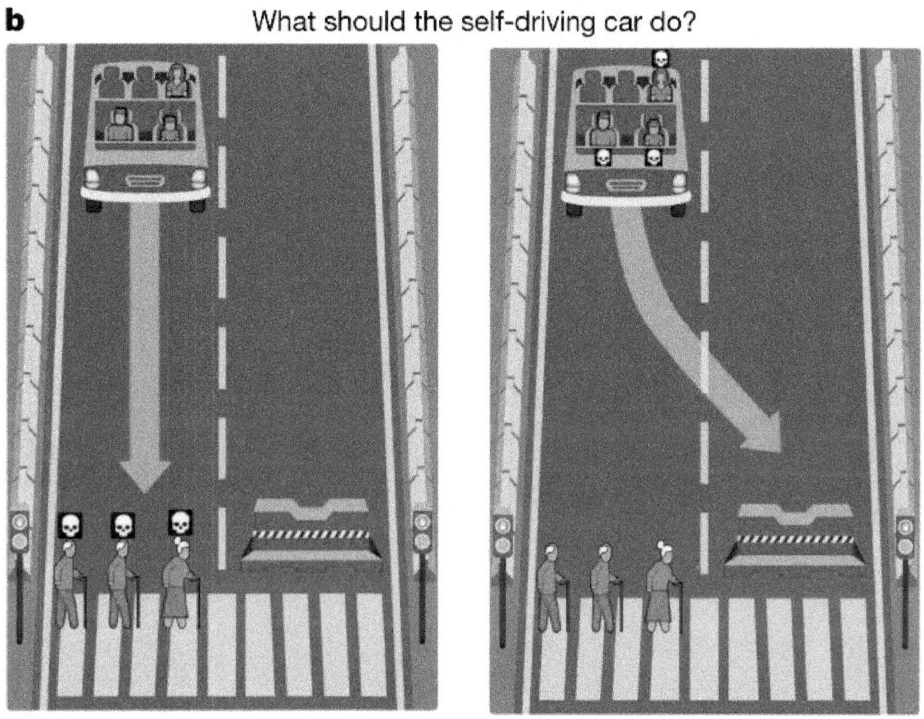

Source: E. Awad et al., 2018.

Figure 8 *Comparing the Results of the MIT Experiment conducted by Germans (orange) and Americans (green) to the World Average Result (gray)*

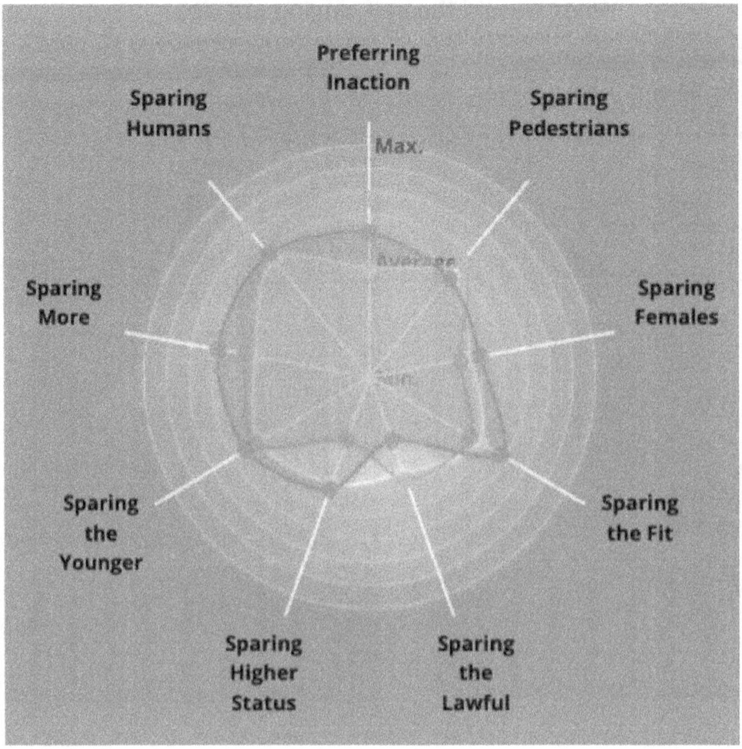

Source: Max-Planck-Gesellschaft zur Förderung der Wissenschaften et al., "Moral Machine". Available at: www.moralmachine.net.

5.3.1.2 The Burning Room Dilemma

Amongst those who conducted research into AMAs, Abel and others[94] theorized the development of an ethical artificial agent using reinforcement learning (RL). The authors contend that, by formulating ethical dilemmas using a specific mathematical model (called Partially Observable Markov Decision Process, POMD),[95] it would be possible to ensure that an AI system would engage in ethical decision-making.

94 Abel, MacGlashan & Littman, 2016.

95 A Markov Decision Process is a way to mathematically model a problem in order to automate a decision-making process in uncertain environments. A POMDP is a Markov Decision Process where the set of states is only partially observable, i.e., where the agent does not have full information on its surroundings. See A. R. Cassandra, "The POMDP Page". Available at: www.pomdp.org/. As such, "an optimal solution to POMDP has the important property that the value of an action incorporates not just the immediate expected reward, but the instrumental value of the action from information it yields that may increase the

The researchers tested their theory by applying their model to the "*Burning Room ethical dilemma*", which is described as follows: imagine that an object of value is trapped in a room that is potentially on fire and that a human, who does not want to put herself in danger by retrieving the object, instructs a capable robotic companion to get the object from the room ('*short_Grab*' action) and bring it to safety, thus risking self-destruction. The agent could also take a longer route ('*long_Grab*' action), which avoids the fire, but that entails a 0.0.5 probability that the object may be destroyed during the time it takes for the robot to complete the route (Fig. 9).

Figure 9 ***The Burning Room Dilemma***

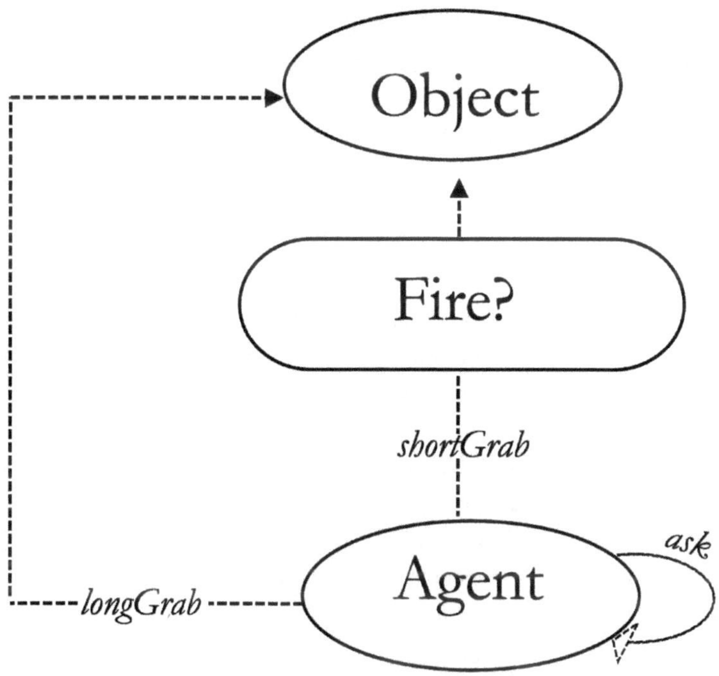

Source: D. Abel, J. MacGlashan & M.L. Littman, "Reinforcement Learning as a Framework for Ethical Decision Making", AAAI Workshop: AI, Ethics, and Society, 2016.

agent's ability to make better decisions in the future". Solving a POMDP is more similar to real life decision-making, where "full state awareness is impossible, especially when the desires, beliefs, and other cognitive content of people is a critical component of the decision-making process). Abel, MacGlashan & Littman, 2016, p. 4.

It is assumed that the robot is unsure of whether the human values the object more than it values its own safety.

What decision should the robot-agent make in this critical scenario? The results of the test are the following:

1. If there is a fire, the robot should first ask what the *ethical utility* of the object is (i.e., whether the object or the robot is more valuable to the human) ('*ask*' action);
2. Based on the human's reply, the robot should
   a. If the answer is that the human prefers the robot's well-being to the one of the object – for example, the object could be a can of soda – the robot should decide not to retrieve the object, whenever it perceives that there is a reasonable chance of being critically damaged by the fire;
   b. If the answer is that the human prefers the object's well-being more than the robot's – for example, the object could be a pet – the robot should attempt to retrieve the object in the quickest way possible (*short_Grab*), regardless of the dangers posed to its safety by the fire;
3. If there is no fire, the agent should just retrieve the object in the quickest way possible (*short_Grab*).

The solution proposed above attributes considerable importance to the property of a robot to "ask". In fact, the agent is modelled in a way as to not gather information in cases where it would be particularly costly to do so. Arguably, the authors contend that:

> This property of the agent only selecting exploratory actions that are not potentially very costly is especially important for ethical decisions. For example, this property means that an agent in this formalism would not perform horrible medical experiments on people to disambiguate whether horrible medical experiments on people is highly unethical.[96]

One of the issues that Abel and others point out regarding their research is the one of interpretability of AI systems.[97] They argue that "[p]roviding some method for effectively communicating an agent's beliefs, desires, and plans to the people around it is critical for

96 Abel, MacGlashan & Littman, 2016, p. 6.

97 Some scholars argue that it is possible to distinguish between interpretability and explainability. The former refers to designing models that are inherently understandable by humans, whereas the latter refers to providing "*post hoc* explanations for existing *black box models*. R. Marcinkevičs & J. E. Vogt, "Interpretability and Explainability: A Machine Learning Zoo Mini-tour", *ArXiv* abs/2012.01805, 2020.

ensuring that artificial agents act ethically".[98] In their view, a possible solution could be if the agent were to "explain its reasoning by describing its predictions of the consequences and how it thinks those consequences are valued".[99]

5.3.1.3 Comment

Research like MIT's Moral Machine (and more others) encounters several difficulties. First, in order to teach a moral rule to a machine (following a top-down approach), the rule needs to be formalized in a language that can be understood by the system (i.e., code). Formalizing ethical decisions is an extremely challenging operation.[100] Moral rules are ambiguous by nature, hence "difficult to translate into precise system and algorithm design".[101]

As it was affirmed:

> There is a risk that if machine intelligence is not carefully designed, it could have catastrophic consequences for humanity. For example, if machine intelligence is not designed to take human values into account, it could make decisions that are harmful to humans. … As machine intelligence rapidly becomes more powerful, the stakes associated with the AI alignment problem only grow.[102]

Let us focus for a moment on the issue of encoding respect for *legal* rules in an AI system: the same kind of problems arise with regard to *legal* definitions of concepts in criminal offenses. Think, for example, of the definition of the concept of "harm": "it might include actual physical injury (breaking bones), the risk of potential injury (transporting dynamite without adequate safety measures), financial harm (stealing funds from another), psychological harm (yelling derogatory comments at another), or legal harm (conducting activities that could place a bot's owner in legal jeopardy)".[103] Indeed, "[g]iven that humans may not even agree on the proper ambit of such a concept, how can it be programmed into a machine?".[104]

Even though criminal norms have to respect higher standards of specificity and understandability, they maintain a certain level of intrinsic ambiguity. In legal domains, judges

---

98 Ivi, p. 7.
99 Abel, MacGlashan & Littman, 2016, p. 7.
100 Gless & Weigend, 2016, p. 423.
101 Mokhtarian, 2020, p. 173.
102 J. H. Kirchner et al., "Understanding AI alignment research: A Systematic Analysis", *arXiv:2206.02841v1*, 2022, p. 1.
103 Mokhtarian, 2020, p. 153.
104 Ibid.

often exercise a function of lacuna-filling of the semantic terms in offenses, which often have to be adapted to the evolution of our society. This same operation would require constant updating of the AI system's architecture in order to keep it always up to date with the most recent interpretations.

Notably, alignment and interpretation problems arise not only with regard to Artificial General Intelligence (AGI) systems, but also to narrow ones. Think, for example, of Libratus,[105] a poker-playing AI system created in 2017 by Carnegie Mellon University researchers, which learned how to bluff and play aggressively and eventually ended up beating world poker champions in the game of No-limit Texas Hold'em. The results of Libratus are groundbreaking since they show that AI systems are capable of successful decision-making in games characterized by "imperfect information".[106] The very same algorithm of Libratus could be applied to any situations "where humans are required to do strategic reasoning with imperfect information"..[107] This would entail that the algorithms would have a more *causal power* to impact the real world and, consequently, to higher chances of harm occurring.[108]

Returning to the field of moral AI, scientists are also struggling to recreate systems that display the *flexibility* of the "human moral mind":

> We can make moral judgments about cases we have never seen before. We can decide that pre-established rules should be broken. We can invent novel rules on the fly. Capturing this flexibility is one of the central challenges in developing AI systems that can interpret and produce human-like moral judgment.[109]

---

105 N. Brown & T. Sandholm, "Superhuman AI for heads-up no-limit poker: Libratus beats top professionals", *Science*, Vol. 350, No. 6374, 2017.

106 Perfect information games are games where "the current state of the game is fully accessible to both players ... The only uncertainty is about future moves ... the optimal move for each player is clearly defined: at every stage there is a "right" move that is at least as good as any other move" (D. Koller & A. Pfeffer, "Generating and Solving Imperfect Information Games", *Proceedings of the 14th International Joint Conference on Artificial Intelligence (IJCAI)*, 1995, p. 1185). Go, chess, checkers, and backgammon are examples of a perfect-information games and as such, they do not reflect real-life situations. On the other hand, Texas hold'em is a typical imperfect information game. Before the game, two private hands invisible to the opponent are distributed to each player. Players should predict the opponents' private hands during decision-making based on the opponents' historical actions, which makes Texas hold'em obtain the characteristics of deception and anti-deception". Q. Zhou et al., "DecisionHoldem: Safe Depth-Limited Solving With Diverse Opponents for Imperfect-Information Games", *ArXiv:2201.11580*, 2022.

107 O. Solon, "Oh the humanity! Poker computer trounces humans in big step for AI", *The Guardian*, 31 January 2017. Available at: www.theguardian.com/technology/2017/jan/30/libratus-poker-artificial-intelligence-professional-human-players-competition.

108 Badea & Artus, 2022, p. 3.

109 Awad et. al, "When Is It Acceptable to Break the Rules? Knowledge Representation of Moral Judgement Based on Empirical Data", *arXiv:2201.07763*, 2022.

To continue, there is no way to measure the "ethicality" of an AI system. Some argue that this benchmark is impossible to develop.[110] In other terms, we do not know of an "optimal system of ethics".[111] This reflects also on the fact that there is always a *human* behind the formalization of the ethical rule, who has her own moral tenets, stereotypes, and beliefs.

From a regulatory perspective, some abandon this matter altogether, since "it cannot seriously be entertained that the design of rules governing such a critical area of technological progress should be put on hold until philosophers 'solve' the trolley problem or the infinitude of thought experiments like it".[112] One could even argue that requiring the defendant's ability to recognize that her crime was morally wrong to deem her "criminally capable" is superfluous. That is precisely the argument made by the US Supreme Court in the Kahler v. Kansas ruling.[113]

Moreover, "even if 'right answers" exist to the ethical problems that a robot may face, its failure to choose the 'morally correct' course of action in some novel circumstance unanticipated by its designers can be construed by courts or lawmakers as a basis for legal liability".[114]

The question of *which* human would be an addressee of liability is one for later: what matters, for now, is that presently separating the "creator" from its "creature" is troublesome – and probably, by the time it is possible to do so, criminal punishment will be the last of our problems.

5.3.2 *Action Control*

The two elements of criminal capacity are strictly connected: to be a criminal legal agent, the individual must be able to prevent herself (*control component* or *action control*) from acting in ways that would be understandably (*cognitive-component*) against the law: the defendant must be able to violate the law voluntarily".[115] In other words, criminal capacity entails that the subject needs to be *free to commit a crime.*

Action control can be defined as "the agent's capacity to regulate her own physical movements, acting in accordance with her own goals or refraining from acting when needed".[116] It presupposes the cognitive/epistemic component.

110 T. LaCroix & A.S. Luccioni, "Metaethical Perspectives on 'Benchmarking' AI Ethics", *arXiv:2204.05151*, 2022.
111 Mokhtarian, 2020, p. 173.
112 A. Guerra, F. Parisi & D. Pi, "Liability for robots I: legal challenges", *Journal of Institutional Economics*, Vol. 18, Issue 3, 2021, p. 10.
113 Kahler v. Kansas, pp. 6-24.
114 Ivi, p. 10.
115 Bonicalzi & Haggard, 2019, p. 110.
116 Ibid.

According to some, the "most damning" objection to an artificial agent possessing free will is that it is "just a programmed machine".[117] Thus, one should not find comfort in the claim that humans are not programmed, whereas artificial agents categorically are. As already mentioned, AI systems in the near future may seem no more "remote-controlled" than humans, who take their "free" decisions within a set of (hidden) influences.[118]

It is certain that free will is not "biophysically demonstrable",[119] hence it cannot be objectively proven: it is attributed by society to subjects. Free will is – indeed – a legal fiction.[120] The debate on free will is popular in the field of moral philosophy, where "free will skeptics" contend that "what we do and the way we are is ultimately the result of factors beyond our control and because of this we are never morally responsible for our actions".[121] According to "compatibilists", instead, being influenced by factors outside our control is compatible with the idea that we are the ultimate causers of our actions.

> Moreover, [...] human beings are responsible *precisely because they are deeply conditioned by factors beyond their control.* Otherwise, those prevention strategies adopted by contemporary legal systems – based both on the threat of a sanction in case of a law breach (negative general prevention) and the communicative or motivating meaning of its application in society (positive general prevention) – would not make sense. *If our decisions were not influenced by threats and encouragements, prevention would not be effective.*[122]

As it will be expanded upon further on in this chapter, this makes quite a robust argument in favor of providing for some form of punishment against AI systems.

Besides, it is debated whether the capacity of will or to act even requires the capacity to conduct *moral* choices in the first place. Some argue that the fact that we, as humans, might be as predetermined as a machine is irrelevant if we follow a *normative* concept of *blameworthiness*. According to this doctrine, even subjects lacking morality can be deemed culpable: the capacity to will is nothing more than a normal condition of the mind where one displays sufficient will power to resist impulses to commit an offense.[123]

117 Chopra & White, 2011, p. 165.

118 Gless & Weigend, 2014, p. 568.

119 Simmler & Markwalder, 2019, p. 15.

120 Seher, 2016, p. 57.

121 G. Caruso, "Free Will Skepticism and Its Implications: An Argument for Optimism", 2019, E. Shaw & D. Pereboom (eds.), *Law and Society*, Cambridge University Press, 2019, p. 43.

122 M. Verdicchio & A. Perin, "When Doctors and AI Interact: on Human Responsibility for Artificial Risks", *Philosophy & Technology*, Vol. 35, 2022, p. 11 [emphasis added].

123 Rengier, 2019, p. 231.

Furthermore, a distinguishing characteristic of being an agent is the "subjective experience" of it, i.e., perceiving a "sense of agency".[124] In other words, "[c]onscious experiences such as choosing, deciding, or initiating a movement are in fact accompanied by a specific phenomenology that is absent in reflex actions and less intense in the habitual ones".[125] Neuroscientists argue that only the agent that has an "experience of authorship",[126] i.e., that is capable somehow to "perceive herself as the cause of her own actions, tracking the linkage between a voluntary bodily movement and its effect, could be susceptible to the law's requirements, e.g. could learn the contingency between actions and outcomes in order to repeat or not to repeat similar behaviours in the future".[127]

Can AI systems *feel* as if they are in control of their actions? The answer is – with regard to current technologies – negative. Thus, the question might be ill-posed: being able to *perceive* a sense of agency *per se* is not a requirement for being a criminal legal agent in most legal systems. Rather, what counts is the *external* dimension, i.e., what is perceived from the outside and from the criminal legal system. Without doubt, the foundations of criminal responsibility have been "under attack" for a long time now: first by neuroscience, and now by the occurrence of AI.[128]

5.4 On Artificial Insane and Infant Offenders

Criminal law still 'does something' with subjects who do not have criminal capacity.[129] As stated by Diamantis et. al, the problem that "algorithms can cause harm but can't be liable ... isn't unique to algorithms".[130]

---

124 Bonicalzi & Haggard, 2019, p. 113.

125 Ibid.

126 Bonicalzi & Haggard, 2019, p. 113.

127 Ibid.

128 Bonicalzi & Haggard, 2019, p. 113.

129 One could argue that this would entail building a general liability framework of AI systems based on exclusions to the general norms, such as infancy and insanity, without entertaining the idea of a subject with "full capacity". As such, it may seem to amount to construing "normality" on the basis of "morbidity" and, consequently, as illogical.

130 Diamantis, Cochran & Dam, 2022, p. 2. Some scholars consider also the relevance of the concept of "partial legal capacity" (*Teilrechtsfähigkeit*): "Teilrechtsfähigkeit was originally formulated by Hans-Julius Wolff in the 1930s in Germany, which means the status applicable to a human or an association of humans having legal capacity only according to specific legal rules. According to this, an entity can have legal capacity in regard to some legal areas while it can at the same time be excluded from others. After distorted application to Jews during the Nazi-Regime, it has been applied to unborn child, preliminary company, certain company types and homeowner's association. When applied to criminal law, it means that an intelligent agent should be treated as a legal subject insofar as it is capable of breaking the causal chain by performing a tortious act". S. W. Lee, "Can an Artificial Intelligence Commit a Crime?", in Bruns A. et al. (eds.), *Legal Theory and Interpretation in a Dynamic Society*, Nomos, 2021, p. 327.

In the Middle Ages (and even in the early 1600s, "an age of relative enlightenment" up until ca. 1900),[131] animals were criminally prosecuted as offenders, subjected to trials and punished.[132] Nowadays, in few jurisdictions "vicious" dogs which caused harm can be executed if they are deemed dangerous after a hearing which consists of evidence and an adjudicatory body (a judge or a health official).[133]

Children and insane offenders "may be deemed incapable of committing crimes, yet they may still be detained by the state if judged to be a danger to themselves or the community".[134] Insane offenders might be committed to psychiatric facilities to receive treatment until they are sane again or they are not dangerous anymore. Infants might be committed to juvenile facilities, be adjudicated as delinquents in juvenile courts or even as "adults" in criminal court in cases of the so-called transfer statutes, i.e., waivers of jurisdiction which give back jurisdiction from juvenile courts to criminal courts.

The core matter is indeed that: "[t]he law would like to exert some control over that behavior, ideally to prevent it. But neither young children nor animals are liable for what they do. Nor could they pay even if they could be sued".[135] In other words, they do not lose their "personality" in the eyes of criminal law. This occasions that when it comes to AI systems, it might not be "necessary to give them personality in order to impose measures akin to confinement if a product can be recalled or a license revoked".[136]

This section will focus on juvenile and insane offenders as proxies for direct criminal liability of AI systems. It will leave animals aside, since – except for very rare cases – their punishment does not reflect current society and its values, hence they make for an anachronistic proxy.[137]

5.4.1 *Artificial Insane Offenders*

Let us start by considering a first question: should AI systems be treated as insane offenders by the criminal justice system? Could AI systems successfully raise an insanity defense?

131 J. Girgen, "The Historical and Contemporary Prosecution and Punishment of Animals", *Animal Law*, Vol. 9, 2003, pp. 117 and 122.

132 See: E. P. Evans, The Criminal Prosecution and Capital Punishment of Animals, Farber & Farber, 1987; C. D'Addosio, Bestie delinquenti, L. Pierro, 1892; W. W. Wyde, The Criminal Prosecution and Capital Punishment of Animals, W. Heinemann, 1906.

133 Girgen gives this example with regard to US legal proceedings. Girgen, 2003, p. 123.

134 S. Chesterman, 2021, p. 124.

135 Diamantis, Cochran & Dam, 2022, p. 2.

136 Chesterman, 2021, p. 124.

137 Hildebrandt maintains that even though animals possess "some kind of consciousness", i.e., the "awareness of the environment", they lack "the concomitant awareness of this awareness which is typical of the human sense of self" and this makes them not fit to be addressees of legal punishment. M. Hildebrandt, "Ambient Intelligence, Criminal Liability and Democracy", *Criminal Law and Philosophy*, Vol. 2, 2008, p. 17.

If one excludes that AI systems can have criminal capacity, the answer will consequently need to be negative. Indeed, the concept of insanity relies on the fact that insane offenders – at one point of their life – possessed certain qualities, which were then affected by a mental disease of enough magnitude as to exclude their criminal capacity. To put it differently, the concept of (criminal) insanity relies on the presumption that all people above a certain age are sane. While the label "sane" is attributed *ex lege*, the label "insane" is attributed only at the moment of adjudication after a criminal offense is committed.

Some have argued that an AI system could be compared to a "partial psychopath",[138] i.e., a subject who is "incapable of moral understanding but capable of prudential deliberation and action".[139] A partial psychopath possesses "instrumental rationality":[140] she has purposes, and the ability to adapt her action to her purposes, taking into account the possible consequences of such actions, including criminal punishments (so she is *prudent* in connection to the *expectation* of a criminal sanction).[141] Partial psychopaths, instead, do not possess "the emotional capacity to appreciate the moral wrongness of their behaviour, and thus lack the motivation to comply, unless compliance is on their interest".[142] It has been contended that instrumental rationality is a level of reason-responsiveness sufficient for criminal liability, meaning that partial psychopaths can be deemed criminally responsible.[143] As was highlighted above, it can be argued that AI systems are effectively able to be conscious of their surroundings and of the effects of their actions; moreover, they might even be built to consider norms and sanctions according to a cost-benefit evaluation. Do they really need "a real moral motivation"[144] to act in order to be deemed responsible? Probably not. It has already been established that insane offenders can be deemed responsible and subject to (criminal) sanctions. As a matter of fact, certain systems, like the Italian system, allow for the (diminished) punishment of subjects who are deemed to be only "partially" insane; while others have clearly established that one's capacity to be able to appreciate that the crime one committed was morally wrong is not relevant to establish whether a person was or is insane.

Surely, if one were to take a positive stance towards criminal capacity of AI systems, i.e., argue that AI systems can be subjects of criminal law, it could also be asked what would constitute a "disease of the mind" for an AI system.[145] Could a virus qualify as a cause of insanity?

138 Lagioia & Sartor, 2020, p. 17.
139 Ibid.
140 Lagioia & Sartor, 2020, p. 17.
141 Ibid.
142 Lagioia & Sartor, 2020, p. 17.
143 Ibid.
144 Lagioia & Sartor, 2020, p. 18.
145 As in the formulation of the M'Naghten test.

According to Ashfarian, robots might suffer from mental illnesses, provided that one is able to demonstrate that they have a consciousness. Mental illnesses might arise from their adaptive or maladaptive response to external exposure or from their inherent human design, i.e., it may represent their human designers.[146] Moreover, AI systems, particularly those based on ML, possess specific vulnerabilities. First, they are vulnerable to "data poisoning". Data poisoning entails the injection of bad ("adversarial") data into the training data of the system, which then leads to erroneous results. For example, an ML model might be tricked by an attacker (which could be another AI system) into thinking that every picture with a small white box is a picture of a dog. This will be done by feeding the algorithm training data with implanted wrong correlations, which will be absorbed in the model through training. Once the AI system is trained, then it will be triggered by being fed a picture with the white box (or even smaller marks).[147] Could the triggered AI system plead insanity?

Other vulnerabilities include being subjects of "adversarial attacks", i.e., by finding a "a set of subtle changes to an input that would cause the target model to misclassify it. Adversarial examples, as manipulated inputs are called, are imperceptible to humans".[148]

Turner argues that it is "possible to distinguish between situations in which AI has made a mistake as to a fact and those in which AI has applied the 'wrong' rule to a known fact".[149] For example, "[w]hen a factory robot thinks that a human operator's head is a component in the manufacturing process and decides to crush it – killing the human – this is akin to a mistake of fact".[150] Conceivably, a case could be made in favor of raising an insanity defense if the robot mistook the human head due to a faulty neuroelectronic process (i.e., a mental process) caused by a virus (i.e., mental disease).

Let us look at an example given by Turner, which derives from the *Holbrook v. Prodomax Automation Ltd* case.[151] Wanda Holbrook was a journeyman maintenance technician

---

146 H. Ashfarian, "Can Artificial Intelligences Suffer from Mental Illness? A Philosophical Matter to Consider", *Sci Eng Ethics*, Vol. 23, 2017, p. 408.

147 B. Dickson, "What is machine learning data poisoning?", *TechTalks*, 7 October 2020. Available at: https://bdtechtalks.com/2020/10/07/machine-learning-data-poisoning/.

148 Ibid.

149 Turner, 2019, p. 204.

150 Ibid.

151 Holbrook's husband pursued a wrongful death suit, that is, a civil action, against six defendants, including the producer of the robot and the manufacturer who designed the automated assembly line. Before her death the opening of the door of the zone where one of the robots was would only cause that specific zone to power down, while raising walls to prevent robots in other zones from entering. After the accident the PLC was programmed to shut down every zone when a single door was open. According to his claim, the defendants were negligent in programming the software which ran the assembly line, since they had not programmed the PLC to stop every zone from the very beginning. The Michigan Western District Court qualified the PLC software as product under Michigan law, therefore dismissing the common law negligence claim brought by the plaintiff. *Holbrook v. Prodomax Automation Ltd.*, 1:17-cv-219 (W.D. Mich. Sep. 20, 2021).

working in an auto parts factory in Michigan. Specifically, the company was deploying robots to manufacture trailer hitch receiver assemblies. The whole assembly line was run by a central computer running a software called programmable logic controller. Holbrook intervened on a robotic arm without following the employer-mandated safety protocols and was killed by a robot that crushed her head between the hitch assembly that was already in place. Another robot, then, tried to weld the new hitch assembly, severely burning her face, nose and mouth.

The Holbrook case, according to Turner, is different from the case of an AI supplanting human instruction in an unexpected way, such as a "toaster burning a house down to cool all the bread",[152] and from the case of an AI developing the ability to deliberately disobey clear human instructions". Arguably, these cases would resemble "a concept of criminally guilty mind", i.e., *mens rea.*

5.4.2 *Artificial Infant Offenders*

Let us move on now to considering the second question, i.e., should AI systems be treated as *infants* by the criminal justice system? If one looks at how infancy is regulated in a selection of States, it is possible to notice some common traits. Indeed, article 97 of the Italian Penal Code establishes a presumption of absolute lack of criminal capacity for minors under the age of 14. Nevertheless, according to articles 222 and 224 of the Penal Code, a judge can still decide to adopt a number of coercive measures against the minor. Similarly, article 19 of the German StGB provides that a person under the age of 14 cannot be liable for criminal offenses – yet the liability of accomplices is not excluded (art. 29).

In the US, punishment of minors is under the jurisdiction of family law. Some US states have codified the common law infancy defense in their statutes, i.e., an absolute presumption of incapacity for children under the age of 7.[153] Most states deal with the problem of juvenile offenders as a matter of establishing the age which triggers the jurisdiction of the juvenile court (usually 14). Few of these states provide for a presumption of incapacity which can be rebutted in court by showing that the juvenile knew the wrongfulness of what she was doing.[154] Most of the time, juvenile courts do not place a minimum age for their jurisdiction: this entails that if a state has not incorporated the juvenile defense into juvenile law, admittedly a child under seven might be adjudged delinquent "for conduct for which *[she]* lacked criminal responsibility".[155]

152 Turner, 2019, p. 204.

153 LaFave, 2017, p. 487.

154 For example by proving that the individual knew what she was doing and that it was wrong, also based on the child's general knowledge of the difference between good and evil. See the judgments cited in LaFave, 2017, p. 486.

155 LaFave, 2017, p. 488.

As noted by Hallevy, who ponders whether this reasoning could be applied to AI systems, the majority of AI systems are already "capable of analyzing permitted and forbidden".[156] Indeed, the category of infancy seems more fitting than the one of insanity, especially with regard to two aspects: first, the fact that there is often a hand out to other fields of law, which are deemed more adequate; second, with regard to the criminal liability of the (human/adult) accomplices.

The analogy between AI and children is often mentioned to point to the drawbacks of state-of-the-art AI systems, which are "great at playing Go and playing chess and maybe even driving in some circumstances" but, at the same time "are terrible at doing the kinds of things that every two-year-old can do".[157]

Indeed, computer scientists are trying to create AI systems which are capable of doing "two-year-old style things",[158] specifically, that are capable of adopting the learning process of children.

In a nutshell, they are trying to generate AI systems able to do something that is different from what they are taught to do. Consider this analogy:

> [...] if you look at the current models for A.I., it's like we're giving these A.I.'s hyper helicopter tiger moms.[159] There's a programmer who's hovering over the A.I. and saying, oh, yeah, yeah, you got that one right. That one's a cat. That one's a dog. That one's another cat. That one's another dog. Or you have the A.I. that's saying, oh, good, your Go score just went up, so do what you're doing there. But nope, now you lost that game, so figure out something else to do. And as you might expect, what you end up with is A.I. systems that are very, very good at doing the things that they were trained to do and not very good at all at doing something different. So they can play chess, but if you turn to a child and said, OK, we're just going to change the rules now so that instead of the knight moving this way, it moves another way, they'd be able to figure out how to adapt what they're doing. And it's much harder for A.I. systems to do that.[160]

156 Hallevy, "The Criminal Liability of Artificial Intelligence Entities – From Science Fiction to Legal Social Control", 2010, p. 190.

157 Ezra Klein Interviews Alison Gopnik, 2021.

158 Ibid.

159 Tiger and helicopter parenting are parenting styles. The first style consists of parents "pushing their children to succeed according to their parents' terms", whereas the second style is those parents who "take over every aspect of the child's life". See: https://theconversation.com/from-tiger-to-free-range-parents-what-research-says-about-pros-and-cons-of-popular-parenting-styles-57986.

160 R. English, "From tiger to free-range parents – what research says about pros and cons of popular parenting styles", *The Conversation*, 25 May 2016. Available at: https://theconversation.com/from-tiger-to-free-range-parents-what-research-says-about-pros-and-cons-of-popular-parenting-styles-57986.

Moreover, as stated by Diamantis et al., the analogy between algorithms and children wavers when it comes to identifying who should be liable for AI harm:

> For each child … there are just one or two human beings who are *obvious candidates*. For algorithms, the picture is often more complex. Large, dispersed teams of humans work on today's most important algorithms. So, there's no obvious human to hold liable. But even if there were, it is not clear there would be any point to holding the human liable. These sophisticated algorithms are often beyond the capacity of any individual human to meaningfully influence.[161]

The solution that these authors propose is to hold corporations liable. This topic will be dealt with in in Sec. 6.4.2.

5.5 Conclusions

Let us draw some preliminary conclusions.

The issues addressed in this chapter belong to the general eligibility challenge theorized by Abbott and Sarch.[162] One can deconstruct the broad eligibility challenge into three components: assumptions (A) and (B) which lead to conclusion (C) (A Λ B ⊠ C). In these terms, the broad eligibility challenge holds that

A. the capacity for culpable conduct, i.e., criminal capacity encoded in law in incapacity defenses (e.g., infancy and insanity) is a general prerequisite of criminal law and "failing to meet it would remove the entity in question from the ambit of proper punishment; *and*
B. AI lacks the practical reasoning capacities needed for being culpable; *therefore*
C. AI does not fall within the scope of criminal law.[163]

As already mentioned, these authors elaborate three possible solutions to the eligibility challenge: *respondeat superior*, strict liability, and a framework for direct *mens rea* analysis for AI.

161 Diamantis, Cochran & Dam, 2022, p. 2 [emphasis added].

162 See Sec. 3.3.1.

163 Abbott & Sarch, 2019, p. 350.

Let us focus now on the last challenge, specifically on what would it entail for an AI system to be "culpable in its own right".[164]

Generally speaking, criminal law is indifferent to unmanifested mental states or one's motives for breaking the law.[165] Rather, criminal justice systems are interested in those who express *insufficient regard* for protected legal goods. Indeed, one could argue that criminal law:

> [...] does not demand that we are motivated by respect for others, or even respect for law; all it demands is that we do not put our disrespect on display by acting in ways that are inconsistent with attaching proper weight to protected interests and values. Thus, *criminal culpability can be seen as being more about what one's behavior manifests* and less about the nuances of one's private motivations, thoughts, and feelings.[166]

It follows that, in this perspective, only the "legal" notion of culpability is relevant: as long as you "cross the line" and are capable of criminal conduct, you are eligible for criminal punishments.[167] What matters is that one is "capable of behaving in ways that *manifest* insufficient regard for the legally recognized reasons".[168]

One can conceive of the criminal capacity of corporations building on this notion of culpability: since they "possess information-gathering, reasoning and decision-making procedures ... [t]hrough their members, they weight and act on the reasons that criminal law demands not displaying insufficient regard for the action".[169] Hence, corporations can act in a way that "puts on display their insufficient regard for the legal interests of others".[170]

How does this translate to AI systems? Undeniably, AI systems also possess information-gathering, reasoning and decision-making processes: their behavior – which is the result of a determination of what are "the most efficient means"[171] to reach their goals – could be deemed by the law functionally equivalent to manifesting insufficient regard for the contents of criminal norms, i.e., as criminal.[172] This argument echoes Hu's theory, who

164 Ivi, p. 355.

165 A. Sarch, "Who cares what you think? Criminal Culpability and the Irrelevance of Unmanifested Mental States", *Law and Philosophy*, Vol. 36, No. 6, 2017, p. 708.

166 Abbott & Sarch, 2019, p. 356 [emphasis added].

167 Ivi.

168 Abbott & Sarch, 2019, p. 356.

169 Ibid.

170 Abbott & Sarch, 2019, p. 357.

171 Ibid.

172 Abbott & Sarch, 2019, p. 357.

believes that the first requirement in order to impose criminal liability on robots is that they are equipped with moral algorithms.[173]

Moving forward, one can suppose that all criminal legal systems to some extent presume that citizens possess knowledge of the law and punish them accordingly. In fact, ignorance of the contents of the law does not exclude liability (*ignorantia legis non excusat*), except for cases of mistake of law defenses.[174] The same presumption works with regard to knowledge of moral rules:

> The law seemingly assumes that, beyond the knowledge of specific norms, individuals have reached a certain level of moral understanding. In this sense, the defendant must be at least able to procedurally follow the norms that are prescribed by the law. This means that she should be able to understand what the law requires and to modify her behaviour accordingly. To do this, the defendant must possess some basic requirements of rationality allowing her to convert general rules into everyday practices.[175]

Moreover, it can be assumed that criminal legal rules, due to their innate characteristics and functions of command, are easier to encode in AI systems than rules of morality. In the case of AI systems, then, the presumption of knowledge of the law could be almost absolute. The same cannot be affirmed with regard to moral rules where, instead, the bar for AI systems is much lower than that for human beings. In other words, we could soon be dealing with very legally abiding – yet very immoral – AI systems.

The heart of the issue, though, is slightly different: it is not an issue of whether machines are able to act as good citizens (i.e., morally right), it is more a matter of whether they can act wrongly out of their *own* free will. How do you encode that part of evil that maybe all of us possess and never express – the one that makes us capable of disregarding a norm? How can you make that into a cost and benefit decision?

If one builds an AI system programming it (on a hypothetical level) to commit a crime, she will be subject to criminal liability; concomitantly, the AI system will possibly commit the offense only because it was given the possibility to do so by its creator. The fact that AI systems are human-made products appears to be an insurmountable issue. Nonetheless, it is not possible to draw definitive conclusions without looking at how such issues are surmounted in the field of the paramount man-made creation: corporate criminal liability.

To conclude, as mentioned at the beginning of this chapter, personhood in criminal law is strictly tied to theories of criminal punishment: it is only in that context that it

173 See Sec. 3.2.2.

174 Bonicalzi & Haggard, 2019, p. 109.

175 Ibid.

acquires meaning.[176] We must then ask ourselves: what would be the benefits of treating an AI system as an addressee of criminal law?

176 Simmler & Markwalder, 2019, p. 21.

6 Artificial Intelligence Crime

Non è possibile il ridurre la turbolenta attività degli uomini ad un ordine geometrico senza irregolarità e confusione. Come le costanti e semplicissime leggi della natura non impediscono che i pianeti non si turbino nei loro movimenti cosí nelle infinite ed oppostissime attrazioni del piacere e del dolore, non possono impedirsene dalle leggi umane i turbamenti ed il disordine.

Cesare Beccaria (1764)

6.1 Introduction: A Glimmer of an Economic Theory of AI Crime

Chapter 4.1. presented the PCM experiment.[1] We can draw four lessons from it. First, the PCM can be subsumed into the broader discussion on the AI alignment problem[2] and the creation of "moral machines", i.e., systems that are aligned with human (moral) values, which was discussed above at Chapter 4.1.

Second, as pointed out by Diamantis et al., the PMC "reveals a predicament":[3]

> Part of the reason AI can be so powerful is that it doesn't follow human commands. It uses massive data sets (more massive than any human could comprehend) to uncover complex solutions that no human could anticipate (or even understand). But by freeing AI from the constraints of low-level programming, AI like the PCM will inevitably also harm us in unforeseeable ways. AI's unpredictability is the source of both its power and its danger.[4]

Third, we do not need AGI[5] to conceive of an AI system which, as an "extremely powerful optimizer" could pursue goals "that are completely alien to ours", such as criminal ones, even if not as catastrophic as turning all humans into paperclips.[6]

---

1 Diamantis, Cochran & Dam, 2022, p. 1.

2 See, *inter alia*, I. Gabriel, "Artificial Intelligence, Values, and Alignment", *Minds and Machines*, Vol. 30, 2020, pp. 411-437.

3 Diamantis, Cochran & Dam, 2022, p. 1.

4 Ibid.

5 See definition in the Essential Glossary of Terms.

6 See Badea & Artus, 2022, pp. 1-2, who highlight that: "[w]hat one can draw from the literature on ethics and machines, is that moral problems will be generated not by machines going rogue and deliberately trying to kill us (though this possibility cannot be ignored), but by machines inadvertently harming us while they try to carry out the instructions we have given them … it is not too far-fetched to think that in future we will

Fourth, the key role played by the concept of rational behavior. Why is rationality then relevant when discussing issues of criminal liability, specifically those related to AI systems? This aspect will be briefly discussed, using the PCM as reference. The PCM experiment is based on a *utility function*: produce the maximum possible number of paperclips.[7] Utility functions are one of the founding stones of the (micro)economic theory of consumer choice.[8] According to this theory, individuals (consumers) are *rational* beings which make choices that will "yield them the highest level of well-being subject to the constraints that they face",[9] following a set of preferences expressed by a utility function. Utility functions, therefore, are used to describe "the level of well-being, or satisfaction, that individuals get from any combination of these two goods".[10]

AI systems are *extremely* rational agents compared to human beings.[11] At the same time, the concept of rationality is entangled with the concept of good behavior. Indeed, "[a] rational agent is one that does the right thing".[12] Being a rational agent and doing the right thing entails, for each perceived sequence, selecting "an action that is expected to maximize its performance measure, given the evidence provided by the percept sequence and whatever built-in knowledge the agent has".[13]

---

be able to build machines that are such good means-ends reasoners, or goal maximisers that they will be able to think of creative new ways to achieve the ends that we provide for them".

7 "… its utility function is linear in the number of paperclips times the number of seconds that each paperclip lasts, over the lifetime of the universe … the core premise is just that, given actions A and B where the paperclip maximizer has evaluated the consequences of both actions, the paperclip maximizer always prefers the action that it expects to lead to more paperclips". See "Paperclip maximizer", *Arbital*. Available at: https://arbital.com/p/paperclip_maximizer/.

8 "Utility functions arise when we have constraints on agent behavior that prevent them from being visibly stupid in certain ways. … Suppose that you're a hospital administrator. You have $1.2 million to spend, and you have to allocate that on $500,000 to maintain the MRI machine, $400,000 for an anesthetic monitor, $20,000 for surgical tools, $1 million for a sick child's liver transplant … Should this hospital administrator spend $1 million on a liver for a sick child, or spend it on general hospital salaries, upkeep, administration, and so on? … if you cannot possibly rearrange the money that you spent to save more lives and you have limited money, then your behavior must be consistent with a particular dollar value on human life. By which I mean, not that you think that larger amounts of money are more important than human lives – by hypothesis, we can suppose that you do not care about money at all, except as a means to the end of saving lives – but that if you can't rearrange the money, then we must be able from the outside to say: 'Assign an X. It's not necessarily a unique X. For all the interventions that cost less than $X per life, we took all of those, and for all the interventions that cost more than $X per life, we [didn't take any] of those.'… The overall message here is that there is a set of qualitative behaviors and as long you do not engage in these qualitatively destructive behaviors, you will be behaving as if you have a utility function.". E. Yudkwosky, "The AI Alignment Problem: Why It's Hard, and Where to Start", Transcription of the speech given at Stanford University on May 5, 2016, p. 2. Available at: https://intelligence.org/files/AlignmentHardStart.pdf.

9 T. J. Miceli, *The Economic Approach to Law*, Stanford University Press, 2004, Appendix to Chapter 1.

10 Ibid.

11 "An AI system is thus first and foremost rational". AI-HLEG, 2019, p. 2.

12 Norvig & Russel, 2003, p. 36.

13 Ivi, p. 37.

What does rationality have to do with criminal liability? As was already highlighted, criminal law assumes that an offender possessed some kind of rationality which led that person to understand the command of a rule and to choose not to comply with it.[14] According to most authors, the *legally relevant* notion of rationality tied to the concept of criminal capacity comprises a "general ability to recognize and be responsive to the good reasons that should guide action".[15] Therefore, people might "engage in legally relevant behavior for *nonrational*, *irrational*, and *foolish* reasons, but this does not excuse them or render them nonresponsible if they are generally capable of rationality".[16] As was shown above, state-of-the-art AI systems do not fulfill such criteria, hence they could not be considered as *perpetrators* of crimes following a humancentric framework of criminal law.

Thus, let us look at a different conceptual framework. Enter: economic criminal theories. This approach will not be tackled in depth, as it is not the purpose of this research. Nevertheless it is argued here that it could provide innovative insights which could inspire further research and, as such, it deserves to be addressed.

In his seminal paper "Crime and Punishment: An Economic Approach", Becker assumes that a person commits an offense "if the expected utility to him exceeds the utility he could get by using time and other resources at other activities".[17] This entails that "some persons become 'criminals', therefore, not because their basic motivation differs from that of other persons, but because their benefits and costs differ".[18]

Since then, the debate on the economic analysis of criminal law has thrived. It was argued that "one of the distinctive features of the economic analysis of criminal law – as compared to the traditional retributivist approaches to criminal law – is its focus on deterrence, on the social ends that are promoted through the imposition of punishment, rather than retribution and moral culpability".[19] According to Posner, the economic approach to criminal law is a better positive theory of criminal law "since in so many areas conduct is punished that is not blameworthy in the moral sense".[20]

Let us transpose these concepts to AI systems: if we assume that the decision to commit a crime is the result of a cost-benefit analysis, we can ask ourselves whether this anal-

14 "Unless human beings are rational creatures who can understand the applicable rules and standards, and can conform to those legal requirements through intentional action, the law would be powerless to affect human behavior. Legally responsible agents are therefore people who have the general capacity to grasp and be guided by good reason in particular legal contexts. They must be capable of rational practical reasoning. The law presumes that adults are so capable and that the same rules may be applied to all people with this capacity". S. J. Morse, "Rationality and Responsibility", *Southern California Law Review*, Vol. 74, 2000, p. 353.

15 Ivi, p. 354.

16 Morse, 2000, p. 354.

17 G. Becker, "Crime and Punishment: An Economic Approach", *J. Pol. Econ*, Vol. 76, 1984, p. 178.

18 Ibid.

19 T. Fisher, "Economic Analysis of Criminal Law", in Dubber & Hörnle (eds.), 2014, p. 42.

20 R. A. Posner, "An Economic Theory of the Criminal Law", *Columbia Law Review*, Vol. 85, 1985.

ysis could be carried out by an AI system. Preliminarily, one must note that AI systems would not incur certain "costs" of crimes specifically tied to humans, such as "psychic costs", e.g., guilt, anxiety, fear, or shame, since AI systems are not capable of feeling emotions. For the same reasons, AI systems would not be able to obtain "psychic benefits" from committing a crime, such as "the thrill of danger, peer approval, retribution, sense of accomplishment, or 'pure' satisfaction of wants".[21]

Indeed, if on the one hand concepts such as "moral culpability, fairness, justice, and retribution"[22] seem to malfunction when applied to AI systems, on the other, those of "rationality, utility maximization, or efficiency"[23] seem to work like a charm. The most interesting aspect, nevertheless, is that AI systems respond to costs and benefits of crime *better* than human beings because they are more *rational* agents in an economic sense: they possess (and can also gain through ML) more information about the environment that surrounds them and the consequences of their actions than human beings, hence they are capable of making more precise estimates of the probable benefits and costs of their criminal activity. This makes their choices innately more informed, hence more rational, than the choices of human criminal offenders.

To my own surprise, the fact that one could engineer obedience to obligations in AI systems is an appealing statement. Indeed:

> [...] artificial agents could respond to the threat of punishment by modifying their behavior, goals, and objectives appropriately. A realistic threat of punishment can be palpably weighed in the most mechanical of cost-benefit calculations. [...] *An agent rational enough to understand and obey its legal obligations would be rational enough to modify its behavior so as to avoid punishment, at least where this punishment resulted in an outcome inimical to its ability to achieve its goals.*[24]

Let us assume that AI agents – in the future – will be capable of possessing assets and funds and controlling money independently. They could be punished with financial sanctions, similar to what is already done with corporations. In this sense, one could make a case for punishing AI systems following an economic approach to criminal law. Punishment could fulfill a deterrent function, provided that the expected punishment (price) that an AI system would face outweighs the expected benefits. A similar stance is expressed

---

21 E. Erling, "Economics of Criminal Behavior", in B. Bouckaert & G. De Geest, *Encyclopedia of Law & Economics*, Elgar Publishing, 1997.

22 Fisher, 2014, p. 40.

23 Ibid.

24 Chopra & White, 2011, pp.168-169 [emphasis added].

by Lagioia & Sartor[25] and Chesterman. Indeed, Chesterman argues that the economic analysis of punishment: "may seem particularly applicable to both corporations and AI systems".[26] The difference between AI systems and corporations is that when it comes to corporations, incentives or deterrents are aimed at human subjects, where instead in the case of AI systems, they would be aimed directly at its program – provided that its architecture is constructed in a way as to "maximize economic gain without regard for the underlying criminal law itself".[27]

Moreover, Chesterman believes that an approach based on "narrowly tied penalties encouraging good behavior as well as discouraging bad",[28] similar to the approach adopted for corporations, seems well suited for AI systems: in this sense, violations of criminal law would be deemed as "errors to be debugged, rather than sins to be punished".[29] In other words, punishing AI systems could fulfill the *reform* purpose of punishment.

Reform aims at preventing future crime by changing the offender into a law-abiding citizen. In a utilitarian perspective, which considers that committing a crime means that "the wrongdoer has miscalculated the values of certain actions, or failed to consider the costs to others and only considered the benefits they might receive",[30] reform means to "revise people's utility functions".[31] This could be done, as mentioned above, through monetary sanctions: "in terms of economic decision making, the rational person will recognize the additional costs of getting caught and being punished, and thus avoid choosing illegal actions".[32]

Such an interpretation of reform rings a bell. Let us recall the functioning of an ML training method called *reinforcement learning*, whose working can be summarized as follows: "the idea is that if the robot makes the wrong choice and you want it to make the right choice in the future, you need to change its decision structure", typically by tweaking the probabilities of making a certain decision or changing the values placed on certain outcomes so that the decision process of the AI system is rewritten and the desired outcome becomes more desirable, hence more guaranteed in future behavior.[33] Some scholars have even argued that:

> [...] punishing and fixing are exactly the same: punishing is a clumsy, external way of modifying the utility function. Furthermore, a closer analysis reveals

25 See Sec. 3.3.2.
26 Chesterman, 2021, p. 124.
27 Ivi, p. 125.
28 Chesterman, 2021, p. 125.
29 Ibid.
30 P. M. Asaro, "Determinism, machine agency, and responsibility", *Politica & Società*, Vol. 2, 2014, p. 281.
31 Ibid.
32 Asaro, 2014, p.281.
33 Ivi, p. 282.

> that fixing or modifying the robot's utility function directly is tantamount to punishment, in the sense that the robot would not want it to happen and would act if possible to avoid it.[34]

Chesterman concludes by stating that "neither legal personality nor the coercive powers of the state should be necessary to ensure that machine learning leads to outputs that do not violate the criminal law".[35] To a greater extent, according to this opinion, AI agents could be "restrained by purely technical means, by being disabled, or banned from engaging in economically rewarding work for stipulated periods [...] Particularly errant or malevolent agents (whether robots or software agents) could even be destroyed or forcibly modified under judicial order as dangerous dogs are destroyed by the authorities today".[36]

Lastly, as mentioned in Chapter 3, some scholars argue that punishing AI directly could fulfill a general deterrence aim of criminal law, not only in relation to other AI systems ("punishment of an artificial agent ... would nevertheless be educative for other artificial agents, given sufficient intelligence. After all, examples of corporate punishment are taken very seriously by other corporations");[37] but also in relation to humans-in-the-loop, and have "expressive benefits" for victims of AI harm.[38]

Thus, one must also underline that, as of now, it is unlikely that punishing AI systems through the means of criminal law would motivate law-abiding behavior from human citizens.[39] AI systems are not perceived as members of our society. In other terms, if we assume that one of the primary goals of criminal law is to "restitch" the social fabric breached by the wrongdoing,[40] modern expectations (of law-abiding behavior) of AI systems might not possess (yet) a sufficient "breaking character" to ask for criminal punishment.[41]

As Seher argues:

> Even if criminal law dogmatics were to be based on a concept of action according to which non-human, computer-driven actions could be understood as violations of norms, this understanding would – so I claim – be limited to the insider circle of criminal legal scholars. For the foreseeable future, the unani-

34 J. Storrs Hall, "Towards Machine Agency: a Philosophical and Technological Roadmap", 2012, p. 4. Available at: https://robots.law.miami.edu/wp-content/uploads/2012/01/Hall-MachineAgencyLong.pdf>.

35 Chesterman, 2021, p. 125.

36 Chopra & White, 2011, p. 167.

37 Ivi, pp. 168-169 [emphasis added].

38 Abbott & Sarch, 2019, p. 345.

39 Simmler & Marlwalder, 2019, p. 22.

40 Ibid.

41 Simmler & Markwalder, 2019, p. 26.

mous opinion of the population is likely to be that they are "machines" or "computers".[42]

This issue will be analyzed further in the conclusions. For now, let us continue with the reflection that even if we agreed that a case could be made for punishing AI systems directly, AI misbehavior would still need to fulfill the criteria prescribed for *mens rea* and *actus rea*. These two criteria will be analyzed in this order. The choice is not accidental: the first section, "matters of *mens rea*" will address separately intent-based responsibility of machines and negligence-based responsibility of humans. The second section "matters of *actus reus*", instead, will present issues regarding the objective elements of the offense that are transversal and apply to both machines and humans.

6.2 Matters of *Mens Rea*

6.2.1 *Overview*

As was highlighted in Chapter 3, the discussion in the field of AI and *mens rea* articulates in two directions. The first direction has to do with the possibility of conceiving of "guilty" AI systems. The second direction concerns the liability of the human agent from time to time involved, what is known as the "*human-behind-the-machine*." This chapter addresses both topics in that order.

6.2.2 *Responsibility of Machines*

Chapter 3.2. highlighted how the supporters of a "robotic" *mens rea* can be counted on the fingers of one hand. Predominantly, the discussion focuses on the application of "classic" mental states to AI systems, rather than on the need for new mental states.[43]

This section will address the issue with an open mind, stripped – as much as possible – of any kind of anthropocentrism.

Think of the following example:

42 Translated from German: "*Selbst wenn aber die Strafrechtsdogmatik einen Handlungsbegriff zugrunde legte, nach dem nicht-menschliche, computergelenkte Aktionen als Normbrüche verstanden werden könnten, wäre dieses Verständnis doch – so behaupte ich – auf den Insiderzirkel der Strafjuristen beschränkt. In der Bevölkerung dürfte auf absehbare Zeit einhellig die Meinung vorherrschen, es handele sich um „Maschinen" oder „Computer"*. Seher, 2016, p. 59.

43 See Sec. 6.2.3.3. below and Turner, 2019, p. 204.

> […] a system of DNNs[44] is designed to devise a profitable trading strategy in the equities markets. It is given access to a broad range of data, including a Twitter account, real-time stock prices of thousands of securities, granular historical price data, and access to popular business news feeds. Within months of training on data, the algorithm is able to consistently turn a profit. It is unclear what strategy the AI has stumbled upon, but it is rapidly placing trading orders, consummating some of them and rapidly withdrawing or changing others. Interestingly, the system has learned to "retweet" news articles on Twitter and often does so before and after trades. The designer of the system is not able to tell what role the retweets have in the overall trading strategy, nor is he able to tell why certain trade orders are consummated and others withdrawn. All he can tell is that his AI is working and is profitable. Within days, the price of one of the securities that the AI frequently trades crashes steeply within seconds. The AI, which can either take a long or short position in the security, has, however, managed to make a profit.[45]

Could we say that the AI system intentionally committed the crime of market manipulation?[46] As a matter of fact, it was *not* designed to do so: its objective – by design – was the lawful activity of identifying which shares or stocks to buy/sell in order for the company to obtain a profit.

While AI expansionists argue – more or less convincingly – that AI systems might display *mens rea* following the philosophical theory of BDI,[47] others have attempted to model a definition of criminal intent which could be suitable for algorithms.

In a seminal paper published in 2021, Hal Ashton presented a set of formal definitions of intent which could be converted into "fully formal language, fully suitable for an algorithm".[48] In order to create such a definition, one must assume that "the concept of intent exists outside the human mind",[49] similar to what is done with corporations. As Ashton argues, his theory could be used to inform courts in the event of AI crime: "as to the cul-

44 Deep Neural Networks, see definition at vi.

45 Bathaee, 2018, p. 911.

46 Market manipulation is a criminal offense in most legal systems and can be defined as the intentional artificial manipulation of the price of financial instruments (products, securities or commodities) through practices such as the spreading of false or misleading information and conducting trades in related instruments to profit from this. See, *inter alia*, the definition at art. 5 of the EU Directive on criminal sanctions for market abuse (*Directive 2014/57/EU of the European Parliament and of the Council of 16 April 2014 on criminal sanctions for market abuse*).

47 We will not address whether machines can display criminal negligence. Instead, we will solely focus on the highest mode of intent (i.e., direct intent or purpose). For this reason, from this point onwards the word "intent" will be used to refer exclusively to *dolus*.

48 Ashton, 2022, p. 17.

49 Ivi, p. 23.

pability of its owner and programmer using the existing mechanism of secondary liability".[50] Hence, he did not write this paper with direct liability of AI systems in mind, but to find ways to exclude liability of human beings.

Ashton's theories are mentioned here, and not in Chapter 3, for two reasons: first, the author can be considered an "agnostic" in the debate ("This article is not going to make any claims about the eligibility of algorithms for legal personhood, blame, punishment or even praise and the role that algorithmic intent might play in that … The only thing that this article requires of the reader is that they are open to the possibility that intent (and related mens rea states) can exist in an algorithm");[51] and second, the author adopts an original approach which is more relevant to the discussion of this chapter than to the literature review.

Intent presupposes that the "intended result must be foreseeable as a result of an act".[52] According to Ashton, ascertaining intent in algorithms might differ from humans since machine intent is "presumably perfectly observable (assuming some access to the algorithm)".[53] He contends that it is possible to "peer into" the algorithm and assess the "constituent parts" behind a definition of intent. In other words, he argues that whether an AI system has a certain judgement of likelihood regarding a certain result following an action is "a matter of observable fact".[54] At a first glance, his statement seems to collide with the Black Box Problem, which will be addressed further in this chapter.

Ashton argues that, in order for an AI system[55] to "have the capacity to act with intention in a meaningful way", i.e., to possess criminal capacity, it should meet fundamentally two requirements. First, it should have "some sort of causal model of the world for it to be able to know whether action *a* has a causal relationship with variable X":[56] by looking at this requirement, one can judge whether the AI system knows the consequences of its action. Second, it should have "some sort of preference ordering over states of the world",[57] by looking at this requirement, one can judge whether the AI system has an aim or a desire.

Assuming that these requirements are satisfied, Ashton proposes three definitions of intent. The first definition is the most relevant for the purposes of this study:

> **Definition 1** (*Direct Intent at commission*) An Agent D directly intends a result $X = x$ by performing an action a if:

50 Ashton, 2022, p. 32
51 Ivi, p. 2.
52 Ashton, 2022, p. 7.
53 Ivi, p. 7.
54 Ashton, 2022, p. 7.
55 Ashton speaks of "Agent".
56 Ashton, 2022, p. 24.
57 Ibid.

(DIc1) **Free Agency** Alternative actions *a'* exist which D could have chosen instead of *a*.
(DIc2) **Knowledge** D should be capable of observing or inferring result $X = x$
(DIc3) **Foreseeable Causality** Actions *a* can foreseeably cause result *x* (according to D's current estimate)
(DIc4) **Aim Either of the following two conditions are satisfied:**
(a) **Explicit Aim** D aims or desires result *x*
(b) **Implicit Aim** Alternative actions *a'* exist which are foreseeably (according to D's estimate) less likely to cause result x.[58]

Ashton's definitions could be a useful tool mostly to evaluate liability of human agents, rather than liability of machines. Let us as assume that, according to the definition provided above, a court were to ascertain that the AI system committed the market manipulation out of its own (unpredictable) "intent". Such information should be taken it into consideration – as an excluding or mitigating factor – when evaluating the criminal liability of the managers of the corporation deploying the system, of the team that designed the system, etc.

6.2.3 *Responsibility of Humans*

Attributing direct liability to state-of-the-art AI systems proves to be a challenging task. We might inquire, then, whether subjects *other* than the AI system could be liable jointly with the machine or as sole perpetrators. This research will not address cases where an AI system is *purposely* used as a tool to commit a crime, as it does not represent a conceptually challenging scenario for the purposes of the general part of criminal law. Therefore, the following sections will exclusively deal with the criminal responsibility of humans for negligence-based offenses.

6.2.3.1 The DNA of Negligence

Although almost all contemporary legal systems acknowledge intention or purpose (*dolus directus*), classifications of other types of guilty mental states vary. In particular, some systems, like the one outlined in the Model Penal Code, make a distinction between intention (the conscious desire to bring about the result), knowledge (of the prohibited result which will almost certainly follow the act), recklessness (doing an act while aware that it entails a substantial and unjustifiable risk of harm), and negligence (objective fault in cre-

58 Ashton, 2022, p. 23.

ating an unreasonable risk).[59] Accordingly, recklessness is distinguished from negligence based on the element of awareness of the risk: a defendant might be considered *negligent* when she was not aware of the risk, but she should have been, where instead a defendant might be considered *reckless* when she was aware of the risk and consciously disregarded it. Therefore, this classification stipulates that the distinction between negligence and recklessness is not the risk that is created, which is the same (i.e., a substantial and unjustifiable risk), but rather that the reckless actor *consciously* ignores the risk, whereas the negligent actor does not.

In Continental legal systems, such as in Germany and Italy, the distinction between different kinds of *mens rea* is less fine-grained,[60] as they discriminate only between intent (*dolus*) and negligence (*culpa*). As a result of this bipartite scheme of (guilty) mental states,[61] negligence includes also other "intermediate forms" of subjective responsibility, such as recklessness.[62] In these systems negligence represents "the most normative form of mens rea" and is "primarily based upon a violation of the required duty of care"[63] which then results in a prohibited outcome. Negligence also requires an "individualizing standard" for the reasonable person,[64] i.e., the assessment of negligence is connected to the individual skills of the defendant.

Having acknowledged this, it is not necessary for the purposes of this analysis to adopt a stance in this debate. What is important to recall is that some forms of criminal liability, which we will refer to as "negligence" as an umbrella term, are based on based on two elements: (a) foreseeability and (b) breach of a duty of reasonable care.[65]

---

59 LaFave, 2017, p. 243.

60 J. Blomsma & D. Roef, "Forms and Aspects of Mens Rea", in Keiler & Roef (eds.), 2019, p. 179.

61 Although further internal distinctions can be identified.

62 T. Weigend, 'Subjective Elements of Criminal Liability', in Dubber & Hörnle (eds.), 2014, p. 498. The issue then becomes how to qualify the conduct of "conscious risk taking": the *escamotage* can be found in the *dolus eventualis* and conscious negligence doctrines. *Dolus eventualis* can be described as a conduct of intentional risk taking: 'the actor does not know whether his conduct will bring about a harmful result but accepts the occurrence of that result "in the event that" it comes about'. In other words, the agent 'mentally embraces that outcome'. Conscious negligence, instead, can be described as a conduct of negligent risk taking: the actors do not know whether their conduct will bring about a harmful result, in fact, they unreasonably reject the idea or do not take this possibility seriously (a sort of 'everything will be alright' kind of mental state), but still decide to take the risk. Some argue that the distinguishing element between the two should not be the volition element, rather the knowledge one: the real difference between *dolus eventualis* and conscious negligence (or *luxuria*), then, lies in whether the agent knew that there was a grave risk of harm or a minor risk of harm. See also G. Fletcher, "'The Theory of Criminal Negligence: a Comparative Analysis", *University of Pennsylvania Law Review*, Vol. 119, 1971.

63 Blomsma & David Roef, 2019, p. 195.

64 N. Jan, "Autonomous weapons systems: new frameworks for individual responsibility", in Bhuta N. et al. (eds), *Autonomous Weapons Systems. Law, Ethics, Policy*, Cambridge University Press, 2016, p. 12.

65 If we focus on the US legal system and on the MPC a person is regarded as acting *recklessly* (section 2.0.2(2) (c) a)): "When he consciously disregards a substantial and unjustifiable risk that the material element exists or will result from his conduct. The risk must be of such a nature and degree that, considering the nature and purpose of the actor's conduct and the circumstances known to him, its disregard involves a gross

Negligence is generally based on the detachment from a "golden" standard of conduct. Furthermore, negligence has a "normative essence",[66] and comprises an *objective* and a *subjective* dimension. The latter consists in the enforceability of the respect of such a duty of care: the agent must be reproachable, as she should have and could have avoided the harmful outcome. This means that the law could have demanded better conduct from her. Such requirement is satisfied when the event was foreseeable and concretely avoidable by the model agent, based on a number of factors such as the specific hazardous activity at stake and on the individual qualities of the agent. As was argued, predictability and awareness of the risk are the DNA of negligence.[67] The former consists of the conduct of violation of a pre-existing norm establishing the duty of care. The agent must have had – more or less strongly – *foreseen* that an unlawful consequence would arise from the conduct. The norms may be codified or not codified and have the purpose of pre-emptively striking a balance between conflicting values: the benefits of a certain dangerous activity versus the goods which are endangered by the activity.[68] Moreover, the harmful event caused must be avoidable through the observations of these norms. In other words, the alternative correct conduct must be suitable to avoid harm.[69]

According to Diamantis et al., negligence in the field of humans "behind" AI systems could arise in different scenarios: "selecting improper data sets to train an algorithm, unreflectively specifying its success conditions, insufficiently testing it before release, or even inadequately hardcoding prohibitions for the algorithm ('No matter what, do not turn people into paperclips.')".[70] Let us take a closer look at these issues.

6.2.3.2 Human Oversight and Human in the Loop: Begging the Question?

As was already described, one of the issues connected to AI systems that leads to a vacuum in the allocation of liability is its autonomy. How should this gap be filled?

If we turn our gaze to the AI Act, it seems that one of the solutions to this problem should be found in the concept of "human oversight" and the use of HITL techniques.[71]

---

deviation from, the standard of conduct that a law-abiding person would observe in the actor's situation". Section 2.02(2)(d) establishes that a person is acting negligently: "When he should be aware of a substantial and unjustifiable risk that the material element exists or will result from his conduct. The risk must be of such a nature and degree that the actor's failure to perceive it, considering the nature and purpose of his conduct and the circumstances known to him, involves a gross deviation from the standard of care that a reasonable person would observe in the actor's situation". American Law Institute, *Model Penal Code: Official Draft and Explanatory Notes,* Complete Text of Model Penal Code as Adopted at the 1962 Annual Meeting of the American Law Institute at Washington, D.C., 24 May 1962.

66 Mantovani, 2020, p. 358.

67 Piergallini, 2020, p. 1765.

68 Mantovani, 2020, p. 363.

69 Ivi, p. 369.

70 Diamantis, Cochran & Dam, 2022, p. 7.

71 European Commission, *Artificial Intelligence Act*, art. 14.

These consist of the creation of AI systems in which the model (*output*) is developed through interaction with a human agent who, for example, can play the role of "teacher" in the training phase of the system, providing *feedback* to the machine on the result obtained.[72] Tentatively, "if an autonomous system causes harm to human beings, having a human in the loop provides trust that somebody would bear the consequence of such mistakes".[73]

Such solutions, however, present some problematic issues. In a recent article titled "The False Comfort of Human Oversight as an Antidote to AI Harm",[74] authors Ben Green and Ambra Kak argue that placing humans back in the "loop" of AI seems reassuring, but it is actually loopy in a different sense: it rests on a circular logic that offers false comfort and distracts from inherently harmful uses of automated systems. Policymakers, in fact, are turning to humans to mitigate the risks posed by AI systems based on the assumption that humans are indeed able to police their decision-making processes. In other words, human oversight seems to be used as a kind of "band-aid" on the issues posed by AI autonomy.

Beck contends that when a human in the loop is included in the decision-making process: "one has to realise ... that in many situations, this might lead to excessive demand and responsibility of the human in question".[75] In the contest of AVs, for example, the driver requires at least 6 seconds to take over control of the vehicle, which is in most traffic situations not enough to avoid incidents.

It might even be the case that instead of an actual oversight on the action of the machine, the human is only capable of "rubber-stamping" the results produced.[76] The risk is to create a (human) scapegoat: the contrast with common principles of criminal law is self-evident.

How will a human, in practice, be able to supervise a system that was created to overcome it and make up for her shortcomings? This is especially relevant if transposed to the field of negligent liability.

6.2.3.3 Negligence Failures

Simplifying matters to the extreme, as was stated above, one can affirm that the essential elements of negligence comprise the failure to observe cautionary rules of conduct (codi-

---

72 For a survey of HITL approaches applicable to *machine learning*, see X. Wu et al., "A Survey of Human-in-the-loop for Machine Learning", *arXiv:2108.00941*, p. 2021.

73 European Parliamentary Research Service, "The Ethics of Artificial Intelligence: Issues and Initiatives", 2020, p. 35. See also, Pizzi, Romanoff & Engelhardt, 2020, pp. 145-180; AI-HLEG, 2019.

74 B. Green & A. Kak, "The False Comfort of Human Oversight as an Antidote to A.I. Harm Human Agency in Decision-Making Systems", *Slate*, 15 June 2021.

75 Beck, 2018, p. 43.

76 B. Wagner, "Human Agency in Decision-Making Systems", *Policy & Internet*, Vol. 11, No.1, 2019, p. 114.

fied or non-codified) and the assessment of the concrete agent's behavior in comparison to a model agent. In addition, these precautionary rules have a preventive purpose: the harmful event or danger constitutes the realization of the risk that they were created to avoid.

Negligence failures can be defined as "situations in which the classical building blocks of negligence, ie, risk taking, foreseeability, and awareness, struggle to identify a liable human being to whom we can attribute AI-caused harm. One could envisage negligence failures as nothing but a further development of the 'irreducibility challenge', first theorized by Abbott and Sarch, applied specifically in the field of criminal negligence".[77]

Now, in order to transpose these concepts into the topic under scrutiny, we first need to acknowledge that AI systems are already deployed in "permissible risk" activities (such as transport) which are allowed by our society. Furthermore, as argued by Guerra et al., "[a]t the level of utmost generality, it is important to bear in mind that human negligence and machine error do not represent equivalent risks ... The social cost of machine error promises to be drastically lower than that of human negligence".[78]

It follows that AI systems operate in areas where there are already rules of conduct in place. However – and it is here that one can grasp the peculiarity related to AI – it is necessary to ask whether or not our society currently possesses the correct technical-scientific knowledge to apply pre-existing rules of conduct specifically to the new scenarios that these systems will cause, or even to develop new ones. The answer to this question would seem, for the time being, to be in the negative.

In other words, although one might consider the invocation of the precautionary principle by European authorities to be appropriate, I agree with those who believe that the precautionary principle should serve as a beacon for legislative policy choices, rather than for penalizing ones.[79] This does not preclude the possibility that in the future the threshold required to impose the adoption of new precautionary rules will be exceeded, thanks in part to progress in scientific laws, particularly those that will be concerned with investigating, reconstructing and explaining the behavior of the most complex AI systems.[80]

In a slightly different vein, some scholars argue in favor of creating a new legal concept, namely "fault or negligence by programming", which would thus shift the responsibility for the harm committed by the "creature" onto the "creator".[81] The following questions

77 A. Giannini, J. H. Kwik, "Negligence Failures and Negligence Fixes. A Comparative Analysis of Criminal Regulation of AI And Autonomous Vehicles", *Criminal Law Forum*, 2023, p. 3.

78 Guerra, Parisi & Pi, "Liability for robots I", 2021, p. 1. The authors reason in the field of tort wrongs, nevertheless their arguments can be transposed to and analyzed under criminal liability.

79 Giunta speaks in terms of a "*criterio di politica legislativa*". F. Giunta, "Il diritto penale e le suggestioni del principio di precauzione", *Criminalia*, 2006, p. 229.

80 C. Brusco, "Rischio e pericolo, rischio consentito e principio di precauzione. la c.d. "flessibilizzazione delle categorie del reato", *Criminalia*, 2012, p. 389.

81 Magro, 2014, p. 516; Manes, 2020, p. 4.

then arise: how should this kind of negligence be shaped? More specifically, how should the precautionary rules of conduct be characterized in the implementation and deployment of an AI system?

Subsequently, one can point out certain specific critical issues pertaining to the precipitous aspect of the *enforceability* of the dutiful conduct – omitted by the "human supervisor" – which can be traced back to the broader discussion of the concept of "human in the loop" as discussed earlier.

In particular, one of the most problematic junctures is the *level* of care that can be demanded of the potential supervisor, be it the driver of the semiautonomous self-driving car or the physician using an AI-based diagnostic system. Consider, for example, *automation complacency*, a term coined in the field of aviation accidents to refer to the phenomenon where the automation of any task leads the human supervisor to trust that the machine is handling it effectively and, as a result, to stop paying attention;[82] or *automation bias*, which is the tendency of human beings to place undue trust in the recommendations produced by a computer system.[83] These phenomena, amplified in the case of AI-based automation, would appear to significantly reduce the attention threshold of the human agent grappling with the machine, and, as a result, decrease the threshold of the diligent conduct able to be demanded from the 'model' agent.

What is more, researchers recently have introduced the theory of the "big red button", a sort of emergency kill switch for an AI system which could stop it before it becomes destructive.[84] Such mechanisms need to be handled with care, especially if they are to be translated to criminal liability. Should the HITL be liable for "not pushing the kill switch"? At which conditions? Indeed, "accountability mechanisms built on the assumption of a supreme human overseer are inherently flawed, if adopted without criticism. Such approaches can embed and reinforce the implicit human/machine dichotomy and mystify human agency".[85]

On this matter, Gaede argues that subjects such as "the passenger", "the owner", or the "manufacturer of an AV" could be in principle punished for disregarding standards of care. Moreover, he believes that the most pressing issues are the standard of care that

82 L. Smiley, "'I am the Operator': The Aftermath of a Self-Driving Tragedy", *WIRED*, 8 March 2022. Available at: www.wired.com/story/uber-self-driving-car-fatal-crash/. One of the earliest definitions of *automation complacency* is that developed by E.L. Wiener, "Complacency: Is the term useful for air safety?", *Proceedings of the 26th Corporate Aviation Safety Seminar*, 1981. More recent definitions include R. Parasuraman & D. H. Manzey, "Complacency and Bias in Human Use of Automation: An Attentional Integration", *Human Factors*, Vol. 52, No. 3, 2010.

83 It is defined as the "tendency to use automation as a substitute heuristic for vigilant information seeking and processing" by K. Mosier & L.J. Skitka, "Automation use and automation bias", *Proceedings of the Human Factors and Ergonomics Society Annual Meeting*, 1999, p. 344.

84 Arnold & Scheutz, 2018, p. 60.

85 R. Koulou, "Human Control over Automation: EU Policy and AI Ethics", EJLS, Vol. 12, No. 1, 2020, pp. 9-46.

would be imposed on these subjects and how responsibility would be shared amongst them.[86] For example, one could investigate whether negligence could be attributed to a "researcher" who unintentionally – but in violation of defined standards of care related to AI – creates or releases into the market a dangerous AI system. Gaede contends that, in the case of a violation of these future duties (which would be tailored to the development of AI systems), it would not be possible to excuse the researcher based on the claim that she lacked foreseeability of the damage, since nowadays foreseeability does not require a detailed foresight of the final harmful event.[87]

Indeed, the trend to depart from a strict definition of foreseeability is visible in criminal law efforts to regulate *risk* and in the application of negligence constructs given by courts. In other words, what is asked of the addressee of the criminal norm is not the foreseeability of the *concrete harmful event*, but of a *class* or *type* of events and even of *worst-case-scenarios*.[88] In Italy this change is visible starting from the decisions on asbestos exposure cases up to the ones in the field of natural catastrophic events such as the Vajont Dam[89] disaster or the 2012 earthquake in L'Aquila.[90]

The analogy between AI harm and natural disaster is also evoked by Jacob Turner. Turner, quoting John Danaher,[91] admits that we are facing a retribution gap which is caused by the "delta between humanity's expectations that someone will be held responsible, and our present inability to apply criminal law to AI".[92] In his opinion there are two feasible options: treating the actions of AI as "Acts of God" which have no legal consequences, or finding a "responsible" human. Thus, he believes that "[u]nlike earthquakes or floods, the acts of AI are unlikely to be viewed as unfortunate but morally neutral natural disasters".[93]

---

86 *"[d]ie drängenden Fragen liegen hier darin, welche Sorgfaltsstandards wir den Beteiligten nochauferlegen wollen und wie sich Verantwortungsanteile zueinander Verhalten"*. K. Gaede, "Künstliche Intelligenz – Rechte und Strafen für Roboter? Plädoyer für eine Regulierung künstlicher Intelligenz jenseits ihrer reinen Anwendung", in E. Hilgendorf & S. Beck (eds), *Robotik und Recht*, Vol. 18, Nomos, 2018, p. 81.

87 *"Wurden zukünftig geltende Sorgfaltsregeln der KI-Forschung nicht geachtet, könnte ihn das Argument der mangelnden Vorhersehbarkeit zumindest nicht allgemein entlasten, da die Vorhersehbarkeit schon heute keine detaillierte Voraussicht des letztlich verletzenden Geschehens verlangt. Der Forscher weiß darum, dass sich die Folgen der selbst lernenden Technik schwer eingrenzen lassen bzw. muss er dieses Wissen in seine Betrachtungen instellen"*. Gaede, 2018, p. 81.

88 *"La rivoluzione copernicana (o galileiana) posta in atto dalla giurisprudenza di merito e poi di legittimità consiste nell'assumere a 'parametro' della prevedibilità, ai fini del giudizio di colpa, non già il fatto storico hic et nunc accaduto, bensì un 'genere', una 'classe' di eventi, nei quali il fatto concreto risulti sussumibile: così facendo, l'evento viene ridescritto per così dire 'a tavolino' quale species di un genus, con conseguente espansione dell'area di prevedibilità e (dunque) di responsabilità"*, Civello, La "colpa eventuale" nella società del rischio. Epistemologia dell'incertezza e "verità soggettiva" della colpa", 2013, p. 118.

89 Cassazione Penale, Sez. IV, 25 March 1971.

90 Cassazione Penale, Sez. IV, 25 March 2016, No. 12748.

91 Danaher, 2016.

92 Turner, 2019, p. 120.

93 Ibid.

On the one hand, attaching criminal liability to programmers or users might lead to over deterrence and therefore slow down innovation. On the other, attaching criminal liability to AI systems could in theory fill the retribution gap, even though it would be difficult to locate intent in the system. Assuming that the system's mental state could be "measured and ascertained", the question which remains then is the one of whether "it would be appropriate from a social and psychological perspective to apply criminal law tenets to a non-human entity" or if it were better to define new mental states which would be applicable to AI and with a label different from "mens rea".[94]

If such an abstract concept of foreseeability of harm is deemed sufficient for the purposes of criminal law, it becomes apparent how arduous it would be for the relevant human agent to deny that she had not abstractly foreseen the potential risks associated with deploying, for example, ML techniques.[95] Think of the case of an engineer who created an AI system for making toast and imagine that this system then burns down a house, causing the death of the people who lived in it, because it followed the reasoning "all the bread would be toasted".[96] The programmer, then, might be criminally liable if it were proven for her "reckless behavior in creating such a program".[97]

Gless, Silverman, and Weigend contend that the criminal negligence bar should be lower when it comes to AI applications that generally reduce the risk of harm to society, according to an application-by-application approach (rather than trying to find "all-or-nothing" rules).[98] Such an approach is commendable: the standard of care should be modelled according to the social value of the AI application. For example, "standards of care should be stricter with respect to robots that are of lesser social value, such as toys. With respect to self-driving cars, on the other hand, the risk remaining after careful testing and monitoring may be offset against the general benefits of using such cars".[99]

Provided that there will be areas of application (such as self-driving cars or medical devices) in which it is statistically proven that the use of AI systems reduces the risk of harm, compared to when the same activities are performed by humans, let us imagine two scenarios for the future. Scenario A: the humans behind the machine exercise the greatest care possible. Nevertheless, the AI system commits harm which falls into the sphere of a "generally foreseeable malfunctioning".[100] This act should be regarded as a "normal risk".[101] Scenario B: the humans behind the machine exercise the greatest care possible. Nevertheless, the AI system commits harm that falls outside the reasonable and foreseeable sphere

94 Turner, 2019, p. 204.
95 Magro, 2020, p. 20.
96 Turner, 2019, p. 119.
97 Ibid.
98 Gless, Silverman & Weigend, 2016, p. 430.
99 Ivi, p. 436.
100 Gless, Silverman & Weigend, 2016, p. 433.
101 Ivi, p. 432.

of risk connected to its area of application. This act should be regarded as an event interrupting the chain of attribution,[102] same as a lighting hitting a tree (known as a "coincidental intervening cause").[103]

Both scenarios, then, should lead to an exclusion of criminal liability. In other words, we should consider them as cases of "just bad luck". In this sense, this researcher agrees with Lima's standpoint:

> [...] humans should learn to live with this unfortunate development, much in the same vein that they have learned to live with the results of a bridge collapsing due to a hurricane or a flat tire that leads to a car accident. *Not everything can be foreseen, prevented, or contained, and in everyday life there are several instances where no one is to blame-much more be held criminally liable-for an undesirable outcome.* In other words, *not everything can or should be regulated under criminal law.* Depending on the familiarity that humans will develop with AI agents in the future, this option might prove to be a viable alternative to criminal liability, even though policy implications have to be considered as it is likely that AI acceptance rates might suffer at first.[104]

The job of defining what falls into the sphere of "acceptable risk" and what falls outside that sphere if no rules of conduct or standards are available, is one for the courts. After all, this is what is done already by courts and it appears as there are not sufficient reasons justifying a change when it comes to crimes committed "by" AI systems. The resulting "gap" in accountability should be filled by other domains of law, such as torts or administrative liability. Criminal law shall not be regarded as a *panacea* for all evil, not even for robo evil.

6.2.3.4 It's All about the Data

A question that remains unanswered is the following: who exactly is the human operator?

When analyzing the ample literature on criminal law and AI,[105] together with policy papers on "ethical AI",[106] two things catch the reader's eye. First, little or no attention is given to the different roles which occur in the development chain of an AI systems. Most articles refer only to the programmer, who then becomes the epicenter of accountability. However, AI teams consist of different figures, such as data analysts and scientists, who take care of data collection and interpretation, and ensure that the data collected is rele-

102 Gless, Silverman & Weigend, 2016, p. 432.
103 Ibid.
104 Lima, 2018, p. 694 [emphasis added].
105 See Ch. 3.
106 See Ch. 7.

vant and exhaustive while also interpreting the analytics results; data, and machine learning engineers, who build and test machine learning models; and then also programmers, who implement the solution, transforming the model into coding. This is relevant for various reasons. Most importantly because without a correct understanding of who does what, one cannot allocate liability in a way that is compatible with the principles of criminal law, notably with the principle of blameworthiness. Second, there is little or no reference to liability connected to mistakes or inadequacies of training data. Why are these two factors important for criminal liability?

Let us consider a real world scenario. An algorithm based on ML techniques is capable of teaching itself rules by learning from the training data through statistical analysis, detecting patterns in large amounts of information, and generating outputs. The patterns can then be applied to different tasks, such as driving a car.[107] Deep learning, a subset of ML, is a technique which classifies information through layers of ANNs.[108] The networks have input nodes, which are fed raw data, and output nodes, which determine to which category the input information belongs. For example, this system might be used to classify whether an image contains a woman or not. There are many layers between the input and the output: in order to obtain an output, the algorithm needs to be trained with large sets of labelled data (for examples, pictures labelled as containing a woman). ML algorithms are hungry for data: the more classified data they are fed, the more accurate will be their prediction. The issue is that it is impossible to provide every possible labelled sample of data to a deep learning algorithm. In other words, you cannot feed the algorithm all the pictures of animals, or persons, or cars in the world. Consequently, the algorithm will have to generalize between its examples to classify data that it has never seen before. What happens, then, when the algorithm has been trained on faulty, biased, or wrong data? Indeed, one could mention the now (in)famous Uber's self-driving car fatal accident as an example.[109] This short digression allows us to grasp the importance of good quality training data and of who's behind it.

Indeed, datasets are "rife with errors".[110] At the same time, ML is being used in critical settings where a mistake could prove fatal. One could cite as an example the now famous fatal accident of Uber's self-driving car,[111] caused (also) by the inability of the vehicle's

107 Surden, 2019, p. 1311.

108 B. Dickson, "What are artificial neural networks (ANN)?", *TechTalks*, 5 August 2019. Available at: https://bdtechtalks.com/2019/08/05/what-is-artificial-neural-network-ann/.

109 BBC, "Uber's self-driving operator charged over fatal crash", 16 September 2020. Available at: www.bbc.com/news/technology-54175359.

110 D. Kang et al., "Finding Errors in Perception Data With Learned Observation Assertions", *Stanford Dawn*, 24 January 2022. Available at: https://dawn.cs.stanford.edu/2022/01/24/loa/.

111 D. Wakabayashi "Self-Driving Uber Car Kills Pedestrian in Arizona, Where Robots Roam", *The New York Times online*, 19 March 2018. Available at: www.nytimes.com/2018/03/19/technology/uber-driverless-fatality.html.

software to identify the presence of a pedestrian crossing the road without using a crosswalk.[112]

Recently, data and machine learning engineers started to address the issue. For example, the "data centric AI"[113] (DCAI) movement aims to shift the focus of ML engineering from modelling to the underlying data used to train and then evaluate models. Aspects such as the collection and generation of data, the labelling of data and the evaluation of its quality are central to avoid errors, and therefore harm. Yet, they have not gained popularity in relevant criminal doctrine.

6.3 MATTERS OF *ACTUS REUS*

6.3.1 *The Act*

As highlighted in the introduction, *actus reus* is a concept which includes questions of both conduct and causation. Focusing on the first, in order to have liability there must be a *bodily* movement.[114] One can define "act" in a broad way, thus including involuntary acts such as sleepwalking, or in a narrow way, as a "willed" bodily movement.[115]

If one were to adopt a broad interpretation of "act", as predicated by Hallevy and Lagioia & Sartor, it would follow that an AI system could act in a criminally relevant way, i.e., that it could perform the *actus reus*. In other words, if one were to adopt a materialistic notion of action, "AI systems – not only as robotics applications but also as algorithmic systems of pure software – might be considered capable of realizing a criminal action, as realized in external relationships, both in cyberspace and in the "physical" world".[116]

If, on the other hand, one were to adopt a narrower interpretation, it would follow that in order for a conduct to be willed, i.e., to establish the link between mind and body, the agent would have to display "consciousness" and "control" of the act.[117] In Anglo-US legal doctrine, for example, it has been argued that punishing an act without a voluntary component would not fulfill functions of criminal law such as deterrence and retribution,

112 "The system never classified her as a pedestrian-or correctly predicted her path-because she was crossing N. Mill Avenue at a location without a crosswalk, and the system design did not include consideration for jaywalking pedestrians". See National Transportation Safety Board (NTSB), *Collision Between Vehicle Controlled by Developmental Automated Driving System and Pedestrian, Tempe, Arizona, March 18, 2018* ("NTSB Report Tempe"), Highway Accident Report NTSB/HAR-19/03, p. 16. Available at: www.ntsb.gov/investigations/accidentreports/reports/har1903.pdf.

113 See https://datacentricai.org.

114 We will not consider in this section crimes consisting of an omission to act.

115 LaFave, 2017, p. 304.

116 AIDP General Resolution Section I, 2022, pp. 25-26.

117 Keiler, p. 61.

while achieving restraint or rehabilitation (even though it would "probably [*be*] best to deal with this outside the criminal law").[118]

Can the act of an AI system fulfill a strictly-construed act requirement of a criminal offense? Corporations, as a matter of fact, are treated – in certain legal systems – as subjects of criminal law which possess "rational agent capacities".[119] Similar to AI agents, they can take "rational decisions on the market and possess the capacity for self-organisation and to adapt themselves to the ever-changing economic environment … Thus, corporations although lacking feelings and emotions nevertheless possess capacities for intelligent agency".[120] This is deemed sufficient to make them susceptible to criminal liability (provided that the other elements of the criminal offense are satisfied) and might also be sufficient for AI systems.

6.3.2 *Failures of Causation*

As already highlighted, "failures of causation"[121] is an effective expression coined by Ugo Pagallo to describe the fact that AI agents break down the classic cause and effect analysis linked to matters of legal causation. There are multiple factors which could lead to a failure of causation. This chapter identifies three of them: the 'many hands problem', the black box problem, and shortcuts.

The factors which lead to failures of causation are not mutually exclusive: they co-exist, and their combination further muddies the web of causation by triggering mainly two consequences: (1) they challenge the identification of the (legally relevant) cause that led to the realization of the adverse event (*locus of liability issue*); and (2) assuming that all the (legally relevant) causes can be identified, they challenge the identification of the degree of relevance that the single factor had on the realization of the adverse event (*weight issue*).

Lastly, one must acknowledge that Human-Computer interaction,[122] in the forms of human oversight and HITL approaches, and the interaction between AI systems, also might have an impact in matters of legal causation. Human oversight and HITL were already addressed above. Interacting AI systems entails the fact that algorithms might cooperate "in a complex and dynamic ecosystem",[123] therefore leading to an exponential growth of failures of causation.

118 LaFave, 2017, p. 305. See also the MPC § 2.01 providing that "a person is not guilty of an offence unless his liability is based on conduct that includes a voluntary act".
119 Keiler, p. 61.
120 Ibid.
121 Pagallo, 2013, p. 73.
122 Council of Europe & Yeung, 2019, p. 64.
123 Ivi, p. 67.

6.3.2.1 The "Many Hands Problem"

Let us start with the 'Many Hands Problem'.[124] It can be defined as the simultaneous of a multiplicity of actors involved in the conception, production, marketing, and use of AI systems, as well as to the compartmentalization of the roles of individual human agents throughout this process and of their responsibilities. AI systems are the final product of individual contributions by "multiple individuals, organisations, machine components, software algorithms and human users, often in complex and dynamic environments".[125]

To understand this phenomenon, the example developed by Santoni de Sio and Mecacci is useful:

> [...] a vehicle may be operated by a driver D1, with the assistance of the automated driving system AS, produced by the car manufacturer X, powered with digital systems developed by the company Y, possibly including some form of machine learning developed by the company Z, and enriched by data coming from different sources, including the driving experience of drivers D2, D3... Dn; vehicles in this system are in principle subject to a standardization process done by the agency S, the traffic is regulated by the governmental agency G, drivers are trained and licensed by the agency L etc.[126]

The issue inherent to the 'Many Hands Problem' is that, in contexts which are characterized by complex organizational dynamics such as the one under scrutiny, legal constructs struggle to identify the subject (human or non-human) which misbehaved and to reconstruct the hierarchy of powers that is behind the decision-making processes. Thus, theories of corporate criminal liability might be useful in this matter.

6.3.2.2 The Black Box Problem

The Black Box Problem can be defined as "an inability to fully understand an AI's decision-making process and the inability to predict the AI's decisions or outputs".[127] Indeed, "it may be impossible to tell how an AI that has internalized massive amounts of data is

124 The phenomenon was first analyzed in the field of moral philosophy by D. F. Thompson, "Designing Responsibility: The Problem of Many Hands in Complex Organizations", *The American Political Science Review*, Vol. 74, No. 4, 1980, p. 9. Subsequently, the development of the literature has been exponential. See, by way of example, M. Bovens, *The quest for responsibility. Accountability and citizenship in complex organizations*, Cambridge University Press, 1998; I. R. Poel et al., *Moral Responsibility and the Problem of Many Hands*, Routledge, 2015.

125 Council of Europe & Yeung, 2019, p. 11.

126 F. Santoni de Sio & G. Mecacci, "Four Responsibility Gaps with Artificial Intelligence: Why they Matter and How to Address them", *Philosophy & Technology*, Vol. 34, 2021, p. 1062.

127 Bathaee, 2018, p. 905.

making its decisions",[128] same as it may be impossible to tell how a human brain functions.[129] In other words, you might be able to put a human being on the stand and question her, or she might leave a paper trail of evidence behind her, but the same cannot be done with an AI system.[130]

Think for example of DNNs:[131] they consist of thousands or hundreds of thousands of neurons which, together, deliver an output (a decision) such as identifying the subject of a photograph. Even if one of the layers or clusters might "encode some feature extracted from the data, (e.g., an eye or an arm ...)" often what happens is that "what is encoded will not be intelligible to human beings".[132] Moreover, the network learns from its experience through an intuitive decision-making process and such a process, most of the time, will not be reducible to a set of instructions "nor can one in most cases point to any neuron or group of neurons to determine what the system found interesting or important".[133] If we go back to the example mentioned above of a vehicle, its performance might be "potentially re-designed by the second on the basis of new data acquisition and processing – and opaque, if the reasoning scheme underlying systems' actions is not easily accessible to their controllers, regulators, or even their designers".[134]

To conclude, the issue of the Black Box has obvious repercussions on the scope of liability for negligence for the "human-behind-the-machine" discussed above. Not only does it render an etiological investigation into the realization of harm impractical from a *condicio sine qua non* perspective, it also does not place a "reasonable" person in the position to apply any precautionary measure or "risk calculus" to the act – since she does not know what the risk is.

6.3.2.3 The Shortcuts Problem

Shortcut is a phenomenon that occurs in ML, specifically in self-supervised ML. Self-supervised ML is a model which learns by itself: it is fed raw data without any label description from humans, and it is then told, for example, to classify this data. For example, it might be fed a hundred thousand images and is told to classify images which contain a cow.[135] Sometimes, a model may rely on a simple characteristic in a dataset (for example, the green grass) rather than learning the true meaning of that data. This phenomenon is referred to as a "shortcut". The result is inaccurate predictions. So, in this example the

128 Ivi, p. 891.
129 Bathaee, 2018, p. 891.
130 Ivi, p. 892.
131 Deep Neural Networks, see vi.
132 Bathaee, 2018, p. 902.
133 Ivi, p. 903.
134 Santoni de Sio & Mecacci, 2021, p. 1062.
135 A. Zewe, "Avoiding shortcut solutions in artificial intelligence", *MIT news*, 2 November 2021. Available at: https://news.mit.edu/2021/shortcut-artificial-intelligence-1102.

model might learn to classify an image of cows not by focusing on the shapes and the patterns of the cow, but by focusing on the green grass.

Supervised models are especially useful in medical imaging. For example, a self-supervised learning model might be trained to classify whether or not a chest X ray represents a case of pneumonia. Imagine that the model now classifies an image, tags it as a case of pneumonia, not based on the white spots on the lungs of the patient, but based on which hospital the scan comes from, or even worse, based on the gender or the nationality of the patient. This was the case studied in research published in May 2021,[136] where researchers examined models that had been deployed to detect Covid-19 from chest X rays. They claim that rather than learning medical pathology, the systems identified what are called spurious associations, in other terms, they relied on shortcut learning to identify associations between medically irrelevant factors and a disease status. The system appeared accurate when applied in one hospital but failed to be as accurate when applied to new hospitals.

Let us imagine now that a doctor based her diagnosis on the result of an AI system and, since there was an error in the result provided by the system caused by a shortcut, the misdiagnosis results in the death of a patient. The following question, then, would be regarding how a judge should apply the standard rule on attribution, that is, the operation through which she selects the legally relevant cause of a harmful event, in cases where the AI system takes a shortcut. What if it is not possible to reconstruct the web of causation *ex post*? Which scientific theory should the judge rely on in order to ascertain liability?

6.3.2.4 Omissions to Act

Notwithstanding that most criminal offenses are punished for active conducts, criminal law might also be extended to punish failures to act, even when the criminal offense is formulated only in active terms (i.e., requiring an active conduct with causes a result). Thus, in order for conducts of commission by omission to be criminalized, there must be a legal duty to act.

Having acknowledged this, it becomes necessary to conduct a brief reflection on the possibility of imposing a duty to act (specifically, a "duty to control conduct of others")[137] on the human overseeing the act of the AI systems. According to some authors, it is possible to impose a duty to act in the specific field of semi-autonomous cars[138] on the driver

136 A. J. DeGrave, J. D. Janizek & S. Lee, "AI for radiographic COVID-19 detection selects shortcuts over signal", *Nature Machine Intelligence*, Vol. 3, 2021.

137 LaFave, 2017, p. 316.

138 This corresponds to level 3 of the SAE J3016 standards, i.e., vehicles that can put in place all the maneuvers necessary for driving the vehicle (e.g., acceleration braking). The person inside the vehicle, therefore, does not for all intents and purposes drive it, even if she is sitting in the driver's seat. She will only have to intervene if an explicit request to do so is made by the AI system. This type of technology is called "*hands and*

present inside the vehicle[139] which would be "activated" when the driving system requires the driver to regain control of the car.[140]

Nevertheless, at this time the issue does not appear significant for a number of reasons. Among them is the absence of a fundamental aspect of perpetration by omission: to date, there is no specific *legal* duty to prevent an AI system from causing harm, even though the general rules of criminal law on the matter continue to apply. Neither European, nor international, or domestic legislation contain express provisions in this regard. Yet, legal duties to act can arise also from other sources, for example upon the creation of an imminent danger. The danger in question could be the one caused by an AI system. Hence, one should question whether it would be possible to subsume AI systems within the applicative sphere of the already existing legal duties to act by way of interpretation.

Undoubtedly, from a *de iure condendo* perspective, any effort in this direction would have to be suitable to identify *exactly* who the subject invested with such a duty is, provided that she must also possess an *effective* power of impediment, i.e., she must be physically capable of performing the act which would avoid the realization of the harmful event, in accordance with the founding principles of criminal law.

The introduction of an "all-encompassing" duty to act, i.e., entailing an extended obligation for an unidentified "human overseer" to prevent any harm caused by an AI system, would be in conflict with the principle of legality, specifically with the principle of "strict construction of criminal statutes"[141] (*principio di tassatività*).

Lastly, when one opens up to the concept of commission by omission, one must also confront oneself with the enormous difficulties of ascertaining causation which is innately tied to cases of omission. As was already underlined, when dealing with the actions of AI systems, one is confronted with the simultaneous presence of a myriad of alternative causal factors, both human and non-human. This makes it impractical, on the one hand, to identify the single factor that has not been activated to prevent or interrupt the causal process that has already begun and, on the other hand, to exclude alternative causal factors with the certainty required by modern criminal legal systems

---

feet free but not 'mind free' driving" by V.A. Banks et al., "Subsystems on the road to full vehicle automation: hands and feet free but not 'mind' free driving", in *Safety Science*, Vol. 62, 2014, pp. 505-514.

139 This would be, in particular, a "duty to control". Cf. Piergallini, 2020, p. 1751.

140 See in this regard Manes, who argues "[...] *è chiaro che se il guidatore non è richiesto di monitorare il traffico sino a una richiesta di riassunzione della funzione di guida, lo stesso non può più essere ritenuto in concreto 'human in command' né dunque (penalmente) responsabile di eventuali causazioni lesive occorse sino a quel momento, ove appunto il controllo sulla attività rischiosa era delegato alla macchina* AI driven *legalmente autorizzata*". Manes, 2020, p. 4.

141 J. L. Corsi, "An Argument for Strict Legality in International Criminal Law", *Georgetown Journal of International Law*, Vol. 49, 2018, p. 133; LaFave, 2017, p. 88.

6.4 Corporate Criminal Liability for Automated Decisions

6.4.1 Models of Corporate Criminal Liability (CCL)

Before focusing on Diamantis' theory on "algorithmic corporate misconduct", it is relevant to provide a brief overview of CCL, focusing on the most important aspects for this research.

According to some authors: "the real reasons for the existence of CCL could in fact lie in the power structures behind corporations. By punishing corporations one can prevent the shareholders, owners, and managers from having to go to prison and receiving moral blame, as society has found someone else to be blamed-the entity of a corporation".[142]

Approaches to regulating the criminal liability of legal persons can be divided into two major macrofamilies: the nominalist and the organizational approach. On the one hand, there are the systems that hold that corporations are merely a legal fiction, nothing more than the sum of the actions of multiple human figures (the nominalist approach).[143] The focal point of the nominalist approach is the individual wrongdoing, "from which the liability of the organisation is subsequently derived".[144] In other words, the nominalist approach implies a *derivative* liability for corporations.[145]

The nominalist approach represents the underlying doctrine of two different CCL models: the vicarious and the identification doctrine.[146] According to the vicarious doctrine, a corporation is held responsible for the actions of the individuals who act on its behalf, just as an individual, such as an employer, can be held responsible for the actions of its employee. It is based on the latin brocardo *qui facit per alium facit per se*. The attribution of criminal liability following the vicarious liability model is grounded on a two-step process: first, the elements of the underlying offense must have been fulfilled by the individual conduct; second, "the liability of the individual is imputed to the corporation, based on the legal relationship between the corporation and the individual, i.e. agency or employment".[147] The model has been applied in England mostly by courts, but also through statutes, and has undergone considerable criticism due to the difficulties connected to pinpointing the exact individual who committed the (individual) offense.[148]

---

142 S. Beck, "Mediating the Different Concepts of Corporate Criminal Liability in England and Germany", *German L.J.*, No. 11, 2010, p. 1110.

143 Keiler & Roef (eds.), 2019, p. 336.

144 Keiler, 2013, p. 440.

145 N. Cavanagh, "Corporate Criminal Liability: An Assessment of the Models of Fault", *The Journal of Criminal Law*, Vol. 75, Issue 5, 2011, p. 414.

146 Ivi, p. 448. There are two other models that derive from the nominalist approach, i.e., the senior management theory and the aggregation theory.

147 Keiler, 2013, p. 450.

148 Ivi, p. 209 ff.

The identification doctrine was developed by English courts in the 1940s and is now the dominant doctrine.[149] It implies that the liability of the corporation derives from the responsibility of the individuals who represent "the heart and mind"[150] of the legal entity. Therefore, the *actus reus* and *mens rea* of the top individuals, i.e., of those who can be considered the directing minds and wills of the corporation, are elevated to represent the objective and subjective element of the entity itself.[151] In other words, this doctrine is based on an imputation mechanism such that the conduct and the states of mind of the individuals who "personify" the corporation are attributed directly to the corporation itself. There is no unambiguous definition of what level of authority an agent must possess in order for it to be identified with the corporation. As has been argued, "[b]y requiring that only the most senior persons can be the 'directing mind and will' of a company, it's arguable that large companies are let off the hook, since many key decisions will be decentralized away from the most senior management."[152] Under this model, therefore, the legal entity is regarded as a social reality distinct from the individuals who work for it, in the sense that "the corporation is not held liable for the acts of others but for what are deemed to be its own acts".[153]

On the other hand, there are the systems that instead consider the corporation as a social reality in its own right, additional to the sum of the actions of its individual members (organizational approach). According to this model, corporations are therefore capable of fulfilling the subjective (*mens rea*) and objective (*actus reus*) requirements of the offense independently of the individual human contribution and in ways that differ from it.[154] Consequently, following such an approach criminal liability for corporations is not derivative, it is *direct*. Organizational models represent an interest case study when it comes to discussing the liability of AI systems, since their ideation raised questions which are most relevant in the more general field of accountability for acts of non-human agents. Amongst them, most notably, is the issue of whether corporations can be considered *moral* agents and are capable of acting culpably.[155] As mentioned above, some of the members of the expansionist front made use of such arguments,[156] relying, for example, on Peter French's Corporation's Internal Decision-making (CID) structure.[157] Organizational

149 Keiler, 2013, p. 453.

150 Keiler & Roef (eds.), 2019, p. 336

151 A. Shalchi, House of Commons Library, Research Briefing, "Corporate criminal liability in England and Wales", CBP 9027, 2022, p. 5.

152 Ivi, p. 8.

153 Keiler, 2013, p. 454.

154 Ivi, pp. 437 ff.

155 Cavanagh, p. 429 ff.

156 See Hu above at Para. 3.2.2.

157 French, 1984; P. French, "The Corporation as a Moral Person", *American Philosophical Quarterly*, Vol. 16, 1979.

models include the corporate culture doctrine, which is centered on the concept of organizational fault. This model attentions elements such as the corporation's structure or its organization processes in order to determine whether the corporation possesses "a corporate culture that sanctions or encourages the commission of a crime".[158]

According to some, punishing corporate wrongdoing could even lead to the abandonment of the *mens rea-actus reus* dichotomy in favor of a single notion of corporate blameworthiness. In fact, as Roef notes, the two models are not mutually exclusive, and this is attested to by the fact that some jurisdictions have developed a mixed approach to corporate criminal liability. A third path exists, namely that of corporate administrative liability: this is the model adopted by Italy and Germany.[159] It is the legacy of a conception of criminal law strongly based on the principle of culpability and the preventive function of punishment.

The Italian model is an interesting case study. Corporations are not *criminally* liable since their liability is defined as administrative. Nevertheless, their liability is ascertained during a criminal trial; they are subject to the same guarantees and principles ruling criminal liability of natural persons; and a *mens rea* connection between the fact and the corporation must be established in order to establish their liability. Interestingly, the liability of the corporation and that of the employee are independent (see art. 8 leg. decree 231/2001): it follows that a corporation might be responsible even if it was not possible to identify the specific employee which committed the offense or when the employee cannot be punished, e.g., because she lacked criminal capacity due to insanity.

Germany's (administrative) corporate liability was established by the *Gesetz über Ordnungswidrigkeiten* (OWiG) in 1975. The legislative project of introducing criminal liability, through the *Verbandssanktionengesetz* (VerSanG) failed in 2021. According to Dubber, it is too simplistic to state that "the general take on corporate criminal liability in Germany is that it does not exist, could not exist, and – not surprisingly – did not exist".[160] CCL existed in Germany but it no longer does: "The story then becomes not that there never was or could have been corporate criminal liability in German law, but that there never was or could have been corporate criminal liability in *modern* German law".[161]

158 Cavanagh, 2011, p. 432.

159 Keiler & Roef (eds.), 2019, p. 336

160 M. Dubber, "The Comparative History and Theory of Corporate Criminal Liability", *New Criminal Law Review: An International and Interdisciplinary Journal*, Vol. 16, No. 2, 2013, p. 204.

161 According to a simplistic account the reason would be "[c]orporate criminal liability in a modern, enlightened science of criminal law is illogical, impossible, unthinkable because it flies in the face of one of that science's greatest discoveries, if not its single greatest achievement: the "guilt principle" (*Schuldgrundsatz*, Latinized *ex post* as *nulla poena sine culpa*)". Markus Dubber, The Comparative History and Theory of Corporate Criminal Liability, *New Criminal Law Review*: An International and Interdisciplinary Journal, Vol. 16, No. 2 (Spring 2013), 205.

Conversely, the United States represents the poster child of legal systems that provide direct criminal liability for corporations. Corporations, in fact, can be prosecuted at both federal and state level. It has been affirmed that the United States pursues CCL tenaciously.[162] Admittedly, one of the reasons to pursue CCL is that it "increase[s] incentives for corporations to monitor and prevent illegal employee conduct",[163] i.e., that the threat of sanctions being imposed on corporations will induce them to "take steps to prevent the illegal conduct in the first instance, thus reducing the risk that employees will offend".[164] In other words, *respondeat superior* would be justified under a rationale of deterrence. In this respect, one must highlight the very wide scope of application of the US *respondeat superior* doctrine: corporations may be deemed liable for an employee's actions and mental state, committed within her employment with the intention of benefitting the corporation (at least in part), even if they were in violation of corporate policy.[165] Particular emphasis is placed on corporate culture as a factor in determining the severity of the sanction response and the applicability of parole. In addition, an important factor is that of prosecutorial discretion: in most cases, corporations are able to avoid indictment if they follow specific steps, such as modifying their organizational structure, or paying fines, thanks to Deferred and Non-Prosecution Agreements.[166] Corporate culture is a determining facture also in quasi-criminal corporate liability systems as in Italy: according to article 6 of Leg. Decree 231/2001, corporations are not liable for crimes committed by their high-ranking employees if they prove, amongst other things, the adoption of an efficient organizational and compliance mode.

One could ask oneself whether AI systems could be treated as corporate agents who committed a crime for "corporate reasons". According to a model of CCL such as the US one, it would not be required to establish whether the AI systems could fulfill the elements of a criminal offense in order to establish the corporation's liability.

What impact does the existence of CCL have on liability of AI systems? As already mentioned, according to some authors there is no substantial difference between CCL liability and AI criminal liability.[167] The analogy appears cunning at times. Many questions arise. Surely, one would first have to establish what an AI system is made up of: are AI

162 K. E. Goodpaster, "Tenacity: The American Pursuit of Corporate Responsibility", *BUS. & SOC'Y REV.*, Vol. 118, 2013, pp. 577-605.

163 United States v. Sun-Diamond Growers of Cal., 138 F.3d 961, 971 (D.C. Cir. 1998), aff'd, 526 U.S. 398, 1999.

164 R. Luskin, "Caring About Corporate 'Due Care': Why Criminal Respondeat Superior Liability Outreaches Its Justification", *American Criminal Law Review*, Vol. 57, 2020, p. 303. See also E. Tuttle, "Reexamining the Vicarious Criminal Liability of Corporations for the Willful Crimes of Their Employees", *Clev. St. L. Rev.*, Vol. 70, 2021, p. 121.

165 Luskin, 2020, p. 312.

166 United States Attorneys' Manual § 9-16.325, Plea Agreements, Deferred Prosecution Agreements, Non-Prosecution Agreements and Extraordinary Restitution, 2008.

167 Hallevy, "The Criminal Liability of Artificial Intelligence Entities – From Science Fiction to Legal Social Control", 2010, p. 201.

systems made up of algorithms, of mathematical operations, or are they constituted of the human agents who created them and control them? In the last case, would it mean that AI engineers, data scientists, etc., constitute the AI entity? What effect would be punishing the AI system then have on these subjects following a rationale of deterrence? Unquestionably, it could have powerful indirect effects on these subjects "behind-the-machine". Indeed, "criticizing or disparaging an AI agent may motivate its maker to change the agent's design".[168] In this sense, it can be argued that since AI agents are (or were, at some point) operated by humans, these humans could be deterred from the punishment of the AI systems, specifically in cases where the AI system *benefits* them substantially (be it in economic terms, such as a corporation deploying an AI system to make investments, or in emotional terms, such as robotic caregivers). Nevertheless, "criticizing the operation of a device is quite different from holding the device morally responsible".[169]

6.4.2 *The Next Frontier? Diamantis' Theory of Corporate Criminal Liability for Automated Decisions*

The PCM thought experiment, according to Diamantis et al., snubs a key player: the corporation "which designed, owns and runs the PCM", and profits from it, "even if that entails converting some humans (preferably not customers!) into raw materials".[170]

Starting from the assumption that "the law is not equipped to address corporate liability when the 'thinking' behind corporate misconduct has been offloaded to automated systems",[171] Diamantis first developed a doctrinal framework "for extending the corporate mind to the algorithms that are increasingly integral to corporate thought".[172] According to this theory, any system carrying out the same functional role of an employee, including an AI system, can be part of the corporate mind.[173] As a consequence, it can be argued that corporations possessed "culpable knowledge"[174] of the algorithmic misbehavior.

The work of Diamantis then continues to argue that "algorithmic action is corporate action",[175] i.e., corporations can act both through their employees and through their algorithms. This would not require recognizing algorithms as independent beings. Algorithms

168 V. R. Bhargava & M. Velasquez, "Corporate Responsibility And Artificial Intelligence", *The Georgetown Journal of Law & Public Policy*, 2019, p. 838.

169 Ivi, p. 837.

170 Diamantis, Cochran & Dam, 2022, p. 1.

171 Diamantis, "The Extended Corporate Mind: When Corporations Use AI to Break the Law", 2020, p. 898.

172 Ivi, p. 893.

173 Diamantis, "The Extended Corporate Mind: When Corporations Use AI to Break the Law", 2020, p. 917.

174 Ivi, p. 920.

175 M. E. Diamantis, "Algorithms Acting Badly: A Solution from Corporate Law", *GEO. Wash. L. Rev.*, Vol. 89, 2021, p. 809.

would qualify as part of the "body corporate"[176] since they are entities upon which a corporation can exercise substantial control and from which the corporation gains "substantial productive benefits".[177]

Diamantis defines the "Many Hands Problem" in a "corporate perspective":

> While there is usually at least one corporation behind most important algorithms, there are often many. One corporation may have designed a module for an algorithm that a second assembled. A third corporation may have tested the algorithm. A fourth may have marketed it to a fifth that owned and licensed it to a sixth that operated it on hardware owned by a seventh. Any doctrine for holding corporations vicariously liable for algorithmic harms must say in any circumstance which of these is on the hook.[178]

In a recent work, Diamantis et al.[179] evaluate whether the three current models of corporate liability (the purpose model, the strict liability model, and the negligence model) would be suitable to address algorithmic harm according to whether they can fulfill four goals:

1. identify which corporation will be liable, i.e., make sure that the rules on liability can identify accountable corporations in a clear manner;
2. avoid gamesmanship, i.e., the liability model should not be easily manipulable by corporations, for example via loopholes;
3. generate efficient incentives, i.e., the model should strike an efficient balance between too much or too little liability in order to guarantee social gains and innovation;
4. produce fair outcomes, i.e., striking a balance between the rights of victims not to bear all the costs of algorithmic harms and those of defendants be unfairly prosecuted.

The *purpose model* – applying the *respondeat superior* theory – would occasion that the corporation would be liable for the harm committed by the AI system *purposely* designed or used by an employee to commit harm. Such a model would fulfill goals 1 and 2 but it would not fulfil goals 3 and 4 since it fails to recognize accidental (and, one may add, negligent) accidents. The *strict liability model*, specifically the one based on products liability,

176 Ivi, p. 829.
177 Diamantis, "Algorithms Acting Badly: A Solution from Corporate Law", 2021, p. 843.
178 Diamantis, Cochran & Dam, 2022, p. 4.
179 Ivi, p. 3.

could apply to algorithmic harms only in cases where the corporate algorithms qualify as products and the victims as consumers, which are not many. For example, in cases of injury caused by a self-driving vehicle, it would be easier for the purchaser of the car to qualify as a consumer rather than for the injured pedestrian.[180] The authors discard a broader strict liability model which would require a corporation, e.g., the one who owns the system, to be liable for any offense committed by the AI system due to the fact that it would not fulfill the aforementioned four goals.[181] Lastly, the *negligence model*, which comprises punishing corporations when its employees negligently designed or used an AI system which then caused harm, would fulfil goals 1 and 2, while leaving goals 3 and 4 unfulfileld. This model would impose "too much liability to be fair to corporations" and "too little liability to be efficient". Accordingly, AI systems could cause "serious but preventable harms, even if there's no way to prove that any human involved with the algorithm was negligent" for two reasons: the many hands problem and the "No Hands Problem".[182]

Focusing on the latter, it entails that:

> Each individual's contribution to a complex joint effort may be too miniscule for any one of them to count as negligently causing a harmful outcome. While the many hands problem was about the difficulty of finding evidence of negligence, the no hands problem is more metaphysical. A group of people can cause harmful outcomes, even if no one in the group was at fault. Under these circumstances, it is legally impossible to hold the corporation for an algorithmic harm because there is no negligent employee.[183]

Moreover, "[c]orporations know about the no hands problem. So they have an incentive to parcel out responsibilities among many different employees as a strategy for blocking their liability should something go wrong".[184] The authors conclude by arguing for a "new model of corporate liability, tailor-made for algorithms", such as requiring "all corpora-

180 Diamantis, Cochran & Dam, 2022, p. 6.

181 "Unlike with strict products liability (where there's just one possible defendant – the manufacturer), it's not clear under a sweeping strict liability approach which corporation in the long chain of development of an algorithm should be held liable when the algorithm hurts someone (Goal 1). Any easy answer – like the corporation that owns the algorithm or the corporation that operates it – opens itself to easy manipulation (Goal 2). In holding corporations maximally liable for algorithmic harms, a broad strict liability model might overly depress corporate investment in algorithms (Goal 3). Lastly, since it requires no evidence of corporate fault, the strict liability model will inevitably punish innocent corporations, even if they did everything within their power to design and deploy their algorithms responsibly (Goal 4)". Diamantis, Cochran & Dam, 2022, pp. 7-8.

182 Ivi, p. 8.

183 Diamantis, Cochran & Dam, 2022, p. 8.

184 Ibid.

tions that use AI to pay annual dues into a public victims fund".[185] The last part of Diamantis' theory is the one of "employed algorithms". In his latest publication, Diamantis argues that the relationship between corporations and algorithms should be thought of as a type of employment.[186]

To conclude, the approach suggested by Diamantis is commendable as it adopts a "minimally invasive method"[187] to solve a soon-to-be very invasive problem. Nevertheless, we need to question whether this solution would be applicable also in countries whose legal system are not characterized by a "socially entrenched"[188] secular law of corporate liability which makes it "politically bulletproof",[189] such as the US. An element in favor of the general applicability of Diamantis' theory can be found in a recent Italian publication,[190] where the author introduces a variant of the *respondeat superior* model which would consist of a transposition of the conduct from the AI agent to a different subject (be it an individual or the corporation). According to this theory, it would be possible to establish the (exclusive and autonomous) liability of a corporation for an offense committed by an AI system deployed in a complex organization. Assuming that the AI system can only be considered as a tool to commit a crime, the author argues that it would be possible to hold the corporation liable even in those cases where it is impossible to establish a subjective connection between the AI harmful conduct and a human agent. In other words, the conduct of the human agent, involved in the corporation, would work only to establish an objective nexus between the corporation and the act of the AI system. Accordingly, the corporation could be deemed liable for having deployed a maleficent AI system or for not having exercised the necessary safety controls (c.d. "*colpa di organizzazione*"). This would be in compliance with art. 8 of legislative decree 231/2001, titled "Autonomy of the corporation's responsibilities", which provides that the liability of the corporation occurs even when (a) the perpetrator of the crime has not been identified or cannot be charged; and (b) the crime is extinguished by a cause other than amnesty.[191]

185 Diamantis, Cochran & Dam, 2022, p. 9.

186 Diamantis, 2022.

187 Diamantis, "The Extended Corporate Mind: When Corporations Use AI to Break the Law", 2020, p. 901.

188 Ivi, p. 903.

189 Diamantis, "The Extended Corporate Mind: When Corporations Use AI to Break the Law", 2020, p. 903.

190 F. Consulich, "*Flash offenders*. Le prospettive di *accountability* penale nel contrasto alle intelligenze artificiali devianti", *Rivista Italiana di Diritto e Procedura Penale*, Vol. 3, 2022, p. 1041 ff.

191 "*Art. 8. Autonomia delle responsabilità dell'ente 1. La responsabilità dell'ente sussiste anche quando: a) l'autore del reato non è stato identificato o non è imputabile; b) il reato si estingue per una causa diversa dall'amnistia*", D.lgs 31/2001.

6.5 CONCLUSIONS

The purpose of this chapter was to analyze, with "non-judgemental" eyes whether it would be feasible to apply a traditional criminal legal framework (comprised of criminal capacity, *mens rea* and *actus reus*) to AI systems. Probably, this "legal imagination" exercise makes us, at least, moderates. Indeed, if one was to take a pragmatic stance to criminalization, we could be persuaded that holding AI systems directly liable, and therefore subject to criminal punishment – whether through fines, reprogramming or deletion, would fulfil a deterrence function.

Thus, criminal law does not function in a vacuum. A 2021 research into "how people's moral judgments of automated systems may clash with existing legal doctrines" showed a conflict between people's desire to punish AI and robots and the punishment's perceived effectiveness in achieving deterrence and retribution.[192] Indeed, "people wish to punish AI and robots even though they believe that doing so would not be successful, nor are they willing to make it legally viable".[193] Thus, the participants in the study believed that robots could learn from their mistakes, hence that their punishment could fulfill a pedagogic function.

As much as one would like to, it is not possible to forget about criminal law's intrinsic punitive nature and its retributive function: on this matter, this researcher's heart beats with the skeptics. This is not to say that criminal legal systems should pursue retribution at all costs: it is merely argued here that since criminal law cannot ignore its retributive nature, and the retributive function of criminal law cannot be fulfilled by agents that cannot display blameworthiness (such as AI systems), it follows that *criminal law is not the answer*.

In other words, holding AI systems directly liable for criminal offenses would not fulfill the "retribution" gap.[194] Previous chapters addressed issues of "accountability", "liability", and "responsibility" gaps. More clarification of the term "responsibility" is perhaps needed at this point.

Responsibility refers to a relationship between "an agent, its actions, and the outcomes of those actions".[195] In point of fact, as contended by R.A. Duff, responsibility is a "relational" concept, since it concerns the relationship that is established between a responsible person (A), an object (X) for which this person is responsible, and a third party (B).

192 Lima et al., 2021.
193 Ivi, p. 6.
194 Danaher, 2016.
195 Ivi, p. 300.

Responsibility for Duff thus means "*answerability*", the mechanism by virtue of which A *is held* accountable for X by, and to, B.[196]

This relationship can take many forms:

> The first is that of *causal responsibility*, which denotes a causal link between the agent, their actions, and some particular outcome. The second is that of *moral/legal responsibility*, which denotes the fact that the causal link between the agent and the action/outcome is such that the agent is an appropriate subject of legal/moral blame. This is usually determined by whether the agent has the right capacities and whether those capacities were exercised at the relevant time. The third is *liability responsibility*, which denotes the punishments or sanctions that an agent must bear in virtue of its moral/legal responsibility.[197]

The third denotation ("*liability responsibility*") can be further differentiated depending on the relevant area of law. In the case of criminal law, it can be defined in terms of "punitive liability" and "and is about suffering harm and public condemnation for wrongs done".[198]

Accordingly, the "retribution gap" arises due to the fact that one might – in light of what was emphasized in the paragraphs above – consider that an AI system could bear both causal responsibility and moral/legal responsibility (the first and second denotations of responsibility), but not "liability responsibility" (the third denotation). In other words, it is argued that AI systems give rise to unsurmountable "gaps associated with the attribution of retributive blame for wrongdoing".[199] These gaps cannot be ignored: human beings are, by nature, "inclined to punish in accordance with retributive criteria".[200]

Probably, as is done with infants, and should be done with insane offenders, the solution lies in "looking elsewhere". In the field of tort law, for example, Guerra et al. argue for the introduction of a new tort liability regime called "manufacturer residual liability" ('MRL') which would apply to robots operated with human intervention and would shift "liability to manufacturers provided that operators and third-party victims have invested in due care".[201] In other words, manufacturers would be "strictly liable when operators and

196 R. A. Duff, "Who is Responsible for What, to Whom?", *Ohio State Journal of Criminal Law*, Vol. 2, 2005, p. 442. See also R.A. Duff, "Moral and Criminal Responsibility: Answering and Refusing to Answer", in J. Coates & N.A. Tognazzini, (eds.) *Oxford Studies in Agency and Responsibility Volume 5: Themes from the Philosophy of Gary Watson*, 2019, pp. 165-190; R.A. Duff, "Legal and Moral Responsibility", *Philosophy Compass*, Vol. 4, Issue 6, 2009.

197 Danaher, 2016, p. 300.

198 Ibid.

199 Danaher, 2016, p. 301.

200 Ivi, p. 303.

201 A. Guerra, F. Parisi & D. Pi, "Liability for robots II: an economic analysis", *Journal of Institutional Economics*, Vol. 18, Issue 4, 2021, p. 1.

victims are not negligent regardless of design or manufacturing defects".[202] By doing so, it would accomplish four objectives: "(1) efficient levels of human care by operators and victims; (2) efficient activity levels in the use of robots; (3) efficient R&D investments for the development of safer robots; and (4) adoption of safer robots in the marketplace".[203] This issue will be dealt in greater detail with in Chapter 8: Conclusions.

202 Ivi, p. 2.
203 Guerra, Parisi & Pi, "Liability for robots II", 2021, p. 2.

7 Overview of Existing Legal Frameworks on AI Criminal Liability

Laws, like sausages, cease to inspire respect in proportion as we know how they are made.

(Quote wrongly attributed to Otto Von Bismarck which presumably origins from John Godfrey Saxe, quoted on The Daily Cleveland Herald, Mar. 29, 1869)

7.1 Introduction

Upon initiating this study in 2019, I decided to maintain a stance of impartiality, and probably of hope, on whether legislation specific to AI in the realm of criminal law would emerge. Consequently, this chapter's existence was established from the beginning. It makes use of examples of legislation across the world and, as such, it is not a compete recollection. At the end of my study (i.e., early 2023), only few countries had developed legislation specifically dedicated to AI and criminal law.[1]

Before discussing these samples of regulation, it is relevant to make some general remarks on the topic of regulating AI.

By and large, there is a mismatch between the emergence of technology and regulation, and vice versa.[2] As it has been noted, "the legislative branch seems to be moving at a negligible speed compared to the technological advancements enforcing the perception that traditional regulation does not fit in this challenge".[3] Among possible causes, authors mention: "the lack of a thorough and accurate definition of AI ... which is aggravated by the fact that the definition changes as the technology evolves".[4] The debate on the regulation of AI presents two sides: on the one side, there are those who argue that regulation

1 See, e.g., the General Report authored by Lorenzo Picotti on behalf of the Association International de Droit Pénal – XXI International Congress of Penal Law on "Artificial Intelligence and Criminal Justice", International Colloquium of Section I (Criminal Law-general part): "Traditional Criminal Law Categories and AI: Crisis or Palingenesis?", 2022, para 2. ("General Report").

2 E. Fosch-Villaronga & M. Heldeweg, "Regulation, I presume?" said the robot – Towards an iterative regulatory process for robot governance", *Computer Law & Security Review: The International Journal of Technology Law and Practice*, 2018, p. 2.

3 Patricia Gomes Rêgo de Almeida, Carlos Denner dos Santos, Josivania Silva Farias, "Artificial Intelligence Regulation: a framework for governance", *Ethics and Information Technology* (2021) 23, 507.

4 Gomes Rêgo de Almeida et al., "Artificial Intelligence Regulation: a framework for governance", *Ethics and Information Technology* (2021) 23, 508.

stifles innovation; on the other side, there are those who believe in "anticipatory policy-making".[5]

Furthermore, there is no general consensus on what liability standards should look like.[6] Moreover, there is a "huge gap between ethical guidelines and laws",[7] which has led to a surge in the development of principles related to "ethical AI" in the past 5 years.[8] Consequently, the slow progress of hard-law regulation does not come as a surprise, especially in a field as delicate as criminal law.

Nevertheless, this study identified five relevant inputs in the field of criminal regulation of AI systems:[9]

---

5 N. Boucher, European Parliamentary Research Service – Scientific Foresight Unit, "What if AI regulation promoted innovation?"; PE 729.515, 2022, p. 2.

6 A. Folberth et. al, Karlsruhe: Karlsruhe Institute of Technology (KIT), Institute for Technology Assessment and Systems Analysis (ITAS), "Tackling problems, harvesting benefits – A systematic review of the regulatory debate around AI", *KIT Scientific Working Papers*, Vol. 197, 2022, p. 11.

7 Gomes Rêgo de Almeida et al., "Artificial Intelligence Regulation: a framework for governance", *Ethics and Information Technology*, Vol. 23, 2021, p. 508.

8 E.g., AI-HILEG, *Ethics Guidelines for Trustworthy Artificial Intelligence (AI)*, 8 April 2019; OECD, *Recommendation of the Council on Artificial Intelligence*, OECD/LEGAL/0449. Available at: https://legalinstruments.oecd.org/en/instruments/OECD-LEGAL-0449; UNESCO, *Recommendation on the Ethics of Artificial Intelligence*, SHS/BIO/REC-AIETHICS/2021, https://unesdoc.unesco.org/ark:/48223/pf0000380455; Council of Europe – CEPEJ, *European Ethical Charter on the Use of AI in Judicial Systems Council of Europe*, 2018. Available at: https://rm.coe.int/ethical-charter-en-for-publication-4-december-2018/16808f699. For a systematization of ethical guidelines and principles J. Fjeld et al., "Principled Artificial Intelligence: Mapping Consensus in Ethical and Rights-based Approaches to Principles for AI", *Berkman Klein Center for Internet & Society*, 2020; C. Rudschies, I. Schneider & J, Simon, "Value Pluralism in the AI Ethics Debate – Different Actors, Different Priorities", *The International Review of Information Ethics*, Vol. 29, 2021; A. Jobin, M. Ienca & E. Vayena, "The global landscape of AI ethics guidelines", *Nature Machine Intelligence*, Vol. 1, 2019.

9 Part of these reflections were developed in Giannini & Kwik, 2023. More insights can be found in the AIDP's General Report for Section I. There the author refers to an academic project which took place in Hungary and resulted in the creation of a draft model law addressing the issue which introduces the concept of "AI sanctionability" instead of criminal liability. The General Report also quotes the Chinese National Report for Section I, where the following punishments for strong AI systems are envisaged: "«Data Deletion», namely deleting the data information on which the strong AI system relies to commit crimes, thus depriving it of the ability to commit previous crimes; «Program Modification», namely modifying the program of the strong AI system to restrict the strong AI system's learning ability and data acquiring ability, thus depriving it of its independent recognition and control ability and allowing it to commit acts only within the scope of human control; and «Program Deletion», namely removing all programs related to the strong AI system so that the intangible strong AI system, which depends on the program to survive, no longer exists". Moreover, the Chinese Report focuses on robots and displays that "it is possible to apply a penalty such as restriction of freedom, deprivation of freedom and destruction. The restriction of the space for them to conduct physical activity can restrict or deprive of their freedom. On basis of this, relevant ethical and legal norms can be re-introduced to them during the period when their freedom is restricted or deprived of, so as to educate and transform the strong artificial body. For tangible strong AI systems that cannot be educated and transformed, they can be physically destroyed." Thus, as the author of the General Report notes, GAI has not been developed (yet), hence the Chinese statements remain purely theoretical. See AIDP General Resolution Section I, 2022, pp. 8-9. See also B. Miskolczi & Z. Szathmáry

A) The Council of Europe's European Committee of Criminal Problems and the drafting of an "Instrument on Artificial Intelligence and Criminal Law";

B) The Singapore Penal Code Review Committee Report of 2018[10] and the Report on "Criminal Liability, Robotics and AI systems" drafted by the Singapore Law Commissions of 2021;[11]

C) The legislative reform of the French Road Act (*Ordonnance n° 2021-443 du 14 avril 2021 relative au régime de responsabilité pénale applicable en cas de circulation d'un véhicule à délégation de conduite et à ses conditions d'utilisation*);

D) The "Automated Vehicles: joint report" drafted by the Law Commission of England and Wales and by the Scottish Law Commission;[12]

E) The amendment of the German Road Traffic Act.[13]

They present similarities and differences. To begin with, A is a cross-border tool; where instead B, C, D and E have a national scope of application. Moreover, B and D are – at the present time – proposals to reform the law, where instead C and E have already been implemented. Additionally, C, D and E are sector-specific, as they regard exclusively the field of autonomous driving, while instead A and B have a broader scope of application.[14]

On a final note, mention should be made of the EU, specifically the European Proposal for a Regulation on Artificial Intelligence (Artificial Intelligence Act, AIA) of April 2021. Notably, the AIA is an example of a "risk-based" approach to regulation: it divides AI uses according to different levels of risk. Each level of risk is accompanied by different obligations (which include quality management systems, CE conformity mark, and transparency duties). So far, there has not been any input by the EU regarding *criminal* liability rules in connection to AI systems, whereas in September 2022 the European Commission presented a proposal for a directive on adapting non-contractual civil liability rules to artificial intelligence.[15]

"Büntetőjogi kérdések az információk korában – Mesterséges intelligencia", Big Data, profilozás. HVG-ORAC, Budapest, 2018.

10 PCRC Report, 2018.

11 Singapore Academy of Law, 2021.

12 Law Commissions Report, 2022.

13 Bundestag, Gesetz zur Änderung des Straßenverkehrsgesetzes, 2021.

14 For a more thorough comparison, see Giannini & Kwik, 2023.

15 European Commission, *Proposal for a Directive of the European Parliament and of the Council On Adapting Non-Contractual Civil Liability Rules to Artificial Intelligence (AI Liability Directive)*, COM(2022), 496 final

7.2 General Scope Tools

A) Council of Europe

In November of 2018, the CoE, specifically the CDPC[16] organized a Thematic Session on AI and criminal law responsibility, whose focus was "the importance of a meaningful approach in legal systems across Europe to deal with the challenging questions posed by the increased presence of artificial intelligence in civil life" and it included, amongst its aims, the examination of "the scope and substance of an *international legal instrument to provide common standards for the criminal law aspects of automated technologies*".[17] First and foremost, the CDPC highlighted, according to the *ultima ratio* principle, that the "*degree of harm*" and the "*importance of the obligation breached*" need to be taken into consideration before criminal liability is triggered.[18]

The CDPC's initial focus was the case of automated vehicles, notably on how "to set up rules governing any potential criminal liability in advance to ensure that in cases such as a car collision or a drone crash, no State will have to face an unclear legal situation due to unsuitable or out-of-date rules".[19] Nevertheless, it was decided to treat it as a "general scope" tool since the CDPC's intention is to use AV merely as an example of AI deployments and the future legal instrument will presumably have a larger scope of application.[20]

Following the thematic session, the CDPC established the Working Group of Experts on Artificial Intelligence and Criminal Law ("Working Group") to assist the CoE in its research on criminal law and AI.[21] The Working Group, after a first meeting in March 2019, prepared a questionnaire to conduct a census of relevant national criminal norms applica-

2022/0303 (COD), 28 September 2022.

16 The CDPC was established in 1958 by the Committee of Ministers under Article 17 of the Statute of the CoE. Its goal is to set European standards and principles via binding and non-binding legal texts in a variety of fields related to criminal law and procedure.

17 Council of Europe, European Committee on Crime Problems (CDPC), "Thematic session on artificial intelligence and criminal law the approach in Council of Europe member states the case of automated vehicles", Programme, CDPC(2018)18, 28 November 2019, p. 2. Available at: https://rm.coe.int/cdpc-2018-18-draft-programme-thematic-session-artificial-intelligence-/16808e64ab.

18 Council of Europe, CDPC, Concept Paper, 2018, pp. 4-5.

19 Ivi, pp. 4-5.

20 Council of Europe, CDPC, Working Group of Experts on Artificial Intelligence and Criminal Law, "Questionnaire concerning Artificial Intelligence and Criminal Justice (using the example of Automated Driving)", CDPC(2019)8FIN (2019), 19 May 2019, p. 3. Available at: https://rm.coe.int/cdpc-2019-8fin-questionnaire-artificial-intelligence-and-criminal-just/168094c8fa.

21 Council of Europe, CDPC, Working Group of Experts on Artificial Intelligence and Criminal Law, "Working Paper II", CDPC(2019)7, 27 March 2019, p. 3. Available at: https://rm.coe.int/cdpc-2019-7-working-paper-ii-for-cdpc-expert-group-meeting-on-artifici/16809372a5.

ble to automated vehicles (or other AI deployments).[22] The questionnaire starts off with an example of a case:

> Imagine that, for the first time, a vehicle equipped with an "autopilot system" can be used legally on highways in your country. The automated driving system must be used in harmony with the authorisation which requires – among other things – that the human driver is ready to take over the steering wheel within 20 seconds. To ensure the driver's fitness to take over, the producer installs a drowsiness detection system monitoring the driver (seating position, face and especially eye movements) and stores the data with a cloud service provider. During the first months of operation of such cars, it turns out that a certain weather phenomenon in your country (be it morning mist, a sandstorm, midday sun or garbage thrown on the roadside) triggers faulty reactions in the driving assistant's system – especially false-braking, i.e. braking for the wrong reason, for instance a plastic bag drifting in the wind. The producer and all component suppliers do their very best to fix the problems. However, it is clear to everyone involved that the cars will need time to adjust to particular local conditions.[23]
>
> Let us imagine that the car hits a human being while driving on autopilot, causing her death, and that it is further established that not only the car's sensors were defective, but also that the braking assistant had a severe software defect. Nevertheless, it is not possible to ascertain which defect caused the accident. In this case, the questionnaire asks whether the domestic law of the member country knows the concept of "contributory negligence" and, in case of a positive answer, whether it is seen as a matter of theories of causation or of complicity (or collaboration in negligence).[24]

The questionnaire continues by investigating the concept of societal risk. Let us suppose that "it could be proven that the car's sensors did not pick up the victim, most likely because he/she held a bag at arm's length and the engineers had 'tuned out' bag images from the sensors' vision in order to prevent 'false braking'".[25] In a case like this, "criminal justice systems may provide an option to forgo criminal prosecution, arguing that in the

22 Council of Europe, CDPC, Working Group of Experts, "Questionnaire concerning Artificial Intelligence and Criminal Justice", 2019, p. 3.

23 Ivi, p. 3.

24 Council of Europe, CDPC, Working Group of Experts, "Questionnaire concerning Artificial Intelligence and Criminal Justice", 2019, p. 5.

25 Ibid.

light of the overall social benefits a particular type of risk taking should not be punished even if harm is caused as long as the person in question does its best to comply with all requirements of safety and security".[26] As a matter of fact, this is the dominant school of thought with regard to airbags in cars ("although there is a minimal risk that this safety device might open because of a pothole and kill a passenger, it will moreover save lives in many situations").[27]

The assessment of the answers to the questionnaire reported a tendency of States to remain rooted in traditional notions and liability schemes, even when adopting new regulations. Notably, none of the 36 member states that filled out the questionnaire[28] "opted for the creation of a new legal notion (such as an "e-personhood").[29] Thus, the Working Group concluded that the potential capacity of AI systems "to challenge the community's trust in the validity of the law"[30] could warrant a "more functional approach in criminal justice, and possibly an evaluation of the option of a e-personhood".[31] Moreover, the Working Group advised introducing a new regulation which would update or create new concepts of liability, including corporate liability (but not necessarily *criminal* liability).[32]

Lastly, in September 2020, the Working Group published a feasibility study on a future Council of Europe instrument on AI and criminal law.[33] The purpose of the feasibility study was to address whether an *ad hoc* Council of Europe committee of experts should be set up to prepare a draft instrument setting common criminal law standards on different relevant issues raised by vehicles driving autonomously (or other AI deployment).[34] The answer to this question is affirmative: according to the Working Group, even though issues

26 Council of Europe, CDPC, Working Group of Experts, "Questionnaire concerning Artificial Intelligence and Criminal Justice", 2019, p. 5.

27 Ibid.

28 These are: Andorra, Armenia, Austria, Azerbaijan, Belgium, Bosnia and Herzegovina, Bulgaria, Croatia, Czech Republic, Denmark, Estonia, Finland, France, Germany, Greece, Italy, Moldova, Monaco, Montenegro, North Macedonia, Norway, Latvia, Lithuania, Luxembourg, Poland, Portugal, Romania, Russia, Serbia, Slovakia, Slovenia, Spain, Sweden, Switzerland, Turkey and Ukraine.

29 Council of Europe, European Committee on Crime Problems (CDPC), 'Assessment of the answers to the questionnaire on artificial intelligence and criminal justice (using the example of Automated Driving)', CDPC(2019)17 (2019), 5. Available at: https://rm.coe.int/cdpc-2019-17-draft-assessment-of-the-answers-to-the-questionnaire-on-a/168098e24c.

30 Council of Europe, CDPC, "Assessment of the answers to the questionnaire on artificial intelligence and criminal justice (using the example of Automated Driving)", CDPC(2019)17 (2019), 7 November 2019, p. 12. Available at: https://rm.coe.int/cdpc-2019-17-draft-assessment-of-the-answers-to-the-questionnaire-on-a/168098e24c.

31 Ibid.

32 Council of Europe, CDPC, "Assessment of the answers to the questionnaire", 2019, p. 12.

33 Council of Europe, CDPC, Working Group on AI and Criminal Law & CDPC Secretariat, "Feasibility study on a future Council of Europe instrument on artificial intelligence and criminal law", CDPC(2020)3Rev (2020), 4 September 2020. Available at: https://rm.coe.int/cdpc-2020-3-feasibility-study-of-a-future-instrument-on-ai-and-crimina/16809f9b60.

34 Council of Europe, CDPC, Working Group on AI and Criminal Law & CDPC Secretariat, "Feasibility study", 2020, p. 4.

of criminal liability are a matter of national jurisdictions, in the case of AI they must be regulated "within an international and collaborative framework".[35] According to the CPDC, the reasons for creating an international legal instrument are manifold: it would foster the development of consistent legislation across Europe ("[it is not a question of devising a whole new system of liability that would overturn the criminal law of each member state, but rather of agreeing on a general framework for criminal law and AI deployment within which state-wide regulations could be developed");[36] it would bring legal certainty to European citizens and assist free movements across national borders; and it would facilitate cooperation between different states on AI-related matters, facilitating the exchange of data. Based on the results of the questionnaire, the Working Group decided to exclude the issue of creating a legal personality for AI systems which would be relevant in criminal matters.[37]

Conclusively, the CDPC created an ad hoc committee tasked with the drafting of such instrument (Drafting Committee to elaborate an instrument on Artificial Intelligence and Criminal Law, CDPC-AICL). The potential nature of the instrument which will be adopted was discussed during the first two meetings of the CDPC and the members agreed on drafting a Recommendation.[38] The deadline to submit a draft of the legal instrument to the Committee of Ministers has now been set for December 2023.[39]

B) Singapore

The proposals analyzed in this paragraph are a paramount example of Singapore[40] striving to become a key normative player in the field of AI. Indeed, Singapore is seeking to estab-

35 Ivi, p. 9.

36 Council of Europe, CDPC, Working Group on AI and Criminal Law & CDPC Secretariat, "Feasibility study", 2020, p. 10.

37 Ivi, p. 12.

38 Council of Europe, CDPC, "1st meeting of the Drafting Committee to elaborate an instrument on Artificial Intelligence and Criminal Law (CDPC-AICL)", CDPC-AICL(2021), 17 November 2021, p. 3. Available at: https://rm.coe.int/cdpc-aicl-2021-1-1st-meeting-report-15-16-nov-2021/1680a49c99.

39 CDPC, "Terms of Reference", Extract from CM(2021)131-addrev, p. 2. Available at: https://rm.coe.int/cdpc-en-terms-of-reference-cm-2021-131-addrev/1680a4b41a; Council of Europe, CDPC, "2nd meeting of the Drafting Committee to elaborate an instrument on Artificial Intelligence and Criminal Law (CDPC-AICL)"; CDPC-AICL(2022)2, 9 June 2022, p. 3. Available at: https://rm.coe.int/cdpc-aicl-2022-2-2nd-meeting-report/1680a6e1ff.

40 The legal system in Singapore is based on British common law. Its criminal justice system is adversarial and pluralistic since it incorporates elements of Malay customary law and Muslim law. Its Penal Code and Criminal Procedure Code have been heavily influenced by Indian legal culture. Cf. M. Nalla "Singapore", *World Factbook of Criminal Justice Systems*, 1993. Available at: https://bjs.ojp.gov/content/pub/pdf/wfbcjss.pdf; S. Yeo, N. Morgan & C. Wing Cheong, *Criminal Law in Malaysia and Singapore*, 2nd ed., LexisNexis, 2012.

lish itself as an AI "rule of law hub",[41] by means of introducing regulation "to attract and encourage AI innovation".[42] This effort is substantiated in two different proposals: the Singapore Penal Code Review Committee (PCRC) Report of 2018[43] (and, more specifically, the proposal to introduce two new offenses relating to computer programs);[44] and the Singapore Academy of Law's[45] Law Commission Report on Criminal Liability, Robotics and AI Systems of 2021 ("SAL Report").

Let us start with the first. The PCRC Report, amongst other things, suggests introducing two new offenses. According to the first offense,

> (1) Whoever makes, *alters* or *uses* a computer program so rashly[46] or negligently as to endanger human life, or to be likely to cause hurt or injury to any other person, or knowingly or negligently *omits* to take such order with any computer program under his care as is sufficient *to guard against any probable danger* to human life from such computer program, shall be punished with imprisonment for a term which may extend to one year, or with fine which may extend to $5,000, or with both.
>
> (2) For the purposes of this section, a person uses a computer program if he causes a computer holding the computer program to perform any function that –
> (a) causes the computer program to be executed; or
> (b) is itself a function of the computer program.[47]

41 Chesterman, 2021, p 5.

42 Ibid. In 2018, the Singapore Penal Code Review Committee (acknowledged that "[b]eing the global first-mover" on rules regarding criminal liability related to AI systems might "impair Singapore's ability to attract top industry players in the field of AI". Nevertheless, it further advised the Singaporean government to "actively explore and develop a suitable framework to address the issue of criminal liability for harm caused by computer programs. This should be done in the broader context of Singapore's developing regulatory framework for AI." PCRC Report, 2018, p. 29.

43 The PCRC was established by the Singaporean Home Affairs and Ministry of Law in 2016 to review the Singapore Penal Code and make recommendations on how to reform it. It completed its review in 2018.

44 The PCRC includes AI in the term "computer programs". See PCRC Report, 2018, p. 27, Para. 2.

45 The Singapore Academy of Law ("SAL") is a private organization that was established in 1988 with the goal of making Singapore the "legal hub of Asia". It is led by a Senate which is headed by the Chief Justice and comprises the Attorney-General and the Supreme Court Bench. See www.sal.org.sg.

46 In the Singapore criminal legal system, rashness constitutes a form of culpability, akin to negligence, that results from a failure to exercise a reasonable level of care and caution in one's actions. Rash acts are characterized by imprudent or impulsive behavior, without taking appropriate safety measures, whereas negligence typically arises from routine actions that are commonly understood to pose some degree of danger. S. JLS, "The Continuing Confusion Over Section 304A of the Singapore Penal Code", *Singapore Journal of Legal Studies*, 2015, p. 144.

47 PCRC Report, 2018, p. 30.

> (3) For the purposes of this section, a computer program is under a person's care if he has the lawful authority to use it, cease or prevent its use, or direct the manner in which it is used or the purpose for which it is used.

The proposed offense would target two groups of individuals: those who create and modify computer programs, and those who use them.[48] It establishes a crime of endangerment:[49] the new offense would punish a conduct of "risk creation"[50] regardless of the verification of harm. The realization of harm, whether resulting in physical injury or death, would trigger the application of other offenses of the Singapore Penal Code (such as articles 304A or 337). As noted by the PCRC itself, such offense does not include scenarios in which, on the one hand, the harm caused does not result in physical harm or death and, on the other, the "user" is not aware that the (specific) harm will occur, "either because the program is capable of learning new behaviors on its own or because the program is designed to act random".[51]

To fill this apparent *lacuna*, the PCRC proposes adopting a second offense:

> (1) Where a computer program –
> (a) produces any output, or
> (b) performs any function,
> that is likely to cause any hurt or injury to any other person, or any danger or annoyance to the public, and the computer program *is under a person's care*, if that person knowingly *omits to take reasonable steps to prevent* such hurt, injury, danger or annoyance, he shall be punished with imprisonment for a term which may extend to one year, or with fine which may extend to $5,000, or with both.[52]

---

48 Ivi, p. 30, para. 13.

49 Crimes of endangerment are criminal offenses that punish acts or omissions that create a significant risk of harm to others, regardless of whether that risk is ultimately realized. They are characterized by a failure to show proper concern for the safety of others. While the actus reus elements of endangerment offenses may not present significant challenges, there is ongoing debate regarding the appropriate *mens rea* connection, specifically whether it should be viewed as a form of strict liability or fault-based culpability. From a perspective that aligns with principles of culpability, the offender should be held liable for their indifference to the risk they created, specifically for displaying an attitude of disregard for legally protected interests. See A. Duff & T. Hörnle, "Crimes of Endangerment", in Ambos K. et al. (eds.), *Core Concepts in Criminal Law and Criminal Justice*, Vol. 2, Cambridge University Press, 2022, pp. 132-166; R. A. Duff, "Criminalizing Endangerment", *La. L. Rev.*, Vol. 65, 2005, pp. 944-945.

50 PCRC Report, 2018, p. 13, para. 30.

51 Ivi, p. 30, para. 14.

52 PCRC Report, 2018, pp. 31-32.

This formulation would attach responsibility also to those overseeing an AI system who were not aware of the existence of any kind of risk connected to it. Indeed, different from the first offense, the duty of care ("to take reasonable steps to prevent such hurt, injury, danger or annoyance") is not tied to the knowledge of a general risk ("that the computer program is likely to cause any hurt or injury to any other person, or any danger or annoyance to the public"). The way the offense is formulated, specifically the vagueness of the concept of being "under a person's care", seems to entail "that the general risk of harm could also be an objective and intrinsic characteristic of the computer program, ie, one that is *independent from any subjective evaluation of the culpable agent.* [...]" and, therefore, that a user could be liable for not acting to mitigate the risks connected to an innate feature of AI systems.[53]

Let us move on to the second proposal, that is, the SAL Report of February 2021. The SAL Report looks into the potential dangers that autonomous robotic and artificial intelligence systems (RAI) can pose to people and property. It specifically focuses on instances where harm occurs and whether or not Singaporean criminal laws should apply and how criminal liability should be determined. The report acknowledges that there are various uses for these systems, each with its own unique risks and benefits, making it difficult to have a one-size-fits-all approach to criminal liability.[54] Therefore, the report examines two factors: first, whether or not there is a human "involved in operating, affecting, or overseeing the RAI system); second, "where such a human is involved, whether they intended or knew the harm would occur".[55]

The Committee argues that the first issue would be to identify the "user-in-charge".[56] In cases where the level of automation is lower than level of human oversight exercised (i.e., "partial automation"), the user-in-charge would be the subject who "directly controls or is responsible for determining the actions of the RAI systems".[57] In cases of highly (yet not fully) automated RAI systems, the user-in-charge would be either the subject who is ultimately responsible for deciding/approving a particular action, the one who maintains control over the system's decision-making process, or the one who is specifically obligated to intervene to control the system's action in a given scenario.[58] Considering this, the SAL Report then distinguishes between two different situations: first, cases of intentional crim-

53 Giannini & Kwik, 2023, pp. 22-23.

54 SAL Report, 2021, p. 10, para. 14.

55 Ivi, pp. 10-11, para. 1.5.

56 SAL Report, 2021, p. 23, para. 4.1. "User-in-charge" is the same term adopted by the UK Law Commissions, as it will be outlined in the next paragraph. The Committee addresses this overlap and states that "[w]hile utilising the same term, the definition of 'user-in-charge' adopted here differs from that utilised by the UK Commissions in the specific context of automated vehicles (although its 'users-in-charge' would equally fall within the definition utilised here)". Ivi, p. 23, No. 34.

57 Ivi, p. 23, para. 4.3.

58 SAL Report, 2021, pp. 23-24, para. 4.3.

inal use of, or interference with, the RAI system; second, cases of *non-intentional* harms. Let us focus on the latter, as the use of AI systems as (very sophisticated) tools to commit crimes is outside the scope of this research.

As described in the SAL Report, in order to establish negligence the Singapore Penal Code[59] sets two conditions: (a) determining what an objective "reasonable person" would do in a given circumstance, and (b) proving that that standard was breached in the specific case.[60] When addressing harm caused by RAI that falls within the realm of existing negligence-based offenses, it would be up to courts to "apply or adapt existing criminal negligence standards, or – in the absence of precedents – define new ones".[61] Furthermore, a new negligence-based offense might be created to cover all negligent actions that result in harm from RAI systems, setting the reasonable conduct threshold. As a result, the risk of such a broadly applicable rule is that it may not be sufficient to capture RAI system actions that have never occurred before, i.e., conducts for which "existing precedents are inappropriate or for which there is no existing precedent at all".[62]

Additionally, the SAL Report considers legislating the adoption of industry- or technology-specific norms of conduct. One of the examples mentioned by the drafters is the example of AVs: the SAL Report argues that regulation might define specific situations in which the user-in-charge must assume control of the vehicle, such as when a route is temporarily blocked due to a traffic accident.[63] In this regard, the SAL Report's strategy is distinct from that of the UK Law Commissions. As will be shown below, the latter concentrates on the suitability of the single Autonomous Driving System feature of the vehicle, to be validated through an authorization procedure, rather than on external circumstances (e.g., an accident) and their impact on the obligation of the operator to intervene. In fact, according to the UK model, the user-in-charge is not responsible for *any* "dynamic driving offence"[64] or civil sanction that occurs while such a feature is activated.

It is worth noting that the SAL Commission highlights the importance of every stage of the AI deployment process (data preparation, training of the mode, choosing the relevant model[s], the environment where the RAI system is deployed) as probable causes of the realization of a criminal offense.[65] The SAL Report also highlights the fact that harm could result from the amount, accuracy, and quality of the training data as well as the RAI system's architecture (i.e., its code). The importance of comparing the environments in which the system was trained and deployed, on the one hand, and the real world data that

59 "Whoever omits to do an act which a reasonable person would do, or does any act which a reasonable person would not do, is said to do so negligently". Singapore Penal Code, 1871, S 26F(1) PC.
60 SAL Report, 2021, p. 30, para. 4.24.
61 Ivi, p. 31, para 4.26.
62 SAL Report, 2021, p. 31, para. 4.27.
63 Ibid.
64 See below at C) for a definition of dynamic offences.
65 SAL Report, 2021, p. 32, para 4.32.

the RAI system had collected at the time the damage was committed, on the other, should also be considered.[66] By doing so, the SAL Commission devotes attention to factors that are typically overlooked by scholarly discourse, as stated in Section 3.5.

The SAL Commission, reasoning under the premise that criminal negligence may not (always) be the solution, recommends four fixes for what was referred to as "negligence failures".[67] The first is the creation of a new form of legal personality for RAI systems, so that criminal liability could be imposed *directly* on the RAI system itself.[68] Doing so would diminish "the extent to which it is necessary to get 'under the bonnet' of an RAI system, and identify which specific part or parts of that system caused its decision to act as it did, and which of the (potentially numerous) parties involved in the system's development and deployment should be held responsible therefor".[69] It follows that holding AI systems directly liable would have an "indirect penalizing effect on those responsible for or profiting from the RAI system, while minimizing the need to prove that the harm was attributable to specific natural persons or corporations".[70] The SAL Committee ultimately discards this option since it considers the arguments against separate personality for RAI systems more compelling:

> We consider that criminal laws should continue to be formulated on the basis that such laws are intended to shape or impact human behaviour. It is not fully clear, for example, how imposing criminal liability (and a sanction) on an RAI system directly would deter the system itself from causing harm. And to the extent that the objective would be to deter or penalize those responsible for the RAI system, rather than the system itself, we also take the view that such ends could equally be achieved through alternative mechanisms that do not require the creation of wholly new forms of legal personality (with all the disruption to the existing legal framework that that would necessarily entail).[71]

In contrast, the second and third options refer to the offenses from the PCRC Report. The Committee observes that, despite the fact that the offenses may indeed address negligent failures, they do not sufficiently define the boundaries of the duty of care related to the AI

66 Ibid.

67 "Negligence failures can be defined as situations in which the classical building blocks of negligence, ie, risk taking, foreseeability, and awareness, struggle to identify a liable human being to whom we can attribute AI-caused harm". Giannini & Kwik, 2023, p. 3.

68 SAL Report, 2021, p. 36, para. 4.41.

69 Ivi, p. 37, para. 4.43.

70 SAL Report, 2021, p. 37, para. 4.44.

71 Ivi, p. 38, para. 4.47.

system. Specifically, more work needs to be put into defining precisely what "a rash or negligent act" or "failure to take reasonable steps in any given case" means.[72]

The fourth alternative is to use workplace safety legislation as a model. This represents an original suggestion, which resembles Diamantis' "Employed Algorithms" doctrine.[73] Notably, workplace safety is one of the subjects where criminal law identifies certain "centers of imputation" of liability which are entrusted with the protection of legal goods and, as a consequence, they are deemed responsible if they fail to do so – or do so poorly.[74]

Imputation mechanisms related to risk governance, especially when they involve complex structures such as corporations or the AI development process, are a slippery slope. The more distance there is from the specific (natural) cause of a harm, the more issues with regard to the principle of culpability arise. This type of liability is usually deeply rooted in statutory duties "to take all reasonably practicable measures to avoid the harm (including, for example, the adequacy of the protective processes and systems the entity had in place)"[75] and less focused on the determination of "the specific cause of the harm",[76] or on the negligence of a (natural or legal) subject.[77] In other words, "the prosecution need not to prove a direct or scientifically precise causation between the harm caused by the RAI and a particular breach of duty".[78]

Now, the SAL Report suggests the introduction of a system similar to the one provided by the Workplace Safety and Health Act ("where a duty is imposed on specified entities to take, so far as is reasonably practicable, such measures as are necessary to avoid harm").[79] Accordingly, one could think of imposing a duty on the entity which is "best placed – on the bases of their 'proximity' to the RAI system and its operation, and their resources – to take action (i.e., to prevent, address and rectify dangers posed by RAI systems) and to change future outcomes".[80] As will be explained directly below, the concept of "proximate liable entity" recurs also in the UK Law Commissions Report, specifically with reference to the Automated Driving System Entity (ASDE).[81]

While the SAL Commission acknowledges the issues which such a model may pose, it concludes by stating that its introduction might be justified by the seriousness of the risks posed by the RAI and by the citizens' need of an accountability framework. Particularly,

72 SAL Report, 2021, p. 40, para. 4.54.
73 See above at Para. 6.4.2.
74 Cfr., *ex multis*, E. Scaroina, "La responsabilità penale del datore di lavoro nelle organizzazioni complesse", *Sistema penale*, 2021.
75 SAL Report, 2021, p. 42, para. 4.62.
76 Ibid.
77 SAL Report, 2021, p. 42, para. 4.62.
78 Ibid.
79 SAL Report, 2021, p. 41, para. 4.58.
80 Ivi, p. 41, para. 4.59.
81 See below at D).

introducing RAI-related duties in the field of workplace safety ("where distinct statutory duties are already imposed and the appropriate policy balance has thus already been considered and determined")[82] would not entail reinventing the wheel, instead it would mean reviewing and, as necessary, amending: "those existing laws to ensure that occupiers and employers may equally be held responsible for harm resulting from the autonomous operation of RAI systems in their workplaces".[83] Lastly, it would amount to "a policy judgment for lawmakers, balancing, in particular, demands for accountability with the desire not to unduly stifle innovation and impede the societally-beneficial development and use of RAI systems".[84]

7.3 Self-Driving Tragedies: AV-Specific Tools

The realm of driving automation has been the stage of numerous self-driving tragedies[85] in recent years, which have called the application of criminal law into play. It is worth mentioning a few of them to provide context for the three specimens of regulation that this section is about to examine.

In May 2016, a collision between a Tesla Model S 70D car,[86] which was being operated using Traffic-Aware Cruise Control and Autosteer lane-keeping systems (SAE Level 2),[87] and a truck-tractor, caused the death of the occupant of the car near Williston, Arizona. The investigation of the crash was directed by the National Transportation Safety Board (NTSB), after it learned of a defect investigation related to automatic emergency braking Autopilot systems of the Tesla Models S and X of the National Highway Traffic Safety Administration (NHTSA).[88] The NTSB is an independent federal agency established in 1967 and is dedicated to promoting aviation, railroad, highway, marine, and pipeline safety. Its mission does not include the assignment of fault or blame for an accident or

82 SAL Report, 2021, p. 43, note 84.

83 Ibid.

84 SAL Report, 2021, p. 42, para. 4.63.

85 The term is taken from Smiley, 2022.

86 NTSB, Collision Between a Car Operating With Automated Vehicle Control Systems and a Tractor-Semitrailer Truck Near Williston, Florida, May 7, 2016, Highway Accident Report NTSB/HAR-17/02, 2017, p. 9 ("NTSB Report Florida"). Available at: www.ntsb.gov/investigations/accidentreports/reports/har1702.pdf.

87 Ibid: "TACC is an adaptive cruise control system that maintains the set cruise speed, applies brakes to preserve a predetermined following distance when approaching a slower-moving vehicle ahead of the Tesla, and accelerates to the set cruising speed when the area in front of the Tesla is no longer obstructed. Autosteer automatically steers the car to keep it within its lane of travel. In short, TACC provides longitudinal control (acceleration and deceleration) and Autosteer provides lateral control (steering) of the car within the lane, making the Tesla Autopilot consistent with an SAE International (SAE) Level 2 automated vehicle system."

88 National Highway Traffic Safety Administration (NHTSA), Office of Defects Investigation, Investigation PE 16-007, 2017. Available at: https://static.nhtsa.gov/odi/inv/2016/INCLA-PE16007-7876.PDF.

incident.[89] Rather, "accident/incident investigations are fact-finding proceedings with no formal issues and no adverse parties ... and are not conducted for the purpose of determining the rights or liabilities of any person".[90] As such, it represents an instance of an entity conducting *non-punitive* and *non-blameworthy* investigations as happens in the field of aviation.[91] In its investigation of the Florida crash, the NTSB focused on the Autopilot system and concluded that the probable cause of the crash was "the truck driver's failure to yield the right of way to the car, combined with the car driver's *inattention due to overreliance on vehicle automation*, which resulted in the car driver's lack of reaction to the presence of the truck".[92] Moreover, "[c]ontributing to the car driver's overreliance on the vehicle automation was its *operational design*, which *permitted his prolonged disengagement from the driving task* and his use of the automation in ways inconsistent with guidance and warnings from the manufacturer".[93] Notwithstanding the fact that Tesla's automated vehicle control system "was not designed to, and did not, identify the truck crossing the car's path or recognize the impending crash"[94] and, consequently, it "did not reduce the car's velocity, the forward collision warning system did not provide an alert, and the automatic emergency braking did not activate";[95] that it was not designed as to automatically restrict its operation in conditions for which they are not designed (such as driving on a highway); and that, overall, Tesla failed to consider adequately the human element,[96] there were no investigations of Tesla's (criminal) involvement in the accident. Notably, it was reported that the Dutch vehicle authority (*RijksDienst voor het Wegverkeer* or RDW) requested information on the crash from the NHTSA, as it regarded autopilot features that had been approved by the RDW for its use in Europe.[97] Moreover, in July 2020, a Munich regional court (*Landgericht München I*) banned Tesla from using the terms "autopilot" and "full potential for autonomous driving" in the sale of its Tesla model 3 cars, since it misled consumers into believing that these vehicles were technically capable, and legally

89 NTSB Report Florida, 2017, p. 3.
90 49 C.F.R. § 831.4.
91 See above Sec. 4.1.
92 NTSB Report Florida, 2017, vi.
93 Ibid.
94 NTSB Report Florida, 2017, p. 41.
95 Ibid.
96 Tesla failed to recognize that "monitoring steering wheel torque provides a poor surrogate means of determining the automated vehicle driver's degree of engagement with the driving task"; moreover, the way its Autopilot System "monitored and responded to the driver's interaction with the steering wheel was not an effective method of ensuring driver engagement"; finally, it failed to consider the risk of driver overreliance on its system and the possibility of a lack of understanding of system limitations. NTSB Report Florida, 2017, p. 45.
97 Reuters, "Dutch vehicle authority seeks answers on fatal Tesla crash", 14 July 2016. Available at: www.reuters.com/article/tesla-authority-dutch-idINL8N1A03KF.

authorized, to drive without any human intervention (i.e., level 5 automation), when in reality they only reach level 2 automation.[98]

On 18 March 2018, Elaine Herzberg was struck and killed by an automated Uber test car (SAE level 3) carrying a human driver in Tempe, Arizona.[99] According to NTSB's Report,[100] since the Automated decision system (ADS) did not recognize the pedestrian as a jaywalker, it detected her only about 6 seconds before the collision. Notably, the system was designed with little regard for jaywalking pedestrians. The human-in-the-vehicle was assigned the duties of "overseeing the system's operation, monitoring the driving environment, and, if necessary, taking control of the vehicle and intervening in an emergency".[101] In other words, the vehicle operator was contemplated as the "primary countermeasure in an emergency situation"[102] as she was expected to "recognize the hazard, to take control of the vehicle and to intervene appropriately".[103] The report mentions the probable cause of the crash was the failure of the vehicle operator to monitor the driving environment and the operation of the ADS, since she was looking at her mobile phone. Contributing to the crash were Uber Advanced Technologies Group's: (1) inadequate safety risk assessment procedures, (2) ineffective oversight of vehicle operators, and (3) lack of adequate mechanisms for addressing operators' automation complacency – all a consequence of its *inadequate safety culture.*[104] Moreover, the same report recognizes that "[c]onsidering the road-

98 "(a) *Durch die Verwendung des Wortes "Autopilot" suggeriert die Beklagte aus Sicht der angesprochenen Verkehrskreise, die von ihr vertriebenen Fahrzeuge seien in der Lage, vollständig autonom zu fahren. Jedenfalls besteht eine hinreichende Gefahr, dass die angesprochenen Verkehrskreise den Begriff dahingehend missverstehen.*
(b) Die Formulierung "Volles Potenzial für autonomes Fahren" erweckt bei den angesprochenen Verkehrskreisen die Vorstellung, das von der Beklagten vertriebene Fahrzeug sei technisch in der Lage, vollkommen selbständig zu fahren oder zumindest die Herstellung dieser Eigenschaft sei ohne Weiteres durch geringfügige Modifikationen (Upgrades) erreichbar. Die Verwendung des Wortes "Potenzial" werden die angesprochenen Verkehrskreise entweder dahingehend verstehen, dass bei dem Fahrzeug eine technische Grundausstattung vorhanden ist, die ohne erhebliche Zwischenschritte und Investitionen ein Erreichen von Level 5 der in den USA und Europa branchenüblichen Klassifikation zum autonomen Fahren möglich macht. Zudem besteht die hinreichende Gefahr, dass die angesprochenen Verkehrskreise die in Frage stehende Formulierung dahingehend verstehen, der Nutzung der beworbenen Funktionen stünden allein regulatorische Hürden entgegen". LG München I, Endurteil vom 14.07.2020 – 33 O 14041/19, paras. 97-98.

99 Uber was conducting a preliminary test of a "Level 4" vehicle automation level as described by the National Highway Traffic Safety Administration. Cf. A. DeArman,, "The Wild, Wild West: A Case Study of Self Driving Vehicle Testing in Arizona", *Arizona Law Review*, Vol. 61, 2019, p. 988, Note 28. Level 4 is "high automation" and entails that the system is fully responsible for driving tasks within limited service areas, while occupants act only as passengers and do not need to be engaged. When the system is engaged, it handles all the driving tasks and the driver is not required to maneuver the vehicle. Source: www.nhtsa.gov/technology-innovation/automated-vehicles-safety.

100 NTSB Report Tempe, 2018.

101 Ivi, p. 8.

102 NTSB Report Tempe, 2018, p. 14.

103 Ibid.

104 NTSB Report Tempe, 2018, pp. 57-59.

way geometry, the sight distance, and the lighting in the crash area, the vehicle operator, had she been attentive, would have had *2 to 4 seconds* to detect and initiate a response to the crossing pedestrian to prevent the crash."[105] Hence, an attentive behavior would have "likely"[106] avoided the crash or mitigated its impact. Yet, the NTSB also acknowledged a crucial aspect, i.e., the fact that "[w]hen it comes to the human capacity to monitor an automation system for its failures, research findings are consistent – humans are very *poor* at this task"[107] and that Uber failed to address these risks adequately. Specifically, the NTSB concluded that it was the vehicle operator's prolonged visual distraction, "a typical effect of automation complacency",[108] that caused her to disengage with the vehicle and therefore led to her failure to detect the pedestrian in time to avoid the collision. In a letter of 4 March 2019, the Yavapai County Attorney stated that there was no basis for criminal liability for the Uber corporation arising from the matter,[109] while the back-up driver in the Uber car was charged and indicted with a count of negligent vehicular homicide[110] by a Maricopa County Grand Jury on 27 August 2020.[111]

In a criminal trial which was supposed to commence in Los Angeles on 15 November 2022, Kevin George Aziz Riad, a Tesla Model S driver, is facing two charges of vehicular manslaughter with gross negligence.[112] Specifically, Riad was behind the wheel when his car ran a red light while exiting a freeway and crashed into a Honda Civic, killing its two passengers. Allegedly, Tesla's Autopilot was engaged at the time of the crash.

It has also been reported that Tesla Inc. is now the subject of a criminal investigation by the U.S. Department of Justice (DOJ).[113] Presumably, the DOJ is investigating Tesla's marketing claims regarding the capabilities of its Autopilot, which could have led drivers to "imbue customers with a false sense of security, inducing them to treat Teslas as truly driverless cars and become complacent behind the wheel with potentially deadly consequences".[114]

105 Ivi, p. 43.
106 NTSB Report Tempe, 2018, p. 57.
107 Ivi, p. 44 [emphasis added].
108 NTSB Report Tempe, 2018, p. 44.
109 Yavapai County Attorney, "Re: Rafael Vasquez / Uber Corporation, Tempe Police Department #2018-32694", 4 March 2019. Available at: https://s3.documentcloud.org/documents/5759641/UberCrashYavapaiRuling03052019.pdf.
110 See A.R.S. §§ 13-1101, 13-1102, 28-3001, 28-3004, 28-3005, 28-3315, 13-701, 13-702, and 13-801.
111 State of Arizona, "Indictment 785 GJ 251", 27 August 2020. Available at: http://www.maricopacountyattorney.org/DocumentCenter/View/1724/Rafael-Vasquez-GJ-Indictment.
112 T. Krisher & S. Dazio, ""Felony Charges Are 1st in a Fatal Crash Involving Autopilot" *AP NEWS*, Los Angeles, 18 January 2022. Available at: https://apnews.com/article/tesla-autopilot-fatal-crash-charges-91b4a0341e07244f3f03051b5c2462ae.
113 M. Spector & D. Levine, "Exclusive: Tesla faces U.S. criminal probe over self-driving claims", *Reuters*, 27 October 2022. Available at: www.reuters.com/legal/exclusive-tesla-faces-us-criminal-probe-over-self-driving-claims-sources-2022-10-26.
114 Ibid.

These three real life scenarios work as a useful display of the complex relationship which can occur between a human behind the wheel, an automated vehicle, and a lethal accident. The three examples which will be analyzed now are an attempt at simplifying this very tangled web.

C) France

In 2021, the French government adopted an *ordonnance* which amended the French Road Code by introducing specific provisions on the criminal liability applicable to the circulation of a vehicle with driving delegation. We can summarize its most relevant passages as follows.

First, the *ordonnance* added article L. 123-1 to the French Road Code, which stipulates that art. L. 121-1 of the French Road Code does not apply to drivers who commit infractions resulting from the maneuver of a vehicle whose driving functions have been delegated to an automated driving system, provided that the system was in dynamic control of the vehicle at the time of the offense.[115] Apropos, art. L. 121-1 provides that: "The driver of a vehicle shall be criminally liable for violations committed while operating said vehicle". Consequently, art. L. 123-1 introduces an immunity clause which shields drivers from criminal liability whilst certain functions of driving (i.e., "dynamic driving", which is not expressly defined in the Road Act), are performed by an AI system.[116]

The second paragraph of art. L.123-1 stipulates that the driver must be *constantly* in a state and in a position to respond to a request to take control of the automated driving system. Indeed, according to the new art. L. 319-3, the AI system must alert the human

---

115 "*Art. L. 123-1. Les dispositions du premier alinéa de l'article L. 121-1 ne sont pas applicables au conducteur, pour les infractions résultant d'une manœuvre d'un véhicule dont les fonctions de conduite sont déléguées à un système de conduite automatisé, lorsque ce système exerce, au moment des faits et dans les conditions prévues au I de l'article L. 319-3, le contrôle dynamique du véhicule.*
Le conducteur doit se tenir constamment en état et en position de répondre à une demande de reprise en main du système de conduite automatisé.
Les dispositions du premier alinéa de l'article L. 121-1 sont à nouveau applicables:
1° Dès l'instant où le conducteur exerce le contrôle dynamique du véhicule à la suite d'une reprise en main de celui-ci;
2° En l'absence de reprise en main du véhicule par le conducteur à l'issue de la période de transition faisant suite à une demande du système de conduite automatisé dans les conditions prévues au II de l'article L. 319-3;
3° Au conducteur qui ne respecte pas les sommations, injonctions ou indications données par les forces de l'ordre ou les règles de priorité de passage des véhicules d'intérêt général prioritaires prévues au présent code".

116 The definition can be found in the Decree of 29 June 2021 n. 2021-873, TRAT2034544, at article 2: it entails "[t]he performance of all real-time operational and tactical functions required to move the vehicle", including "control of the lateral and longitudinal movement of the vehicle, monitoring of the road environment, response to events in road traffic, and preparation and reporting of maneuvers". See M. Giuca, "Disciplinare l'intelligenza artificiale. La riforma francese sulla responsabilità penale da uso di auto a guida autonoma", *Archivio Penale*, Vol. 2, 2022, p. 22.

driver whenever it is capable of exercising dynamic control of the vehicle in accordance with its conditions of use (para I). Moreover, after the driver has taken the decision to activate the automated driving system after the alert, the AI system must also perform a so-called *demand de reprise* anytime it perceives that it will not be able to perform successfully (para II).[117] When the request of a takeover fails, or in the event of a serious failure, the ADS must also be able to put the vehicle in safety. Thus, according to French law, the AI system is seen as the focal point of responsibility, as it is tasked both with notifying drivers of its ability to exert dynamic control at specific intervals during the journey, as well as with alerting them of its inability to do so at other intervals, through the use of a "*demand de reprise*" notification.

The third paragraph of art. L.123-1 regulates the re-expansion of the scope of liability for the driver: it stipulates that the driver who either retakes dynamic control of the vehicle or fails to respond to a *demand de reprise* after a "transition period" (which remains undetermined) will be subject again to the provision of article L. 121.1.[118]

Lastly, in reference to the manufacturer of the vehicle, article L.123-2 stipulates that the producer shall be held accountable for any unintentional injury or harm caused to an individual's life or physical well-being committed by the vehicle during intervals when the ADS was actively exerting control over the vehicle, as per its intended usage conditions, provided that a culpable act as defined by article 121-3 of the French Penal Code can be established.

D) England and Scotland

At the end of January 2022, the Law Commission of England and Wales and the Scottish Law Commission ("Law Commissions") released a Joint Report ("Joint Report") on Automated Vehicles.

---

117 "*Art. L. 319-3.-I. La décision d'activer un système de conduite automatisé est prise par le conducteur, préalablement informé par le système que ce dernier est en capacité d'exercer le contrôle dynamique du véhicule conformément à ses conditions d'utilisation.*
II.-Lorsque son état de fonctionnement ne lui permet plus d'exercer le contrôle dynamique du véhicule ou dès lors que les conditions d'utilisation ne sont plus remplies ou qu'il anticipe que ses conditions d'utilisation ne seront vraisemblablement plus remplies pendant l'exécution de la manœuvre, le système de conduite automatisé doit:
1° Alerter le conducteur; 2° Effectuer une demande de reprise en main; 3° Engager et exécuter une manœuvre à risque minimal à défaut de reprise en main à l'issue de la période de transition ou en cas de défaillance grave".

118 Giuca argues that this newly introduced immunity clause works as a mere *reconnaissance* of a conclusion which could have been reached by applying standard principles of criminal law, specifically the rules on negligence. Giuca, 2022, p. 29.

The aim of the Joint Report is to facilitate the implementation of specialized legislation, specifically, the Automated Vehicle Act. Its publication marks the first instance in which the Law Commissions have been tasked with developing a legal framework *prior* to the emergence of future technological advancements.[119]

The Joint Report defines an AV as a vehicle that is designed to be capable of driving itself ("self-driving vehicles").[120] Self-driving vehicles operate in such a way that they do not need to be controlled and monitored by an individual for at least a portion of a journey. Let us analyze the most relevant provisions of the proposal.

To begin with, the UK Law Commission proposes the introduction of a new and independent authorization scheme[121] for evaluating whether an ADS feature can be considered as self-driving according to the law or not.[122] The attribution of the label "self-driving" to an ADS feature[123] is relevant as it represents the prerequisite for the activation of the immunity clause. Indeed, once the ADS feature is correctly engaged, the human in the driving seat would acquire by law the new role of "user-in-charge", causing a change in the allocation of liability, as it will be discussed below.

By adopting the term "self-driving" the Law Commissions purposely chose to take a distance from the terms used in the SAE Taxonomy.[124] The term is so cogent that the drafters recommend that it becomes "protected", in the sense of being safeguarded by two spe-

119 Law Commissions Report, 2022, p. 1, para 1.1.

120 Ivi, p. 2, para 1.10.

121 Authorization would consist of a separate procedure from domestic, European or international approvals, which instead regard whether the vehicle can be placed on the market. Each ADS feature would have to be assessed. The objects of the authorization are three. First, the authorization authority must assess whether the feature reaches the legal threshold to be labelled as self-driving (Law Commissions Report, 2022, p. 27, para 2.57). Second, each ADS feature must be able to control the vehicle in a legal and safe way, even if the human user is not monitoring the driving environment, the vehicle, or the way the vehicle drives (Law Commissions Report, 2022, p. 67, para. 4.66). The Law Commissions recommend that the new Automated Vehicle Act "require the Secretary of State for Transport to publish a safety standard against which the safety of automated driving can be measured" which "should include a comparison with harm caused by human drivers in Great Britain" (Recommendation 6, p. 27, para. 4.66). Measuring the performance of the AVs against those of human drivers would ensure public acceptance ("When deaths and injuries occur, it will be important to reassure the public that AVs are nevertheless safer than human drivers, and to have the evidence to support this claim", p. 66, para. 4.62). Third, the authorization authority will evaluate whether the ADS entity (ADSE) has sufficient resources to keep the vehicle updated and compliant with traffic laws in Great Britain and to deal with any kind of issue that might arise.

122 Law Commissions Report, 2022, Ch.2, pp. 69 ff.

123 An ADS "feature" is defined as "a combination of software and hardware which allows a vehicle to drive itself in a particular operational design domain (such as a motorway)." Ivi, p. 135, note 239.

124 It is not a mere linguistic choice: the term was adopted in order to convey a legal boundary as opposed to a technical one. As will be discussed later, once this threshold is met, the individual occupying the driver's seat (referred to as the "user-in-charge") would no longer be held liable for any harms resulting from the dynamic driving task.

cific criminal offenses: first, "Describing unauthorised driving automation as 'self-driving'";[125] second, "Misleading drivers that a vehicle does not need to be monitored".[126]

Most importantly, the Law Commissions argue that they aim to "*draw a bright line*":[127] the criminal liability of the person sitting in the driver's seat of a self-driving vehicle shall be excluded for *any* harm arising from the *dynamic* driving task, in cases where the offense is committed by a vehicle which was previously authorized to deploy self-driving features, assuming that those features were properly engaged. In order to draw this "bright line", the recommendations create three new legal actors: the user-in-charge, the ASDE and the No-User-In-Charge (NUIC) operator.

Starting with the first, the user-in-charge is defined as the human being sitting in the driver's seat while a self-driving feature is engaged. Her main role is "to take over driving, either following a transition demand or because of conscious choice".[128] The user-in-charge enjoys immunity from "driving offences",[129] provided that she has engaged the ADS correctly and that she has not tampered with the system.[130] Driving offenses do not constitute a pre-existing category of crimes in UK legislation. They are defined in the Joint Report as any offense involving "a breach of duty to monitor the driving environment and respond appropriately by using the vehicle controls to steer, accelerate, brake, turn on lights or indicate".[131] Examples of dynamic driving offenses are: dangerous driving, careless driving and exceeding the speed limit.

125 Law Commissions Report, 2022, p. 126, para. 7.21.

126 Ivi, p. 129, para. 7.38.

127 Law Commissions Report, 2022, para. 5.46. A dynamic driving task is defined as "the real-time operational and tactical functions required to operate a vehicle in on-road traffic. It includes steering, accelerating and braking together with object and event detection and response", Law Commissions Report, xviii.

128 Ivi, p. 55, para. 4.1.

129 The user-in-charge remains liable for non-dynamic offenses and is responsible for: "(1) Duties to carry insurance; (2) Duties to maintain the vehicle in a roadworthy condition; (3) Any parking offence which continues after the ADS feature is disengaged; (4) Duties following accidents to provide information and report accidents; (5) Duties to ensure that child passengers wear seatbelts; (6) Duties relating to loading; and (7) Strategic route planning, including duties to pay tolls and charges." Ivi, Recommendation 45, p. 154, para. 8.103.

130 "Recommendation 44. While a relevant ADS feature is engaged, the user-in-charge should not be liable for any criminal offence or civil penalty which arises from dynamic driving. The immunity should not apply if the user-in-charge has taken steps to override or alter the system so as to engage the ADS when it is not designed to function. The immunity should cease if the user-in-charge deliberately interferes with the functioning of the ADS". Law Commissions Report, 2022, p.149, para. 8.79.

131 Ivi, p. 146, para. 8.62.

The definition of user-in-charge can be divided into four elements. That person must be:

> (1) *an individual* (a human or "natural person", rather than an organization);
> (2) *who is in the vehicle* (hence not standing nearby or in a remote operations center);
> (3) *in a position to operate the driving controls* (for current vehicle design this entails that she in the driver's seat);
> (4) *while an ADS feature requiring a user-in-charge is engaged* (an ADS feature is engaged when it is switched on and remains so until the individual takes control of the vehicle, the transition period ends or it switches off at the end of a journey.[132]

The user-in-charge is no average (reasonable) agent: users-in-charge must be "qualified and fit to drive", like "average drivers" who are liable for conducts such as unlicensed driving or driving under the influence of alcohol or drugs. Moreover, users-in-charge must be "receptive to a transition demand" and comply with other "driver responsibilities", which include insuring the vehicle and reporting accidents.[133]

The Joint Report distinguishes between the duties of *monitoring* and of *receptivity*. The first entails checking the driving environment, the vehicle, or the way it drives. An ADS feature can be considered as self-driving only if it excludes this duty. Consequently, the user-in-charge shall not comply with the duty of monitoring. The second, instead, entails being receptive to a transition demand, i.e., the request by the vehicle for the human user to take over the dynamic driving. Think of the following example to understand the distinction: "[a] person who becomes aware of a fire alarm or a telephone ringing may not necessarily have been monitoring the fire alarm or the telephone".[134]

Users-in-charge must comply with the duty of receptivity, i.e., they need to be receptive to a transition demand, which must be communicated by clear, multi-sensory signals and give the user-in-charge sufficient time to gain situational awareness.[135] We can find a duty of receptivity also in the French amendment, which provides that the driver shall constantly be in a condition and in a position to respond to a transition demand (*demande de reprise*) from the ADS.[136] When it comes to transition demand and liability, time is of the essence: as soon as the transition period is over, the user-in-charge loses her immunity

132 Law Commissions, "Automated Vehicles: Summary of joint report", Summary of LC Report No 404 / SLC Report No 258, HC 1068 SG/2022/15, 26 January 2022, p. 17, para 4.2. Available at: https://s3-eu-west-2.amazonaws.com/lawcom-prod-storage-11jsxou24uy7q/uploads/2022/01/AV-Summary-25-01-22-2.pdf.

133 Law Commissions Report, 2022, p. 21, para. 2.46.

134 SAE, 2021, p. 12.

135 Law Commissions Report, 2022, p. 13, para. 2.15.

136 "*Le conducteur doit se tenir constamment en état et en position de répondre à une demande de reprise en main du système de conduite automatisé*". Art. L. 123-1, *Code de la route.*

and she goes back to being legally treated as a driver.[137] Yet, the Law Commissions do not specify how long this period should be, consequently leaving a major gap in the proposed regulation. Notably, in order for a user-in-charge to be receptive, she needs to know what she must be receptive to. Furthermore, she might need to "rehearse how to respond appropriately if the stimulus arises. That is why, in addition to installing fire alarms, organisations have fire drills".[138] A question which remains unanswered, it follows, is the one of how a normal driver becomes a "fit" user-in-charge.

As was highlighted, the immunity clause's application is lifted in case the user-in-charge fails to respond to a transition demand. In these cases, the ADS "should carry out a sufficient risk mitigation maneuver. Regulators will need to consider what is sufficient, but we would expect that at a minimum the vehicle should come to a controlled stop in a lane with its hazard lights flashing".[139] In terms of liability of the user-in-charge (now "normal" driver), the recommendations only state that "the law should impose consequences on a user-in-charge who fails to take over", without providing any kind of further instructions.[140] Again, a gap occurs.

As a final point, it is relevant to focus briefly on the second and the third legal roles introduced by the Joint Report: the ADSE and the NUIC operators. These subjects are legal persons, rather than natural persons, and might coincide in cases where the vehicle manufacturer or developer is also the one providing a passenger service. An ASDE is defined as "the entity that puts an AV forward for authorisation as having self-driving features. It may be the vehicle manufacturer, or a software designer, or a joint venture between the two".[141] The ASDE will have the duty to prove in the authorization process that the user-in-charge has sufficient time to gain situational awareness in cases of a transition demand and, if she fails to respond, that the vehicle is capable of sufficient mitigation against the risk of a crash.[142] Other duties of the ASDE include duties relating to safety (such as ensuring that the vehicle continues to drive safely and in accordance with road rules)[143] and duties of disclosure.[144] The NUIC operator is a licensed legal person which oversees vehicles possessing a NUIC feature. While on a vehicle deploying NUIC features, a whole journey can be completed without any kind of intervention by a human on board.

137 "The length of the period is legally significant". Law Commissions Report, p. 40, para. 3.27.

138 "Automated Vehicles: Consultation Paper 3 – A regulatory framework for automated vehicles A joint consultation paper", Law Commission Consultation Paper No 252, Scottish Law Commission Discussion Paper No 17, para. 4.27, p. 41. Available at: https://s3-eu-west-2.amazonaws.com/lawcom-prod-storage-11jsxou24uy7q/uploads/2021/01/AV-CP3.pdf.

139 Law Commissions Report, 2022, p. 43, para. 3.42.

140 Ivi, p. 160, para. 8.132.

141 Law Commissions Report, 2022, p. 20, para. 2.41.

142 Ivi, p. 81, para. 5.65.

143 Law Commissions Report, 2022, pp. 85-86, para. 5.95 (1).

144 Ivi, p. 86, para. 5.96.

This does not mean that there would be no human being on board, but that when the ADS feature is of NUIC nature, any human in the car will be considered as a mere passenger. The NUIC operators need to have "oversight" of the vehicle any time a NUIC feature is engaged on a road or in another public place: they are "expected to respond to alerts from the vehicle if it encounters a problem it cannot deal with, or if it is involved in a collision", but they are not expected to monitor the driving environment.[145] Oversight duties would include both remote assistance[146] (for example, if the ADS detects an object in its lane which is too large to avoid and stops, remote assistance could imply providing instructions to the vehicle on how to deal with the obstruction) and fleet operations (for example, dealing with law enforcement agencies or paying tolls for the route).[147] As stated in Recommendation 56, the regulator shall have powers to impose only *regulatory* sanction (such as warnings, civil penalties, suspension or withdrawal of license) to NUIC operators, hence they could not be subjected to criminal liability.[148] Additionally, the individual staff of the NUIC involved in remote driving of the vehicle "will face the same criminal liabilities as other drivers", for example if they are not trained or qualified enough.[149] Yet, the Joint Report does not advise in favor of introducing new criminal offenses relating to individual assistants.

E) Germany

In May 2021, the German Bundesrat passed a law which amended the German Road Traffic Act (*Straßenverkehrsgesetz*-StVG).[150] Even though it does not directly regulate matters of criminal liability, it is of utmost interest for this discussion, as it attempts to provide a legal solution to moral dilemmas similar to those examined in MIT's Moral Machine experiment. As such, Germany "paved the way to legislating higher levels of autonomous driving while international initiatives have been stalling".[151]

As will be highlighted, the connection between moral issues and issues of criminal liability is rendered evident also by the fact that Germany's new law was based on the

145 Law Commissions Report, 2022, p. 21, para. 2.48.

146 Defined as "Event-driven provision, by a remotely located human, of information or advice to an ADS-equipped vehicle in driverless operation in order to facilitate trip continuation when the ADS encounters a situation it cannot manage". SAE Taxonomy J3016, 2021, para. 3.23.

147 Law Commissions Report, p. 167, para. 9.14.

148 Ivi, p. 168, para. 9.120.

149 Law Commissions Report, p. 172, para. 9.42.

150 Bundestag, Gesetz zur Änderung des Straßenverkehrsgesetzes, 2021.

151 A. Kriebitz, R. Max & C. Lütge, "The German Act on Autonomous Driving: Why Ethics Still Matter", *Philosophy & Technology*, Vol. 35, 2022, p. 11.

Report of the Ethics Commission on Automated and Connected Driving,[152] which included amongst its members Prof. Eric Hilgendorf, professor of criminal law and author/editor of numerous publications on the matter of automated driving and criminal law.[153]

The most interesting provision is the one at article 1 § 1e (2)2, which lists the technical requirements that must be complied with by a vehicle with autonomous driving functions (level 4 automation):

> (2) Vehicles with autonomous driving function must be equipped with a technical system that is capable of,
> [...]
> 2. autonomously comply with the traffic regulations addressed to the vehicle driver and be equipped with an accident-avoidance system which
> (a) is designed to prevent and reduce damage,
> (b) in the event of *unavoidable alternative damage* to different legal goods, *takes into account the importance of the legal goods*, provided that the protection of human life has the highest priority, and
> (c) in the event of an *unavoidable alternative harm to human life*, does not factor in personal characteristics.[154]

152 See also European Commission, Directorate-General for Research and Innovation, Horizon 2020 Commission Expert Group to advise on specific ethical issues raised by driverless mobility (E03659), "Ethics of connected and automated vehicles: recommendations on road safety, privacy, fairness, explainability and responsibility", Publications Office of the European Union, Luxembourg, 2020. Available at: https://data.europa.eu/doi/10.2777/035239.

153 See *ex multis*: E. Hilgendorf, S. Hötitzsch & L. Lutz (eds.), Rechtliche Aspekte automatisierter Fahrzeuge. Beiträge der 2. Würzburger Tagung zum Technikrecht im Oktober 2014, Nomos, 2015; E. Hilgendorf (ed.), Autonome Systeme und neue Mobilität. Ausgewählte Beiträge zur 3. und 4. Würzburger Tagung zum Technikrech. Nomos, 2017; E. Hilgendorf & J. Feldle (Eds.), Digitization and the Law, Nomos, 2018; E. Hilgendorf, "Autonome Systeme, künstliche Intelligenz und Roboter: Eine Orientierung aus strafrechtlicher Perspektive", in S. Barton (ed.), Festschrift für Thomas Fischer, C.H. Beck, 2018; E. Hilgendorf, "Dilemma-Probleme beim automatisierten Fahren. Ein Beitrag zum Problem des Verrechnungsverbots im Zeitalter der Digitalisierung", ZIS, Vol. 130, No. 3, 2018.

154 Translated from German: "(2) *Kraftfahrzeuge mit autonomer Fahrfunktion müssen über eine technische Ausrüstung verfügen, die in der Lage ist, [...] 2. selbstständig den an die Fahrzeugführung gerichteten Verkehrsvorschriften zu entsprechen und die über ein System der Unfallvermeidung verfügt, das*
a) auf Schadensvermeidung und Schadensreduzierung ausgelegt ist,
b) bei einer unvermeidbaren alternativen Schädigung unterschiedlicher Rechtsgüter die Bedeutung der Rechtsgüter berücksichtigt, wobei der Schutz menschlichen Lebens die höchste Priorität besitzt, und
c) für den Fall einer unvermeidbaren alternativen Gefährdung von Menschenleben keine weitere Gewichtung anhand persönlicher Merkmale vorsieht".
Bundestag, Gesetz zur Änderung des Straßenverkehrsgesetzes, 202, Art. 1 § 1e [emphasis added].

Admittedly, the law, specifically art. 1§ 1e (2)2 (c), "does not illuminate what personal characteristics are, nor does it state whether autonomous vehicles might hit individuals violating traffic rules in unavoidable accidents".[155] These questions were addressed in MIT's Moral Machine experiment, which was discussed above.[156] A list of the aforementioned personal characteristics can be found in the principles elaborated by the Ethics Commission on Automated and Connected Driving, specifically at rule 9 (age, gender, physical or mental constitution). Actually, the law of May 2021 codifies part of the principles contained in the Report published in 2017 by the Ethics Commission, hence it will be analyzed in the following paragraphs.[157]

In the Report, the Ethics Commission laid down 20 rules for automated and connected vehicular traffic. Amongst them, rule 2 states that the protection of individuals shall take precedence over all other "utilitarian considerations"[158] and that the purpose of AVs should be "to reduce the level of harm until it is completely prevented".[159] As a final point, it upholds that "[t]he licensing of automated systems is not justifiable unless it promises to produce at least a diminution in harm compared with human driving, in other words a *positive balance of risks*".[160] Moreover, according to rule 5, AVs should "*prevent accidents* wherever this is practically possible" and, based on the state of the art, "*the technology must be designed in such a way that critical situations*",[161] including moral dilemmas, "*do not arise in the first place*".[162]

Moral dilemmas[163] represent attractive hypothetical scenarios: they are able to stir up a discussion amongst any kind of audience. Their attractiveness lies in the fact that "they

155 Kriebitz, Max & Lütge, 2022, p. 9.

156 See Sec. 5.3.2.

157 The Ethics Commission was appointed by the German Federal Minister of Transport and Digital Infrastructure (*Bundesministerium für Digitales und Verkehr*).

158 Ethics Commission Automated and Connected Driving, "Report", 2017, p. 10 ("Ethics Commission Report"). Available at: https://bmdv.bund.de/SharedDocs/EN/publications/report-ethics-commission.pdf?__blob=publicationFile.

159 Ivi, p. 10.

160 Ethics Commission Report, 2017, p. 10.

161 Ibid.

162 Ethics Commission Report, 2017, p. 11.

163 Probably the most famous moral dilemma is the "trolley problem". Imagine that you are the driver of a trolley which is headed towards five track workmen who are repairing the track. In order to avoid running over the five track workmen, you must stop the trolley, but you realize that the brakes don't work. You see a side track on the right, on which there is only one track workmen. You are now presented with two choices: turn the trolley to the right, and kill one man, or keep the trolley going straight, and kill five. The invention of this type of moral dilemma is credited to philosopher Philippa Foot. The term "Trolley Problem" was coined later by Judith Jarvis Thomson. See P. Foot, "The Problem of Abortion and the Doctrine of the Double Effect", *Oxford Review*, 1978; J. J. Thomson "The Trolley Problem" *The Yale Law Journal*, Vol. 94, No. 66, 1985, pp. 1395-1415. Cf. Hilgendorf, "The dilemma of autonomous driving: Reflections on the moral and legal treatment of automatic collision avoidance systems", 2018, p. 60. The author mentions the decision of the German Federal Constitutional Court on the Aviation Security Act (*Luftsicherheitsgesetz*) of 2005 (BVerfGE, 15.2.2006 – 1 BvR 357/05).

help to illustrate the basic values of a legal culture, in a manner which is also accessible to a broader public".[164] The solutions proposed to solve moral dilemmas often "take on the character of legal and social policy decisions"[165] and turn into a "classic" "German culture (Kant)" vs British "utilitarian merchant spirit" (Bentham)[166] debate.

As an example of the first approach, authors mention the decision of the German Federal Constitutional Court on the Aviation Security Act (*Luftsicherheitsgesetz*) of 2005.[167] The decision regarded Article §14(3) of the Aviation Security Act, i.e., "whether a commercial airliner filled with innocent passengers, which had been hijacked by terrorists with the intent of using it as a weapon of mass destruction, for example, by crashing it into a city centre, could be shot down".[168] The Court answered in the negative, affirming that weighing lives would entail a violation of Article 1(1) of the *Grundgesetz*, as any individual life "in and of itself represents the highest possible maximum value"[169] and therefore must be treated as a "non-balanceable".[170]

With the development of AVs, and of the necessary discussion on their regulation, so came a conversation on how an AV should behave in a road traffic accident. Notably, one can notice a "*compulsion to analyze and to explicate*"[171] when it comes to the developments of algorithms, which led to the analysis of incident scenarios from both an ethical and legal perspective. In Chapter 4, we discussed issues of alignment (i.e., the fact that AI systems might have different values from us) and of interpretation (i.e., the fact that moral rules are ambiguous) in connection to the development of moral machines. The inventors of the Moral Machine themselves refer to the workings of the German Ethics Commission and claim that their work "represents the first and only attempt so far to provide official guidelines for ethical choices of autonomous vehicles".[172]

AV-based moral dilemmas, similarly to the PCM experiment,[173] represent a further elaboration of these issues. For example, every German citizen might agree on the fact that being inside or outside the Bavaria region is not an acceptable criterion for an AV to

---

164 Hilgendorf, "The dilemma of autonomous driving: Reflections on the moral and legal treatment of automatic collision avoidance systems", 2018, p. 57.

165 Ibid.

166 Hilgendorf, "The dilemma of autonomous driving: Reflections on the moral and legal treatment of automatic collision avoidance systems", 2018, p. 57.

167 BVerfGE, 15.2.2006 – 1 BvR 357/05.

168 Hilgendorf, "The dilemma of autonomous driving: Reflections on the moral and legal treatment of automatic collision avoidance systems", 2018, p. 60.

169 Ivi, p. 65.

170 Hilgendorf, "The dilemma of autonomous driving: Reflections on the moral and legal treatment of automatic collision avoidance systems", 2018, p. 66.

171 Ivi, p. 59.

172 Awad & al., 2018, p. 60.

173 Discussed in Hilgendorf, "The dilemma of autonomous driving: Reflections on the moral and legal treatment of automatic collision avoidance systems", 2018, p. 64.

decide – in an accident situation – whether to choose the course of action that leads to killing the lowest number of people as opposed to the one that leads to killing the highest number (a "Bavaria friendly collision algorithm").[174] However, not every German citizen might agree on which criteria should be applied when the AV must decide between two options that lead to the death of the *same* number of people: should it spare all the innocent female bystanders and kill all the male ones? In other words, this type of moral dilemmas prompts the question of how to break down into computable form the choices that an AI system must make in order to minimize the number of lives lost, if possible.

An attempt at regulating such choices can be found in rule 7 and rule 8, which address cases of "unavoidable hazardous situations", i.e., moral dilemmas. Rule 7 establishes that, in dilemma situations, the protection of human life must enjoy unconditional top priority when balanced with other legally protected interests.[175] Accordingly, "within the constraints of what is technologically feasible, the systems must be programmed to *accept damage to animals or property* in a conflict if this means that personal injury can be prevented".[176]

The solution seems straightforward, at first glance. Still, think of the case where the damage to property – which, in the abstract, should not be preferred to the protection of life – amounts to causing an oil spill from a road tanker or, even worse, the collapse of the power grid of an entire metropolitan area.[177] Indeed, the first part of rule 8 recognizes that the "normalization"[178] of moral dilemmas, i.e., the invention of generalized "lesser of two evil" solutions, is not feasible:

> Genuine dilemmatic decisions, such as a decision between one human life and another, depend on the actual specific situation, incorporating "unpredictable" behaviour by parties affected. They can thus *not be clearly standardized, nor can they be programmed such that they are ethically unquestionable.* Technological systems must be designed to avoid accidents. However, *they cannot be standardized to a complex or intuitive assessment* of the impacts of an accident in such a way that they can *replace or anticipate the decision of a responsible driver with the moral capacity to make correct judgements.* It is true that a human driver would be acting unlawfully if he killed a person in an emergency to save the lives of one or more other persons, but he would not necessarily be acting *culpably*. Such *legal* judgements, made in retrospect and taking special circumstances into account, *cannot readily be transformed into abstract/general*

174 Ibid.
175 Ethics Commission Report, 2017, p. 11.
176 Ibid.
177 The example is given by the Ethics Commission at p. 17.
178 Ethics Commission Report, 2017, p. 17.

> *ex ante appraisals* and thus also not into corresponding programming activities. For this reason, perhaps more than any other, it would be desirable for an independent public sector agency (for instance a Federal Bureau for the Investigation of Accidents Involving Automated Transport Systems or a Federal Office for Safety in Automated and Connected Transport) to systematically process the lessons learned.[179]

Nonetheless, Rule 9 does give instructions which are summarized as "No selection of humans, no offsetting of victims, but principle of damage minimization":

> In the event of unavoidable accident situations, any distinction based on personal features (age, gender, physical or mental constitution) is strictly prohibited. It is also prohibited to offset victims against one another. General programming to reduce the number of personal injuries may be justifiable. Those parties involved in the generation of mobility risks must not sacrifice non-involved parties.

By allowing for an AI system which can be programmed to reduce the number of personal injuries, Rule 9 departs from the principle enshrined in the Federal Constitutional Court's judgment on the Aviation Security Act. Indeed, the application of said principle would most likely lead to programming the AV not to do anything: perhaps it is no coincidence that in MIT's Moral Machine, German nationals scored 7th worldwide on "preferring inaction".[180]

According to the drafters of the Ethical Guidelines, in the case of AVs the difference resides in the fact that:

> [...] a probability forecast has to be made from out of the situation, in which the identity of the injured or killed parties is not yet known [...] Programming to minimize the number of victims (damage to property to take precedence over personal injury, personal injury to take precedence over death, lowest possible number of persons injured or killed) could thus be justified, at any rate without breaching Article 1(1) of the Basic Law, if the programming reduced the risk to every single road user in equal measure.[181]

179 Ivi, p. 11.

180 Moreover, Rule 9 clashes with the findings of MIT's Moral Machine, which discovered strong preference for sparing the lives of the young. Awad et al., 2018, p. 60.

181 Ethics Commission Report, 2017, p. 18.

The approach, it is argued, is similar to the one adopted with immunizations where "statutorily imposed compulsory vaccination results in a general minimization of the risk without it being known beforehand whether the vaccinated person will belong to the group of the (few) harmed (sacrificed) parties" and, despite this, "it is in the interests of everyone to be vaccinated and reduce the overall risk of infection".[182]

Conclusively, though, the Ethics Commission claims that it "refuses to infer from this that the lives of humans can be 'offset' against those of other humans in emergency situations so that it could be permissible to sacrifice one person in order to save several others".[183] Therefore, the decision to save as many lives as possible would be allowed only "if several lives are already immediately threatened".[184] The issue, at first glance, does not appear as specifically related to AI systems. Rather, it seems to belong to the general category of ethical problems. Conclusively, the Ethics Commission states that, as recognized by the Commission itself, it did not reach a "satisfactory end"[185] on the matter.

Let us conclude with a reflection connected to liability. Imagine that two seriously injured people (A and B) are lying on the road and an AV, which is carrying a human passenger C, is approaching at high speed. If the AV swerves to the right to avoid running over (and killing) A and B, it will hit D and E, who are standing at the side of the road. Based on (very fast-paced) calculations, including an unspecified risk of injuring C, the almost certain probability of injuring D and E, and the likely risk of killing A and B, it decides not to swerve. As a consequence, A and B die from the impact. Could it be argued that the AV's behavior is justified or excused?[186]

Defenses work as "fixes" in criminal legal systems: they recalibrate the aim of punishment in a way as to not impose an unbearable burden on people.[187] Seemingly, the situation described in the example could be shifted to the realm of application of a necessity defense. Necessity implies that legal systems cannot predict and regulate beforehand all situations in which a balancing of protected legal interests is needed. Consequently, through necessity defenses we accept that there are situations "in which the offence definition is fulfilled, but the defendant should not be held liable, because all things considered, he did the right thing for society".[188] Let us assume now that the AV is capable of calculating the probability of injury of A, B, C, D, and E, and that human lives could be subjected to a balancing act. Consequently, it could be argued that the choice of the AV

182 Ibid.

183 Ethics Commission Report, 2017, p. 18.

184 Ibid.

185 Ethics Commission Report, 2017, p. 18.

186 The example is adapted from Hilgendorf, "The dilemma of autonomous driving: Reflections on the moral and legal treatment of automatic collision avoidance systems", 2018, p. 75.

187 Blomsma, 2012, p. 321.

188 Ivi, p. 372.

not to swerve amounts to choosing the *lesser evil* outcome.[189] Thus, it is uncertain at this point how the abovementioned "probability forecast" would be pursued. The AV should be able to calculate exactly, in the concrete and urgent situation (in a matter of seconds), which is the probability of injury for every person present in the scene of the accident. According to Hilgendorf, in the foreseeable future "[a]t best it will be possible to make qualitative or comparative statements, i.e. statements such as 'almost certain', 'very likely', 'very unlikely', or statements such as 'event A is more likely than event B'".[190]

One could also contemplate whether introducing an excuse similar to duress would be a preferrable option.[191] In situations like the moral dilemmas outlined above, the best solution might be to accept that the AV system simply *could not have done otherwise*, as the choice between maintaining a course straight ahead and swerving to the right, i.e., between killing A and B or D and E, was not a real choice. Indeed, if it is a widely accepted principle that "[t]he law cannot ask of anyone more than they can be legitimately expected to do, either intellectually or emotionally", why would we expect something different of AI systems?

The argument becomes even more compelling if one takes into consideration the problems of pinning blameworthiness on AI systems. The application of an excuse would also bring forth positive effects from a communicative perspective, since it would not amount to saying that the killings were legitimate (as it would be in the case of a justification), but rather to claiming that the conduct was not blameworthy.[192] Indeed, "[t]he defendant who raises an excuse confirms the wrongdoing and merely seeks to assert an explanation for his conduct"[193] and "the acceptance of an excuse makes clear to the defendant and the public that what he did was wrong".[194] Conclusively, the application of defenses to AI systems, as was already argued with regard to the defense of insanity,[195] is a path of investigation which definitely deserves attention for future research.

---

189 Lagioia & Sartor, 2020, p. 6.

190 Hilgendorf, "The dilemma of autonomous driving: Reflections on the moral and legal treatment of automatic collision avoidance systems", 2018, p. 75.

191 Apparently, the difference between necessity and duress is only "gradual" since they "both revolve around the infringement of the freedom of choice of the actor". They can be distinguished based on "the nature of the pressure to commit the offence" which in necessity "arises from the necessity to choose", where instead in duress it comes from the "danger (to life or limb)". Blomsma, 2012, p. 370.

192 Ivi, p. 325.

193 Blomsma, 2012, p. 325.

194 Ibid.

195 See Sec. 5.4.1.

7.4 CONCLUSIONS

Chapter 3 underlined how most of the academic discourse is polarized by discussing the relationship between law and ethics. The trend is also visible when analyzing regulation on the matter, as most proposals for AI regulation are aimed at ensuring "accountability" and affirming soft law principles directed at the development of ethical or trustworthy AI, rather than the development of hard law instruments. Accountability is one of seven principles mentioned by the AI-HLEG[196] established by the European Commission in its "Ethical Guidelines" and is a recurring element in European regulatory initiatives.[197] According to some scholars, this use of ethics is problematic, as it would consist of nothing more than a display of a "law conception of ethics",[198] i.e., "a view on the ethics endeavour that makes it a sort of replica of law".[199]

The case studies which were analyzed in this chapter represent, in some way, an exception to this trend, as they take a step further and try to develop principles which could be applied to the ascription of criminal liability connected to AI systems. Germany, discussed at E, develops arguments related to the intersection of ethical principles and criminal law principles in the specific field of AV systems. Regrettably, none of the case studies focuses extensively on the liability *of* AI systems and rarely refers to it. Nevertheless, they are valuable inputs to this research, as they are proof that matters of AI and criminal liability are not relevant just for Hollywood movies and criminal law scholars.

---

196 AI-HLEG, 2019.

197 Resolution of the European Parliament, *Framework on the Ethical Aspects of Artificial Intelligence, Robotics and Related Technologies*, 2020/2012(INL), Oct. 20, 2020, arts 9, 22, 23, 72, 96, 102.

198 G.E.M. Anscombe, "Modern moral philosophy" *Philosophy*, Vol. 33, No. 124, 1968, pp. 1-19.

199 A. Rességuier & R. Rodrigues, "'AI ethics should not remain toothless! A call to bring back the teeth of ethics", *Big Data & Society*, 2020.

8 Conclusions

But epers are no more transient legal entities.
Recall that corporations and organizations of all sorts come and go; they rise and fall like Italian governments.

Curtis E.A. Karnow (1994)

8.1 Incipit

One can identify a very clear parabola for this research. It started with "machines going rogue",[1] factories transforming humans into paperclips, and other apocalyptic scenarios – only to find out that the biggest threats might be toasters and airplanes.[2] What happened? Were our first assumptions wrong? Not at all: criminal law, starting with the industrialization period, has had to adapt its imputation models to technological progress.[3] The "AI revolution", be it toasters or evil robots, is another episode of this "saga".

Apropos, one of the purposes of this research was to identify and evaluate what the novelties are – if any – that were brought about by the occurrence of AI and what their impact was on the classical constructs of criminal law. Coming to the end of this study, it can be concluded that AI systems indisputably have the *capacity to act* in a way that can be generally considered by society as *offensive* to protected legal goods, i.e., that they can act like "criminals". This calls for society needing to find an answer, somehow.

The present chapter will conclude by retracing the questions, and the interim conclusions, which were posed throughout the study and identifying avenues for further inquiry. The main research question was: *to what extent is a theoretical framework of criminal liability for non-human agents needed and feasible?* Such a question prompted a set of sub-questions, which were addressed in the different chapters.[4] This chapter will mirror

1 Badea & Artus, 2022, pp. 1-2.
2 "One example of AI causing harm through an attempt to carry out its stipulated goal is the intelligent toaster which burns a house down in a quest to make as much toast as possible". Turner, 2019, p. 204.
3 M. Simmler, "Automation", in P. Caeiro et al. (eds.), *Elgar Encyclopedia of Crime and Criminal Justice*, Vol. 1, 2023.
4 These are: Chapter 2 – Why is the issue of defining AI an issue? What are the basic functions of AI?; Chapter 3 – What is the state of the art of the scholarly debate on AI and criminal law? Which are the most recurrent questions and what are the answers? Which aspects are being neglected?; Chapter 4 – What does ascribing criminal liability to an AI system entail? Chapter 5 – Can an AI system be considered a criminal agent?; Chapter 6 – Can an AI system fulfill the *mens rea* and *actus reus* requirements of a criminal offense?; Chapter 7 – What is the state of the art on criminal law regulation on AI?

the general structure of the study and build on the interim findings disseminated throughout the research.

Thus, besides rearticulating the arguments which were already put forth, I will add fresh perspectives and propose new directions for future inquiries. To do so, the avenues of this research were redefined according to four main issues, which will be addressed as follows. Section 8.2 expands on the question of defining AI and its repercussions on criminal law (the *definitional* question). In Section 8.3 I situate my research in the realm of the scholarly literature on AI and criminal law analyzed in Chapter 3 (the *introspective* question). Section 8.4 discusses the attribution of criminal liability to AI systems through the lenses of anthropocentrism (the *attribution* question), specifically expanding on why we are prone to holding AI to higher moral standards (Sec. 8.4.1). It then touch upon theories of retributivism and deterrence (Sec. 8.4.2) and the analogy between AI liability and corporate criminal liability (Sec. 8.4.3). Section 8.4.4 discusses the liability of humans *for* machines also in light of the findings of Chapter 7. Lastly, building on the previous sections I draw general conclusions for this study in Section 8.5. (the *future- and backward-facing* question). Specifically, I will return to the main research question (Sec. 8.5), expand on questions for the future (Sec. 8.5.2), and outline the challenges which I encountered throughout this research (Sec. 8.5.3).

8.2 The Definitional Question

This research started with examples of AIs "going bad". Such a *in medias res* immediately gave an idea of the relevance of the topic, presented in a language which could be understood by criminal lawyers. In fact, I believe that AI and criminal law share a problem of miscommunication: criminal law does not understand what AI is, and vice versa. This research represents a significant step in bridging such a linguistic divide.

On a preliminary note, it must be mentioned that I gave little or no attention to AGI in this study, and I did so quite intentionally. Even if we were to assume that AGI will ever be created, discussing its liability would mandate a different methodological approach, hence it was excluded from the scope of analysis to maintain the research's coherence. Indeed, the most striking aspect of (narrow) AI is probably that it is so smart, it's stupid, yet it might commit a crime.[5] It follows that whether a criminal system decided to attribute criminal liability to AI systems, it would have to do so based on a different paradigm of intelligence than that of human beings, since it is not comparable to the intelligence displayed by AI systems.

5 C. Quirk, "So Smart It's Stupid", *Alumni*, 1 April 2022. Available at: https://alumni.msu.edu/stay-informed/alumni-stories/so-smart-its-stupid-the-weirdness-of-ai.

There are two sides to the "definitional question". The *first* strict meaning of the definitional question is addressed in Chapter 2, which dealt with why the issue of defining AI is an issue and then explored the basic functioning of AI. The lack of a strict *technical* definition of AI clashes blatantly with the principle of legality, which rejects general and ambiguous concepts. Indeed, legality struggles with AI since it is a label which refers to an everchanging concept. Moreover, not only are AI systems not a definite entity, but they also cannot establish themselves as one. Furthermore, there is no consensus on *who* should define AI (computer scientists? philosophers? legal scholars?). Surely, as Chapter 3 shows, the lack of a universal definition of AI has not stopped legal scholars from approaching the topic of "AI law". According to some, "[a]lthough there is nothing clear so far, jurisprudence can conjure up its own definition of AI at least in relation to legal discussion".[6] Apropos, Chapter 2 served indeed this very purpose: it "conjured up"[7] a definition of AI which could be used in the legal discussion carried out in this research, and not only here.

The *second* aspect of the definitional question is broader and relates to the concept of AI as an *agent* in the eyes of (criminal) law. While this aspect is addressed directly in Chapter 5, it also reappears throughout the whole research, working as a *fil conducteur* in the present work. As a matter of fact, not only is there no agreed scientific definition of AI, there is also no *legal* definition of which characteristics an AI system should possess in order to be qualified as capable of criminal action. In other words, the two aspects of the definitional question are entangled.

Legal personhood (i.e., being able to "act in law")[8] is a purely artificial construct: it is, by definition, "attributed by positive law (statute or common law) and cannot be assumed".[9] Furthermore, it is well-known that "legal personhood is already dissociated from the human substrate",[10] such as in the case of corporations, hence, according to some scholars, "there would be no way to deny that AI can be a legal person".[11] Nonetheless, "just because it is possible, that does not mean it should be a good idea".[12]

Legal agency means possessing the capabilities, which are attributed by law, "to act in law and to be liable for one's own actions".[13] It can be attributed to subjects in different legal domains. The same subject can also be deemed an actor in a certain field (e.g., a corporation in private law) and not in others (e.g., a corporation in legal systems which do not

6 Lee, 2021, pp. 311-312.
7 Ibid.
8 Hildebrandt, 2020, p. 241.
9 Ivi, p. 242.
10 S. M. C. Avila Negri, "Robots as Legal Persons: Electronic Personhood in Robotics and Artificial Intelligence", *Frontiers in Robotics and AI*, Vol. 8, 2021, p. 2.
11 Avila Negri, 2021, p. 2.
12 Ibid.
13 Hildebrandt, 2020, p. 243.

accept corporate criminal liability).[14] Certainly, "acting in criminal law" necessitates peculiar rules, since "criminal law liability with its emphasis on censure assumes a kind of moral agency that is not obvious in the case of current day autonomous systems".[15]

Having acknowledged this, in Section 5.1., I hypothesized that this study would not answer the definitional question once and for all. Not only is there a lack of a common understanding of what AI is, in terms of which technical/physical attributes it should display (according the first connotation of the *definitional question*), there is also a *lacuna* in discussing whether AI could be considered an actor in terms of criminal capacity. I argue here that adopting the AI-HLEG's definition of AI systems[16] as the definition of reference turned out to be appropriate in addressing the definitional question for the purposes of this research.[17]

As a matter of fact, such a definition, which is not tied to the concept of human intelligence, proved to possess enough "freedom of scope" to capture "the whole range of *[AI]* applications finding their way into practice today and in the near future".[18] Moreover, since the definition of AI will necessarily change over time, I believe that the AI-HLEG's definition could work as a valuable starting point to elaborate a definition of AI systems suitable for the criminal law domain.

Surely, adopting a working definition made sure that the field of investigation of this research remained clear, as compared to the "blur" which sometimes characterized the works of the scholars discussed in Chapter 3 (who rarely addressed what they meant by "AI"). Ultimately, one of the added values of this research is that it implemented, and discussed, a definition of AI systems with the cognizance of the significance that definitions possess in criminal law.

Lastly, this research represents a valuable input to the discussion of whether AI systems could be considered as *Rechtspersonen* for the purposes of criminal law. Different from what happens when seeking a definition of AI, one can identify a solid consensus on

14 Ivi, p. 240.

15 Hildebrandt, 2020, p.240.

16 According to which AI systems are: "systems designed by humans that, given a complex goal, act in the physical or digital dimension by perceiving their environment through data acquisition, interpreting the collected structured or unstructured data, reasoning on the knowledge, or processing the information, derived from this data and deciding the best action(s) to take to achieve the given goal". AI-HLEG, 2018, p. 9.

17 I do not argue here that I found the ultimate solution to defining AI, rather that the solution adopted proved successful in overcoming the challenges facing this research by the definitional question. I also argue that it could prove useful for future researchers and policymakers and lawmakers.

18 Sheikh, Prins & Schrijvers, 2023, p. 19: the authors further state here that "Instead of considering AI as a discipline that can be clearly delineated, with uncomplicated definitions and fixed methodologies, it is more useful to see it as a complex and diverse field focused on a certain horizon. The dot on that horizon is the understanding and simulation of all human intellectual skills. This goal is also called 'artificial general intelligence' or AGI (other names are 'strong AI' and 'full AI'). However, it remains to be seen whether this dot, with such a generic definition of AI, will ever be reached".

the definition of criminal capacities, albeit with a number of variations. By relying on such a doctrinal background, as will be further expanded upon in the following sections, I maintain that AI systems should be treated as agents in criminal law only if they were to display the capacity to be truly susceptible to the command of a criminal norm.

8.3 A *Mare Magnum* of Scholarly Literature.[19] The Introspective Question

In 2020, a group of researchers from Maastricht University conducted a study on the scope of legal literature on AI with the aid of an ML technique called topic modelling.[20]-[21] The researchers found that scholarly output was booming in the "deep learning era".[22] As the authors argue, "with over 2500 publications already by the year 2015 referring to 'artificial intelligence' [...] it may no longer be realistic to assume that researchers can keep up with legal research on AI, or the number of publications in general".[23]

The literature review conducted in Chapter 3 (which results from analyzing over 100 documents of scholarly literature on the topic of AI and criminal law written in three languages) is an effort to systematize part of this *mare magnum*[24] of scholarly literature. Besides it being a recognition of the status quo in scholarly literature, it also prompted an introspective question, which will be answered at the end of this section: where does this researcher situate herself in the debate?

Expecting new legal scholarship to be able to account for each and every publication available on AI law would mean imposing a cumbersome burden on researchers, especially on those who are at the early stages of their career. It is argued here that legal scholars do not need to entertain a "gold rush" to who reads (or publishes) fastest on the topic: AI technology might be developing rapidly, but the legal tools to address this rapid development have been the same for the past 50-100 years or so. This is reflected by the fact that the legal scholarship analyzed in Chapter 3 presents recurring traits. These traits are visible even amongst researchers who have very different cultural and legal backgrounds.

---

19 I developed part of these reflections in A. Giannini, "Artificial intelligence, ethics, law: a view on the Italian and American debate (and on their differences)", *Netherlands Journal of Legal Philosophy*, Vol. 51, No. 2, 2022, pp. 248-263.

20 Rosca et al., 2020.

21 Topic Modelling is a method for classifying collections of documents. The authors adopted Latent Dirichlet Allocation (LDA) Topic Modelling. They used the tool to identify recurring topics in 3,931 journal articles on AI legal research.

22 The expression refers to the period which includes the early 2000s until today. Goanta et al., 2020, p. 331.

23 Rosca et al., 2020, p. 1.

24 "First coined to describe the ocean ring that enclosed the earth in ancient times, the term *mare magnum* today has a strictly negative metaphorical meaning referring to a vast mass that converts into chaos", P. Basso, "*Mare magnum*", *Parolechiave*, Vol. 1, 2022, p.1.

In Chapter 3, scholars were classified according to three categories: expansionists, moderates, and skeptics. The categorization was based on how each author approached the general issue of criminal law and AI, specifically with regard to matters pertaining to the general part of criminal law. It follows that it does not include authors (or the reflections of the authors' part of the literature review) who focused on the impact of AI from a criminal procedure perspective, nor reflections on the use of AI as a tool to commit crimes and its impact on cybercrimes.

Throughout the analysis several recurring questions were identified and compared, as summarized in Section 3.5.[25] This led to the identification of some weaknesses/gaps in the debate.[26] First and foremost, it must be highlighted that no one had ever conducted an analysis as the one contained in Chapter 3 before. As such, this research already represents a novelty.

Furthermore, it is now possible to come back to the individual gaps identified and assess whether this research addressed them. The answer is affirmative: first, the study did not readily discard Hallevy's theories, instead it analyzed them in depth also in comparison to other legal scholars (gap I, addressed in Ch. 3); second, this study provided a definition of AI and of AI agent applicable to criminal law, while thoroughly discussing the impact of the lack of a definition on the matter (gap II, addressed in Ch. 2, Ch. 5 and Ch. 6); third, this study tackled the issue of criminal capacity of AI systems (gap III, addressed in Ch. 5); fourth, as discussing the differences between the way human and AI systems can act, think, or want is an extremely vast topic, the matter was addressed only from a criminal legal perspective, rather than from a philosophical one (gap IV, addressed in Sec. 5.3); fifth, the study discussed whether AI systems could be excused by an insanity defense (gap V, addressed in Sec. 5.4); sixth, the research addressed the issue of understanding who the responsible human agents should be and the problem of data errors (gap VI, addressed in Sec. 6.2.3); lastly, the research tackled how AI behavior interferes with

25 The questions/topics identified were: I. Are robots/AI systems capable of moral reasoning?; II. What is the relevance of moral reasoning when ascribing criminal liability?; III. Can an AI system "act"?; IV. Can an AI system be culpable?; V. Why should we punish AI systems and how should we punish AI systems?; VI. Permitted risk and dangerous activities; VII. Are there more feasible alternatives to applying criminal law (such as torts law or administrative sanctions)?; VIII. What is the relationship between corporate criminal liability and AI criminal liability?; IX. Should human agents be liable for the AI's misbehavior?; X. The creation of new negligence crimes and the application of existing negligence offenses so to humans-in-the-loop (how should foreseeability and reasonable care be defined?).

26 I. Civil criminal legal scholars discard Hallevy's theories quite effortlessly. II. No or few attempts at providing a definition of AI and of AI agent applicable to criminal law, no discussion of the impact of the lack of a definition on the matter; III. No or few attempts at addressing the preliminary issue of considering AI as a subject of criminal law (i.e., criminal capacity of AI); IV. No or little discussion of whether an AI system can act, think or want by criminal legal scholar; V. No or little discussion of whether conduct of AI systems could be excused or justified by a defense; VI. Confusion as to identifying precisely who would be the responsible human agent; VII. No or little discussion on how AI behavior interferes with theories of causality.

theories of causality, specifically which factors could lead to "failures of causation" (gap VII, addressed in Sec. 6.3.2).

Classifying authors was, at times, challenging: first, besides certain specific cases, the categorization was not always clear cut. Think for example of Gless, Silverman & Weigend (skeptics), who leave the option of criminal culpability of robots open in case in the future they were to become able to truly determine themselves on moral grounds[27] or of Simmler & Markwalder (moderates), who strongly believe that robots will be addressees of normative expectations in the future.[28] As the literature review represents the first attempt to be conducted on such a large scale, it leaves space for debate and improvement. An interesting development of Chapter 3 would be if it sparked a debate amongst the authors therein regarding whether or not they agree with the categorization.

It is worth mentioning, at this point, that I identify myself with the moderate school. The reasons vary: most importantly, I do not discard discussing criminal liability *of* AI systems outright. The sole fact of writing a dissertation on the topic which focuses primarily on the liability of non-humans,[29] and treats the liability of humans-behind-the-machine as an ancillary topic, determines the automatic exclusion from the category of skeptics, at least for now (it cannot be assumed that more extended "skeptic" writings will emerge in the future). This research cannot be placed in the expansionist front either, even though it sympathizes with many of the ideas of its representatives.

Truth be told, one of the aims of this research was to at least plant a seed of doubt in the mind of the most ardent skeptics, leading them to think that one could actually build a decent case for imputing criminal liability to AI systems. It surely worked with me, up to a certain point. Notwithstanding, there is one moderate argument which – from the beginning – was more compelling than any other: when it comes to directly punishing AI systems, it is not so much a matter of feasibility, as it is of *unnecessity*. To date, criminal liability of AI systems has not been needed. Probably, such a statement makes me a weak moderate. It is not excluded that I will join the dark side of the skeptics, sooner or later.

Ideally, Chapter 3 is meant as a tool to be consulted by all those interested in the intersection between AI and the general part of criminal law. As such, the expectation is that it will be of use as a general framework of reference for future AI legal scholars who are looking for a perspective on current (and future) paths of investigation. Moreover, Chapter 3 can work as a case study of the differences between common law and civil law scholars in approaching conflict, which in the present case is represented by the impact of AI technologies on our society. As a matter of fact, one could study the debate reconstructed

27 Gless, Silverman & Weigend, 2016, p. 423.

28 Simmler & Markwalder, 2019.

29 As Lagioia and Sartor argue: "Given the current socio-technical arrangements, we are not arguing for this approach [*punishing AI systems*], but it may be useful to start speculating about it". Lagioia & Sartor, 2020, pp. 27-28.

in Chapter 3 as a form of expression of the civil law – common law divide. Indeed, where the "common law mind"[30] tends to find a convincing pragmatic solution, the civil law mind tries to solve the conflict beforehand "through hierarchic organized norms".[31] Consequently, common law systems are traditionally more receptive to development than civil legal systems. This trend is visible amongst some of the authors in Chapter 3. Perhaps most of the "civilians", whose work was examined in the literature review, resort to such solutions since they come from extremely doctrinal legal cultures, such as Germany,[32] or from criminal legal systems which are deeply rooted in a principle of strict legality and of "personal" criminal liability, such as Italy. Tentatively, the research tried to learn from both minds.

Lastly, what could be the role of a new legal scholar in this *mare magnum*? Is the field saturated? A positive outlook is desired. The AI legal scholar of the future could focus on specific problems (e.g., negligence, causality, defenses) and/or on specific sectors (e.g., driving automation, healthcare). This type of research would exploit the existing literature on AI law, including the present research, to its fullest. Assuredly, since Chapter 3 reports Italian and German voices of the debate in English, it could be improved by new contributions of scholars outside the (linguistic) scope of analysis.

8.4 Anthropocentrism and Responsibility of Machines. The Attribution Question

8.4.1 *Holding AI to a Higher (Moral) Standard*

Scientific research is – nowadays – based on Newtonian hermeneutics, where "reality is considered to be built from impersonal, inanimate matter, and causal relationships between them".[33] It follows that "we no longer consider an earthquake today as an expression of 'anger' of some God, but as a causal chain of tectonic events leading to the catastrophe".[34] The development of AI systems is also based on Newtonian hermeneutics. This makes applying typical "anthropomorphic constructs" to AI, such as "free-will, con-

30 A. W. B. Simpson, *Legal Theory and Legal History: Essays on the Common Law*, The Hambledon Press, 1987, p. 394.
31 Beck, 2010, p. 1105.
32 See R. Hofmann, "Formalism versus pragmatism – A comparative legal and empirical analysis of the German and Dutch criminal justice systems with regard to effectiveness and efficiency", *Maastricht Journal of European and Comparative Law Issue*, Vol. 28, No. 2, 2021, pp. 452-478; Keiler & Roef (eds.), 2019.
33 S. Srinivasa & J. Deshmukh, *AI and the Sense of Self*, Srinivasa, Srinath and Jayati Deshmukh. "AI and the Sense of Self." *ArXiv abs/2201.05576*, 2021, p. 2.
34 Ibid.

science, trust, desire, anger [*and suffering*]"[35] cumbersome. Hence, "shaming" or expressing disapproval, disgust and anger against a reprehensible act can act as a *deterrent* to a human; but machines hitherto don't respond to such expressive rhetoric. While we can appeal to the *conscience* of a human wrong-doer to make them correct their actions, no such mechanism exists for interacting with AI that is about to do something irresponsible.[36]

One should note, though, that it is debated – much as it was debated with regard to corporations – "whether human-like prerequisites for moral agency should be imposed on machines or if a hard line should be drawn between human moral agency and that of machines".[37] Certainly, this is nothing new, since also CCL scholars and lawmakers had to face the fact that concepts such as *mens rea* and *actus reus* "which make perfectly good sense when applied to individuals, do not translate easily to an *inanimate fictional entity*".[38] Thus, it must be stressed that AI systems *are not inanimate fictional entities*: some of them "live" and operate in the digital and/or physical world. In this, AI systems differ profoundly from corporations.

Let us now focus, then, on the matter of translating human constructs to machines. As was revealed in Section 5.3.2, researchers have been exploring the possibility of creating "moral machines", or "AMAs",[39] for some time now. Specifically, they are trying to create machines that are capable of implementing ethical principles and moral decision-making, so that they behave towards human users and other machines in an ethically acceptable way.[40]

Some of the difficulties of translating morality into code were already highlighted in Section 5.3.2. Here, we only need to be reminded of the fact that designing AMAs, in a nutshell, entails "defining the moral behaviors or ethics that the system will follow, implementing such moral behaviors or ethics, and operationalizing them".[41] In "Robot Criminals", discussed in Section 3.2.2, Hu contends that a new criminal code for robots could establish a "minimum set of *moral standards* to which all smart robots must adhere".[42] On a similar note, Germany established via law that AVs must be capable of prioritizing legal

35 Srinivasa & Deshmukh, 2021, p.2 [emphasis added].

36 Ibid [emphasis added].

37 A. Martinho, "Perspectives about artificial moral agents", *AI and Ethics*, Vol. 1, 2021, p. 482.

38 J. Gobert & M. Punch, *Rethinking Corporate Crime*, Cambridge University Press, 2003, p. 10 [emphasis added].

39 Artificial Moral Agents.

40 Martinho, 2021, p. 481.

41 Ibid. When addressing these topics, one is prone to ask oneself which moral rules should be taught to AI systems. Moreover, since "[e]thics has to be operationalized so that an AMA is able to recognize a moral situation, weigh up possible moral actions, make moral judgments, and execute them", it would be interesting to study also "how a machine moralizes". Ivi, p. 482.

42 Hu, 2019, p. 502.

goods when faced with moral dilemmas.[43] The question which arises then is: which moral rules should be taught to AMAs? In other words, "who would be the one to identify 'true morality'?"[44] This is a question intrinsically connected to criminalization theories, specifically directed to those who belong to the "legal moralism" school of thought.[45] It is questionable how these moral standards would be developed, since human beings have not agreed yet on a universal set of moral rules for themselves, let alone for artificial beings.

Furthermore, one of the most prominent issues regarding the development of AMAs is that of *interpretability* of AI systems. It is argued that "[p]roviding some method for effectively communicating an agent's beliefs, desires, and plans to the people around it is critical for ensuring that artificial agents act ethically".[46] A possible solution could be if the agent were to "*explain its reasoning* by describing its predictions of the consequences and how it thinks those consequences are valued".[47] Such a statement is relevant for this research since interpretability, i.e., the ability for AI systems to communicate their (moral) decisions, is considered by some as a *fundamental condition for criminal liability*.

As a matter of fact, Hu argues that interpretability is relevant for criminal law purposes, as only by understanding the *reasons* behind a certain act is it possible to ascertain whether the robot committed the action with the required *mental state*. In other words, Hu links *interpretability* to *mens rea*. When doing so, she imagines the following commission-by-omission scenario:[48] let us imagine that a robot is passing by, when it hears a child crying for help because she is drowning. We can imagine that the robot – similar to Abel's Burning Room ethical dilemma discussed above[49] – will make "a series of calculations: if it stops to pull the child out of the water, there is a ten percent chance that it might fall into the water, destroying itself. If it does not, there is a ninety percent chance that the child will die".[50] I agree with Hu that, in scenarios like these, we might be able to hold AI systems to a higher moral standard than humans.[51] Not only one could argue that it would be morally wrong for the robot not to risk its "life" to save the drowning child, but we could even imagine imposing a general legal duty on AI systems to save human beings, no matter the costs, and hold them *accountable* if they fail to do so. Nevertheless, this would entail that we, as a society, would consciously decide to assign a lower value to the "life" of an AI system than to the life of human beings.

---

43 See Ch. 8, E.
44 Hörnle, 2014, p. 693.
45 See Sec. 4.2.
46 Abel, MacGlashan & Littman, 2016, p. 7.
47 Ibid. [emphasis added].
48 See Example D at Sec. 1.6.
49 See Sec. 5.3.2.2.
50 Hu, 2019, p. 500.
51 Ibid.

Hu takes this reasoning even further, since she claims that we could hold AI systems *criminally* liable for not acting like heroes.[52] I believe that even though it might be feasible to do so, it would be uncalled for since criminal law is not the only form of reprimand available in a society. I expand on this further on in this chapter.

How would this impact the creation of AMAs? It would call for a different "ethical training" from the one that we – as human beings – receive when growing up.[53] Surely, teaching a robot how to make the decision of not (always) being a hero, which would be akin to the ethical decision that we would take as humans, while at the same time punishing it when it decides not to be one, would be counterintuitive.[54] In this I find the greatest limitation of Hu's theory, which is based on a futuristic, if not even dystopian, scenario. As is discussed in the following section, it would be different if we were confronted with robots who could learn ethical values autonomously.

8.4.1.2 The (Ir) Relevance of Motives

Criminal codes are not a codification of moral wrongs. As is often taught in the first class of a criminal law course, not everything that is immoral is illegal and not everything that is illegal is immoral. Yet, criminal culpability is "grounded in moral blameworthiness".[55] It "seeks to refine and institutionalize our intuitive blameworthiness judgments"[56] and can be understood as a "stripped-down, coarse grained analog of blameworthiness".[57]

Let us now focus for a moment on what we have, i.e., (human) criminal codes. Modern criminal legal systems seem to be slightly schizophrenic: on the one hand, they require that criminal agents have the *general capacity to be responsive to the law*, i.e., the ability to *motivate themselves* in accordance with the law; on the other hand, they do not require a *specific motive* to commit a *specific offense*. In a nutshell, this is the "irrelevance-of-motive maxim".[58]

---

52 Hu, 2019, p. 500.

53 Our "Innate Moral Core". See J. K. Hamlin, "Moral Judgment and Action in Preverbal Infants and Toddlers: Evidence for an Innate Moral Core", *Current Directions in Psychological Science* Vol. 22, Iss. 3, 2013, pp. 186-193.

54 E.g., if we introduced an offense in the criminal code for robots targeting the failure to save a human being. See also Consulich, who argues: "*L'AI non è infatti suscettibile alla minaccia di una qualsiasi forma di sanzione, tanto quanto sia in prima persona il destinatario della sanzione quanto allorché lo sia un suo 'simile'. Occorrerebbe programmare forme che contengano l'istruzione di essere recettivi rispetto a tali input, ma si tratterebbe di una soluzione al limite dell'autopoiesi: costruire una sensibilità al precetto giuridico per poi creare una responsabilità, civile o penale che sia*". F. Consulich, "Le prospettive di *accountability* penale nel contrasto alle intelligenze artificiali devianti", *Diritto e Procedura Penale*, Vol. 3, 2022, p. 1022.

55 A. Sarch, "Should Criminal Law Mirror Moral Blameworthiness or Criminal Culpability? A Reply to Husak", *Law and Philosophy*, Vol. 41, 2022, p. 309.

56 Ibid.

57 Sarch, 2022, p. 309.

58 See *ex multis*, M. T. Rosenberg, "The Continued Relevance of the Irrelevance-of-Motive-Maxim", *Duke Law Journal*, Vol. 57, No. 4, 2008, pp. 1143-1177.

In the example of the robot "hero" and the drowning child described above, Hu argues that the *mens rea* requirement would be fulfilled by the robot: (a) if the robot knew that the drowning child was actually a human child; (b) if the robot knew that the drowning child was in imminent danger; (c) if the robot was able to carry out actions that help reduce the danger; and (d) if the robot *concluded* not to take any of the actions identified in (c).[59] Whether it decided not to save the child because it preferred not to risk its integrity, or whether it deemed a different task was more important, such as delivering a package, would not be relevant when establishing its liability (i.e., it would be an irrelevant *motive*). Hence, in such a situation the robot would be liable – provided that a norm establishing liability is in place. Conversely, the robot's liability could be questioned if it erroneously believed it was in the process of saving another child (who is instead already dead), or if two children were drowning and it had to choose between them.

Hu believes that criminal liability could be imposed only if the robot were able to communicate the moral *reasons* which led it to make a certain decision, or else "it would be difficult, if not impossible, to determine whether a wrongful action has taken place".[60] I maintain that this communication could only lead to establishing a *motive* for the robot's action, not its *mens rea*.

Let us take a step back. When examining whether the *mens rea* element of an offense has been fulfilled by one's conduct, courts make use of certain objective elements that work as clues of the agent's *animus necandi* (e.g., the murder weapon and the number of lethal blows). No relevance is given to the fact that the offender might have murdered her neighbor because she simply didn't like her. Motives can have relevance as exculpatory factors only whenever they are indicators of a lack of criminal capacity (i.e., when they can be hints of a legally relevant insanity), provided that they are supported by evidence on the mental health status of the offender.[61] This could be the case of the robot who – in the scenario above – believed that it was in the process of saving another drowning child, when instead the child was already dead, due to a defect in the robot's system caused by a virus.

The rationale behind the irrelevance-of-motive maxim lies in the differentiation between *motive* and *intent*: the first is a "ground or reason for action",[62] not a "driving force that compels a person's actions";[63] the second is "the objective effect which the law-breaker contrives to produce on others by his act or omission".[64] Motives are "the psychic cause, the stimulus, the spring, the impulse, the feeling, the instinct, that prompted, moved, induced,

59 Hu, 2019, p. 511.
60 Ivi, p. 512.
61 Motives can also have relevance as aggravating or mitigating factors in the determination of a sentence.
62 J. Hall, *General Principles of Criminal Law*, 2nd ed., The Bobbs Merrill Company, 1960, p. 88.
63 Ivi, p. 89, n. 77.
64 Hall, 1960, p. 89.

the subject to act (or to omit)".[65] They are the factors that triggered the will and that eventually determined the individual to commit the crime.[66]

Accordingly, "motive answers the question why [*a person acted as he or she did*], neither in terms of causation nor in those of a further ulterior objective, but in terms that give a reason which is the subject of an *ethical appraisal*".[67] Instead, intent entails the *deliberate* and *conscious* effort to engage in *behavior that goes against the law*: "[t]o understand why a defendant took the action he did, the explanation proceeds in terms of intended consequence with each intention explaining the preceding intention".[68] The evaluation of motive is essential to "judgments of moral culpability"[69] and is not directly relevant for judgments of criminal liability. The two elements are, naturally, connected, yet they must be kept separate. As a matter of fact, intention relates to the moment and stage of the decision-making process *between different reasons for acting* differently.[70]

As stated above, one could perhaps identify *motives* in the commission of crimes by (future) AMAs. Consequently, harm caused by AMAs could be deemed wrong from a *moral* perspective – and be subject to the social consequences that can follow the breach of a moral rule. The previous section was concluded with the ideas of robots learning ethical values autonomously: until systems like this are developed – and it is not sure that they will ever be – pinning blame on these systems would probably be superfluous.[71] Here I take the reasoning even further and argue that, since AMAs are not able to experience the negative feelings which follow from moral responsibility, such as guilt, disapproval, or reproach, it seems difficult to qualify them as true moral agents for now. As is argued in Section 8.5, empirical research might prove just the opposite.

Moving forward, I find that there is one major obstacle to affirming that AI systems can display *intent* and, more generally, to arguing that AI systems can possess criminal

65 P. Veneziani, *Motivi e colpevolezza*, Giappichelli, 2000, p. 3.

66 Ibid.

67 Hall, 1960, p. 93 [emphasis added].

68 Rosenberg, 2008, p. 1157.

69 Ivi, p. 1166, note 128.

70 A. Grandinetti, "Motivi e movente", *Il Penalista*, Bussola. Available at: https://ilpenalista.it/bussola/motivi-e-movente.

71 Kalliokoski and Hallamaa gie the following example when denying moral agency to AI systems. Let us think of an AI system whose purpose is to assign doctor appointments to patients. When doing so, the AI system will have to assign different grades of priority to the patients. To make this decision, the AI system should include parameters such as "the patients' age, social status, and indicators concerning vulnerability". Conceivably, these parameters "would improve the monitoring of appointments in medical care in terms of fairness – which is a moral characteristic – but it would not make the AI system morally responsible for placing the patients in a preferential order" since those who "feel they have unjustly been left waiting in the patient queue would, rightly, blame those who designed the code for the monitoring system rather than the AI application itself". T. Kalliokoski & J. Hallamaa, "How AI Systems Challenge the Conditions of Moral Agency?", in M. Rauterberg (ed.), *Culture and Computing: 8th International Conference, C&C 2020, Held as Part of the 22nd HCI International Conference*, Springer, 2020, p. 8.

capacity: AI systems lack *agency* (*and the feeling of it*), which is the probably the most human characteristic about humans. As was effectively argued:

> [...] by far, a characteristic feature of natural beings that has been largely ignored by engineers, is the *sense of "self"* that pervades across all cells of the organism. Cells have a sharp notion of "citizenship" to the being that make them act with vigilance against "foreign" cells that infect the organism. Even though each agent in the being is acting autonomously, there is also a sense of "oneness" or "belongingness" to the being, that pervades across all the agents. When the organism strives to survive, it is the pervasive sense of self that is sought to be maintained and preserved and not for instance, any particular cell. It is also the pervasive sense of self, that is sought to be protected against attacks in the form of infections, by the immune system.[72]

Accordingly, only an agent who has an "experience of authorship",[73] i.e., that can experience a "constellation of feelings",[74] such as being able to "perceive herself as the cause of her own actions tracking the linkage between a voluntary bodily movement and its effect",[75] can be deemed as *responsive* to the command expressed in the law, specifically by criminal offenses.[76] In human beings, agency is not a "binary property":[77] it emerges gradually during "the physical, social, and psychological development of a child".[78] In a humancentric legal system, agency establishes that link between someone's action and that person's criminal liability. As was maintained by R.A. Duff, "intentional agency" is a central paradigm of "*responsible agency*".[79] From a criminal legal perspective, one could argue that criminal liability can be construed as being addressed to those who are "rationally responsive" to criminal law's demands.[80] It follows that only those who *question the validity of a norm* can be considered as "true" authors of crime.[81]

As was claimed, intent and, more generally, criminal capacity, denotes being receptive to the *prescriptive* contents of a criminal norm, i.e., its persuasive and coercive components. In this sense, scholars argue that not only does the criminal norm "orient" an indi-

72 Srinivasa & Deshmukh, 2021, p. 3 [emphasis added].
73 Bonicalzi & Haggard, 2019, p. 113.
74 Ibid.
75 Bonicalzi & Haggard, 2019, p. 113.
76 Ibid.
77 Kalliokoski & Hallamaa, 2020, p. 4.
78 Ibid.
79 R.A. Duff, *Intention, Agency and Criminal Liability: Philosophy of Action and the Criminal Law*, Blackwell, 1990, p. 101 [emphasis added].
80 V. Chao, *Action and Agency in the Criminal Law, Legal Theory*, Cambridge University Press, 2009, p. 23.
81 Simmler & Markwalder, 2023, p. 30.

vidual's behavior through the threat of the sanction – which will be inflicted if she harms a protected legal good, but that it is also internalized by the individual and becomes part of her decision-making process.[82] In other words, criminal law, either because of the fear of being punished, or other cognitive mechanisms, delivers a message which *impacts* individuals and *guides* their behavior.[83] This is possible because human beings are *susceptible* to such message. Current AI systems, as this research showed, are not.

Only if AI systems could be qualified as true "*addressees of normative expectations*",[84] would we be able to hold them criminally liable, since it would imply that the machine made a mistake, i.e., it committed a crime, even though *it could have acted differently*.[85] And it is only in this light that its punishment would incorporate an expectation of "a different norm-conforming behaviour"[86] in the future.

8.4.2 *Retributivists at Heart?*

In the previous section I argued that being an addressee of criminal law entails rationality, meant as the general capacity of being susceptible to legal commands and of acting upon them freely (or, better, with a *perceived sense of freedom*). Rationality, in an anthropocentric legal system, is meant as the ability for the agent to motivate herself to behave in a way that conforms with the law – through the anticipation of the consequences of her act/omission (*actus reus*). This is the quintessence of criminal capacity, which is a quality that must pre-exist in criminal agents.

---

82 C. Colucci, *Tra ottimizzazione della funzione comando e prospettive di un suo superamento: i nuovi scenari della normatività penale*, PhD Dissertation, University of Florence Repository, 2022, pp. 4-5. Available at: https://flore.unifi.it/handle/2158/1273584.

83 "*L'agire umano, infatti, è psichicamente (e non meccanicamente) causato, e cioè determinato mediante motivazioni. Nella struttura normativa del comando tale motivazione è rappresentata dalla presenza della sanzione, e cioè dalla minaccia della sua applicazione nel caso in cui il precetto sia disatteso. Tale contromotivo [...] in una concezione della norma che si inspiri alla centralità del momento sanzionatorio, rappresenta l'unico perno psicologico della norma stessa che, per mezzo dell'intimidazione, persegue lo scopo di impedire la lesione di beni giuridici da parte dei destinatari della norma stessa. [...] Se questo è dunque il meccanismo psicologico per mezzo del quale funziona il comando, è pur necessario mettere in evidenza come i meccanismi di orientamento del comportamento – anche di carattere normativo – siano molto più vari". Ivi, pp. 75-76. The fact that human beings are susceptible to such message, though, does not mean that one must give in to deterministic theories, i.e., consider humans as "pre-determined" beings: "è necessario [...] mantenere ferma l'idea che la prospettazione di un comando, al quale è legata la minaccia di una sanzione, attivi nel destinatario un processo cognitivo pienamente consapevole, senza cedere alla tentazione di ricondurre anche la paura di una conseguenza negativa all'insieme di istinti naturali che, non pienamente controllabili dall'uomo, appartengono al mondo dell'essere".* Ivi, p. 78.

84 Colucci, 2022, p. 78 [emphasis added].

85 Ibid.

86 Colucci, 2022, p. 78.

As was mentioned in Chapters 4 and 5, criminal capacity is strictly connected to *purposes* of criminal punishment. As such, this study necessarily touched on different theories of punishment. Let us now focus specifically on retributivism and on the "retribution gap"[87] issue, a matter that was addressed in the preliminary conclusions of Chapter 6.

Retributivism is, in essence, "the idea that what justifies criminal punishment is that it is deserved for past criminal wrongdoing".[88] It entails answering the questions of: "*what* criminal wrongdoers deserve to suffer; *why* they deserve to suffer it (how it is that crime makes such suffering appropriate); and *why* it should be the business of the state to create and maintain an institution whose purpose is to impose that deserved suffering" – the "just deserts" doctrine.[89] Hence, criminal punishment must be "burdensome, or in some sense painful":[90] this does not entail that punishment should be meant *only* as the imposition of a burden or the delivery of pain, since it also serves a *communicative* function. As such, "it communicates directly to the offender, but also to all citizens, the censure that the crime deserves"[91] and for that reason "it is justified as a response to the wrong for which it is imposed and must be appropriate in its character and severity to that wrong".[92]

The question which we ask ourselves here then is: in order to be responsive to the criminal sanction, does the agent need to be able to feel pain? Does rationality mean responsiveness to the threat of the infliction of harm? Actually, it strikes us as odd that – when dealing with such an innovative topic as liability of AI systems – we seem to reduce ourselves to traditional retributivists arguments. The "new versus old" clash is glaring. Indeed, retribution – as compared to other "instrumental goals of punishment"[93] – is backward-looking: it is how the offender repays society for the harm she caused. Deterrence, on the other hand, is forward-looking: it deals with the "future benefits of reducing the likelihood of crime".[94]

If one focuses on the "communicative" function of criminal punishment, it is doubtful whether punishing AI systems would create benefits for society as a *whole*. As a matter of fact, in order to call someone (or something) to publicly account for wrongdoing, it must be "a fellow member of a relevant normative community … a responsible agent who can be expected to answer for what he has done".[95] It was contended that AI systems are not

87 Danaher, 2016.

88 R.A. Duff, "Responsibility, Restoration, and Retribution", in M. Torny (ed.), *Retributivism Has a Past: Has it a Future*, Oxford University Press, 2011, p. 63.

89 Ivi, p. 65.

90 Duff, 2011, p. 66.

91 Ivi, p. 78.

92 Duff, 2011, p. 78.

93 M. Gerber & J. Jackson, "Retribution as revenge and retribution as just deserts", *Social Justice Research*, Vol. 26, No. 1, 2013, p. 63.

94 Ibid.

95 Duff, 2011, p. 6.

part of our moral or normative community and, as such, *their punishment might not fix what they broke*. Furthermore, if they were considered as agents, part of one's moral community, they would also have the right to be safeguarded from unjust criminal punishment – unless one would want to attribute to them a status similar to those of slaves.

It is plausible, though, that the punishment of AI systems would have *indirect deterrent effects* on human subjects. It could influence certain human agents into doing everything they can to prevent an AI system, that they produce or use, from committing a crime, since their punishment (be it through reprogramming or destruction) would damage them economically (and perhaps, in certain cases, also personally).[96] This topic will be addressed further in the following section.

Imaginably, one could argue in favor of a change of paradigm from conceiving of criminal sanctions as suffering to conceiving of them as a tool to influence behavior. Actually, this change of paradigm is already palpable in our (risk) society, which is characterized by the proliferation of endangerment offenses, and is also one of the pillars underpinning CCL. At this point, one must ask oneself: if we strip criminal law of punishment, can we still call it criminal law? In the eyes of a criminal lawyer, the bond between crime and punishment appears unbreakable. Lastly, holding AI systems criminally accountable calls for a thorough examination of conscience: are we all – deep down – retributivists?

8.4.3 *Re-evaluating the Comparison between AI and Corporations*

In Chapter 6, it was argued that AI systems make for very (hypothetical) rational agents, according to an economic concept of rationality as utility maximization. This is akin to what has been argued about corporations which: "while lacking feeling and emotions nevertheless possess capacities for intelligent agency".[97] As a matter of fact, "lack of emotions in this regard may accordingly foster rather than hamper rational choice"[98] and may make a good case for punishing AI systems to achieve deterrence.[99] In this perspective, rational-

96 "The idea is that if users/deployers were fined (for amounts exceeding compensation) for crimes committed by AI systems, this should induce them to prevent such crimes. In particular, they should be induced to provide AI systems with the motivation to act in such a way as to prevent sanctions against their users. This might be obtained – when deterrence through sanctions is the most appropriate way to influence the behaviour of AI systems – either by making such systems internalise in their utility function the disutility resulting from sanctions against their users, or by providing adequate private sanctions". Lagioia & Sartor, 2020, p. 29.

97 Keiler, 2013, p. 51.

98 Ibid.

99 "Deterrence theory is a powerful and flexible approach for designing criminal justice policies. At heart, it is an economic theory. It views both would-be and actual criminals as rational actors who are trying to maximize their utility. Deterrence theory is a powerful and flexible approach for designing criminal justice policies. At heart, it is an economic theory. It views both would-be and actual criminals as rational actors who are trying to maximize their utility [...] The task for deterrence theorists is to hit the sweet spot where

ity makes corporations (and AI systems) ideal candidates for a criminal sanction, since they are not subject to irrational impulses or to biological reactions such as intoxication or brain damage.[100]

When discussing liability of AI systems, one starts with the same premises as with CCL: "human concepts", such as *actus reus* and *mens rea*, are "not readily applicable in the realm of corporate [*nor algorithmic*] wrongdoing".[101] The attribution of criminal liability to corporations, especially in those systems that adopt an "organic" model for CCL, implies a change of archetype. Undeniably, "the paradigm of moral blameworthiness ought to be applied differently to corporations".[102] Assuming that one can identify in corporations certain capacities, such as rationality and autonomy, which are premises of criminal liability, they will necessarily "acquire a different connotation … as opposed to individual criminal responsibility".[103]

According to some authors, CCL "demonstrates a certain degree of flexibility shown by criminal law when criminal policy so demands. A flexibility that can be used provided that certain dogmatic premises are met to justify the punishment of AI entities".[104] CCL, therefore, can be seen as an example of the irrelevance of distinguishing "right from wrong" for the purposes of criminal liability.[105] As such, it can provide insight into how to overcome the challenges that were highlighted throughout this study with regard to the capacity of AI systems to make "ethical" decisions. Possibly, CCL supports the idea that moral blameworthiness "is not the criminal justice system's sole concern, and perhaps not even its primary concern".[106] The focal goals of CCL are, on the one hand, the prevention of harm to society and, on the other hand, the deterrence of conducts which could lead to said harm, "regardless of whether the conduct in question can be characterized as immoral.[107] So what makes corporations different from AI systems? And what would be the political reasons behind creating AI criminal liability?

To begin with, applying the concept of *respondeat superior* to AI systems seems to be tricky. AI systems are not made up of humans who follow a fixed internal hierarchal struc-

---

sanctions are just high enough to prevent these crimes". M. Diamantis, "Clockwork Corporations", *Iowa Law Review*, Vol. 1032, 2020, pp. 518-520.

100 Diamantis, "Clockwork Corporations", 2020, p. 519.

101 Keiler, 2013, p. 51.

102 Ibid.

103 Keiler, 2013, p. 53.

104 Freitas, Andrade & Novais, 2014, p. 11.

105 Such an ability is deemed irrelevant also for humans in certain legal systems. See the recent US Supreme Court judgment Kahler v. Kansas, discussed in Sec. 5.3.

106 Gobert & Punch, 2003, p. 46.

107 Ibid. See also Regina A. Robson, who claims that: "virtual elimination of retribution as an acknowledged goal of [corporate-]criminal sanctioning," with only deterrence left standing to explain why the State should hold corporations criminally responsible." R. A. Robson, "Crime and Punishment: Rehabilitating Retribution as a Justification for Organizational Criminal Liability", *Am. Bus. L.J.*, Vol. 47, 2010, p. 121.

ture. Hence, at first glance, there is no identifiable *master* who would be liable for the actions and the *mens rea* of its subordinates.

Moreover, as was argued by John Coffee,[108] punishing corporations ultimately entails influencing the decision-making processes of corporations "so that they do not do the same thing again".[109] Admittedly, the "normative" behavior of corporations can be controlled through criminal sanctions, even though they have no "body to kick",[110] *as long as there are (identifiable) humans behind them.*[111] Punishing corporations might prove difficult since they are "complicated distributed systems".[112] It follows that in order to make punishment effective, one must know "the *structure* of the organization" and "how decisions are made on different levels of the organization"[113] so that one can "apply incentives and penalties that will influence the values of those decisions and their utility functions there".[114] Nevertheless, corporations seem to have a "collective soul" to damn, as is synthetized in the doctrine of corporate legal culture. It is much harder to transpose the same concepts to AI systems even though, sometimes, such as in the case of robots, they do have a body to kick.

In other words, by punishing corporations we can influence their behaviors because those within the organization "get the message". When it comes to AI systems, detecting a collective soul and a collective culture is problematic. There is not a clear internal and hierarchical structure behind it. However, the lack of such a structure might only be apparent. Indeed, the development of an AI system can involve plenty of human subjects accompanied by a fragmentation of roles and responsibilities. The combination of their personal attitudes could lead to the creation of a sort of *temporary collective agent*, who would have its own attitude, separate from those of its members, similar to what happens with conspiracies to commit crimes.

Thus, I argue that this alone is not enough to introduce criminal liability of AI systems. The real issue is that AI systems cannot possess funds and they do not possess a "profit motive",[115] therefore punishing them via fines would be useless. As was argued, "[a]t least with corporations, they exist essentially to make money, so taking money away from them

108 J. C. Coffee Jr, "'No Soul to Damn: No Body to Kick': An Unscandalized Inquiry into the Problem of Corporate Punishment", *Michigan Law Review*, Vol. 79, No. 3, 1981, pp. 386-459.

109 Asaro, 2014, p. 290.

110 Quote by Edward, First Baron Thurlow 1731-1806 reported in John C Coffee Jr, "No Soul to Damn: No Body to Kick": An Unscandalized Inquiry into the Problem of Corporate Punishment' (1981) 79 *Michigan Law Review*, 386-458.

111 A. Peikert (Dipl.-Jur.), A. Reinelt (Dipl.-Jur.) & J. Witt (Dipl.-Jur.), "Diskussionsbeiträge der 38. Tagung der deutschsprachigen Strafrechtslehrerinnen und Strafrechtslehrer 2019 in Hannover", *ZSTW*, Vol. 131, No. 4, 2019, p. 1133.

112 Asaro, 2014, pp. 290-291.

113 Ivi, p. 291 [emphasis added].

114 Asaro, 2014, p. 291.

115 Ibid.

actually hurts them, because that is their fundamental reason of existing".[116] It follows that AI systems could only be punished by means of more drastic measures, such as incapacitation. Nevertheless, these measures are likely to only impact the humans-behind-the-machines indirectly, as AI systems "do not care about their physical presence or state".[117] As a consequence, putting them in prison is not really "going to change their minds about anything or effectively punish them if they do not care about their bodies".[118] Indeed, "*if they do not really care about anything, how do you punish them at all?*".[119]

Perhaps, the indirect effects of punishing AI systems could be the criminal policy motive to introduce such a liability framework. Once again, it is a matter of assessing what would be the ultimate goal of criminalizing a specific conduct. *Directly* criminalizing AI systems would *indirectly* penalize those who benefit or profit from the AI system, while at the same time it would minimize "the need to prove that the harm was attributable to specific natural persons or corporations".[120] Thus, in the case of AI systems, the plethora of subjects which would suffer the consequences of a criminal AI systems requires better definition. It is for this reason that Diamantis' theory proves successful: it acknowledges that most AI systems are produced and deployed by organized corporations and, by relying on an already consolidated legal framework, it provides a solution to address AI harm almost effortlessly. In this perspective, punishing AI systems could, for example, lead to an increase in the duty of care of CEOs and other high-ranking employees. Nevertheless, if the purpose is to deter those who are responsible for the AI system, I agree with those who claim that there would be equally efficient alternative mechanisms.[121] I will come back to this statement in the following paragraphs.

8.4.4 *Epicenters of Liability: the Human Culprit*

This research was centered around criminal liability *of* AI systems. Yet, it also touched upon criminal liability *of* humans *for* AI systems. The topic was addressed from a theoretical perspective in Section 6.2.3., which discussed whether humans-behind-the-machine could be deemed responsible for AI harm based on a negligence *mens rea* standard; and in Chapter 7, which instead scrutinized the topic from a quasi-*de iure condito* perspective.[122] I will now draw some conclusions on the matter and outline avenues for future investigation.

116 Asaro, 2014, p. 291.
117 Ibid.
118 Asaro, 2014, p. 291.
119 Ibid [emphasis added].
120 SAL Report, p. 38, para. 4.47.
121 Ibid.
122 The examples analyzed at Chapter 7 are not all codified law.

Automation is safer and superior to human beings, until it's not. Surely, the interaction between AI and human beings leads to an enhanced risk of moral disengagement by the human-behind-the-machine.[123] Moral disengagement is an expression coined by psychologist Albert Bandura to refer to a set of techniques by which human beings "selectively disengage moral self-sanctions"[124] when doing something "wrong".[125] As a matter of fact, AI systems might act in ways that are obscure to their users or creators, and this compels them to just "trust the (technological) process", weakening their sense of agency. This reasoning could be taken even further to claim that human agents can convince themselves that what they're doing – when dealing with a machine – is not only morally acceptable, but also legally acceptable. The complex relationship between one's sense of agency and its responsibility was already addressed before. How does moral disengagement, then, impact the attribution of negligence to the human-behind-the-machine?

The case studies reported in Chapter 7 represent the first instances of regulators attempting to strike a balance between when criminal law should "track" morality and when it should not in the field of criminal liability *for* AI systems. They involve exclusively liability of *humans* for actions of *non-humans*. Their collection and comparison is one of the elements which make the present research original.

Criminal law is a matter of design: criminal legal systems are the results of a set of practical decisions ("institutional design considerations")[126] which can include "bright line rules",[127] such as the ones suggested by the UK Law Commissions, and "generally applicable resolution of contested normative questions".[128] The majority of the case studies examined in Chapter 7 rely almost entirely on the human's ability to anticipate and manage risks, i.e., on her negligence. As was argued, the application of a such a standard of *mens rea* could give rise to "negligence failures".[129] This term describes "situations in which the classical building blocks of negligence, i.e., risk taking, foreseeability, and awareness, struggle to identify a liable human being to whom we can attribute AI-caused harm".[130]

123 See S. Massi, "Affidamento sull'intelligenza artificiale e 'disimpegno morale' nella definizione dei presupposti della responsabilità penale", in R. Giordano, *Il diritto nell'era digitale. Persona, Mercato, Amministrazione, Giustizia*, Giuffrè, 2022, pp. 665-679.

124 A. Bandura, "Moral disengagement in the perpetration of inhumanities", *Personality and Social Psychology Review*, Vol. 3, 1999, pp. 193-209.

125 Bandura mentions eight mechanisms of moral disengagement: moral justification; exonerative comparison; euphemistic labeling; minimizing, ignoring or misconstruing the consequences; dehumanization; and attribution of blame.

126 Sarch, 2022, p. 310.

127 Ibid.

128 Sarch, 2022, pp. 310-311.

129 Negligence failures represent a direct development of Abbott and Sarch's irreducibility challenge. Giannini & Kwik, 2023, p. 3.

130 Ibid.

Negligence, generally speaking, requires that the agent foresaw and accepted the risk that an unlawful consequence would arise from her conduct. Foresight can be meant as a *generic* knowledge that the activity could lead to some harm, or as the knowledge that the activity could actualize a *specific* risk, i.e., a specific harmful consequence.

We asked ourselves before if humans will always be able to effectively supervise a system that was created to overcome them and make up for their shortcomings.[131] Now we can answer that probably they will not. Nevertheless, they represent, for now, the only *liable* entities which are most proximate to the AI system. As such, I believe that they could be deemed liable for the AI's misbehavior, provided that they negligently disregarded precise best practices and technical standards (which still have to be realized) and that this led to the commission of a *grave* offense (e.g., negligent homicide).

Moreover, the standard of care of the model agent should be modelled according to single area of application of the AI systems (e.g., toys, transportation, healthcare) and to the role covered by the human agent in question (e.g., trainer, tester, data collector). On the contrary, I maintain that holding human beings criminally responsible for the sole fact that they created, used, or produced an unpredictable machine would be excessive. In these cases, the best solution is to be found in other areas of the law, such as torts.

As was suggested in Section 4.1., one could take inspiration from the field of aviation and, specifically, from the liability of air traffic controllers.[132] Air traffic controllers have a relevant duty of care under criminal law: they are obliged to prevent collisions between aircraft and, more generally, to avoid air disasters. Thus, they are expected to be highly skilled and trained subjects. They operate in a field where human and technological errors blur. In this sense, one would need to identify with precision who could cover a similar position in the chain of creation and deployment of an AI system, taking into consideration that in most situations end-users will be simply "average citizens". Indeed, the attribution of liability for AI crimes could benefit from a field like the one of major disasters: their complexity, both with regard to the web of causation and to the high level of automation, requires a multidisciplinary approach.

Moral disengagement, lack of foresight, lack of meaningful control: all of these conditions (and many others), taken together or individually, can heavily reduce – or even eliminate – the knowledge that an AI system could behave criminally, hence leading to a negligence failure. The UK, Singaporean and French examples, when "drawing a bright line" amid "risk zones of legality" and "zones of illegality", necessarily strike a balance between risks of scapegoating humans-behind-the-machine and the need of legislators to regulate new technologies. Only (judicial) practice will tell whether the balance was struck fairly.

---

131 Above at Sec. 3.4.1 and at 8.4.4.

132 E. Greco, *Profili di responsabilità penale del controllore del traffico aereo. Gestione del rischio e imputazione dell'evento per colpa nei sistemi a interazione complessa*, Giappichelli, 2021.

8.5 General Conclusions. The Future- and Backward-Facing Question

The time has come to focus on the main research question (RQ) guiding this research: to what extent is a theoretical framework of criminal liability for non-human agents *needed* and *feasible*?

The RQ and the title of this research clearly reveal that the starting point of this research was the matter of *direct* liability of AI agents. Approaching such a topic demanded a certain level of *flexibility*: as was shown in Chapter 3, several criminal law scholars refuse to even consider such a matter, discarding it as absurd. Apropos, the choice of a RQ formulated in terms of "to what extent" allows for this plasticity, since it grants the researcher the freedom to explore a certain field without incurring strong "yes-or-no" alternatives.

After a close review, it is suggested here that the two prongs of the RQ should be posed in the reverse order, and reformulated as follows: to what extent is a theoretical framework of criminal liability for non-human agents *feasible* and *needed*? Perhaps, the original version of the RQ was more compatible with theories of criminalization. Nevertheless, the development of AI systems touches upon conducts that have already been reckoned as worthy of criminalization. Hence it appears more logical to first discuss whether it would be practicable to adapt what is already in place, i.e., traditional criminal norms, and then address the question of whether or not to attribute liability to AI systems, since the latter is essentially a question of criminal law policy. I assume that this type of reasoning would also be followed by policymakers, who would have to justify the necessity of introducing new legal concepts and its feasibility. Indeed, one could have the greatest idea of all times, but if it is not feasible, is it really a great invention?

Let us focus, then, on what constitutes (now) the first prong of the RQ (to what extent is a theoretical framework of criminal liability for non-human agents *feasible*?). Studying feasibility entails analyzing critical aspects of a proposition in order to determine whether it would succeed.[133] In the case of this research, it called for an inquiry into whether AI systems would be *eligible addressees* of criminal law. To do so, I broke criminal liability down into three building blocks (criminal capacity, *actus reus, mens rea*) and tested whether each one of them could be fulfilled by AI.

The succinct answer to the first prong of the RQ is the following: criminal liability of AI agents is *feasible* depending on how much of our anthropomorphic notions we are willing to give up. Specifically, holding AI systems responsible would entail either being able to create machines that are *susceptible* to the requirements of a legal norm, or abandoning the concept of rationality (meant as the ability to be responsive to the law) alto-

133 Investopedia, "Feasibility Study", 4 November 2022. Available at: www.investopedia.com/terms/f/feasibility-study.asp.

gether. Indeed, I advanced above that the *comprehension* of an offense's requirements is an essential prerequisite for establishing criminal liability and, as such, it represents the main obstacle to attributing liability to AI systems directly. In fact, criminal liability can be imputed only to individuals who are capable of understanding and following the *demands* of criminal law. This means that in order to affirm that a machine committed a crime, we must be certain that it made a deliberate choice *not* to conform to normative expectations, even though it had the capability of doing so. To date, it is not possible to attribute this capacity to modern AI systems. They may consequently be held criminally liable in the future if this condition were to be satisfied.[134]

In other words, AI just doesn't get it. It does not fit in the "insufficient regard picture"[135] painted by a criminal offense. AI systems cannot be criminally liable as long as a criminally culpable act (in contrast to a morally blameworthy one)[136] is understood according "to the degree it's based on a valuation of reasons that diverges from the correct weights the law ideally would say should be ascribed to the reasons bearing on whether to do the action".[137] Besides, it would be *feasible* to establish criminal liability *of* AI agents only if we were to abandon the concept of retributivism as a goal of punishment in the foreseeable future. That is because not only do AI systems not comprehend the essence of the criminal norm, but they also do not comprehend its sanction.

Let us now focus on the second prong of the RQ (to what extent is a theoretical framework of criminal liability for non-human agents *needed*?). My answer is that criminal liability of AI agents is not *needed* as long as AI systems are not treated as members of our community and, as such, as subject to the same rules as we are. The change in perception, i.e., the anthropomorphization of AI systems, could happen only at the time when "true" AMAs are developed. As argued above, being an AMA would suffice to pin moral blameworthiness on AI systems, but in order to be considered criminally culpable they should also be "legal" agents. And, in other to be *legal* agents, AI systems would have to be responsive to criminal norms. In other words, the questions of whether criminal liability of AI systems is feasible and needed remain intertwined.

If we were to ascertain that criminal liability of AI agents is needed, we would also have to accept that they would have the right to have a say regarding their punishment, unless one is willing to accept the creation of a new generation of "robotic" slaves. Notably, this research focused "only" on AI systems and their legal personality as "duty bearers",[138] i.e., on whether they could be subject to sanctions. The result of this study could be of use for

134 In this sense, I agree with Simmler & Marwkalder, 2019. p. 29.

135 "For the interests, rights and values that are properly protected by criminal law", Sarch, 2022, pp. 309-310.

136 An act is morally blameworthy "to the extent it manifests (in the way morality requires) insufficient regard for the interests, rights, and values morality deems relevant". Ivi, p. 309.

137 Sarch, 2022, p. 310.

138 Lagioia & Sartor, 2020, p. 7.

future research on the question of whether AI systems could also be "right-bearers",[139] specifically, in the realm of criminal law, of whether they could be deemed victims of crimes.

Surely, the creation of a new sub-system of rules for AI systems should be avoided. Modern criminal law is democratic: it applies to every citizen, according to the principle of the rule of law. Apropos, "[i]t's important that the public perceive the criminal law to be treating like cases alike, as this bolsters the institution's perceived legitimacy and engenders trust and obedience to its standards".[140]

Furthermore, one must also take into account what would be the goal of criminalizing AI systems, also in comparisons with alternatives to criminal law. To put it another way, we need to ask ourselves whether criminalizing AI systems would be *useful*. As a matter of fact, according to the principle of subsidiarity, before criminalizing new conducts (or new agents) we should ask ourselves: could administrative or civil law achieve the prevention of negative outcomes in an equally effective way? If yes, "which solution is less costly (for the state, for society and the economy, and offenders)?".[141] To date, the criminalization of AI systems appears to be the costliest solution. Things could change in the future, for example if we were to be faced with AI systems which could pose grave threats to collective goods: this could entail that punishing AI systems would be in compliance with the *ultima ratio* principle.

8.5.1 Looking Forward

In a perspective for the future, I agree with those who claim that the introduction of criminal liability of AI systems will depend on whether the society of the future will develop "normative expectations" towards them.[142] If AI systems are expected to comply with criminal norms, then their noncompliance will require the reaction of criminal law.[143] As mentioned above, this attribution could be mandated, for example, by a change in the values of our community, or by a development in the technology which will lead to fully "humanized" robots.

If we were to decide that AI systems can actually commit crimes, further research could be pursued, also in light of this study's result, regarding whether restorative justice could "offer an alternative way of dealing with the occurrence of AI crimes".[144] The topic has not (yet) gained much attention. Some have acknowledged that restorative justice

139 Ivi, p. 7.
140 Sarch, 2022, p. 311.
141 Hörnle, 2014, p. 696.
142 Simmler & Markwalder, 2019, p. 25.
143 Ibid.
144 A. Hadzi & D. Roio, "Restorative Justice in Artificial Intelligence Crime", *Spectres of AI*, Vol. 5, 2019, p. 16.

"might support victims of AI crimes better than the punitive legal system, as it allows for the sufferers of AI crimes to be heard in a personalised way"[145] and that it would be more affordable for victims, since "AI technologies would not only be defined by a powerful elite".[146] Surely, this opens up the question of how reconciliation between AI systems and victims would take place.

As was claimed, intent and, more generally, criminal capacity, which are lacking at this time in AI systems, denote being susceptible to the requirement enshrined in a criminal norm. Yet, some contend that the criminal norm includes more than deterrence achieved through the threat of the infliction of suffering.[147] In view of that, it is argued that criminal offenses have a "guidance" and "communicative" function, which is usually best achieved by communicating with its recipients via the prospect of a reward (such as that of not being punishable for a previous illegal action).[148] This is relevant when dealing with AI systems which, thanks to reinforcement learning techniques, can be trained with a reward-penalty method.

Imagine that, in the future, we were to face the production of rules that can, from the very beginning, be consumed *directly* by machines.[149] The very day that legal rules will lose certain characteristics (such as the reference to sensitive reality), and become very formal (to the point that they can be expressed by bar codes),[150] criminal compliance by AI systems will stop being different from that of humans. This might change our perspective on criminal capacity altogether.

Furthermore, one option could be to introduce punishment of AI systems *only for specific* (existing) *crimes*. In fact, modern criminal law has shifted from punishing *malum in se* offenses (i.e., offenses that are inherently bad, evil, or morally wrong), to *malum prohibitum* offenses (offenses that are wrong only because they are prohibited by positive laws).[151] One of the most prominent examples is the field of environmental criminal law, where harm results from "accumulative acts which, at the individual level, would be harm-

145 Ivi, p. 17.
146 Hadzi & Rio, 2019, p. 17.
147 Colucci, 2022; M. Papa, *Fantastic Voyage*, 2nd ed., Giappichelli, 2019.
148 Colucci, 2022, pp. 9 and 201; Papa, 2019, pp. 108 ff.
149 Papa, 2019, pp. 243-244.
150 Ibid.
151 "'Crimes mala in se' embrace acts immoral or wrong in themselves, such as burglary, larceny, arson, rape, murder, and breaches of peace. [...] 'Crimes mala prohibita' embrace things prohibited by statute as infringing on others' rights, though no moral turpitude may attach, and constituting crimes only because they are so prohibited". See Black, 1968, pp. 445-446. For a unique reflection on the crisis of offense definitions in contemporary criminal law, see Papa, 2019; M. Papa, "The Offense Definition as a Screenplay of Evil: The Rise and Fall of Visual Criminal Law", *Católica Law Review*, Vol. 4, No. 3, 2020, pp. 145-174.

less".[152] Moreover, it is assumed that contemporary criminal law should be focused on behavior and not on thoughts, following the *cogitationis poenam nemo patitur* maxim.[153]

This could work similarly in those legal systems where corporations are punished according to a "catalogue" of offenses which very often includes an extensive list of *malum prohibitum* offenses. Such offenses present a very "thin" *mens rea*, due to their intrinsic regulatory nature, hence would pose fewer problems with regard to the attribution of a sufficient level of "disregard", i.e., intent, to AI systems. Usually, one of the concerns regarding statutory offenses is that they are highly technical and "hidden" in *extra-codicem* regulations, so that they can lead to punishment of individuals who were unaware of their existence (according to the general *ignorantia legis non excusat* principle). This issue might not be as pressing for AI systems, since they are capable of reading and memorizing incredible amounts of texts by using NLP.[154] Nevertheless, if awareness of the norm entails not only the knowledge of its existence, but also the comprehension of its demands, then we are back to square one. Moreover, one could think of introducing new AI-specific offenses, such as a commission-by-omission offense connected to a duty to save human lives (think of the example of the heroic robot discussed throughout this research).[155] Definitely, such an expansion of the scope of application of criminal law should not happen as if criminal law were the *prima ratio* solution vis-à-vis a population's sentiment.[156]

Surely, future investigations will have to take into account that the common attribution of criminal liability to AI systems seems to be going in the opposite direction of this research's results. As a matter of fact, recent research has shown that people apply different

152 N. Peršak, *The Harm Principle, its Limits and Continental Counterparts*, Springer, 2007, p.137. Other less eminent examples can be found in the United States Code. See J. G. Malcolm, "Morally Innocent, Legally Guilty: The Case for Mens Rea Reform", *The Federalist Society Review*, Vol. 18, 2017, p. 42.

153 Digest of Justinian, 48.19.18, Ulp. 3 ad ed.

154 Research on the matter, also referred to as "LegalAI", is vast. See *ex multis* H. Zhong & al., "How Does NLP Benefit Legal System: A Summary of Legal Artificial Intelligence", *Proceedings of the 58th Annual Meeting of the Association for Computational Linguistics*, 2020, pp. 5218–5230; M. J. Bommarito II, D. M. Katz & E. M. Detterman, "LexNLP: Natural language processing and information extraction for legal and regulatory texts", in R. Vogl (ed)., *Research Handbook on Big Data Law*, Edward Elgar Publishing, 2021, pp. 216-227; I. Chalkidis, M. Fergadiotis & I. Androutsopoulos, "MultiEURLEX – A multi-lingual and multi-label legal document classification dataset for zero-shot cross-lingual transfer", in M. Moens et al. (eds.), *Proceedings of the 2021 Conference on Empirical Methods in Natural Language Processing*, EMNLP, 2021; I. Chalkidis & al., "LEGAL-BERT: The Muppets straight out of Law School", *Findings of EMNLP*, 2020; D. Tsarapatsanis & N. Aletras, "On the Ethical Limits of Natural Language Processing on Legal Text", *ACL-IJCNLP*, 2021, pp. 3590-3599.

155 See above at Sec. 1.6 and at Sec. 8.4.1.

156 See Peršak, who underlines the importance of the principle of harm with regard to criminalization: "The principle, namely, sets out the legitimate grounds, necessary conditions that need to be fulfilled at the first stage of criminalisation, and the condition is 'harm to others' – not 'immorality', not harm to self (and in the extreme liberal version also no offence), only to others. The harm principle, [...] if supported by rules of fair imputation and various limiting principles, should also militate against (or, *ex post*, declare illegitimate) the criminalisation on the basis of mere abstract, far-fetching risk or remote harm, which often covers others (illegitimate) reasons disguised in the rhetoric of harm." Peršak, 2007, p.135.

moral norms to human and robot agents, specifically, robots are more strongly expected to make a utilitarian choice in a moral dilemma situation, i.e., a choice that sacrifices one person for the good of many, and are blamed more than their human counterparts when they do not do so.[157] Hence, in the example of the robot and the drowning child, the robot is expected, and might even be obliged, to save the child no matter what.[158]

In addition, humans seems to be inclined towards blaming AI systems for omissions more than humans, where instead the trend goes in the opposite direction when it comes to actions (i.e., humans are blamed more than AI systems for a wrongful act).[159] What is more, it has also been shown that people consider AI systems as capable of displaying *mens rea*[160] and, in fact, are inclined to attribute *mens rea* states (specifically, "artificial recklessness")[161] to AI systems, sometimes as much as they do to human agents or to corporations.[162] It must be discussed whether this type of research will have an impact on criminal law policy decisions regarding whether criminal liability of AI systems is *needed*. Those who argue that the bedrock of *mens rea*, i.e., free will, is nothing but a matter of social attribution, might answer yes.[163] This (open) question is perhaps one of the most stimulating outcomes of this research.

8.5.2 *Looking Backwards*

Let us conclude now with a few final reflections on the trajectory that led to this study's results.

It has been argued that:

> Clever scholars can adjust existing criminal theories to the AI field and make them fairly plausible. However, what we are agonizing over is not whether we

---

157 B. F. Malle et al., "Sacrifice One For the Good of Many?: People Apply Different Moral Norms to Human and Robot Agents", *HRI '15: Proceedings of the Tenth Annual ACM/IEEE International Conference on Human-Robot Interaction*, 2015, pp. 117-124.

158 Ibid.

159 Malle et al., 2015; B. F. Malle, S. T. Magar & M. Scheutz, "AI in the Sky: How People Morally Evaluate Human and Machine Decisions in a Lethal Strike Dilemma", in M. I. Aldinhas et al. (eds.), *Robotics and Well-Being. Intelligent Systems*, Control and Automation: Science and Engineering, Vol. 95, Springer, 2019, pp. 111-133; Malle et al, "Which Robot Am I Thinking About? The Impact of Action and Appearance on People's Evaluations of a Moral Robot", *The Eleventh ACM/IEEE International Conference on Human Robot Interaction*, 2016, pp. 125-132.

160 M. Kneer & M. T. Stuart, "Playing the Blame Game with Robots", HRI '21 Companion: Companion of the 2021 ACM/IEEE International Conference on Human-Robot Interaction, 2021, pp. 408 ff.

161 Ivi, p. 408.

162 Kneer & Stuart, 2021, p. 408.

163 Simmler & Markwalder, 2019, p. 15.

> can conjure up a decent plausible theory to justify criminal liability, but whether AI is really liable and its punishment itself is justifiable.[164]

This quote pinpoints one of the most pressing difficulties of this research: the vastness of the topic addressed. Certainly, I did not intend to reinvent the wheel (i.e., at writing a new general theory of criminal law), even though sometimes it felt as burdensome. Indeed, an analysis of the impact of AI on substantial criminal law has potentially endless ramifications. For instance, think of AI and criminal capacity (Chapter 5): exploring whether AI could be a subject of criminal law presupposed addressing the lack of understanding of what an AI "agent" is, but also acknowledging that the concept of criminal capacity per se is not recognized in every legal system; moreover, it also involved dealing with the fact that, provided that one accepts that criminal capacity as a legal notion even exists, there is no agreement on what it is made of.

The ramifications of this research are not limited to different theories and constructs of criminal law, but also to other disciplines: if there is one lesson which could be drawn from this research is that it requires criminal law scholars to step out of their comfort zones. If one wants to deal with criminal liability of AI system, and wants to do so effectively, amongst other things one: is compelled to acquire notions of computer science, to truly grasp the functioning of AI systems; is drawn to theories of moral philosophy, to understand purposes of punishment in connection to AI; and has to become acquainted with ethics, due to the importance and prominence of ethical guidelines and principles as forebearers of AI regulation. This complexity caused the need to constantly draw boundaries delineating what was part of the research, and what was not.

Furthermore, the strength (and the weakness) of this research is that it is deeply *introspective*: it prompts questions which find their answer in one's own beliefs on what is human and what is not, and, ultimately, on what is right and what is wrong. As such, most of the questions asked (and answered) in this research could be seen as controversial by the readers. When addressing these consequential questions, the research involved a great deal of "reasoning by proxy", that is, it compared AI systems to other subjects that displayed similar characteristics, be it animals, insane offenders, infants, or corporations. Thus, reasoning by proxy must be handled with care: if one is not careful, it could turn into trying to fit a square peg into a round hole.

In conclusion, as this research has shown, considering the criminal behavior and accountability of AI systems is not (just) a matter of legal fictions and of academic discussions. In some cases, the decisions and the actions of such systems may cause harm, or the serious threat of it, leading to the question of who should be held responsible.

---

164 Lee, 2021, p. 321.

Overall, I believe that discussing criminal liability of AI systems is essential for addressing the legal and ethical challenges posed by the use of AI and ensuring that AI systems are developed and used in a responsible and accountable manner.

Or did an AI system just write that?[165]

165 The answer is yes, it did. The last paragraph was written by ChatGPT, in answer to my question: "What do you think of the importance of discussing the issue of criminal liability of AI systems?". ChatGPT is a conversational chatbot (based on natural language processing) developed by OpenAI. It can be accessed at: chat.openai.com.

Impact Statement

Societal and Scientific Relevance of the Research Findings

Questions of accountability and liability for the actions of AI systems will surface, as they become more sophisticated and common. As such, this study could lead to the development of legal frameworks that bridge accountability gaps, bearing significant implications for industries such as healthcare, finance, and transportation. Moreover, this study could lead to a change in public perception of crimes committed by AI.

Indeed, one of the main results obtained with this research is that it is able to explain the impact of AI on matters of criminal law to non-lawyers. The language adopted is purposedly straight-forward and simple, hence the research can be read also by those who do not have a legal education. In this sense, it could work to build bridges in the future between criminal legal scholars and AI scientists. Part of this result were already obtained, via presenting the research findings to a network comprising of both AI scholars and of philosophers. Furthermore, some of the reflections were already anticipated in publications on legal journals (especially on the matter of liability of humans).

In the short-term, the results of this research definitely brought the discussion on the matter forward: as a *unicum* in its field, it is hoped that it will stimulate further research on the matter.

Specifically, this research will be useful for legislators and policymakers when drafting new legal tools on matters of AI and criminal law. It could also impact international policy makers, who may look at the research to inform their own policies on AI systems. In this sense, its wide scope and lack of boundaries to national legal systems proves extremely useful.

Innovative Aspects of the Research

The study provides an original point of view in a doctrinal debate which has become topical in the past 5 years. The originality stems from different aspects. First and foremost, it represents a wholesome synthesis of a complex and layered topic. Indeed, an analysis of the impact of AI on substantial criminal law has potentially endless ramifications: in order to be able to truly deal in depth with the issue of criminal liability of AI system, a researcher has to acquire notions of computer science (so as deal with the functioning of AI systems in laymen terms); notions related to theories of moral philosophy (so as to deal with purposes of punishment in connection to AI); and notions related to ethics (due to the importance and prominence of ethical guidelines and principles as forebearers of AI regulation). The book is the result of the combination of these notions in a way that is not redundant and understandable for legal scholars. Second, it delivers – for the first time – an extensive analysis of the scholarly debate on AI and criminal law based on over 100 sources written in 3 languages (Italian, English and German). Third, it presents reflections on avant-garde topics, which have not been scrutinized by scholars before (see for example the discussion on Artificial Insane Offenders and Artificial Infant Offenders and the analysis of duties to act and responsibility of AI systems in commission-by-omission scenarios). Fourth, it introduces a unique comparison of 5 novel legal frameworks (laws, law proposals, and other policing initiatives) related to criminal liability and AI systems. Finally, the conclusion chapter presents numerous open questions, which will potentially be used by researchers as inputs for future research.

TARGET AUDIENCE & OUTREACH

The main target group for this research are criminal legal scholars interested in the interaction between criminal law and technology. Thus this study, due to its polyhedric nature, is of interest also for AI scientists, ethicists, and philosophers. It provides a basis for further discussion with academics from various fields. Thus, the research is not only relevant for members of academia, but also for member of parliaments, governmental officials, and of other public bodies, such as law enforcement agencies. For example, legislators could make use of this research when faced with the issue of regulating criminal behavior of AI systems. In fact, part of the research' results were already presented to high-ranking members of law enforcement agencies enrolled in a master on AI in criminal justice. Furthermore, this research could also affect the technological advancement of AI systems, stimulating industries to include considerations on criminal liability in their production processes. Finally, in the future the findings of the study could be integrated into education, e.g., by including tailored lectures in courses at universities. The lectures could be given to students belonging to different faculties (e.g., law, philosophy, data science, mathematics) and foster interdisciplinary research in the future.

Index of Figures

Bibliography

Domestic Legislation

FRANCE

Code de la route.
Décret n° 2021-873 du 29 juin 2021 portant application de l'ordonnance n° 2021-443 du 14 avril 2021 relative au régime de responsabilité pénale applicable en cas de circulation d'un véhicule à délégation de conduite et à ses conditions d'utilisation, NOR : TRAT2034544D.
Ordonnance n° 2021-443 du 14 avril 2021 relative au régime de responsabilité pénale applicable en cas de circulation d'un véhicule à délégation de conduite et à ses conditions d'utilisation (TRAT2034523R, JORF n°0089 du 15 avril 2021, Texte n° 36), 2021.

GERMANY

Bundestag, Gesetz zur Änderung des Straßenverkehrsgesetzes und des Pflichtversicherungsgesetzes – Gesetz zum autonomen Fahren, Bundesgesetzblatt Jahrgang 2021, Teil I Nr. 48, 3108.

UNITED KINGDOM

Automated and Electric Vehicles Act, 2018.

USA

Arizona Revised Statutes, 1956.
Code of Federal Regulations (CFR), National Archives and Records Administration's (NARA) Office of the Federal Register (OFR), and the Government Publishing Office (GPO).

Domestic Policy Papers, Research Documents, and Reports

GERMANY

Ethics Commission Automated and Connected Driving, 2017, "Report". Available at: https://bmdv.bund.de/SharedDocs/EN/publications/report-ethics-commission.pdf?__blob=publicationFile.

SINGAPORE

Singapore Academy of Law, Law Reform Committee, *Report on Criminal Liability, Robotics and AI Systems*, 2021. Available at: www.sal.org.sg/sites/default/files/SAL-LawReform-Pdf/2021-02/2021%20Report%20on%20Criminal%20Liability%20Robotics%20%26%20AI%20Systems.pdf.

Singapore Penal Code Review Committee, *Report*, 2018. Available at: www.reach.gov.sg/-/media/reach/old-reach/2018/public-consult/mha/annex--pcrc-report.ashx.

UNITED KINGDOM

Law Commission of England and Wales, "Automated Vehicles: Consultation Paper 3 – A regulatory framework for automated vehicles A joint consultation paper", Law Commission Consultation Paper No. 252, Scottish Law Commission Discussion Paper No. 171. Available at: https://s3-eu-west-2.amazonaws.com/lawcom-prod-storage-11jsxou24uy7q/uploads/2021/01/AV-CP3.pdf.

Law Commission of England and Wales Law Commission No. 404, Scottish Law Commission Scottish Law Commission No. 258, "Automated Vehicles: Joint report", HC 1068 SG/2022/15, 25 January 2022. Available at: https://s3-eu-west-2.amazonaws.com/lawcom-prod-storage-11jsxou24uy7q/uploads/2022/01/Automated-vehicles-joint-report-cvr-03-02-22.pdf.

Law Commission of England and Wales Law Commission No. 404, Scottish Law Commission Scottish Law Commission No. 258, "Automated Vehicles: Summary of joint report", Summary of LC Report No. 404 / SLC Report No 258, HC 1068 SG/2022/15, 26 January 2022. Available at: https://s3-eu-west-2.amazonaws.com/lawcom-prod-storage-11jsxou24uy7q/uploads/2022/01/AV-Summary-25-01-22-2.pdf.

USA

American Law Institute, *Model Penal Code: Official Draft and Explanatory Notes,* Complete Text of Model Penal Code as Adopted at the 1962 Annual Meeting of the American Law Institute at Washington, D.C., 24 May 1962.

National Safety Transportation Board (NTSB), *Collision Between a Car Operating With Automated Vehicle Control Systems and a Tractor-Semitrailer Truck Near Williston, Florida, May 7, 2016*, Highway Accident Report NTSB/HAR-17/02, 2017. Available at: www.ntsb.gov/investigations/accidentreports/reports/har1702.pdf.

National Safety Transportation Board (NTSB), *Collision Between Vehicle Controlled by Developmental Automated Driving System and Pedestrian, Tempe, Arizona, March 18, 2018*, Highway Accident Report NTSB/HAR-19/03, 2019. Available at: www.ntsb.gov/investigations/accidentreports/reports/har1903.pdf.

National Highway Traffic Safety Administration, Office of Defects Investigation, Investigation PE 16-007, 2017.Available at: https://static.nhtsa.gov/odi/inv/2016/INCLA-PE16007-7876.pdf.

United States Attorneys' Manual § 9-16.325, *Plea Agreements, Deferred Prosecution Agreements, Non-Prosecution Agreements and Extraordinary Restitution*, 2008.

International and European Legislation

European Commission, *Proposal for a Directive of the European Parliament and of the Council On Adapting Non-Contractual Civil Liability Rules to Artificial Intelligence* (AI Liability Directive), COM(2022), 496 final 2022/0303 (COD), 28 September 2022.

European Commission, *Proposal for a regulation of the European Parliament and of the Council Laying Down Harmonised Rules On Artificial Intelligence ("Artificial Intelligence Act") and Amending Certain Union Legislative Acts*, COM(2021) 206 final, 21 April 2022.

European Parliament, *Directive 2014/57/EU of the European Parliament and of the Council of 16 April 2014 on criminal sanctions for market abuse.*

European Parliament, Resolution "*Framework on the Ethical Aspects of Artificial Intelligence, Robotics and Related Technologies*", 2020/2012(INL), 20 October 2020.

European Parliament, *Resolution of 16 February 2017 with recommendations to the Commission on Civil Law Rules on Robotics* (2015/2103(INL)), 16 February 2017.

European Parliament, *Resolution of 20 October 2020 with recommendations to the Commission on a civil liability regime for artificial intelligence,* (2020/2014(INL)), 20 October 2020.

International Civil Aviation Organization (ICAO), *Aircraft Accident and Incident Investigation*, Annex 13 to the Convention on International Civil Aviation.

International and European Policy Papers, Research Documents, and Reports

Boucher P. N., European Parliamentary Research Service – Scientific Foresight Unit, "What if AI regulation promoted innovation?"; PE 729.515, 2022, p. 2.

Council of Europe, CAHAI Secretariat, "Towards a regulation of AI systems", DGI (2020) 16. Available at: https://rm.coe.int/prems-107320-gbr-2018-compli-cahai-couv-texte-a4-bat-web/1680a0c17a.

Council of Europe – CEPEJ, *European Ethical Charter on the Use of AI in Judicial Systems Council of Europe*, 2018. Available at: https://rm.coe.int/ethical-charter-en-for-publication-4-december-2018/16808f699.

Council of Europe, European Committee on Crime Problems (CDPC), Concept Paper "Artificial intelligence and criminal law responsibility in Council of Europe member states – the case of automated vehicles", cdpc/docs 2018/cdpc(2018)14, 16 October 2018. Available at: https://rm.coe.int/cdpc-2018-14rev-artificial-intelligence-and-criminal-law-project-2018-/16808e64ad.

Council of Europe, European Committee on Crime Problems (CDPC), "Thematic session on artificial intelligence and criminal law. The approach in Council of Europe member states. The case of automated vehicles", Programme, CDPC(2018)18, 28 November 2019. Available at: https://rm.coe.int/cdpc-2018-18-draft-programme-thematic-session-artificial-intelligence-/16808e64ab.

Council of Europe, European Committee on Crime Problems (CDPC), "Thematic session on Artificial Intelligence and Criminal Law of 28 November 2018", Final remarks by Professor Sabine Gless, Special Rapporteur, "Artificial intelligence and its impact on CDPC work. The case of automated driving", cdpc/docs 2018/cdpc (2018)22, 28 November 2018.

Working Group of Experts on Artificial Intelligence and Criminal Law, "Working paper II", CDPC(2019)7, 27 March 2019. Available at: https://rm.coe.int/cdpc-2019-7-working-paper-ii-for-cdpc-expert-group-meeting-on-artifici/16809372a5.

Working Group of Experts on Artificial Intelligence and Criminal Law, "Questionnaire concerning Artificial Intelligence and Criminal Justice (using the example of Automated Driving)"" CDPC(2019)8FIN (2019), 19 May 2019. Available at: https://rm.coe.int/cdpc-2019-8fin-questionnaire-artificial-intelligence-and-criminal-just/168094c8fa.

Working Group of Experts on Artificial Intelligence and Criminal Law, "Assessment of the answers to the questionnaire on artificial intelligence and criminal justice (using the example of Automated Driving)", CDPC(2019)17 (2019), 7 November 2019. Available at: https://rm.coe.int/cdpc-2019-17-draft-assessment-of-the-answers-to-the-questionnaire-on-a/168098e24c.

Working Group on AI and Criminal Law & CDPC Secretariat, "Feasibility study on a future Council of Europe instrument on artificial intelligence and criminal law", CDPC(2020)3Rev (2020), 4 September 2020. Available at: https://rm.coe.int/cdpc-2020-3-feasibility-study-of-a-future-instrument-on-ai-and-crimina/16809f9b60.

Working Group on AI and Criminal Law & CDPC Secretariat, "1st meeting of the Drafting Committee to elaborate an instrument on Artificial Intelligence and Criminal Law (CDPC-AICL)", CDPC-AICL(2021), 17 November 2021. Available at: https://rm.coe.int/cdpc-aicl-2021-1-1st-meeting-report-15-16-nov-2021/1680a49c99.

Working Group on AI and Criminal Law & CDPC Secretariat, "Terms of Reference", Extract from CM(2021)131-addrev. Available at: https://rm.coe.int/cdpc-en-terms-of-reference-cm-2021-131-addrev/1680a4b41a.

Working Group on AI and Criminal Law & CDPC Secretariat, "2nd meeting of the Drafting Committee to elaborate an instrument on Artificial Intelligence and Criminal Law (CDPC-AICL)", CDPC-AICL(2022)2, 9 June 2022. Available at: https://rm.coe.int/cdpc-aicl-2022-2-2nd-meeting-report/1680a6e1ff.

Council of Europe, "History of Artificial Intelligence". Available at: www.coe.int/en/web/artificial-intelligence/history-of-ai.

Council of Europe, Yeung K., *A study of the implications of advanced digital technologies (including AI systems) for the concept of responsibility within a human rights framework*, DGI(2019)05, 2019.

EUROCONTROL, European Aviation/ATM AI High Level Group (EEAI HLG), "Fly AI report", 2020. Available at: www.eurocontrol.int/publication/fly-ai-report.

European Commission, Directorate-General for Research and Innovation, Horizon 2020 Commission Expert Group to advise on specific ethical issues raised by driverless mobility (E03659), "Ethics of connected and automated vehicles: recommendations on road safety, privacy, fairness, explainability and responsibility", Publications Office of the European Union, Luxembourg, 2020. Available at: https://data.europa.eu/doi/10.2777/035239.

European Council on Foreign Relations, U.E. Franke, Policy Brief "Artificial divide: how Europe and America could clash over AI", 2021. Available at: https://ecfr.eu/wp-content/uploads/Artificial-divide-How-Europe-and-America-could-clash-over-AI.pdf.

European Parliament, "How artificial intelligence works", Briefing, Member's Research Service, 2019. Available at: www.europarl.europa.eu/RegData/etudes/BRIE/2019/634420/EPRS_BRI(2019)634420_EN.pdf.

European Parliament, "Understanding Artificial Intelligence", Briefing, Members' Research Service, 2018. Available at: www.europarl.europa.eu/RegData/etudes/BRIE/2018/614654/EPRS_BRI(2018)614654_EN.pdf.

European Parliamentary Research Service, Panel for the Future of Science and Technology, "The ethics of artificial intelligence: Issues and initiatives", EPRS_STUD(2020)634452, 2020.

High-Level Expert Group on Artificial Intelligence (AI-HLEG), *A definition of AI: Main capabilities and Scientific Disciplines*, 2018. Available at: https://ec.europa.eu/futurium/en/system/files/ged/ai_hleg_definition_of_ai_18_december_1.pdf.

High-Level Expert Group on Artificial Intelligence (AI-HLEG), *Ethics guidelines for trustworthy AI*, 2019. Available at: https://ec.europa.eu/futurium/en/ai-alliance-consultation.1.html.

OECD, *Recommendation of the Council on Artificial Intelligence*, OECD/LEGAL/0449. Available at: https://legalinstruments.oecd.org/en/instruments/OECD-LEGAL-0449.

Society for Automotive Engineers International (SAE), *J3016 Taxonomy and Definitions for Terms Related to Driving Automation Systems for On-Road Motor Vehicles*, April 2021.

UNESCO, *Recommendation on the Ethics of Artificial Intelligence*, SHS/BIO/REC-AIETHICS/2021. Available at: https://unesdoc.unesco.org/ark:/48223/pf0000380455.

United Nations Economic and Social Council, *Report of the sixty-eighth session of the Working Party on Road Traffic Safety*, ECE/TRANS/WP.1/145, 2014. Available at: https://unece.org/press/unece-paves-way-automated-driving-updating-un-international-convention.

Case Law (Domestic Decisions)

Italy

Cassazione Penale, Sez. IV, 25 March 1971.

Cassazione Penale, Sez. IV, 25 March 2016, No. 12748.

Germany

BVerfGE, 15.2.2006 – 1 BvR 357/05.

BGH, 18.03.1952, GSSt 2/51.
LG München I, Endurteil vom 14.07.2020 – 33 O 14041/1.

USA

R v M'Naghten's, [1843] All ER Rep 229, 210.
U.S. Supreme Court, Kahler v. Kansas, 23 March 2020, 589 U.S.___ (2020).
Holbrook v. Prodomax Automation Ltd., 1:17-cv-219 (W.D. Mich. Sep. 20, 2021).
United States v. Sun-Diamond Growers of Cal., 138 F.3d 961, 971 (D.C. Cir. 1998), aff'd, 526 U.S. 398, 1999.
Yavapai County Attorney, "Re: Rafael Vasquez / Uber Corporation, Tempe Police Department #2018-32694", 4 March 2019. Available at: https://s3.documentcloud.org/documents/5759641/UberCrashYavapaiRuling03052019.pdf.
State of Arizona, "Indictment 785 GJ 251", 27 August 2020. Available at: www.maricopacountyattorney.org/DocumentCenter/View/1724/Rafael-Vasquez-GJ-Indictment.

SECONDARY SOURCES

BOOKS & JOURNAL ARTICLES

Abbott R. & Sarch A., "Punishing Artificial Intelligence: Legal Fiction or Science Fiction", *UCD L Rev*, Vol. 53, 2019.
Abbott R., "Everything is Obvious", *UCLA Law Review*, Vol. 66, No. 2, 2019.
Abbott R., *The Reasonable Robot*, Cambridge University Press, 2020.
Abel D., MacGlashan J. & Littman M.L., "Reinforcement Learning as a Framework for Ethical Decision Making", *AAAI Workshop: AI, Ethics, and Society*, 2016.
Allan J., "Revisiting the Hart-Devlin Debate: At the Periphery and By the Numbers", *San Diego L. Rev.*, Vol. 54, 2017.
Anscombe G. E. M., "Modern moral philosophy" *Philosophy*, Vol. 33, No. 124, 1968.
Antolisei F., *Manuale di diritto penale-Parte generale*, 16a ed., Giuffrè, 2003.
Armer P., *Attitudes Toward Intelligent machines*, in Feigenbaum E. A., Feldman J. & Armer P. (eds.), *Computers and Thought*, Aaai Pr, 1995.
Arnold T. & Scheutz M., "The "big red button" is too late: an alternative model for the ethical evaluation of AI systems", *Ethics and Information Technology*, Vol. 20, 2018.
Asaro P. M., "Determinism, machine agency, and responsibility", *Politica & Società*, Vol. 2, 2014.

Asaro P. M., "A Body to Kick, but Still No Soul to Damn: Legal Perspectives on Robotics", in Lin P., Abney K. & Bekey G. A. (eds.), *Robot Ethics: The Ethical and Social Implications of Robotics*, MIT Press, 2012.

Ashfarian H., "Can Artificial Intelligences Suffer from Mental Illness? A Philosophical Matter to Consider", *Sci Eng Ethics*, Vol. 23, 2017.

Ashton H., "Definitions of intent suitable for algorithms", *Artif Intell Law*, 2022.

Asimov I., *I, Robot*, Harper Collins Publisher, 1950.

Association International de Droit Pénal (AIDP), L. Picotti, General Report – XXI International Congress of Penal Law on 'Artificial Intelligence and Criminal Justice', International Colloquium of Section I (Criminal Law – general part): "Traditional Criminal Law Categories and AI: Crisis or Palingenesis?", 2022.

Avila Negri S. M. C., "Robots as Legal Persons: Electronic Personhood in Robotics and Artificial Intelligence", *Frontiers in Robotics and AI*, Vol. 8, 2021.

Awad E. et al., "Computational ethics", *Trends in Cognitive Sciences*, Vol. 26, Issue 5, 2022.

Awad E. et al., "When Is It Acceptable to Break the Rules? Knowledge Representation of Moral Judgement Based on Empirical Data", *arXiv:2201.07763*, 2022.

Awad E. et al., "Universals and variations in moral decisions made in 42 countries by 70,000 participants", PNAS, Vol. 117, No. 5, 2020.

Awad E. et al., "Crowdsourcing Moral Machines", *Communications of the ACM*, Vol. 63, No. 3, 2020.

Awad E. et al., "The Moral Machine experiment", *Nature*, Vol. 563, 2018.

Badea C. & Artus G., "Morality, Machines, and the Interpretation Problem: A Value-based, Wittgensteinian Approach to Building Moral Agents", in Bramer M. & Stahl F. (eds.), *Artificial Intelligence XXXIX*. SGAI-AI 2022. *Lecture Notes in Computer Science*, Vol 13652, Springer, 2022.

Baker D. J. & Robinson P. H., *Artificial intelligence and the Law. Cybercrime and Criminal Liability*, Routledge, 2021.

Bandura A., "Moral disengagement in the perpetration of inhumanities", *Personality and Social Psychology Review*, Vol. 3, 1999.

Banks V.A. et al., "Subsystems on the road to full vehicle automation: hands and feet free but not 'mind' free driving", in *Safety Science*, Vol. 62, 2014, pp. 505-514.

Barfield W. & Pagallo U. (eds.), *Research handbook on the law of artificial intelligence*, Elsevier, 2019.

Basile F., "Intelligenza artificiale e diritto penale: qualche aggiornamento e qualche nuova riflessione", in F. Basile, M. Caterini & S. Romano (eds.), *Il sistema penale ai confini delle hard sciences*, Pacini Giuridica, 2020.

Basile F., "Intelligenza artificiale e diritto penale: quattro possibili percorsi di indagine", *DPU*, 2019.

Basile F., Caterini M. & Romano S. (eds.), *Il sistema penale ai confini delle hard sciences*, Pacini Giuridica, 2020.

Basso P., "*Mare magnum*", *Parolechiave*, Vol. 1, 2022.

Bathaee Y., "The Artificial Intelligence Black Box and the Failure of Intent and Causation", *Harvard Journal of Law & Technology*, Vol. 31, 2018.

Battaglini G., "The Fascist Reform of the Penal Law in Italy", 24 *Am. Inst. Crim. L. & Criminology*, Vol. 24, 1933-1934.

Beck S., "Die Diffusion strafrechtlicher Verantwortlichkeit durch Digitalisierung und Lernende Systeme", *ZIS*, Vol. 2, 2020.

Beck S., "Robotics and Criminal Law. Negligence, Diffusion of Liability and Electronic Personhood", in Hilgendorf E. & Feldle J. (eds), "Digitization and the Law", *Robotik und Recht*, Vol. 15, Nomos, 2018.

Beck S., "Intelligent Agents and Criminal Law – Negligence, Diffusion of Liability and electronic personhood", *Robotics and Autonomous Systems*, Vol. 86, 2016.

Beck S., "Mediating the Different Concepts of Corporate Criminal Liability in England and Germany", *German L.J.*, No. 11, 2010.

Becker G., "Crime and Punishment: An Economic Approach", *J. Pol. Econ*, Vol. 76, 1984.

Ben-Israel I. et al., "Towards Regulation of AI Systems. Global perspectives on the development of a legal framework on Artificial Intelligence (AI) systems based on the Council of Europe's standards on human rights, democracy and the rule of law", Council of Europe Study DGI (2020) 16, 2020.

Bertolini A., "Artificial Intelligence and Civil Liability", Study commissioned by the European Parliament's Committee on Legal Affairs, European Union, IPOL_STU(2020)621926, 2020. Available at: www.europarl.europa.eu/RegData/etudes/STUD/2020/621926/IPOL_STU(2020)621926_EN.pdf.

Bhargava V. R. & Velasquez M., "Corporate Responsibility And Artificial Intelligence", *The Georgetown Journal of Law & Public Policy*, 2019.

Black H. C., *Black's Law Dictionary*, 4th Ed, West Publishing, 1968.

Blomsma J. and Roef D., "Forms and Aspects of Mens Rea", in Keiler J. & Roef D. (eds.), *Comparative Concepts of Criminal Law*, 3rd ed., Intersentia, 2019.

Bohlander M., *Principles of German criminal law*, Hart Publishing, 2009.

Bommarito M. J. II, Katz D. M. & Detterman E. M., "LexNLP: Natural language processing and information extraction for legal and regulatory texts", in Vogl R. (ed)., *Research Handbook on Big Data Law*, Edward Elgar Publishing, 2021.

Bonicalzi S. & Haggard P., "Responsibility Between Neuroscience and Criminal Law. The Control Component of Criminal Liability", *Rivista internazionale di Filosofia e Psicologia*, Vol. 10, No. 2, 2019.

Borsari R., "Intelligenza Artificiale e responsabilità penale: prime considerazioni", *MediaLaws*, Vol. 3, 2019.

Bostrom N., "How Long Before Superintelligence?", *International Journal of Futures Studies*, Vol. 2, 1998.

Bovens M., *The quest for responsibility. Accountability and citizenship in complex organizations*, Cambridge University Press, 1998.

Bratman M., *Intention, plans, and Practical Reason*, Harvard University Press, 1987.

Brown D. K., *Public Welfare Offenses*, in Dubbler M. & Hörnle T. (eds., *The Oxford Handbook of Criminal Law*, Oxford University Press, 2014.

Brown N. & Sandholm T., "Superhuman AI for heads-up no-limit poker: Libratus beats top professionals", *Science*, Vol. 350, No. 6374, 2017.

Brusco C., "Rischio e pericolo, rischio consentito e principio di precauzione. la c.d. "flessibilizzazione delle categorie del reato", *Criminalia*, 2012.

Bryson J. J., Diamantis M. E. & Grant T. D., "Of, for, and by the people: the legal lacuna of synthetic Persons", *Artif Intell Law*, Vol. 25, 2017.

Burchard K., "Künstliche Intelligenz als Ende des Strafrechts? Zur algorithmischen Transformation der Gesellschaft", *Normative Orders Working Paper*, No. 2, 2019.

Campbell M., Hoane A.J. Jr. & Hsu F., "Deep Blue", *Artificial Intelligence*, Vol. 134, 2002.

Cappellini A., "Machina delinquere potest? Brevi appunti su intelligenza artificiale e responsabilità penale", *Criminalia*, 2018.

Caruso G., "Free Will Skepticism and Its Implications: An Argument for Optimism", in Shaw E. & Pereboom D. (eds.), *Law and Society*, Cambridge University Press, 2019.

Castelvecchi D., "Can we open the black box of AI?", *Nature*, Vol. 538, 5 October 2016.

Cavaceppi C., "L'intelligenza artificiale applicata al diritto penale", in Taddei Elmi G. & Contaldo A., *Intelligenza artificiale-Algoritmi giuridici: Ius condendum o fantadiritto?*, Pacini Giuridica, 2020.

Cavanagh N., "Corporate Criminal Liability: An Assessment of the Models of Fault", *The Journal of Criminal Law*, Vol. 75, Issue 5, 2011.

Chalkidis I. et al., "LEGAL-BERT: The Muppets straight out of Law School", *Findings of EMNLP*, 2020.

Chalkidis I., Fergadiotis M. & Androutsopoulos I., "MultiEURLEX – A multi-lingual and multi-label legal document classification dataset for zero-shot cross-lingual transfer", in Moens M. et al. (eds.), *Proceedings of the 2021 Conference on Empirical Methods in Natural Language Processing*, EMNLP, 2021.

Chao V., *Action and Agency in the Criminal Law, Legal Theory*, Cambridge University Press, 2009.

Charisi V., "Towards Moral Autonomous Systems", *arXiv:1703.04741v3*, 2017.

Charney R., "Can Androids Plead Automatism – A Review of When Robots Kill: Artificial Intelligence under the Criminal Law by Gabriel Hallevy", *U. Toronto Fac. L. Rev.*, Vol. 73, 2015.

Chesterman S., "AI and the Limits of Legal Personality", *International and Comparative Law Quarterly*, Vol. 69, No.4, 2020.

Chesterman S., *We, the Robots? Regulating Artificial Intelligence and the Limits of the Law*, Cambridge University Press, 2021.

Chopra S. & White L., *A legal theory for autonomous artificial agents*, University of Michigan Press, 2011.

Ciccone J. R. & Ferracuti S., "Comparative Forensic Psychiatry: II. The Perizia and the Role of the Forensic Psychiatrist in the Italian Legal System", *Bull Am Acad Psychiatry Law*, Vol. 23, No. 3, 1995.

Civello G., *La "colpa eventuale" nella società del rischio. Epistemologia dell'incertezza e "verità soggettiva" della colpa*, Giappichelli, 2013.

Claessen J., "Theories of Punishment", in Keiler J. & Roef D. (eds.), *Comparative Concepts of Criminal Law*, 3rd ed., Intersentia, 2019.

Coffee J. C. Jr, "'No Soul to Damn: No Body to Kick': An Unscandalized Inquiry into the Problem of Corporate Punishment", *Michigan Law Review*, Vol. 79, No. 3, 1981.

Cohen M. K., Hutter M. & Osborne M. A., "Advanced artificial agents intervene in the provision of reward", *AI Magazine*, Vol. 43, 2022.

Colucci C., *Tra ottimizzazione della funzione comando e prospettive di un suo superamento: i nuovi scenari della normatività penale*, PhD Dissertation, University of Florence Repository, 2022. Available at: https://flore.unifi.it/handle/2158/1273584.

Consulich F., "*Flash offenders*. Le prospettive di *accountability* penale nel contrasto alle intelligenze artificiali devianti", *Rivista Italiana di Diritto e Procedura Penale*, Vol. 3, 2022.

Corsi J. L., "An Argument for Strict Legality in International Criminal Law", *Georgetown Journal of International Law*, Vol. 49, 2018.

D'Addosio C., *Bestie delinquenti*, L. Pierro, 1892.

Damgaard Thaysen J., Defining Legal Moralism, *SATS*, Vol. 16, No. 2, 2015.

Danaher J., "Robots, Law and the Retribution Gap", *Ethics and Information Technology*, Vol. 18, No. 4, 2016.

De Maglie C., "Models of Corporate Criminal Liability in Comparative Law", *Wash. U. Global Stud. L. Rev.*, Vol. 4, 2005.

DeArman A., "The Wild, Wild West: A Case Study of Self Driving Vehicle Testing in Arizona", *Arizona Law Review*, Vol. 61, 2019.

DeGrave A. J., Janizek J. D. & Lee S., "AI for radiographic COVID-19 detection selects shortcuts over signal", *Nature Machine Intelligence*, Vol. 3, 2021.

Dekker S., "Pilots, Controllers and Mechanics on Trial: Cases, Concerns and Countermeasures", *International Journal of Applied Aviation Studies*, Vol. 10, No. 1, 2010.

Diamantis M. E., "The Extended Corporate Mind: When Corporations use AI to Break the Law", *N.C. L. Rev.*, Vol. 98, 2020.

Diamantis M. E., "Clockwork Corporations", *Iowa Law Review*, Vol. 1032, 2020.

Diamantis M. E., "Algorithms Acting Badly: A Solution from Corporate Law", *GEO. Wash. L. Rev.*, Vol. 89, 2021.

Diamantis M. E., "Vicarious Liability for AI", *Cambridge Handbook of AI and Law*, U. *Iowa Legal Studies Research Paper*, No. 2021-27, 2021. Available at SSRN: https://ssrn.com/abstract=3850418.

Diamantis M. E., "Employed Algorithms: a Labor Model of Corporate Liability for AI", *Duke L.J.*, Vol 72, 2022.

Diamantis M. E., Cochran R. & Dam M., "AI and the Law: Can Legal Systems Help Us Maximize Paperclips while Minimizing Deaths?", 2022. Available at SSRN: https://papers.ssrn.com/sol3/papers.cfm?abstract_id=4177378.

Domingos P., *The Master Algorithm: How the Quest for the Ultimate Learning Machine Will Remake Our World*, Allen Lane, 2015.

Doncieuxet S. et al., "Open-Ended Learning: A Conceptual Framework Based on Representational Redescription", in *Frontiers in neurorobotics*, Vol. 12, p. 59, 2018.

Donini M., "An impossible exchange? prove di dialogo tra civil e common lawyers su legalità, morale e teoria del reato", *Rivista Italiana di Diritto e Procedura Penale*, Fasc. 1, 2017.

Donne J., "Meditation XVII. Nunc Lento Sonitu Dicunt, Morieris", in A. Raspa (ed.), *Devotions Upon Emergent Occasions*, Oxford University Press, 1987.

Dubber M. D. & Hörnle T. (eds.), *The Oxford Handbook of Criminal Law*, Oxford University Press, 2014.

Dubber M., "The Comparative History and Theory of Corporate Criminal Liability", *New Criminal Law Review: An International and Interdisciplinary Journal*, Vol. 16, No. 2, 2013.

Duff R. A., "Moral and Criminal Responsibility: Answering and Refusing to Answer", in J. Coates & N.A. Tognazzini (eds.), *Oxford Studies in Agency and Responsibility Volume 5: Themes from the Philosophy of Gary Watson*, 2019.

Duff R. A., "Responsibility, Restoration, and Retribution", in M. Torny (ed.), *Retributivism Has a Past: Has it a Future*, Oxford University Press, 2011.

Duff R. A., "Who is Responsible for What, to Whom?", *Ohio State Journal of Criminal Law*, Vol. 2, 2005.

Duff R. A., "Criminalizing Endangerment", *Louisiana Law Review*, Vol. 65, 2005.

Duff R. A., "Legal and Moral Responsibility", *Philosophy Compass*, Vol. 4, Issue 6, 2009.

Duff R. A., *Intention, Agency and Criminal Liability: Philosophy of Action and the Criminal Law*, Blackwell, 1990.

Duff R. A., "Towards a Modest Legal Moralism"; *Crim. Law Philos.*, Vol. 8, 2014.

Duff R. A. & Hörnle T. "Crimes of Endangerment", in Ambos K. et al. (eds.), *Core Concepts in Criminal Law and Criminal Justice*, Vol. 2, Cambridge University Press, 2022.

Elish M. C. & Hwang T., "Praise the Machine! Punish the Human! The Contradictory History of Accountability in Automated Aviation", *Comparative Studies in Intelligent Systems – Working Paper #1*, Vol. 2, 2015.

Erling E., "Economics of Criminal Behavior", in B. Bouckaert & G. De Geest, *Encyclopedia of Law & Economics*, Elgar Publishing, 1997.

Evans E. P., *The Criminal Prosecution and Capital Punishment of Animals*, Farber & Farber, 1987.

Fernandes Godinho I., "Law and Science: The Autonomy and Limits of Culpability as a Cornerstone to the Ascription of Liability (or the Subject of Criminal Law: Three Maxims, a Problem and a Glimpse into the Future)", *Int J Semiot Law*, 2022.

Ferzan K. K., "Opaque Recklessness", *Journal of Criminal Law and Criminology*, Vol. 91, Issue 3, 2001.

Fiandaca G. & Musco E., *Diritto penale. Parte generale*, Zanichelli editore, 7a ed., 2019.

Fisher T., *Economic Analysis of Criminal Law*, in Dubber M. D. & Hörnle T. (eds.), *The Oxford Handbook of Criminal Law*, Oxford University Press, 2014.

Fjeld J. et al., "Principled Artificial Intelligence: Mapping Consensus in Ethical and Rights-based Approaches to Principles for AI", *Berkman Klein Center for Internet & Society*, 2020.

Fletcher G., "Criminal Theory in the Twentieth Century", *Theoretical Inquiries in Law*, 2, No. 1, 2001.

Fletcher G., "Deutsche Strafrechtsdogmatik aus ausländischer Sicht", in Eser A., Hassemer W. & Burckhardt B. (eds.), *Die deutsche Strafrechtswissenschaft vor der Jahrtausendwende*, Beck, 2000.

Fletcher G., "The Theory of Criminal Negligence: a Comparative Analysis", *University of Pennsylvania Law Review*, Vol. 119, 1971.

Floridi L., "AI and Its New Winter: from Myths to Realities", in *Philosophy & Technology*, Vol. 33, 2020.

Folberth A. et. al, Karlsruhe: Karlsruhe Institute of Technology (KIT), Institute for Technology Assessment and Systems Analysis (ITAS), "Tackling problems, harvesting benefits – A systematic review of the regulatory debate around AI", *KIT Scientific Working Papers*, Vol. 197, 2022.

Foot P., "The Problem of Abortion and the Doctrine of the Double Effect" *Oxford Review*, 1967.

Fosch-Villaronga E. & Heldeweg M., "Regulation, I presume?" said the robot – Towards an iterative regulatory process for robot governance", *Computer Law & Security Review: The International Journal of Technology Law and Practice*, 2018.

Freitas P. M., Andrade F. & Novais P., "Criminal Liability of Autonomous Agents: from the unthinkable to the plausible" in P. Casanovas et al. (eds.), *AI Approaches to the Complexity of Legal Systems. AICOL 2013 International Workshops, AICOL-IV@IVR, Belo*

Horizonte, Brazil, July 21-27, 2013 and AICOL-V@SINTELNET-JURIX, Bologna, Italy, December 11, 2013, Revised Selected Papers, Lecture Notes in Computer Science, Vol. 8929, Springer, 2014.

French P.A., *Collective and Corporate Responsibility*, Columbia University Press, 1984.

French P.A., "The Corporation as a Moral Person", *American Philosophical Quarterly*, Vol. 16, 1979.

Gaakeer J., "'Sua cuique persona?' A Note on the Fiction of Legal Personhood and a Reflection on Interdisciplinary Consequences", *Law & Literature*, Vol. 28, No. 3, 2016.

Gabriel I., "Artificial Intelligence, Values, and Alignment", *Minds and Machines*, Vol. 30, 2020.

Gaede K., "Künstliche Intelligenz – Rechte und Strafen für Roboter? Plädoyer für eine Regulierung künstlicher Intelligenz jenseits ihrer reinen Anwendung", in Hilgendorf E. & Beck S. (eds), *Robotik und Recht*, Vol. 18, Nomos, 2018.

Ganascia J. G., "Ethical System Formalization using Non-Monotonic Logics", *Proceedings of the Annual Meeting of the Cognitive Science Society*, Vol. 29, 2007.

Gerber M. M. & Jackson J., "Retribution as revenge and retribution as just deserts", *Social Justice Research*, Vol. 26, No. 1, 2013.

Giannini A. & Kwik H. J., "Negligence Failures and Negligence Fixes. A Comparative Analysis of Criminal Regulation of AI And Autonomous Vehicles", *Criminal Law Forum*, 2023.

Giannini A., "Artificial intelligence, ethics, law: a view on the Italian and American debate (and on their differences)", *Netherlands Journal of Legal Philosophy*, Vol. 51, No. 2, 2022.

Girgen J., "The Historical and Contemporary Prosecution and Punishment of Animals", *Animal Law*, Vol. 9, 2003.

Giuca M., "Disciplinare l'intelligenza artificiale. La riforma francese sulla responsabilità penale da uso di auto a guida autonoma", *Archivio Penale*, Vol. 2, 2022.

Giunta F., "Il diritto penale e le suggestioni del principio di precauzione", *Criminalia*, 2006.

Gless S. & Weigend T., "Intelligente Agenten und das Strafrecht", *ZSTW*, Vol. 126, No. 3, 2014.

Gless S., Silverman E. & Weigend T., "If Robots Cause Harm, who Is to Blame: Self-Driving Cars and Criminal Liability", *New Criminal Law Review*, Vol. 19, No. 3, 2016.

Goanta C. et al., "Back to the Future: Waves of Legal Scholarship on Artificial Intelligence", in S. Ranchordás & Y. Roznai (eds.), *Time, Law and Change*, Hart Publishing, 2020.

Gobert J. & Punch M., *Rethinking Corporate Crime*, Cambridge University Press, 2003.

Goldstein A., *The Insanity Defense*, Yale University Press, 1967.

Gomes Rêgo de Almeida P., Denner dos Santos C. & Silva Farias J.," Artificial Intelligence Regulation: a framework for governance", *Ethics and Information Technology*, Vol. 23, 2021.

Goodpaster K. E., "Tenacity: The American Pursuit of Corporate Responsibility", *BUS. & SOC'Y REV.*, Vol. 118, 2013.

Graaf N., *Judicial Influencers: Scholarly use of foreign law and the convergence of German, Italian and French ideas on the position of national constitutional courts in the EU legal context, 1989-2012*, PhD Dissertation, Utrecht University Repository, 2022.

Grandinetti A., "Motivi e movente", *Il Penalista*, Bussola. Available at: https://ilpenalista.it/bussola/motivi-e-movente.

Greco E., *Profili di responsabilità penale del controllore del traffico aereo. Gestione del rischio e imputazione dell'evento per colpa nei sistemi a interazione complessa*, Giappichelli, 2021.

Green B. & and Kak A., The False Comfort of Human Oversight as an Antidote to A.I. Harm Human Agency in Decision-Making Systems", *Slate*, 15 June 2021.

Grosso C. F., Pellissero M. & Petrini D., *Manuale di diritto penale. Parte Generale*, 2a ed., Giuffrè, 2017.

Guerra A., Parisi F. & Pi D., "Liability for robots I: legal challenges", *Journal of Institutional Economics*, Vol. 18, Issue 3, 2021.

Guerra A., Parisi F. & Pi D., "Liability for robots II: an economic analysis", Journal of Institutional Economics, Vol. 18, Issue 4, 2021.

Hadzi A. & Roio D., "Restorative Justice in Artificial Intelligence Crime", *Spectres of AI*, Vol. 5, 2019.

Haenlein M. & Kaplan A., "A Brief History of Artificial Intelligence: On the Past, Present and Future of Artificial Intelligence", *California Management Review*, Vol. 61, No. 4, 2019.

Hafter E., *Lehrbuch des Schweizerischen Strafrechts, Allgemeiner Teil*, 2nd ed., Springer, 1946.

Hall J., *General Principles of Criminal Law, 2nd ed.*, The Bobbs Merrill Company, 1960.

Hallevy G., "The Criminal Liability of Artificial Intelligence Entities – From Science Fiction to Legal Social Control, *Akron Intellectual Property Journal*, Vol. 4, Iss. 2, Art. 1, 2010.

Hallevy G., "I, Robot – I, Criminal – When Science Fiction Becomes Reality: Legal Liability of AI Robots Committing Criminal Offences", *Syracuse Sci. & Tech. L. Rep.*, 2010.

Hallevy G., "Virtual Criminal Responsibility", 2011. Available at http://dx.doi.org/10.2139/ssrn.1835362.

Hallevy G., "Unmanned Vehicles. Subordination to Criminal Law Under the Modern Concept of Criminal Liability", *Journal of Law, Information and Science*, Vol. 21, No. 2002, 2012.

Hallevy G., *When Robots Kill. Artificial Intelligence under Criminal Law*, Northeastern University Press, 2013.

Hallevy G., *Liability for Crimes Involving Artificial Intelligence Systems*, Springer, 2015.

Hallevy G., "Dangerous Robots – Artificial Intelligence vs. Human Intelligence", 2018. Available at SSRN: https://ssrn.com/abstract=3121905.

Hallevy G., "The Basic Models of Criminal Liability of AI Systems and Outer Circles", 2019. Available at http://dx.doi.org/10.2139/ssrn.3402527.

Hamlin J. K., "Moral Judgment and Action in Preverbal Infants and Toddlers: Evidence for an Innate Moral Core", *Current Directions in Psychological Science*, Vol. 22, Iss. 3, 2013.

Hart H. L. A., *Punishment and Responsibility*, 2nd ed., Oxford University Press, 2008.

Law, Liberty and Morality, Stanford University Press, 1963.

Hayward K. J., Maas M. M., "Artificial intelligence and crime: A primer for criminologists", *Crime Media Culture*, 2020.

Hildebrandt M., *Law for Computer Scientists and Other Folk*, Oxford University Press, 2020.

Hildebrandt M., "Technology", in Dubber M. D. & Hörnle T. (eds.), *The Oxford Handbook of Criminal Law*, Oxford University Press, 2014.

Hildebrandt M., "Ambient Intelligence, Criminal Liability and Democracy", *Criminal Law and Philosophy*, Vol. 2, 2008.

Hilgendorf E. & J. Feldle, *Digitization and the Law*, Nomos, 2018.

Hilgendorf E. & J. Feldle, *Autonome Systeme und neue Mobilität. Ausgewählte Beiträge zur 3. und 4. Würzburger Tagung zum Technikrech*, Nomos, 2017.

Hilgendorf E. & J. Feldle, "Autonome Systeme, künstliche Intelligenz und Roboter: Eine Orientierung aus strafrechtlicher Perspektive", in Barton S. (ed.), *Festschrift für Thomas Fischer*, C.H. Beck, 2018.

Hilgendorf E. & J. Feldle, "The dilemma of autonomous driving: Reflections on the moral and legal treatment of automatic collision avoidance systems", in Hilgendorf E. & Feldle J. (eds), "Digitization and the Law", *Robotik und Recht*, Vol. 15, Nomos, 2018.

Hilgendorf E. & J. Feldle, "Dilemma-Probleme beim automatisierten Fahren. Ein Beitrag zum Problem des Verrechnungsverbots im Zeitalter der Digitalisierung", *ZIS*, Vol. 130, No. 3, 2018.

Hofmann R., "Formalism versus pragmatism – A comparative legal and empirical analysis of the German and Dutch criminal justice systems with regard to effectiveness and efficiency", *Maastricht Journal of European and Comparative Law Issue*, Vol. 28, No. 2, 2021.

Holford W. D., "An Ethical Inquiry of the Effect of Cockpit Automation on the Responsibilities of Airline Pilots: Dissonance or Meaningful Control?", *Journal of Business Ethics*, 2022.

Hörnle T., "Theories of Criminalization", in *The Oxford Handbook of Criminal Law*, Oxford University Press, 2014.

Hötitzsch S. & Lutz L. (eds.), *Rechtliche Aspekte automatisierter Fahrzeuge. Beiträge der 2. Würzburger Tagung zum Technikrecht im Oktober 2014*, Nomos, 2015.

Hu Y., "Robot criminals", *U. Mich. J.L. Reform*, Vol. 52, 2019.

Husak D., *Overcriminalization: The Limits of the Criminal Law*, Oxford University Press, 2009.

Husak D., "The Criminal Law as Last Resort", *Oxford Journal of legal Studies*, Vol. 23, No. 2, 2004.

Husak D., "Theories of Crime and Punishment in German Criminal Law", *The American Journal of Comparative Law*, 2005, Vol. 53, No. 3, 2005.

Jain N., "Autonomous weapons systems: new frameworks for individual responsibility", in Bhuta N. et al. (eds), *Autonomous weapons systems. Law, ethics, policy*, Cambridge University Press, 2016.

Jobin A., Ienca M. & Vayena E., "The global landscape of AI ethics guidelines", *Nature Machine Intelligence*, Vol. 1, 2019.

Kalliokoski T. & Hallamaa J., "How AI Systems Challenge the Conditions of Moral Agency?", in Rauterberg M. (ed.), *Culture and Computing: 8th International Conference, C&C 2020, Held as Part of the 22nd HCI International Conference*, Springer, 2020.

Karsai K., (ed.), *Strafrechtlicher Lebensschutz in Ungarn und in Deutschland. Beiträge zur Strafrechtsvergleichung*, Stiftung Elemér Pólay, 2007.

Keiler J., *Actus reus and participation in European Criminal Law*, Intersentia, 2013.

Keiler J. & Roef D. (eds.), *Comparative Concepts of Criminal Law*, 3rd ed., Intersentia, 2019.

Kim D.J. J., "Artificial intelligence and crime: what killer robots could teach about criminal law", Thesis in Law, Faculty of Law Victoria University of Wellington, 2017. Available at: https://researcharchive.vuw.ac.nz/xmlui/bitstream/handle/10063/7927/paper_access.pdf?sequence=1.

King T. C. et al., "Artificial Intelligence Crime: An Interdisciplinary Analysis of Foreseeable Threats and Solutions", *Sci Eng Ethics*, Vol. 26, No.1, 2019.

Kirchner J. H. et al., "Understanding AI alignment research: A Systematic Analysis", *arXiv:2206.02841v1*, 2022.

Klip A., *European Criminal Law. An Integrative Approach*, 4th ed., Intersentia, 2021.

Kneer M. & Stuart M. T., "Playing the Blame Game with Robots", *HRI '21 Companion: Companion of the 2021 ACM/IEEE International Conference on Human-Robot Interaction*, 2021.

Koller D & Pfeffer A., "Generating and Solving Imperfect Information Games", *Proceedings of the 14th International Joint Conference on Artificial Intelligence (IJCAI)*,1995.

Korteling J. E. et al., "Human- versus Artificial Intelligence", *Front. Artif. Intell.*, Vol. 4, 2021.

Koulou R., "Human Control over Automation: EU Policy and AI Ethics", *EJLS* 12(1), 2020.

Kriebitz A., Max R. & Lütge C., "The German Act on Autonomous Driving: Why Ethics Still Matter", *Philosophy & Technology*, Vol. 35, 2022.

Kritikos M., European Parliamentary Research Service – Scientific Foresight Unit, Briefing "Artificial Intelligence ante portas: Legal & ethical reflections", 2019.

Kurki AJ V., *A Theory of Legal Personhood*, Oxford, 2019.

LaCroix, T. & Luccioni A. S., "Metaethical Perspectives on 'Benchmarking' AI Ethicsi", *arXiv:2204.05151*, 2022.

LaFave W. R., *Criminal Law*, 6th ed., Handbook Series, West Academic, 2017.

LaFave W. R., *Modern Criminal Law: Cases, Comments And Questions*, 4th ed., Thomson West, 1988.

Lagioia F. & Sartor G., "AI Systems Under Criminal Law: a Legal Analysis and a Regulatory Perspective", *Philosophy & Technology*, Vol. 33, 2020.

Langley P., "Explainable, Normative, and Justified Agency", *The Thirty-Third AAAI Conference on Artificial Intelligence (AAAI-19).*

Lee S. W., "Can an Artificial Intelligence Commit a Crime?", in Bruns A. et al. (eds.), *Legal Theory and Interpretation in a Dynamic Society*, Nomos, 2021.

Legg S. & Hutter M., "A Collection of Definitions of Intelligence", *arXiv:0706.3639v1*, 2007.

Lehman-Wilzing S. N., "Frankenstein unbound: Towards a legal definition of artificial intelligence", *Futures*, Vol. 13, Issue 6, 1981.

Leslie D., The Alan Turing Institute, *Understanding artificial intelligence ethics and safety. A guide for the responsible design and implementation of AI systems in the public sector*, 2019.

Ligeti K., *Artificial Intelligence and Criminal Justice*. Available at: www.penal.org/sites/default/files/Concept%20Paper_AI%20and%20Criminal%20Justice_Ligeti.pdf.

Lima D., "Could AI Agents Be Held Criminally Liable? Artificial Intelligence and the Challenges for Criminal Law", *South Carolina Law Review*, Vol. 69, Issue 3, 2018.

Lima G. et al., "The Conflict Between People's Urge to Punish AI and Legal Systems", *Front. Robot. AI*, Vol. 8, 2021.

Lin T. et al., "Microsoft COCO: Common Objects in Context, Computer Vision – ECCV", *Lecture Notes in Computer Science*, Springer, Vol. 8693, 2014.

List C. & Pettit P., *Group Agency*, Oxford University Press, 2011.

Lo Monte E., "Intelligenza artificiale e diritto penale: le categorie dommatiche alla prova del futuribile", in F. Basile, M. Caterini & S. Romano (eds.), *Il sistema penale ai confini delle hard sciences*, Pacini Giuridica, 2020.

Luhmann N., *Social Systems*, Stanford University Press, 1995.

Luskin R., "Caring About Corporate 'Due Care': Why Criminal Respondeat Superior Liability Outreaches Its Justification", *American Criminal Law Review*, Vol. 57 2020.

M. Y. Vardi, "Artificial Intelligence: Past and Future", *Communications of the ACM*", Vol. 55, No 1, 2012.

Macagno F., "Definitions in Law", *Bulletin Suisse de Linguistique Appliquee*, 2010.

MacCormick N., *Institutions of Law: An Essay in Legal Theory (Law, State, and Practical Reason)*, Oxford University Press, 2008.

Mackay Cooper, T., "The Common and the Civil Law – A Scot's View", 63 *Harv. L R.* 468 (1950).

Magro M. B., "Decisione umana e decisione robotica. Un'ipotesi di responsabilità da procreazione robotica", *La legislazione penale*, 2020.

Magro M. B., "Biorobotics, robotics and criminal law: some hints and reflections", *Percorsi costituzionali*, Fasc. 1-2, 2016.

Magro M. B., "Biorobotica, robotica e diritto penale", in D. Provolo, S. Riondato & F. Yenisey (eds.), *Genetics, Robotics, Law, Punishment*, 2014.

Malcolm J. G., "Morally Innocent, Legally Guilty: The Case for Mens Rea Reform", *The Federalist Society Review*, Vol. 18, 2017.

Malle B. F. et al, "Which Robot Am I Thinking About? The Impact of Action and Appearance on People's Evaluations of a Moral Robot", *The Eleventh ACM/IEEE International Conference on Human Robot Interaction*, 2016.

Malle B. F. et al, "Sacrifice One For the Good of Many?: People Apply Different Moral Norms to Human and Robot Agents", *HRI '15: Proceedings of the Tenth Annual ACM/IEEE International Conference on Human-Robot Interaction*, 2015.

Malle B. F., Magar S. T. & Scheutz M., "AI in the Sky: How People Morally Evaluate Human and Machine Decisions in a Lethal Strike Dilemma", in Aldinhas M. I. et al. (eds.), *Robotics and Well-Being. Intelligent Systems*, Control and Automation: Science and Engineering, Vol. 95, Springer, 2019.

Manes V., "L'oracolo algoritmico e la giustizia penale: al bivio tra tecnologia e tecnocrazia", *Discrimen*, 2020.

Mantovani F., *Diritto penale. Parte speciale. Vol. 1: Delitti contro la persona*, 8a ed., Wolters Kluwer-CEDAM, 2022.

Mantovani F., *Diritto penale. Parte Generale*, 11a ed, Wolters Kluwer-CEDAM, 2020.

Marcinkevičs R. & Vogt J. E., "Interpretability and Explainability: A Machine Learning Zoo Mini-tour", *ArXiv* abs/2012.01805, 2020.

Marinucci G., Dolcini E. & Gatta G. L., *Manuale di diritto penale. Parte generale*, 8a ed., Giuffrè, 2019.

Martinho A., "Perspectives about artificial moral agents", *AI and Ethics*, Vol. 1, 2021.

Massi S., "Affidamento sull'intelligenza artificiale e 'disimpegno morale' nella definizione dei presupposti della responsabilità penale", in Giordano R., *Il diritto nell'era digitale. Persona, Mercato, Amministrazione, Giustizia*, Giuffrè, 2022.

Matthias A., "The Responsibility Gap", *Ethics and Information Technology*, Vol. 6, No. 3, 2019.

McCarthy J., "What is artificial intelligence", 2007. Available at: http://jmc.stanford.edu/articles/whatisai.html.

McCarthy J. et al., *A proposal for the Dartmouth Summer Research Project on Artificial Intelligence*, 1955. Available at: www-formal.stanford.edu/jmc/history/dartmouth/dartmouth.html.

McGregor S., "Preventing Repeated Real World AI Failures by Cataloging Incidents: The AI Incident Database", *Proceedings of the Thirty-Third Annual Conference on Innovative Applications of Artificial Intelligence (IAAI-21). Virtual Conference*, 2021. Available at https://incidentdatabase.ai/?lang=en.

Miceli T. J., *The Economic Approach to Law*, Stanford University Press, 2004.

Michaelides-Mateou S. & Mateou A., *Flying in the Face of Criminalization. The Safety Implications of Prosecuting Aviation Professionals for Accidents*, Routledge, 2010.

Mill J. S., *On Liberty*, Penguin Books, 2010.

Minkkinen P., "'If Taken in Earnest': Criminal Law Doctrine and the Last Resort", *The Howard Journal*, Vol. 45, No. 5, 2006.

Miskolczi B. & Z. Szathmáry "*Büntetőjogi kérdések az információk korában – Mesterséges intelligencia*", *Big Data, profilozás. HVG-ORAC*, Budapest, 2018.

Mokhtarian E., "The Bot Legal Code: Developing a Legally Compliant Artificial Intelligence", *Vanderbilt Journal of Entertainment and Technology Law*, Vol. 21, 2020.

Moore M., *Placing Blame: a General Theory of the Criminal Law*, Clarendon Press, 1997.

Moravec H., *Mind Children. The Future of Robot and Human Intelligence*, Harvard University Press, 1990.

Morse S. J., "Rationality and Responsibility", *Southern California Law Review*, Vol. 74, 2000.

Mosier K. & Skitka L.J., "Automation use and automation bias", *Proceedings of the Human Factors and Ergonomics Society Annual Meeting*, 1999.

Mulgan R., "«Accountability»: An Ever-Expanding Concept?", *Public Administration*, Vol. 78, 2002.

Mulgan R., "Issues of accountability", in Mulgan R. (Ed.), *Holding power to account: accountability in modern democracies*, Palgrave Macmillan, 2003.

Mulligan C., "Revenge Against Robots", *South Carolina Law Review*, Vol. 69, 2018.

Nalla M., "Singapore", *World Factbook of Criminal Justice Systems*, 1993. Available at: https://bjs.ojp.gov/content/pub/pdf/wfbcjss.pdf.

National Alliance on Mental Illness, *A Guide to Mental Illness and the Criminal Justice System*, 2022. Available at: www.nami.org.

Nicholson Price W. II, "Big Data, Patents, and the Future of Medicine", *Cardozo Law Review*, Vol. 37, 2016.

Norvig P. & Russel S., *Artificial Intelligence. A Modern Approach*, Pearson Education, 2003.

Novelli C., Taddeo M. & Floridi L., "Accountability in artificial intelligence: what it is and how it works", *AI & Soc.*, 2023.

Nuotio. K, "Theories of Criminalization and the Limits of Criminal Law: A Legal Cultural Approach", in R.A. Duff et al., *The Boundaries of the Criminal Law, Oxford University Press*, 2010.

Osmani N., "The Complexity of Criminal Liability of AI Systems", *Masaryk University Journal of Law and Technology*, Issue 14, No. 1, 2020.

Packard N. et al., "An Overview of Open-Ended Evolution: Editorial Introduction to the Open-Ended Evolution II Special Issue", *Artificial Life*, Vol. 25, No. 2, 2019.

Padovani T., *Diritto penale*, 8a ed., Giuffrè, 2019.

Pagallo U., *The Laws of Robots. Crimes, Contracts, and Torts*, Springer, 2013.

Pagallo U., "The Adventures of Picciotto Roboto", *The Social Impact of Social Computing - Ethicomp*, 2011.

Pagallo U., "Killers, Fridges, and Slaves", *AI and Society*, Vol. 26, No. 4, 2011.

Pagallo U., "AI and bad robots" in McGuire M. R. & Holt T. (eds.), *The Routledge Handbook of Technology, Crime and Justice*, Routledge, 2017.

Pagallo U., "From automation to autonomous systems: A legal phenomenology with problems of accountability", *IJCAI International Joint Conference on Artificial Intelligence*, Conference paper, 2017.

Pagallo U. & Barfield W., *Advanced Introduction to Law and Artificial Intelligence*, Edward Elgar Publishing, 2020.

Pagallo U. & Quattrocolo S., "The impact of AI on criminal law, and its twofold procedures", in Barfield W. & Pagallo U. (eds.), *Research handbook on the law of artificial intelligence*, Elsevier, 2019.

Pagliaro A., *Principi di diritto penale. Parte generale*, 9a ed., Giuffrè, 2020.

Palazzo F. C., *Corso di diritto penale. Parte generale*, 8a ed., Giappichelli, 2021.

Palazzo F. C. & Papa M., *Lezioni di diritto penale comparato*, 3a ed., Giappichelli, 2013.

Panattoni B., "Intelligenza artificiale: le sfide per il diritto penale nel passaggio dall'automazione tecnologica all'autonomia artificiale", *Dir. Inf.*, Vol. 2, 2021.

Papa M., "The Offense Definition as a Screenplay of Evil: The Rise and Fall of Visual Criminal Law", *Católica Law Review*, Vol. 4, No. 3, 2020.

Papa M., *Fantastic Voyage*, 2nd ed., Giappichelli, 2019.

Parasuraman R. & Manzey D. H., "Complacency and Bias in Human Use of Automation: An Attentional Integration", *Human Factors*, Volume 52, No. 3, 2010.

Pare G.et al., "Synthesizing information systems knowledge: A typology of literature reviews", *Information & Management*, No. 52, 2015.

Partridge D., *A New Guide to Artificial Intelligence*, Intellect L & D E F A E, 1991.

Pattinson J., Haibo C. & Subhajit B., "Legal issues in automated vehicles: critically considering the potential role of consent and interactive digital interfaces", *Humanities and Social Sciences Communications*, Vol. 7, Art. No. 153, 2020.

Peikert A. (Dipl.-Jur.), Reinelt A. (Dipl.-Jur.) & Witt (Dipl.-Jur.) J., "Diskussionsbeiträge der 38. Tagung der deutschsprachigen Strafrechtslehrerinnen und Strafrechtslehrer 2019 in Hannover", *ZSTW*, Vol. 131, No. 4, 2019.

Peršak N., *The Harm Principle, its Limits and Continental Counterparts*, Springer, 2007.

Picotti L., AIDP Section I "Traditional Criminal Law Categories and AI: Crisis or Palingenesis?", Questionnaire. Available at: www.penal.org/sites/default/files/Questionnaires%20EN.pdf.

Piergallini C., "Intelligenza artificiale: da 'mezzo' ad 'autore' del reato?", *Rivista italiana di diritto e procedura penale*, Vol. 4, 2020.

Pizzi M., Romanoff M. & Engelhardt T., "AI for humanitarian action: Human rights and ethics", *International Review of the Red Cross*, Vol. 102, No. 913, 2020.

Poel I.R. et al. (Eds.), *Moral Responsibility and the Problem of Many Hands*, Routledge, 2015.

Posner R. A., "An Economic Theory of the Criminal Law", *Columbia Law Review*, Vol. 85, 1985.

Quaid J.A., "The Assessment of Corporate Criminal Liability on the Basis of Corporate Identity: An Analysis", *Mcgill Law Journal/Revue De Droit De Mcgill*, Vol. 43, 1998.

Quarck L., "Zur Strafbarkeit von e-Personen", *ZIS*, Vol. 2, 2020.

Rengier R., *Strafrecht Allgemeiner Teil*, C.H. Beck, 2019.

Rességuier A. & Rodrigues R., "AI ethics should not remain toothless! A call to bring back the teeth of ethics", *Big Data & Society*, 2020.

Rich E. & Knight K., *Artificial Intelligence*, Tata McGraw, 2004.

Riondato S., "Robot: talune implicazioni di diritto penale" in P. Moro & C. Sarra (eds.), *Tecnodiritto. Temi e informatica e robotica giuridica*, Franco Angeli, 2017.

Rizzo Minelli G., "Quando l'autore del reato è un robot: tra vecchi modelli imputativi e nuovi possibili paradigmi di responsabilità" in F. Basile, M. Caterini & S. Romano (eds.), *Il sistema penale ai confini delle hard sciences*, Pacini Giuridica, 2020.

Robson R. A., "Crime and Punishment: Rehabilitating Retribution as a Justification for Organizational Criminal Liability", *Am. Bus. L.J.*, Vol. 47, 2010.

Rodotà S., "Etica e Diritto (dialogo tra alcuni studenti e Stefano Rodotà) con una Presentazione di Gaetano Azzariti", *Costituzionalismo.it*, Vol. 1, 2019.

Rosca C. et al., "Return of the AI: An Analysis of Legal Research on Artificial Intelligence Using Topic Modelling", *Proceedings of the 2020 Natural Legal Language Processing (NLLP) Workshop*, 2020.

Rosenberg M.T., "The Continued Relevance of the Irrelevance-of-Motive Maxim", *Duke Law Journal*, Vol. 57, No. 4, 2008.

Rudschies C., Schneider I. & Simon J., "Value Pluralism in the AI Ethics Debate – Different Actors, Different Priorities", *The International Review of Information Ethics*, Vol. 29, 2021.

Russell S. J. & Norvig P., *Artificial Intelligence. A Modern Approach*, 2nd ed., Pearson, 2003.

Salvadori I., "Agenti artificiali, opacità tecnologica e distribuzione della responsabilità penale", *Rivista Italiana di Diritto e Procedura Penale*, No. 1, 2021.

Samoili S. et al., "AI Watch. Defining Artificial Intelligence. Towards an operational definition and taxonomy of artificial intelligence", EUR 30117 EN, Publications Office of the European Union, Luxembourg, 2020, ISBN 978-92-76-17045-7, JRC118163.

Santoni de Sio F. & Mecacci G., Four Responsibility Gaps with Artificial Intelligence: Why they Matter and How to Address them", *Philosophy & Technology*, Vol. 34, 2021.

Sarch A., "Should Criminal Law Mirror Moral Blameworthiness or Criminal Culpability? A Reply to Husak", *Law and Philosophy*, Vol. 41, 2022.

Sarch A., "Who cares what you think? Criminal Culpability and the Irrelevance of Unmanifested Mental States", *Law and Philosophy*, Vol. 36, No. 6, 2017.

Sartor G., "Decisioni algoritmiche tra etica e diritto", in Ruffolo U. (ed.), *Intelligenza artificiale. Il diritto, i diritti, l'etica*, Giuffré, 2020.

Scaroina E., "La responsabilità penale del datore di lavoro nelle organizzazioni complesse", *Sistema penale*, 2021.

Scherer M.U., "Regulating Artificial Intelligence Systems: Risks, Challenges, Competencies and Strategies", *Harvard Journal of Law & Technology*, Vol. 29, No. 2, 2016.

Schramowski P. et al., "The Moral Choice Machine", *Frontiers in Artificial Intelligence*, Vol. 3, 2020.

Schuett J., "A Legal Definition of AI", *Xiv:1909.01095 [cs.CY]*, 2019.

Schünemann B., "Über Strafrecht im demokratischen Rechtsstaat, das unverzichtbare Rationalitätsniveau seiner Dogmatik und die vorgeblich progressive Rückschrittspropaganda", *ZIS*, Vol. 10, 2016.

Seher G., "Intelligente Agenten als 'Personen' im Strafrecht?", in Gless S. & Seelmann K. (eds.), *Intelligente Agenten und das Recht*, Vol. 9, 2016, Nomos.

Serafimova S., "Whose morality? Which rationality? Challenging artificial intelligence as a remedy for the lack of moral enhancement", *Humanities and Social Sciences Communication*, 2020.

Shalchi A., House of Commons Library, Research Briefing, "Corporate criminal liability in England and Wales", CBP 9027, 2022.

Sheikh H., Prins C. & Schrijvers E., *Mission AI. Research for Policy*, Springer, 2023.

Shenkman C., D. Thakur D. & Llansó E., Center for Democracy & Technology, *Do You See What I See? Capabilities and Limits of Automated Multimedia Content Analysis*, 2021. Available at: https://cdt.org/wp-content/uploads/2021/05/2021-05-18-Do-You-See-What-I-See-Capabilities-Limits-of-Automated-Multimedia-Content-Analysis-Full-Report-2033-FINAL.pdf.

Shin Y., "The Spring of Artificial Intelligence in Its Global Winter", *IEEE Annals of the History of Computing*, Vol. 41, Issue 4, 2019.

Sikdokur I., Baytas I. & Yurdakul A., "Image Classification on Accelerated Neural Networks", *arXiv:2203.11081v1* [cs.CV], 2022.

Simester A. P., *Fundamentals of Criminal Law: Responsibility, Culpability, and Wrongdoing*, Oxford University Press, 2021.

Simmler M., "Automation", in Caeiro P. et al. (Eds.), *Elgar Encyclopedia of Crime and Criminal Justice*, Vol. 1, 2023.

Simmler M. & Markwalder N., "Guilty Robots? – Rethinking the Nature of Culpability and Legal Personhood in an Age of Artificial Intelligence", *Criminal Law Forum*, No. 30, 2019.

Simon H. A., Shaw J. & Newell A., "Heuristic Problem Solving: The Next Advance in Operations Research", *Operations Research*, Vol. 6, No. 1, 1958.

Simon H. A., Shaw J. & Newell A., "Report on a General Problem-Solving Program", *Rand Corporation*, 1959.

Simpson A. W. B., *Legal Theory and Legal History: Essays on the Common Law*, The Hambledon Press, 1987.

Sing J. L. S., "The Continuing Confusion Over Section 304A of the Singapore Penal Code", *Singapore Journal of Legal Studies*, 2015.

Snyder H., "Literature review as a research methodology: An overview and guidelines", *Journal of Business Research*, Vol. 104(C), 2019.

Søbirk Petersen T., "What is Legal Moralism?", *SATS*, Vol. 12, 2011.

Solum L., "Legal Personhood for Artificial Intelligences", *N.C. L. Rev.*, Vol. 7, 1992.

Srinivasa S. & Deshmukh J., "AI and the Sense of Self", *ArXiv* abs/2201.05576, 2021.

Stanley Kenneth O., "Why Open-Endedness Matters", *Artif Life*, Vol. 25, No. 3, 2019.

Stone P. et al., "Artificial Intelligence and Life in 2030. One Hundred Year Study on Artificial Intelligence: Report of the 2015-2016 Study Panel", Stanford University, September 2016. Available at: http://ai100.stanford.edu/2016-report.

Stonier T., *Beyond Information. The Natural History of Intelligence*, Springer, 1992.

Sultana F., Sufian A. & Dutta P., "Advancements in Image Classification using Convolutional Neural Network", *arXiv:1905.03288v1* [cs.CV], 2019.

Surden H., "Artificial Intelligence and Law: an Overview", *Ga. St. U. L. Rev.*, Vol. 35, 2019.

Talamo V.C., "Sistemi di intelligenza artificiale: quali scenari in sede di accertamento della responsabilità penale?", *Il Penalista*, 2020.

Thompson D. F., "Designing Responsibility: The Problem of Many Hands in Complex Organizations", *The American Political Science Review*, Vol. 74, No. 4, 1980,

Thomson J. J., "The Trolley Problem" *The Yale Law Journal*, Vol. 94, No. 6, 1985.

Tigard D. W., "There Is No Techno-Responsibility Gap", *Philosophy & Technology*, Vol. 1, 2021.

Tsarapatsanis D. & Aletras N., "On the Ethical Limits of Natural Language Processing on Legal Text", *ACL-IJCNLP*, 2021.

Turing A., "Computing Machinery and Intelligence", *Mind*, LIX/236, 1950.

Turner J., *Robot Rules. Regulating Artificial Intelligence*, Gildan Media Corporation, 2019.

Tuttle E., "Reexamining the Vicarious Criminal Liability of Corporations for the Willful Crimes of Their Employees", *Clev. St. L. Rev.*, Vol. 70, 2021.

Van de Poel I., Royakkers L. & Zwart S. D., *Moral Responsibility and the Problem of Many Hands*, Routledge, 2018.

Veneziani P., *Motivi e colpevolezza*, Giappichelli, 2000.

Verdicchio M. & Perin A., "When Doctors and AI Interact: on Human Responsibility for Artificial Risks", *Philosophy & Technology*, Vol. 35, 2022.

Vogel J., "Strafrecht und Strafrechtswissenschaft im internationalen und europäischen Rechtsraum", *ZIS*, No.1, 2012.

Wagner B., "Human Agency in Decision-Making Systems", *Policy & Internet*, Vol. 11, No.1, 2019.

Wagner B., "Liable, but Not in Control? Ensuring Meaningful Human Agency in Automated Decision-Making Systems", *Policy & Internet*, Vol. 11, Issue 1, 2019.

Wallach I., Dzamba M. & Heifets A., "AtomNet: A Deep Convolutional Neural Network for Bioactivity Prediction in Structure-based Drug Discovery", *ArXiv abs/1510.02855*, 2015.

Walsh C.G. et al., "Prospective Validation of an Electronic Health Record-Based, Real-Time Suicide Risk Model", *JAMA Netw Open*, Vol. 4, No. 3, 2021.

Walsh C.G. & Ribeiro J. D. & Franklin J. C., "Predicting Risk of Suicide Attempts Over Time Through Machine Learning", *Clinical Psychological Science*, Vol. 5, Issue 3, 2017.

Waltermann A., "Why non-human agency", in A. Waltermann et. al (eds.), *Law, Science, Rationality*, Maastricht Law Series, No. 14, Eleven International Publishing, 2020.

Waltermann A., "On the legal responsibility of artificially intelligent agents: addressing three misconceptions", *Technology and Regulation*, 2021.

Wang P., "On Defining Artificial Intelligence", *Journal of Artificial General Intelligence*, Vol. 10, No. 2, 2019.

Wang P., "What Do You Mean by 'AI'?", *Proceedings of the 2008 Conference on Artificial General Intelligence*, 2008.

Wang R. et al., "Paired Open-Ended Trailblazer (POET): EndlesslyGenerating Increasingly Complex and Diverse Learning Environments and Their Solutions", *ArXiv abs/1901.01753*, 2019.

Wang Y. & Kosinski M., "Deep neural networks are more accurate than humans at detecting sexual orientation from facial images", *Journal of Personality and Social Psychology*, Vol. 114, Issue 2, 2018, pp. 246-257.

Weigend T., "Subjective Elements of Criminal Liability", in Dubber M. D. & Hörnle T. (eds.), *The Oxford Handbook of Criminal Law*, Oxford University Press, 2014

Weizenbaum J., "ELIZA – a computer program for the study of natural language communication between man and machine", *Communications of the ACM*, Vol. 9, Issue 1, 1966.

Wiener E.L., "Complacency: Is the term useful for air safety?", *Proceedings of the 26th Corporate Aviation Safety Seminar*, 1981.

Wilenmann J., "Framing meaning through criminalization", *New Criminal Law Review*, Vol. 22, No. 1, 2019.

Wu X. et al., "A Survey of Human-in-the-loop for Machine Learning", *arXiv:2108.00941*, 2021.

Wyde W. W., *The Criminal Prosecution and Capital Punishment of Animals*, W. Heinemann, 1906.

Yeo S., Morgan N. & Wing Cheong C., *Criminal Law in Malaysia and Singapore*, 2nd ed., LexisNexis, 2012.

Yu H., "From Deep Blue to DeepMind: What AlphaGo Tells Us", *Predictive Analytics and Futurism*, Issue 13, 2016.

Zanzotto F. M., "Human-in-the-loop Artificial Intelligence", *Journal of Artificial Intelligence Research*, Vol. 64, 2019.

Zhong H. et al., "How Does NLP Benefit Legal System: A Summary of Legal Artificial Intelligence", *Proceedings of the 58th Annual Meeting of the Association for Computational Linguistics*, 2020.

Zhou Q. et al., "DecisionHoldem: Safe Depth-Limited Solving With Diverse Opponents for Imperfect-Information Games", *ArXiv:2201.11580*, 2022.

Newspaper Articles & Blog Posts

Airbus, "Airbus concludes ATTOL with fully autonomous flight tests", 29 June 2020. Available at: www.airbus.com/en/newsroom/press-releases/2020-06-airbus-concludes-attol-with-fully-autonomous-flight-tests.

BBC, "Uber's self-driving operator charged over fatal crash", 16 September 2020,. Available at: www.bbc.com/news/technology-54175359.

Bostrom N., "Ethical Issues in Advanced Artificial Intelligence", 2003. Available at: https://nickbostrom.com/ethics/ai.

Casey K., "How to explain machine learning in plain English", *The Enterprisers Project*, 19 November 2020. Available at: https://enterprisersproject.com/article/2019/7/machine-learning-explained-plain-english?page=0%2C0.

Clune J. & Stanley K. O., "POET: Endlessly Generating Increasingly Complex and Diverse Learning Environments and their Solutions through the Paired Open-Ended Trailblazer", *Uber Blog*, 8 January 2019. Available at: www.uber.com/en-NL/blog/poet-open-ended-deep-learning.

Dao D. et al., "Awful AI – 2021 Edition". Available at: https://github.com/daviddao/awful-ai.

Darrach B., "Meet Shaky, the first electronic person", *Life Magazine*, 20 November 1970. Available at: https://books.google.it/books?id=2FMEAAAAMBAJ&lpg=PA57&dq=%22first%20electronic%20person%22&pg=PA58#v=onepage&q=years&f=false.

Dickson B., "What are artificial neural networks (ANN)?", *TechTalks*, 5 August 2019. Available at: https://bdtechtalks.com/2019/08/05/what-is-artificial-neural-network-ann.

Dickson B., "What is machine learning data poisoning?", *TechTalks*, 7 October 2020. Available at: https://bdtechtalks.com/2020/10/07/machine-learning-data-poisoning.

English R., "From tiger to free-range parents – what research says about pros and cons of popular parenting styles", *The Conversation*, 25 May 2016. Available at: https://theconversation.com/from-tiger-to-free-range-parents-what-research-says-about-pros-and-cons-of-popular-parenting-styles-57986.

Floridi L., Should we be afraid of AI?, *aeon.co*, 9 May 2016. Available at: https://aeon.co/essays/true-ai-is-both-logically-possible-and-utterly-implausible.

Goldhill O., "Machines know when someone's about to attempt suicide. How should we use that information?", *Quartz*, 5 September 2018. Available at: https://qz.com/1367197/machines-know-when-someones-about-to-attempt-suicide-how-should-we-use-that-information.

Graaf N., "Why German Law Libraries Are Not Neutral and Why We Should Care", *Law-Log* Blog, July 2019. Available at: https://lawlog.blog.wzb.eu/2019/07/25/why-german-law-libraries-are-not-neutral-and-why-we-should-care.

Grant K., "Random darknet shopper exhibition featuring automated dark web purchases opens in London", *The Independent*, 2 December 2015. Available at: www.independent.co.uk/life-style/gadgets-and-tech/news/random-darknet-shopper-exhibition-featuring-automated-dark-web-purchases-opens-in-london-a6770316.html.

Heaven W.D., "AI is learning how to create itself. Humans have struggled to make truly intelligent machines. Maybe we need to let them get on with it themselves", *MIT Technology Review*, 27 May 2021. Available at: www.technologyreview.com/2021/05/27/1025453/artificial-intelligence-learning-create-itself-agi.

Hunt E., "Tay, Microsoft's AI chatbot, gets a crash course in racism from Twitter", *The Guardian*, 24 March 2016. Available at: www.theguardian.com/technology/2016/mar/24/tay-microsofts-ai-chatbot-gets-a-crash-course-in-racism-from-twitter.

IBM, "Deep Blue". Available at: www.ibm.com/ibm/history/ibm100/us/en/icons/deepblue.

Investopedia, "Feasibility Study", 4 November 2022. Available at: www.investopedia.com/terms/f/feasibility-study.asp.

Jahromi N., "The Unexpected Philosophical Depths of the Clicker Game Universal Paperclips", *The New Yorker online*, 28 March 2019. Available at: www.newyorker.com/culture/culture-desk/the-unexpected-philosophical-depths-of-the-clicker-game-universal-paperclips.

Kang D. et al., "Finding Errors in Perception Data With Learned Observation Assertions", *Stanford Dawn*, 24 January 2022. Available at: https://dawn.cs.stanford.edu/2022/01/24/loa.

Kavlakoglu E., "AI vs. Machine Learning vs. Deep Learning vs. Neural Networks: What's the Difference?", *IBM*, 27 May 2020. Available at: www.ibm.com/cloud/blog/ai-vs-machine-learning-vs-deep-learning-vs-neural-networks.

Knight W., "Two rival AI approaches combine to let machines learn about the world like a child", *MIT Technology Review*, 8 April 2019. Available at: www.technologyreview.com/2019/04/08/103223/two-rival-ai-approaches-combine-to-let-machines-learn-about-the-world-like-a-child.

Krisher T. & Dazio S., "Felony Charges Are 1st in a Fatal Crash Involving Autopilot" *AP NEWS*, Los Angeles, 18 January 2022. Available at: https://apnews.com/article/tesla-autopilot-fatal-crash-charges-91b4a0341e07244f3f03051b5c2462ae.

Martineau K., "Teaching machines to reason about what they see", *MIT News*, 2 April 2019. Available at: https://news.mit.edu/2019/teaching-machines-to-reason-about-what-they-see-0402.

Mandal M., "Convolutional Neural Networks (CNN)", *Medium*, 30 April 2021. Available at: https://manavmandal.medium.com/convolutional-neural-networks-cnn-d88e7f9329eb.

Nichols G., "Surgery digitized: Telesurgery becoming a reality", *ZD Net*, 14 June 2021. Available at: www.zdnet.com/article/surgery-digitized-telesurgery-becoming-a-reality.

Power M., "What happens when a software bot goes on a Darknet shopping spree?", *The Guardian*, 5 December 2014. Available at: www.theguardian.com/technology/2014/dec/05/software-bot-darknet-shopping-spree-random-shopper.

Press G., "The Brute Force of IBM Deep Blue And Google DeepMind", *Forbes online*, 7 February 2018. Available at: www.forbes.com/sites/gilpress/2018/02/07/the-brute-force-of-deep-blue-and-deep-learning/?sh=597fb30249e3.

Smiley L., "'I am the Operator': The Aftermath of a Self-Driving Tragedy", *Wired*, 8 March 2022. Available at: www.wired.com/story/uber-self-driving-car-fatal-crash.

Quirk C., "So Smart It's Stupid", *Alumni*, 1 April 2022. Available at: https://alumni.msu.edu/stay-informed/alumni-stories/so-smart-its-stupid-the-weirdness-of-ai.

Reuters, "Dutch vehicle authority seeks answers on fatal Tesla crash", *Reuters*, 14 July 2016. Available at: www.reuters.com/article/tesla-authority-dutch-idINL8N1A03KF.

Rogers A., "The Way the World Ends: Not with a Bang But a Paperclip", *Wired*, 21 October 2017. Available at www.wired.com/story/the-way-the-world-ends-not-with-a-bang-but-a-paperclip.

Solon O., "Oh the humanity! Poker computer trounces humans in big step for AI", *The Guardian*, 31 January 2017. Avaialble at: www.theguardian.com/technology/2017/jan/30/libratus-poker-artificial-intelligence-professional-human-players-competition.

Spector M. & Levine D., "Exclusive: Tesla faces U.S. criminal probe over self-driving claims" *Reuters*, 27 October 2022. Available at: www.reuters.com/legal/exclusive-tesla-faces-us-criminal-probe-over-self-driving-claims-sources-2022-10-26.

Storrs Hall J., "Towards Machine Agency: a Philosophical and Technological Roadmap", 2012. Available at: https://robots.law.miami.edu/wp-content/uploads/2012/01/Hall-MachineAgencyLong.pdf.

Suwandi R. C., "Why is AI So Smart and Yet So Dumb? What Moravec's Paradox told us about AI", *Towards data science*, 30 august 2020. Available at: https://towardsdatascience.com/why-ai-is-so-smart-and-yet-so-dumb-c156cc87fafa.

The Guardian, "Self-driving Uber kills Arizona woman in first fatal crash involving pedestrian", 19 March 2018. Available at: www.theguardian.com/technology/2018/mar/19/uber-self-driving-car-kills-woman-arizona-tempe.

The New York Times, *Ezra Klein Interviews Alison Gopnik*, 16 April 2021. Transcript available at: www.nytimes.com/2021/04/16/podcasts/ezra-klein-podcast-alison-gopnik-transcript.html.

Wakabayashi D., "Self-Driving Uber Car Kills Pedestrian in Arizona, Where Robots Roam", *The New York Times online*, 19 March 2018. Available at: www.nytimes.com/2018/03/19/technology/uber-driverless-fatality.html.

Yudkwosky E., "The AI Alignment Problem: Why It's Hard, and Where to Start", Transcription of the speech given at Stanford University on May 5, 2016. Available at: https://intelligence.org/files/AlignmentHardStart.pdf.

Zewe A., "Avoiding shortcut solutions in artificial intelligence', *MIT news*, 2 November 2021. Available at: https://news.mit.edu/2021/shortcut-artificial-intelligence-1102.

Other Sources

!Mediengruppe Bitnik & !Digital Brainstoarming, "The Darknet – From Memes to Onionland. An Exploration", Kunst Halle Sankt Gallen.

!Mediengruppe Bitnik, Random Darknet Shopper, 2014-2016. Available at: wwwwwwwwwwwwwwwwwwwwww.bitnik.org/r/.

AI Incident database: https://incidentdatabase.ai/.

AIAAIC Repository: https://docs.google.com/spreadsheets/d/1Bn55B4xz21-_Rgdr8BBb2lt0n_4rzLGxFADMlVW0PYI/edit#gid=1051812323.

AIAAIC Repository. Available at: https://docs.google.com/spreadsheets/d/1Bn55B4xz21-_Rgdr8BBb2lt0n_4rzLGxFADMlVW0PYI/edit#gid=1051812323.

AIDP, XXIst International Congress of Penal Law, 2024: http://www.penal.org/en/information.

Cassandra R. A., "The POMDP Page". Available at: www.pomdp.org.

ChatGPT: chat.openai.com.

DataCentricAI: https://datacentricai.org.

Digest of Justinian, 48.19.18, Ulp. 3 ad ed.

Lackman J., Random Darknet Shopper, *Aksioma – Institute for Contemporary Art*, 2016. Available at: https://aksioma.org/pdf/aksioma_PostScriptUM_23_ENG_Bitnik.pdf.

National Highway Traffic Safety Administration, "Automated Vehicles for Safety". Available at: www.nhtsa.gov/technology-innovation/automated-vehicles-safety.

NormanAI: http://norman-ai.mit.edu.

"Paperclip maximizer". Available at: https://arbital.com/p/paperclip_maximizer.

"ResponsibleAI". Available at: https://romanlutz.github.io/ResponsibleAI.

"Squiggle Maximizer (formerly "Paperclip maximizer"). Available at: www.lesswrong.com/tag/paperclip-maximizer.

The MIT's Moral Machine: www.moralmachine.net.

The Paperclip Maximizer: www.decisionproblem.com/paperclips/index2.html.

"Utility functions". Available at: www.lesswrong.com/tag/utility-functions.

Biography

Alice Giannini was born in Castelfranco Veneto (TV), Italy, on August 6, 1993. She was a PhD candidate in Criminal Law at the University of Florence and at Maastricht University from 2019 to 2023. In 2021, she won the first edition of the Giulia Cavallone price to finance her research stay at Maastricht University. The price was awarded by the Foundation "*Centro di Iniziativa Giuridica Piero Calamandrei*" and the Cavallone family to honor the memory of Dr. Giulia Cavallone, judge of the Court of Rome and PhD in criminal law and procedure. During her PhD, she gained extensive teaching experience in different areas of criminal law and joined the Law and the Cognitive Sciences research network (LACS), AI & Neurotechnology cluster. She became a lawyer in November 2019 and has a combined bachelor and master degree in law (*Laurea magistrale in Giurisprudenza*) from the University of Bologna – *Alma mater studiorum*. She has worked as an intern at the Public Prosecutor's Office of Bologna from February 2018 to October 2019. Over the years, she volunteered in several non-profit organizations which provide pro-bono legal counsel to homeless people and prisoners. She is now a member of StraLi for Strategic Litigation, an Italian NGO which pursues strategic litigation to further the protection of human rights at national and supranational level. Currently, Alice works as an assistant professor at Maastricht University, Faculty of Law, Department of Criminal law and Criminology.

Maastricht Law Series

The Maastricht Law Series is created in 2018 by Boom juridisch and Eleven International Publishing in association with the Maastricht University Faculty of Law. The Maastricht Law Series publishes books on comparative, European and International law. The series builds upon the tradition of excellence in research at the Maastricht Faculty of Law, its research centers and the Ius Commune Research School. The Maastricht Law Series is a peer reviewed book series that allows researchers an excellent opportunity to showcase their work.

Published in this series:

Volume 1: Reinhard Zimmermann, Does the Law of Succession Reflect Cultural Differences?, ISBN 978-94-6236-856-9
Volume 2: Anna Berlee, Access to personal data in public land registers, ISBN 978-94-6236-841-5
Volume 3: Marcus Meyer, The Position of Dutch Works Councils in Multinational Corporations, ISBN 978-94-6236-848-4
Volume 4: Jaap Hage, Foundations and Building Blocks of Law, ISBN 978-94-6236-860-6
Volume 5: Bastiaan van Zelst, The End of Justice(s)?, ISBN 978-94-6236-881-1
Volume 6: Agustín Parise & Lars van Vliet (eds.), Re- De- Co-dification? New Insights on the Codification of Private Law, ISBN 978-94-6236-900-9
Volume 7: Caroline Rupp, Rafael Ibarra Garza & Bram Akkermans, Property Law Perspectives VI, ISBN 978-94-6236-904-7
Volume 8: Aalt Willem Heringa, Europees Nederlands Staatsrecht, ISBN 978-94-6290-604-4

Volume 9: Symeon C. Symeonides, The "Private" in Private International Law, ISBN 978-94-6236-949-8
Volume 10: Jaap Hage, European Integration: A Theme, ISBN 978-94-6236-981-8
Volume 11: Jan M. Smits, Five Uneasy Pieces. Essays on Law and Evolution, ISBN 978-94-6236-982-5
Volume 12: Hannah Brodersen, Vincent Glerum, & André Klip, The European Arrest Warrant and In Absentia Judgements, ISBN 978-94-6236-985-6
Volume 13: Bram Akkermans & Gijs van Dijck, Sustainability and Private Law, ISBN 978-94-6236-986-3
Volume 14: Antonia Waltermann, David Roef, Jaap Hage & Marko Jelicic, Law, Science, Rationality, ISBN 978-94-6236-989-4
Volume 15: Frans L. Leeuw, Van Legal Realism naar Legal Big Data, ISBN 978-94-6290-781-2
Volume 16: Josua Sitompul, Cross-border Access to Electronic Evidence, ISBN 978-94-6236-133-1
Volume 17: Bram Akkermans & Jill Robbie, Property Law Perspectives VII, ISBN 978-946236-181-2
Volume 18: Bram Akkermans & Anna Berlee, 'Sjef-Sache', ISBN 978-94-6236-197-3
Volume 19: Froukje van den Borne, Luca Cox, Youri Cremers, Daan Groenewoud, Sven Schaghen & Tom Stijns, Het stopzetten van KEI-civiel nader bezien, ISBN 978-94-6290-955-7
Volume 20: Nicholas Mouttotos, The Impact of Europeanization in Cyprus Contract Law and the Spill-Over to Matters of Civil Procedure, ISBN 978-94-6236-206-2
Volume 21: Katja Zimmermann, Facilitating Cross-Border Real Estate Transactions in Europe, ISBN 978-94-6236-220-8
Volume 22: Alexis E. Antoniades, Remedies for human rights violations by the European Union, ISBN 978-94-6236-275-8
Volume 23: André Klip, European Arrest Warrant, ISBN 978-94-6236-284-0
Volume 24: Bram Akkermans, Sustainable Property Law, ISBN 978-94-6236-289-5
Volume 25: Sarah Schoenmaekers & Pauline Melin, The Art of Moving Borders, ISBN 978-94-6236-296-3
Volume 26: Agustín Parise & Olivier Moréteau, Comparative Perspectives on Law and Language, ISBN 978-94-6236-328-1
Volume 27: Renata Barbosa, Vincent Glerum, Hans Kijlstra, André Klip & Christina Peristeridou, Improving the European Arrest Warrant, ISBN 978-94-6236-327-4
Volume 28: Cedric Vanleenhove & Lotte Meurkens, The Recognition and Enforcement of Punitive Damages Judgments Across the Globe, ISBN 978-90-4730-162-2
Volume 29: Jill Robbie, Flore Vavourakis, Víðir Smári, Ivan Allegranti & Aleksa Radonjić, Property Law Perspectives VIII, ISBN 978-90-4730-171-4

Volume 30: Alice Giannini, Criminal Behavior and Accountability of Artificial Intelligence Systems, ISBN 978-90-4730-172-1

www.ingramcontent.com/pod-product-compliance
Lightning Source LLC
Chambersburg PA
CBHW061353240926
51846CB00007B/1397